W9-AZU-764

THE PHILOSOPHY OF
John Stuart Mill
ETHICAL, POLITICAL
and RELIGIOUS

THE PHILOSOPHY OF
John Stuart Mill

ETHICAL, POLITICAL and RELIGIOUS

edited and with an introduction by Marshall Cohen

THE MODERN LIBRARY

NEW YORK

Random House IS THE PUBLISHER OF The Modern Library

Manufactured in the United States of America by H. Wolff

Acknowledgments

The texts included in this volume are reprinted from the Uniform Library Edition of the Miscellaneous Works of John Stuart Mill published by Henry Holt and Company, 1874-5. This edition omits the lengthy footnotes added by Mill to the third edition of *An Examination of Sir William Hamilton's Philosophy*. Readers interested in Mill's response to Mansel's *The Philosophy of the Conditioned; comprising some remarks on Sir William Hamilton's Philosophy, and on Mr. J. S. Mill's Examination of that Philosophy* are therefore referred to a fuller edition.

It is impossible to make explicit my debt to the many scholars whose work has been exploited in the Introduction. My reliance on the works of W. L. Courtney and M. St. J. Packe for the details of Mill's private life and public career is, however, so great as to require special mention here.

I am grateful for various suggestions concerning this volume to Rogers Albritton, Robert C. Coburn, Walter J. Kaiser, David Kuhn, John E. McNees, and Lowry Nelson, Jr.

M.C.

Cambridge, Massachusetts
October 1960

Contents

THE PHILOSOPHY OF
John Stuart Mill
ETHICAL, POLITICAL
and RELIGIOUS

Introduction

Lady Amberley hoped that John Stuart Mill would not deem it incompatible with his religious principles to bear the relation of godfather to her son. Raising the question indirectly in a letter to Mill's stepdaughter, Helen Taylor, Lady Amberley confided that, "There is no one in whose steps I wd. rather see a boy of mine following in ever such a humble way, than in Mr. Mill's." At the height of his reputation it was common to see him as the wisest and noblest of men—a philosopher without peer, and a saint without God. His *Logic* constituted a definitive refutation of the pernicious *a priori* theories of knowledge and mind which had spread from Königsberg to Craigenputtock. And the *Examination of Sir William Hamilton's Philosophy* had delivered a blow of such force to the Scottish branch of the school that its remnant was sent scurrying for refuge as far afield as Princeton, New Jersey. But his work was not merely destructive. The *Examination* offered empirical solutions to the main metaphysical problems, and the *Logic* finally provided the empirical tradition with a successful analysis of the methods of the physical and social sciences. The development of a social science (to which the *Political Economy* would make an impressive contribution) was of cardinal importance—for it could provide the realistic analysis of means which was required in achieving political ends and applying moral precepts. The fundamental principle of all such activity, the Principle of Utility, had been articulated, and given the sort of proof it was susceptible of, in his *Utilitarianism*. And the Greatest Happiness Principle, as it was also called, enabled Mill to vindicate democracy (in *Representative Government*) and freedom (in *On Liberty*) without appeal to unempirical abstract rights and with a remarkable sense of their manifest properties. The unsettling *Essays on Religion* had not yet appeared.

Nor were Mill's services confined to the higher reaches of speculation. Throughout his life, in critical and polemical essays, the ablest of which were collected in his *Dissertations and Discussions,* he addressed himself to the books and issues of the day with a combined grasp of fact and control of principle which displayed his moral seriousness and intellectual distinction in their most unmistakable form. His letters to many editors, his international correspondence, his administrative and parliamentary careers, were only superfluous evidence that he was, as one of his admirers put it shortly after his death in 1873, "not only the great philosopher, but the great prophet of our time."

Lady Amberley's wishes were granted. Mill agreed to "godfather" Bertrand Russell, and the boy followed in his footsteps; indeed, in some directions, Russell surpassed his spiritual sponsor. Lady Amberley could not, however, have been pleased by Lord Russell's recent assessment of Mill (before the British Academy) as "practically beneficent, but theoretically somewhat incoherent." The remark betrays a certain filial irritation and the tiresome Bloomsbury condescension so characteristic of Russell's generation toward even the most eminent of the Victorians. No doubt female suffrage is a tepid thing in comparison with free love, and it is clear that the *Logic* and the *Political Economy* cannot maintain the reputation they enjoyed before the appearance of Russell's *Principles of Mathematics* or Keynes' *General Theory*. Even writings less vulnerable to technical advance, such as *Utilitarianism* and the essay *On Liberty,* have been damaged by the brilliant, if frequently misconceived, criticisms advanced in G. E. Moore's *Principia Ethica* and in Fitzjames Stephen's *Liberty, Equality, Fraternity.* These developments simply confirm Mill's belief in human fallibility and in the progressive nature of the intelligence. They cannot determine our estimate of his personal achievement.

He would not have wanted his mistakes to be ignored. But his incoherences have for some time now been much exaggerated and too much emphasized. Every departure from the philosophy of Bentham is declared by some intellectual historian to introduce a contradiction into Mill's thought; and academic philosophers have not hesitated to credit themselves with many an unearned dialectical triumph at Mill's expense. Mill's philosophy is, however, neither the catalogue of disastrous concessions nor the handbook of logical howlers many like to pretend. A complex attitude is not necessarily an inconsistent or an indecisive one. And the simple truth will seem fallacious to hectic and hostile readers. When Mill's philosophy ceases to be read as a faint hearted defense of Benthamism and is interpreted with a generosity, even a tact, which is automatically accorded to writings requiring it far more, it can hardly fail to win the interest and command the admiration of contemporary readers. He was the ablest English philosopher of the nineteenth century and, I think it fair to say, the last philosopher of any nationality to cover the whole range of philosophical problems with comparable distinction. His writings, therefore, provide us—particularly those of us who retain any allegiance to the purposes of traditional empiricism or the ideals of democratic liberalism—with a unique opportunity for self-examination.

The definition of his errors is nothing less than the formulation of our own truths, and his permanent successes make a priceless inheritance. Beyond this, he provides for us the embodiment of a great ideal; not the false ideal of the philosopher-king, which he rejected; rather of the student in search of the whole truth and the citizen absolutely devoted to the general good. Even Lord Russell has not quite filled his shoes, and the line threatens to run out.

James Mill was the field marshal of the Philosophical Radicals, and the celebrated education to which he subjected his eldest son was a strategy designed to carry the Benthamite campaign into the next generation. John Stuart Mill began Greek at three, Latin and arithmetic at eight, logic at twelve, and political economy at thirteen. The issues were discussed with his father, and with Radical friends such as Ricardo, Place, and even Bentham himself. The boy was encouraged to draw conclusions. His religious education was ignored, and we may imagine the opinion he can have formed of a God who created pleasure-loving creatures only to consign the majority of them to perpetual pain. He was assigned readings in the poets, but had doubtless been informed of Bentham's dictum that, quantities of pleasure being equal, push-pin is as good as poetry. He learned that social evils proceeded mainly from the ignorance of the many and the "sinister" interests of the few and were to be corrected by universal education and representative government. Rational codification of the law and freedom of speech and of trade were immediately desirable means to the relief of English misery. At the age of fourteen, with a repertory of such ideas at his command, Mill was allowed a busman's holiday in France at the home of Bentham's brother, Sir Samuel Bentham. There he cultivated the French language, and developed a permanent distaste for English manners. On his return, he was set to reading certain books fundamental to Benthamism, including Dumont's redaction of Bentham's *Traité de Législation*. "When I laid down the last volume of the Traité," he tells us in his *Autobiography,* "I had become a different being. The 'principle of utility' understood as Bentham understood it, and applied in the manner in which he applied it . . . , fell exactly into its place as the keystone which held together the detached and fragmentary component parts of my knowledge and beliefs. . . . I now had opinions; a creed, a doctrine, a philosophy; in one of the best senses of the word, a religion; the inculcation and diffusion of which could be made the principal outward purpose of a life. And I had a grand conception laid before me of changes to be effected in the condition of mankind through the doctrine."

There was the question of Mill's career. He read law with Austin, and considered entering Cambridge. But the ancient universities were no more to the radical taste than the Church of England herself. In 1823 he was entered as a clerk in the India House (where he remained until its charter was revoked in 1858). What might have been his leisure in these years was devoted to what he called his "youthful propagandism." He wrote unselfishly for the radical *Westminster Review* and was even briefly jailed for distributing neo-Malthusian literature. (The advance guard wanted the working classes to know that Parson Malthus' moral restraint was not the latest technique in population control.)

In the winter of 1822-23 Mill founded, and named, the Utilitarian Society, which met at the home of Grote, the Radical banker. From half past eight until ten, two mornings a week, the Society discussed logic, psychology, and political economy. Mill also became a leading figure in the London Debating Society, where he was first exposed to the winds of doctrine, Whig and Tory, Comtian and Coleridgian, which were soon to raise so much dust. In his twenty-first year, however, he found himself asking, " 'Suppose that all your objects in life were realized; that all the changes in institutions and opinions which you are looking forward to, could be completely effected at this very instant: would this be a great joy to you?' " To this direct question, "an irrepressible self-consciousness distinctly answered 'No!' At this my heart sank within me: the whole foundation on which my life was constructed fell down."

In the depth of Mill's dejection he felt that he could not support life in this condition for more than a year. But before the term had expired he found himself weeping over an incident recorded in Marmontel's *Mémoires*. The tears convinced Mill that he was no longer "a stick or a stone," and his burden grew lighter. He responded to Wordsworth's *Poems, 1815,* and thought them "the very culture of the feelings." Indeed, he accounts the first years of his acquaintance with Mrs. Taylor, who put Shelley beyond all poets, mainly "years of poetic culture." The reasoning machine threatened to become a sensitive plant. A generation later, in *On Liberty,* he was to write that, "Human nature is not a machine to be built after a model, and set to do exactly the work prescribed for it, but a tree, which requires to grow and develop itself on all sides, according to the tendency of the inward forces which make it a living thing."

The incident in Marmontel's *Mémoires* that had loosed Mill's tears was an account of the death of Marmontel's father. And however we choose to interpret this fact it is clear that we can mark Mill's break with his own father from this time. The Benthamites had underestimated the place of the feelings in human nature, and Mill vowed that in his "new utilitarianism" feeling was to be "at least as valuable as thought, and Poetry not only on a par with, but the necessary condition of, any true and comprehensive Philosophy." In 1829 he allowed himself to see considerable justice in Macaulay's attack on James Mill's essay on *Government,* the political textbook of Philosophical Radicalism. His father's reaction to Macaulay's review seemed to him to exemplify the dictum of Hobbes that when reason is against a man, a man will be against reason. This judgment was confirmed by James Mill's conservative reaction to the events of 1830 in

France and to John's growing affection for Mrs. Taylor, the wife of a London merchant. John Mill's association with certain Saint-Simonian leaders in this period, and his reading of Tocqueville in 1835, only emphasized for him the absolutistic and *a priori* character of his father's political thought. Indeed, by the time of his father's death in 1836, he had opened himself to almost all the influences he associates with the nineteenth-century reaction to the eighteenth. The "half-truths" of each mentality were recorded in the classic essays on Bentham (1838) and Coleridge (1840).

Thoughout the period of his reaction, Mill continued to associate with the Philosophical Radicals. The passing of the Reform Bill of 1832 provided them with the opening, and by 1835 the Radicals held the balance of power in Parliament. But their ability to dictate terms to the hypocritical Whigs was vitiated by a lack of effective parliamentary leadership. Debarred from a parliamentary career by his position in the India House, Mill occupied himself from 1834 to 1840 in writing, mainly for the *London* (later the *London and West-minster*)*Review,* where he essayed the not obviously compatible tasks of giving direction to the party's parliamentary leaders while attempting to free Radicalism of its Benthamite sectarianism. If the parliamentary fortunes of the Radicals had looked brilliant in 1835, the accession of Victoria in 1837 was to destroy them. Although Mill himself succeeded to the editorship of the *London and Westminster Review* in 1838, the publication of the essay on Bentham in that year appeared treasonous to the Radicals, and by 1840 Mill decided that his time could better be spent in the analysis of fundamental philosophical issues. He and Mrs. Taylor withdrew more and more from society, and in the forties he produced his *Logic* (1843) and *Political Economy* (1848). They won for him a pre-eminent place among contemporary thinkers.

It would be false to Mill's understanding of the matter to consider his shift in attention from party politics to logical

investigations as an attenuation of political commitment. Mill
writes in the Bentham essay of "the classification which may
be made of all writers into Progressive and Conservative." And this classification is paralleled by a like division
into Experientialists and Intuitionists. Whatever misgivings
the conservatism of Hume or the liberalism of Kant may have
given him, Mill never doubted that the natural alliance between conservative politics and intuitionist philosophies of
mind would make a powerful vindication of the experientialist
position a major contribution to the cause of progressivism.
He was already at work on his *Logic* when he wrote that
Bentham and Coleridge "were destined to renew a lesson
given to mankind by every age, and always disregarded—to
show that speculative philosophy, which to the superficial
appears a thing so remote from the business of life and the
outward interests of men, is in reality the thing on earth which
most influences them, and, in the long-run, overbears every
other influence save those which it must itself obey." For
whatever he felt Liberals might learn from the Germano-
Coleridgian school, it must be (although it is not always)
remembered that Mill had recommended Coleridge largely on
the ground that he was often "a better Liberal than (the)
Liberals themselves" and that Mill at his most indulgent
never suggested abandoning, but only giving a finer statement
of, the experientialist philosophy. The *Logic* was, after all,
completed within a year of the Coleridge essay. And its con-
cessive tone (dictated in part by strategic considerations)
must not lead us to exaggerate the doctrinal discrepancy
between the essay and the views he announced later in the
Autobiography. He would write there that, "The German, or
a priori view of human knowledge, and of the knowing
faculties, is likely for some time longer (though it may be
hoped in a diminishing degree) to predominate among those
who occupy themselves with such inquiries, both here and
on the Continent. . . . whatever may be the practical value
of a true philosophy of these matters, it is hardly possible to

exaggerate the mischiefs of a false one. The notion that truths external to the mind may be known by intuition or consciousness, independently of observation and experience, is, I am persuaded, in these times, the great intellectual support of false doctrines and bad institutions. By the aid of this theory, every inveterate belief and every intense feeling, of which the origin is not remembered, is enabled to dispense with the obligation of justifying itself by reason, and is erected into its own all-sufficient voucher and justification. There never was such an instrument devised for consecrating all deep-seated prejudices. And the chief strength of this false philosophy in morals, politics, and religion, lies in the appeal which it is accustomed to make to the evidence of mathematics and of the cognate branches of physical science. To expel it from these is to drive it from its stronghold . . ."

In the second book of the *Logic,* and again in the *Examination,* Mill undertook to drive the "Germanic" philosophy from its stronghold in mathematics and the physical sciences and to put them on an experientialist basis. But the German philosophy was not the only false doctrine in the field. Mill had seen the justice in Macaulay's charge that James Mill's method in the essay on *Government* was nothing other than *a priori.* And from the point of view of his own experientialism he could hardly accept the Baconian empiricism of Macaulay as the alternative. He must undermine the methodology of the Tories, and that of the classical Radicals and the Whigs as well. Not only Coleridge, but his father and Macaulay must be corrected.

Macaulay hoped to form a system "as far inferior in pretension" to James Mill's, "and as far superior in its real utility, as the prescriptions of a great physician, varying with every stage of every malady, and with the constitution of every patient, to the pill of the advertising quack which is to cure all human beings, in all climates, of all diseases." The difference between the great physician and the advertising quack was the difference between the Whig's empirical diagnosis and prescription and the Radical's *a priori* administration of political pills. Nor can there be any doubt that at least at crucial stages James Mill's method was *a priori*. From the assumption that human actions are self-interested he would demonstrate that the representative is the best form of government—the cure, in all climates, of all diseases. James Mill contended that only those rulers whose selfish interests coincide with those over whom they rule will govern in their subjects' interests. This would seem to establish direct democracy as the best form of government; for Mill says that "the community cannot have an interest opposite to its interest. To affirm this would be a contradiction in terms." But direct democracy is a practical impossibility. The best form of government must, then, be representative democracy. The people's representatives, unlike an aristocratic class or a monarch, can be "checked," and their interests made to coincide with those whom they govern. Apparently, this argument for representative democracy was applicable equally to the English and the Americans, and to "Bedouins and Malays."

Not only Macaulay's essay, but the writings of Carlyle and Coleridge, of the Saint-Simonians and the French historians, convinced John Mill of the deficiencies of the "abstract and unhistorical" political science of his father. He came to believe that "the human mind has a certain order of possible progress, in which some things must precede others, an order which governments and public instructors can modify to some, but not to an unlimited extent: that all questions of political institutions are relative, not absolute, and that different stages of human progress not only *will* have, but *ought* to have, different institutions . . . that any general theory or philosophy of politics supposes a previous theory of human progress, and that this is the same thing with a philosophy of history."

If Mill's refutation of what in the *Logic* he called his father's "Geometrical" method displayed a sensitivity to Macaulay's criticism, his attack on the "Chemical" method was a direct assault on Macaulay's own procedure. Macaulay's method of appeal to "experience" appeared incompatible with the development of a genuinely scientific philosophy of history of the kind John Mill was to find in Michelet and the French school and with the proper methodology for the social sciences which, under the stimulus of Comte, he was to describe in the final chapters of the *Logic*. Indeed, he viewed Macaulay's attack on his father's political science as an attack on the very notion of political science itself. The "vulgar notion" is, he said, "that all pretension to lay down general truths on politics and society is quackery." There can be no doubt that he had Macaulay and his father in mind when he observed that this prejudice was encouraged by the fact that "a large proportion of those who have laid claim to the character of philosophic politicians have attempted, not to ascertain universal sequences, but to frame universal precepts." Macaulay's words were sounding in his ears a decade after they were written. "They have imagined," he continues, "some one form of government, or system of laws, to fit all cases; a pretension well meriting the ridicule with which it is treated by practitioners, and wholly unsupported by the analogy of the art to which, from the nature of its subject, that of politics must be the most nearly allied. No one now supposes it possible that one remedy can cure all diseases, or even the same disease in all constitutions and habits of body."

By the time Mill published the *Logic* in 1843, poetry and history had been admitted to the "new utilitarianism," and this had entailed a revision of the classical utilitarian conceptions of both human nature and political science. Even the *Political Economy* of 1848, in many ways a "school" book, was not simply an exercise in Smith-Ricardo economics. Mill may have exaggerated the originality (and even the value) of his distinction between laws of the Production of Wealth, which he understood to be "laws of nature," and modes of Distribution, which he held "subject to human will." But his insistence on this ambiguity in the conception of economic law allowed him to display his open-minded attitude on fundamental problems of economic organization, and to communicate his deep concern for their just solution. The new tone introduced into his exposition of the dismal science, and his desire that "the suffering portions of humanity have a voice in the discussions," he attributed to the influence of Mrs. Taylor, whose contribution to all his subsequent writings was so extensive as to qualify her, in his judgment, as their co-author. He was still committed to the principles of private property (which had never been given a fair trial in any country), but in the third edition of the *Political Economy* he could allow himself to assert that, "If . . . the choice were to be made between Communism with all its chances, and the present state of society [1852] with all its sufferings and injustices; if the institution of private property necessarily carried with it as a consequence, that the produce of labour should be apportioned as we now see it, almost in an inverse ratio to the labour—the largest portions to those who have never worked at all, the next largest to those whose work is almost nominal, and so on in a descending scale, the remuneration dwindling as the work grows harder and more disagreeable, until the most fatiguing and exhausting bodily labour cannot count with certainty on being able to earn even the necessaries of life; if this, or Communism, were the alternative, all the difficulties, great or small, of Communism, would be as dust in the balance."

Mill had been introduced to Mrs. Taylor as early as 1830. By 1832 she could write of him as "the type of the possible elevation of humanity" and to be with him seemed to her the "ideal of the noblest fate." He was no less emphatic, and protested that if society offered to women the opportunities it did to men she would have been as distinguished as Shelley or Carlyle. Carlyle and most of Mill's friends were not of the same opinion, and the recent publication of Mill's and Mrs. Taylor's letters does not encourage one to reverse the cooler judgment. Mill and Mrs. Taylor saw one another with regularity in London and on occasion traveled abroad together. Mill's sensitivity about their relationship was such as to lead to permanent ruptures with several close friends who had the temerity to question it and to a complete break with his mother and sisters, who go unmentioned in his *Autobiography*. "They are innocent says Charity, they are guilty says Scandal," observed Carlyle; and Charity was almost certainly correct. But Mill's and Mrs. Taylor's notion that they were sparing John Taylor by their abstinence seems highly unrealistic. Taylor died in 1849, and in 1851, after writing out a statement of their disapproval of the marriage contract as constituted by law, they were married. In 1856, on the retirement of his two superiors, Hill and Thomas Love Peacock (who had done Scottish Economists no favors in *Crotchet Castle*), Mill became Chief Examiner in the India House, an office which, according to his biographer, Packe, carried with it "the responsibility of a Secretary of State." Mill composed the petition requesting a renewal of the company's charter, which was refused, although Lord Grey described it as the ablest state paper he had ever read. Mill retired, declining an honorary position on the new advisory council. It was a cruel blow to him when, in the same year, Mrs. Mill died in Avignon. The leisure that he had expected to enjoy with her he devoted to the composition of the works they had planned together. In the period between her death and his election to Parliament he became "a recluse who reads newspapers" and composed, in addition to the bulk of his *Autobiography* and the *Examination of Sir William Hamilton's Philosophy,* the essay *On Liberty,* the *Utilitarianism,* and the *Considerations on Representative Government,* which constitute his mature restatement of the principles of Utilitarianism.

Despite the refinements which have been introduced into utilitarian theory by Sidgwick, Moore, and recently by John Rawls, Mill's account of the fundamental principle of his philosophy, the Principle of Utility or the Greatest Happiness Principle, remains classic. It can only seem so if it is read, not as an inept defense of Benthamism, but as a powerful independent statement. Mill follows Bentham in allowing "everybody to count for one, nobody for more than one" in his application of the principle "that actions are right in proportion as they tend to produce happiness, wrong as they tend to produce the reverse of happiness." Yet he conceives himself to be offering a defense not simply of Benthamism, but of one of the two main moral theories—a theory held by Bentham and himself, and by Epicurus and Socrates as well. No doubt, he might have strengthened his position by avoiding the equation of happiness with "pleasure, or the absence of pain," an inheritance from Bentham with sources deep in the tradition. But his distinction in kind between higher and lower pleasures is a resourceful innovation, crucial to his entire philosophy. It is presupposed in his defense of liberty and of representative government, and the unity of his philosophy can be appreciated only if this is understood. In making this distinction in the way he does, Mill is deliberately departing from Epicurus as well as from Bentham.

It is usual to criticize Mill's distinction between quantity and quality of pleasure on the ground that it is inconsistent with his own philosophy and a disastrous deviation from Bentham's. It is asserted, for instance, that Mill's distinction between higher and lower pleasures commits him to contradicting his own claim that pleasure is the only thing good in itself. The argument is that the attribute—in this case mentality—in respect of which one pleasure is declared superior to another is *eo ipso* admitted to be good in itself, and Mill's assumption that pleasure is the *only* thing good in itself thereby contradicted. The difficulty, if it were a difficulty, would not depend upon the introduction of the notion of qualities of pleasure; for exactly the same argument might be conducted on the basis of Benthamite quantities alone. One could deduce the contradiction that pleasure is the only good, but that intensity, say, is also a good. In any case, the criticism is fallacious. It simply does not follow from the claim that mental pleasures are better than physical ones that mentality is a good in itself. Consequently, Mill's view cannot be convicted of internal contradiction by this argument.

The question, whether Mill's distinction between quantity and quality of pleasure inadvertently undermines Bentham's calculus, which has long preoccupied commentators, will be of small consequence if Mill is not assumed specifically to be defending Benthamism. But Mill's insistence that the judgment of the man of experience is the only criterion for evaluating pleasures, whether they differ in degree or in kind, will suggest that if Mill does undermine Bentham it is hardly by inadvertence. And even if Mill's distinction is not deemed to justify the inclusion of an element of dissatisfaction in happiness, an argument for the superiority of Socrates to the pig can be made out on cruder utilitarian grounds. Intelligence and other burdens can be justified as means to the general good, even if they are nothing more than sources of pain to those who possess them. Hedonism may, finally, be a swinish philosophy. But the prophets of *Entsagen* and *Härte,* of pain and suffering, who from Teufelsdröckh to Nietzsche have scorned the effeminacy of Mill's ideals, fail to appreciate the role which those qualities may play in a formally hedonistic philosophy. In his essay on *Civilization* Mill can deplore, quite as consistently as Carlyle or Nietzsche, that "there has crept over the refined classes . . . a moral effeminacy, an inaptitude for every kind of struggle. They shrink from all effort, from everything which is troublesome and disagreeable. The same causes which render them sluggish and unenterprising, make them, it is true, for the most part, stoical under inevitable evils. But heroism is an active, not a passive quality; and when it is necessary not to bear pain, but to seek it, little needs be expected from the men of the present day."

Mill's "proof" of the Principle of Utility has cost his reputation more dearly in analytic circles than any other pages of his writing. Both the number of his errors and the importance of this effort in an estimation of Mill's total accomplishment have been much exaggerated. He undertakes to "prove" that pleasure is not only one of the things, but the only thing, desirable as an end. In the course of demonstrating that it is the only thing *desirable* as an end, Mill argues that it is the only thing which can be *desired* as an end. He attempts, that is, to exploit the doctrine of psychological hedonism in the defense of ethical hedonism. I must confess myself hostile to the doctrine of psychological hedonism and warmly disposed toward the criticisms G. E. Moore makes of it in *Principia Ethica.* (It would be better simply to assume the doctrine of ethical hedonism than to prove it by way of psychological hedonism.)

The arguments which have become notorious are, however, those Mill makes in the course of proving the far less ambitious thesis (which might have been assumed in another age) that pleasure is *one* of the things desirable as an end. Neither Bradley's charge that Mill commits the fallacy of composition nor Moore's that he commits the "naturalistic" fallacy can be sustained. The fallacy of composition is supposed to be committed in Mill's assertion that, "No reason can be given why the general happiness is desirable, except that each person . . . desires his own happiness." Bradley assumes that Mill is making the fallacious deduction, *"Because* everybody desires his own pleasure, *therefore* everybody desires the pleasure of everybody else." This interpretation is denied by Mill in a letter published in the second volume of Elliot's collection of Mill's letters (p. 116), and, in any case, Mill's phrasing, "No reason can be given . . . except" is not obviously the phrasing of a writer about to give a deductive proof. So too with the even more celebrated remark that "the only proof capable of being given that an object is visible, is that people actually see it. The only proof that a sound is audible, is that people hear it: and so of the other sources of our experience. In like manner, I apprehend, the sole evidence it is possible to produce that anything is desirable, is that people do actually desire it." Here, it is suggested, by supposing the suffixes to have the same force, Mill has failed to grasp that while visible means *can* be seen, desirable means *ought* to be desired. This failure has led him to suppose that, as it follows from the fact that something is seen that it is visible, it follows from the fact that something is desired that it is desirable. If this were so it would be an empirical question what things were desirable, and ethics would have been established as an empirical science. Again, one may question whether the phrasing "The sole evidence it is possible to produce . . ." is the expression appropriate to a deductive proof. And one may doubt whether Bradley and Moore have sufficiently heeded Mill's insistent remarks in *Utilitarianism* that he is not offering a proof in the ordinary sense of the word, but only "considerations . . . capable of determining the intellect." It is irrelevant to criticize as a deduction what is not offered as one, to point out that it does not *follow* from the fact that something is desired (even universally desired) that it is desirable. (And the harsher view that the consideration of actual desires should in no way *determine* what the intellect finds desirable cannot claim the support of logic, or humanity, or even of Aristotle.) It can be affirmed with certainty that Mill did not believe ethics to be reducible to a science. In the sixth book of the *Logic* he appends to his discussion of the proper methods to be employed in "the social science," the Physical and Historical (rather than the Geometrical or Chemical) methods, a discussion of Moral Knowledge. He does this because "it is customary . . . to include under the term Moral Knowledge, and even (though improperly) under that of Moral Science, an inquiry the results of which do not express themselves in the indicative, but in the imperative mood." The imperative mood he takes to be characteristic of an art, not a science, and it is characteristic of arts to propose ends. The rules of an art are none other than the theorems of the corresponding science, but it is reserved to an art to provide first principles, to assert what is desirable. These assertions are not propositions of science, Mill says. "A proposition of which the predicate is expressed by the words *ought* or *should* be, is generically different from one which is expressed by *is* or *will be*." Every art is thus "a joint result of laws of nature disclosed by science, and of general principles of what has been called Teleology, or the Doctrine of Ends." And he maintains that "the general principle to which all rules of practice ought to conform, and the test by which they shall be tried, is that of conduciveness to the happiness of mankind, or rather, of all sentient beings: in other words, that the promotion of happiness is the ultimate principle of Teleology."

If the happiness of the greatest number is the greatest good, that form of government which satisfies the interest of the greatest number ought to be the best form of government. Mill never repudiates this inherited defense of representative government. But he is able to deepen it in virtue of the high estimate he puts on the contribution that moral and intellectual activity can make to human happiness. Mill's argument, that representative government is "the ideally best polity" because it exercises and enhances the mental and moral qualities of those who practice it, is not an unaccountable addition to the classical utilitarian defense of democracy, but the political consequence of his distinction between higher and lower pleasures. Democracy is the ideally best polity, not simply because it provides the best mechanism for guaranteeing the satisfaction of material interests, but because it is peculiarly suited to expand the class of men who may enjoy "mental" ones. This consideration allows Mill to deny, what the older utilitarians could not and perhaps would not have wanted to deny, "that if a good despot could be insured, despotic monarchy would be the best form of government."

Bentham and James Mill had rejected aristocratic and monarchical political forms because the ruling power would inevitably serve a special interest. But in a direct democracy, or in a properly engineered representative democracy, the interest of the rulers would coincide with that of the community. James Mill thought it a "contradiction in terms" to suppose that a community could have "an interest opposite to its interest." It was an *a priori* truth, then, that in a democratic government no "sinister" interest could prevail, no despotic class dominate. A generation later, in spite of this logical guarantee, John Mill could see, as he indicates in *On Liberty,* that such phrases as "self-government" and "the power of the people over themselves" do not express the true state of the case. The "people" who exercise the power are not the same as those over whom it is exercised. And the "self-government" spoken of is not the government of each by himself, but of each by all the rest. "The will of the people, moreover, practically means the will of the most numerous or the most active *part* of the people; . . . the people, consequently, *may* desire to oppress a part of their number: and precautions are as much needed against this, as against any other abuse of power." Democratic government is not immune to tyranny; its tyranny is the tyranny of the majority. In *Representative Government* he therefore proposes various devices to mitigate a possible tyranny of the working classes over the rest of society. Education qualifications, proportional representation, plural voting (in politics it will no longer be true that everybody is to count for one, nobody for more than one), an open ballot (nothing could have shocked his elders more)—all these are recommended in chapters which have amused or bored more readers than they have convinced.

But it was the existing tyranny of middle-class morality which disturbed Mill even more deeply than the possible political tyranny of the working classes. Macaulay had convinced Mill of the *a priori* nature of his father's political thought, but it was Tocqueville who, in Mill's opinion, produced the first properly scientific study of democracy. Unlike his father's, Tocqueville's treatment of the subject was "inductive and analytical, instead of purely ratiocinative," an exploitation of the Physical, rather than the Geometrical, method in social science. In particular, Tocqueville had exposed Mill's *a priori* argument professing to show that a democratic society could not harbor an interest contrary to its own by producing empirical evidence of its very real tendency toward a "tyranny of the majority." According to Tocqueville this tyranny would not be a political one, but a tyranny more terrible than any of the past political tyrannies. "Under the absolute sway of one man," he wrote, "the body was attacked in order to subdue the soul; but the soul escaped the blows which were directed against it and rose proudly superior. Such is not the course adopted by tyranny in democratic republics; there the body is left free, and the soul is enslaved."

It is for this reason that Mill's most memorable pages on the tyranny of the majority appear, not in *Representative Government,* where he offers political expedients, but in *On Liberty,* where he delivers a social sermon. By the time the second volume of *Democracy in America* appeared in 1840 Mill was convinced, in any case, that Tocqueville had been in error on one fundamental point. Many of the consequences Tocqueville attributed to democracy (by which he understood the equality of conditions rather than any mechanism of government) were in fact the consequences, not of democracy, but of civilization, or modern commercial society. The evils of life under a monolithic middle class in America proceeded not from the extinction of social extremes and the equalization of status, but from the size of this class and its commercial spirit. In his essay on Tocqueville, Mill therefore proposes to combat this evil by lending support to those classes—agricultural, leisured, learned—which might propagate an anti-commercial spirit. And *On Liberty* is an urgent appeal for a relaxation of the middle-class moral pressures which constitute the main threat to freedom in contemporary democratic society. In his great essay Mill attempts to give a utilitarian defense of the value of freedom, forgoing any appeal to "abstract right" which (in Bentham's phrase) he considered "nonsense upon stilts." Bentham had defended freedom as a secondary form of security, and in giving a more high-minded defense of its value Mill is frequently supposed to appeal surreptitiously to the very abstract rights which he officially deplores. All that is true is that one must understand utility to be "grounded on the permanent interests of man as a progressive being" and agree to Mill's assumption that the "free development of individuality is one of the leading essentials of well-being; that it is not only a co-ordinate element with all that is designated by the terms civilization, instruction, education, culture, but is itself a necessary part and condition of all these things." These remarks are wholly in the spirit of Mill's official statement of his own conception of utilitarianism, and they are supplemented by more narrowly utilitarian arguments for the necessity of free speech and the cultivation of genius in discovering, confirming, and diffusing the truth. It is true that Mill does not argue with the energy one might expect for his assumption that the truth is itself useful (as he has not felt pressed to defend the view that freedom is a constituent of happiness). He was, however, safely in his grave when Nietzsche and the Grand Inquisitor proclaimed the transvaluation of his values.

Mill's defense of liberty, and of liberty of speech and the press in particular, is less controversial than his attempt to set proper limits for the moral and legal coercion of personal conduct. According to Mill the only justification for interfering with the liberty of a member of a civilized community "is to prevent harm to others." In asserting this Mill means specifically to deny the view—affirmed not only by platonists, but by utilitarians such as Fitzjames Stephen as well—that, irrespective of a man's own desires, uninvited interference with his conduct may be justified on the ground that it is for his own good, "physical or moral." It is Mill's profound conviction that "in the part which merely concerns himself, his independence is, of right, absolute. Over himself, over

his body and mind, the individual is sovereign." In view of
the centrality of this conviction to Mill's entire political
position, it will be worthwhile to contest the claim that Mill
betrays these views in Chapter V of his essay. The notion that
he does can be found in the earliest notices of his essay
and is repeated in Sir Isaiah Berlin's recent *Two Concepts of
Liberty.* "Even Mill," says Berlin, "is prepared to say that I
may forcibly prevent a man from crossing a bridge if there is
not time to warn him that it is about to collapse, for whatever
his behavior may indicate, I know that he cannot wish to fall
into the water." And others have supposed Mill to be of the
opinion that even if the man does wish to fall into the river I
may prevent him for his own good, physical or moral. Mill,
however, is discussing the question of the prevention of accidents. There is nothing in his discussion of the situation to
justify Berlin's "whatever his behavior may indicate." In
saying that the man does not wish to fall into the river, Mill
is not professing to know better than the man himself what he
desires. He is merely restating the assumption of the discussion: it would be an accident—that is, the man does not
wish it. Nor is Mill suggesting that we may knowingly frustrate
the man's desires for his own good, physical or moral. Interference with the man on the bridge is not justified on the
ground that it is for his own good. It is justified on the ground
that such interference is in accord with what we may rationally
suppose to be his own desire in the matter. Freedom consists
in doing what one wishes, and *ex hypothesi* he does not wish
to fall into the river. Mill's example does not suggest that one
can know another's desire better than he knows it himself
(although this may be true), nor does it suggest that one may
frustrate his desire because it would be for his own good. He
only suggests that in the very special case of accidents one
may interfere with a man's conduct in a manner which there
is every rational reason to believe he would himself approve.
Mill does not here sanction any of the previously rejected
grounds for interference. He does slightly broaden the class of

actions with which one may interfere. The "concession" is, however, not to tyranny, but to common sense. And it is made not only in the name but in the interest of freedom.

If there is a difficulty in Mill's position it arises in his attempt to characterize the class of self-regarding actions. Mill's principle that self-regarding actions are inviolable derives much of its plausibility from his initial characterization of them as actions which concern oneself alone. The principle of non-interference with such actions loses much of its pathos when they are redefined as those which are "directly and in the first instance" of concern to the individual, and some of its informativeness when (in Chapter IV) the class is broadened to include those actions which, although they may indirectly harm others, do not infringe a "distinct and assignable obligation." If the class of self-regarding actions, as reformulated by Mill, does not seem as self-evidently sacrosanct as the class mentioned in his preliminary remarks, it at least provides an answer to those critics who suppose themselves to have justified totalitarianism on Mill's principles when they notice (what they suppose Mill not to have noticed) that virtually all human behavior affects others indirectly. Mill was well aware of this fact and asserted his principle in spite of it. His claim is that one ought not to interfere with actions that affect others only indirectly and (it is crucial to observe) with those that affect them directly only when, and as, utility demands. This principle may lack the precision to justify calling it a criterion, but it expresses a conviction even more important to endorse today than when Mill wrote his essay a century ago.

In view of Mill's status as an oracle in certain circles (or on certain occasions) it is perhaps worth remarking that Mill did not suppose, as many readers have supposed, that the principle set forth in *On Liberty* is incompatible with governmental intervention in economic matters, or even with socialism. His objections to the types of socialism he took seriously derived mainly from his views on economics and not from his views on liberty. If in his youth he ridiculed the Saint-Simonians for wishing to turn the sea into lemonade, in his posthumous *Chapters on Socialism* he endorsed experiments in socialistic living on the scale of the township and the village community. Socialism of the type professed by Owen and Fourier might be the politics of the future, and a rational evaluation must be based on experience. If such experiments were successful, no doctrines about private property should prevent their acceptance. But for those revolutionary socialists who would destroy in hatred, with no knowledge of what the life to follow would be, he felt the profoundest distaste. "It must be acknowledged that those who would play this game on the strength of their own private opinion, unconfirmed as yet by any experimental verification—who would forcibly deprive all who have now a comfortable physical existence of their only present means of preserving it, and would brave the frightful bloodshed and misery that would ensue if the attempt was resisted—must have a serene confidence in their own wisdom on the one hand and a recklessness of other people's suffering on the other, which Robespierre and St. Just, hitherto the typical instances of those united attributes, scarcely came up to."

In 1865 a group of citizens of Westminster asked Mill to become a candidate for Parliament. He was disinclined to seek office (he had refused before), but agreed to stand on condition that he not incur expense, or canvass, during the campaign, that he answer no questions concerning his religious convictions, and that if elected he be free to disregard the special interests of Westminster. Despite the opinion of a local wit "that the Almighty himself could not be elected on such a programme," Mill was returned. In Parliament he spoke for extension of the suffrage to the working class, and in the agitation following the defeat of Gladstone's Reform Bill he bravely faced a working-class mob and quieted what might have developed into another Peterloo Massacre. He exploited the debate on Disraeli's Reform Bill to press his own views on Personal (or Proportional) Representation, and on Female Suffrage. Although his proposal to amend the bill by substituting the word "person" for the word "man" was at first treated as hilarious, he finally secured seventy-three votes for the amendment. Mill's advanced positions on the Irish question won him little English popularity, and he created great enmity for himself with those who took what was called the "damned nigger" view by his implacable attempt to bring Governor Eyre to justice for his brutal conduct in the suppression of the mutiny of Jamaican negroes. His sublime performances were not, however, wholly unappreciated. Gladstone, who had earlier baptized Mill "the Saint of Rationalism," wrote of his parliamentary activity that "what his conduct there principally disclosed, at least to me, was his singular moral elevation. . . . I rejoiced in his advent, and deplored his disappearance. He did us all good. In whatever party, whatever form of opinion, I sorrowfully confess such men rare." Mill was not, however, all pure reason and moral elevation. In reply to an attack made upon him by Sir John Pakington for calling the Conservative party "the stupid party," Mill, admitting the phrase to occur in his *Representative Government*, went on to say, "I never meant to say that the Conservatives are generally stupid. I meant to say that stupid people are generally Conservative. I believe that is so obviously and universally admitted a principle that I hardly think any gentleman will deny it. Suppose any party, in addition to whatever share it may possess of the ability of the community, has nearly the whole of its stupidity, that party must, by the law of its constitution, be the stupidest party; and I do not see why honorable gentlemen should see that position at all offensive to them, for it ensures their being always an extremely powerful party. I know that I am liable to a retort, and an obvious one enough; and as I do not wish to allow any honorable gentleman the credit of making it, I make it myself. It may be said that if stupidity has a tendency to Conservatism, sciolism, or half-knowledge, has a tendency to Liberalism. Something might be said for that, but it is not at all so clear as the other. There is an uncertainty about sciolists; we cannot count upon them; and therefore they are a less dangerous class. But there is so much dense, solid force in sheer stupidity, that any body of able men with that force pressing behind them may ensure victory in many a struggle, and many a victory the Conservative party has gained through that power."

It is perhaps superfluous to record that in the General Election of 1868 Mill was defeated by the Tory candidate. He and his stepdaughter, Helen Taylor, then returned to Avigon. He could soon write to his friend Thornton that "with my herbarium, my virbratory, and my semi-circumgyratory, I am in clover; and you can imagine with what scorn I think of the House of Commons, which, comfortable club as it is said to be, could offer me none of these comforts, or more perfectly speaking, these necessities of life."

During parliamentary recesses he had managed to do only a little writing, a splendid review of Grote's *Plato* and his Inaugural Address to the University of St. Andrews. The students had elected him their Lord Rector without his permission, and he rewarded them with a three-hour disquisition on higher education in which they were urged to cease debating the relative merits of the classics and the sciences in the university curriculum and to devote themselves to the negotiable task of learning both. He had also begun to revise his father's *Analysis of the Phenomena of the Human Mind* and completed this "duty to philosophy and to the memory of my father" in 1869. Despite the distractions of his enormous international correspondence, articles for Morley's *Fortnightly Review* (toward which he felt an obligation), and revisions of the *Logic* and *Political Economy,* Mill managed to bring the *Autobiography* up to date and to complete the essay on *Theism,* which was published posthumously with the earlier essays on *Nature* and the *Utility of Religion* as the third of the *Three Essays on Religion.*

"I have a hundred times heard him say," writes Mill of his father, "that all ages and nations have represented their gods as wicked, in constantly increasing progression, that mankind have gone on adding trait after trait till they reached the most perfect conception of wickedness which the human mind can devise, and have called this God, and prostrated themselves before it. This *ne plus ultra* of wickedness he considered embodied in what is commonly presented to mankind as the creed of Christianity." Mansel's theology seemed to John Stuart Mill to be nothing other than a sophisticated defense (on Hamiltonian principles) of this *ne plus ultra* of wickedness. He thought it "simply the most morally pernicious doctrine now current." A God who could punish the innocent, and give the murderous command to Abraham, was neither good nor just, and to profess such actions compatible with an incomprehensible Infinite Goodness or Justice was to add intellectual insult to moral injury. "Here, then, I take my stand," proclaims Mill, "on the acknowledged principle of logic and morality, that when we mean different things we have no right to call them by the same name, and to apply to them the same predicates, moral and intellectual." Mill's *hier stehe ich* is a challenge not only to Mansel's system which Leslie Stephen in a burst of late Victorian optimism, could pronounce "already extinct fifty years ago," but to the similar theological systems, Lutheran and otherwise, which prevail once again. The punishment of the innocent, and the sacrifice of the guiltless, could not be justified in any civilized human morality, utilitarian or other. And Mansel's device of saying that God's goodness may be different in kind from man's was only a sophistical way of saying that God may not be good or just. "Whatever power such a being may have over me," Mill exclaims, "there is one thing which he shall not do: he shall not compel me to worship him. I will call no being good, who is not what I mean when I apply that epithet to my fellow-creatures; and if such a being can sentence me to hell for not so calling him, then to hell I will go."

It would have been slavish to struggle against the tyrannies of race and class and sex and to have acquiesced in the tyranny of such a God. Fortunately, one did not need to consent either to Mansel's conception of God or to his conception of theological method. God may be possessed of Infinite Attributes, but they differ in degree, not in kind, from those attributes as possessed by men. And if they are inconceivable, it is only in their infinity, not in their other elements. Once this is understood, the question of the Divine Attributes—which can only be answered by revelation in Mansel's system—is returned to natural theology. And Mill's *Theism* is a "strictly scientific" examination of the problems of natural theology. Mill, who said of himself that he was one of the few men in England who had not thrown off religious belief, but never had it, was in a position to conduct the inquiry with perfect impartiality.

The ontological or *a priori* argument for the existence of God Mill dismisses as fallacious, and the cosmological or first-cause argument he allows no support in experience. The argument from design, however, which Hume and Kant had treated with respect, recommends itself to Mill as of genuinely scientific character. The adaptations of Nature, which he is disinclined to explain on the grounds of Darwinian science, do, he thinks, render creation by intelligence a probability. But the very facts which provide the sole evidence of an Author of Nature argue decisively against his omnipotence. Omnipotence has no need of means—however ingenious. Yet the admission of a certain impotency into the divine nature obviates the traditional difficulties in reconciling God's omnipotence with his benevolence. The evils so vividly displayed in the essay on *Nature* are compatible with any degree of benevolence if the Author of Nature is limited in constitution or by conditions. We may, then, assign a low order of probability to a theorem asserting the existence of a benevolent God of finite power. Carlyle was not alone, however, in his refusal to be satisfied with a merely "probable God." And for atheists and agnostics it is always the case that "more than a little is by much too much." If Mill's was the scientific answer, perhaps it was not a scientific question. In any case, the *Theism* is the last elaborate investigation of the problem of natural theology by a major English-speaking philosopher.

Mill's assessment of the truth and utility of religion in the *Theism* is more favorable than one might have expected from the somewhat hostile tone of the earlier essays on *Nature* and the *Utility of Religion*. The evidence for design was at first considered too shadowy and insubstantial; the argument, which he finally accepts as genuinely inductive, a mere inconclusive analogy. But even in the earlier essays Mill thought (James' *Pragmatism* is dedicated to him) that "the wish to believe" might usefully be indulged. Neither his personal idealism nor his Benthamite realism inclined him to assign any large utility to the fear of posthumous pain as a social sanction. But the value of religion to the individual, and through him to society, was never disputed. An awareness of the consolation which the ideal conceptions of the imagination offer to suffering humanity gives way in Mill's final view to an insistence on the inestimable value to be derived from familiarity with "a morally perfect being," particularly if that abstraction is believed to have been made flesh. The rational skeptic may never—and in this he preserves a moral fastidiousness which is not open to the traditional Christian—identify the omnipotent Author of (malevolent) Nature with the (benevolent) Author of the Sermon on the Mount. But he may hope that Christ is "a man charged with a special, express, and unique commission from God to lead mankind to truth and virtue."

Yet such hopes can never constitute religious belief. Nevertheless the rational skeptic, if he is also a utilitarian, may in acknowledging an absolute obligation to the Universal Good, make a commitment which is in the best sense of the word religious. Indeed, this Religion of Humanity, which borrows only its name from Comte, is superior on moral and intellectual grounds to the received supernaturalisms. And it may be embraced in conjunction with the only form of supernatural belief which "stands clear both of intellectual contradiction and moral obliquity," the classical belief that Nature and Life are the product of a struggle between "contriving goodness and an intractable material," between Mill's benevolent but finite God and a world he never made. This supernatural extension of the struggle between Progressives and Conservatives gives to one who aligns himself with the right side the exhilaration and satisfaction of being "a fellow-labourer with the Highest," the sense of "helping God."

Mill's favorite text was "the night cometh when no man can work," and he acknowledged his impending death when he whispered to Helen Taylor, "You know that I have done my work." He died on May 7, 1873, and his body was laid beside that of Helen's mother in Avignon. He had written that he could not perceive that the rational skeptic "loses by his skepticism any real and valuable consolation except one; the hope of reunion with those dear to him who have ended their earthly life before him. That loss, indeed, is neither to be denied not extenuated. In many cases it is beyond the reach of comparison or estimate; and will always suffice to keep alive, in the more sensitive natures, the imaginative hope of a futurity which, if there is nothing to prove, there is as little in our knowledge and experience to contradict."

Bentham

There are two men, recently deceased, to whom their country is indebted not only for the greater part of the important ideas which have been thrown into circulation among its thinking men in their time, but for a revolution in its general modes of thought and investigation. These men, dissimilar in almost all else, agreed in being closet-students—secluded in a peculiar degree, by circumstances and character, from the business and intercourse of the world; and both were, through a large portion of their lives, regarded by those who took the lead in opinion (when they happened to hear of them) with feelings akin to contempt. But they were destined to renew a lesson given to mankind by every age, and always disregarded—to show that speculative philosophy, which to the superficial appears a thing so remote from the business of life and the outward interests of men, is in reality the thing on earth which most influences them, and, in the long-run, overbears every other influence save those which it must itself obey. The writers of whom we speak have never been read by the multitude; except for the more slight of their works, their readers have been few: but they have been the teachers of the teachers; there is hardly to be found in England an individual of any importance in the world of mind, who (whatever opinions he may have afterwards adopted) did not first learn to think from one of these two; and, though their influences have but begun to diffuse themselves through these intermediate channels over society at large, there is already scarcely a publication of any consequence, addressed to the educated classes, which, if these persons had not existed, would not have been different from what it is. These men are Jeremy Bentham and Samuel Taylor Coleridge—the two great seminal minds of England in their age.

No comparison is intended here between the minds or influences of these remarkable men: this were impossible, unless there were first formed a complete judgment of each, considered apart. It is our intention to attempt, on the present occasion, an estimate of one of them; the only one, a complete edition of whose works is yet in progress, and who, in the classification which may be made of all writers into Progressive and Conservative, belongs to the same division with ourselves. For although they were far too great men to be correctly designated by either appellation exclusively, yet, in the main, Bentham was a Progressive philosopher; Coleridge, a Conservative one. The influence of the former has made itself felt chiefly on minds of the Progressive class; of the latter, on those of the Conservative: and the two systems of concentric circles which the shock given by them is spreading over the ocean of mind have only just begun to meet and intersect. The writings of both contain severe lessons, to their own side, on many of the errors and faults they are addicted to: but to Bentham it was given to discern more particularly those truths with which existing doctrines and institutions were at variance; to Coleridge, the neglected truths which lay *in* them.

A man of great knowledge of the world, and of the highest reputation for practical talent and sagacity among the official men of his time (himself no follower of Bentham, nor of any partial or exclusive school whatever), once said to us, as the result of his observation, that to Bentham more than to any other source might be traced the questioning spirit, the disposition to demand the *why* of every thing, which had gained so much ground and was producing such important consequences in these times. The more this assertion is examined, the more true it will be found. Bentham has been in this age and country the great questioner of things established. It is by the influence of the modes of thought with which his writings inoculated a considerable number of thinking men, that the yoke of authority has been broken, and innumerable opinions, formerly received on tradition as incontestable, are put upon their defence, and required to give an account of themselves. Who, before Bentham (whatever controversies might exist on points of detail), dared to speak disrespectfully, in express terms, of the British Constitution or the English law? He did so; and his arguments and his example together encouraged others. We do not mean that his writings caused the Reform Bill, or that the appropriation clause owns him as its parent: the changes which have been made, and the greater changes which will be made, in our institutions, are not the work of philosophers, but of the interests and instincts of large portions of society recently grown into strength. But Bentham gave voice to those interests and instincts: until he spoke out, those who found our institutions unsuited to them did not dare to say so, did not dare consciously to think so; they had never heard the excellence of those institutions questioned by cultivated men, by men of acknowledged intellect; and it is not in the nature of uninstructed minds to resist the united authority of the instructed. Bentham broke the spell. It was not Bentham by his own writings: it was Bentham through the minds and pens which those writings fed—through the men in more direct contact with the world, into whom his spirit passed. If the superstition about ancestorial wisdom has fallen into decay; if the public are grown familiar with the idea that their laws and institutions are in great part, not the product of intellect and virtue, but of modern corruption grafted upon ancient barbarism; if the hardiest innovation is no longer scouted *because* it is an innovation—establishments no longer considered sacred because they are establishments—it will be found that those who have accustomed the public mind to these ideas have learnt them in Bentham's school, and that the assault on ancient institutions has been, and is, carried on for the most part with his weapons. It matters not, although these thinkers, or indeed thinkers of any description, have been but scantily found among the persons prominently and ostensibly at the head of the Reform movement. All movement, except directly revolutionary ones, are headed, not by those who originate them, but by those who know best how to compromise between the old opinions and the new. The father of English innovation, both in doctrines and in institutions, is Bentham: he is the great *subversive,* or, in the language of Continental philosophers, the great *critical,* thinker of his age and country.

We consider this, however, to be not his highest title to fame. Were this all, he were only to be ranked among the lowest order of the potentates of mind—the negative or destructive philosophers; those who can perceive what is false, but not what is true; who awaken the human mind to the inconsistencies and absurdities of time-sanctioned opinions and institutions, but substitute nothing in the place of what they take away. We have no desire to undervalue the services of such persons: mankind have been deeply indebted to them; nor will there ever be a lack of work for them in a world in which so many false things are believed, in which so many which have been true are believed long after they have ceased to be true. The qualities, however, which fit men for perceiving anomalies, without perceiving the truths which would rectify them, are not among the rarest of endowments. Courage, verbal acuteness, command over the forms of argumentation, and a popular style, will make out of the shallowest man, with a sufficient lack of reverence, a considerable negative philosopher. Such men have never been wanting in periods of culture; and the period in which Bentham formed his early impressions was emphatically their reign, in proportion to its barrenness in the more noble products of the human mind. An age of formalism in the Church, and corruption in the State, when the most valuable part of the meaning of traditional doctrines had faded from the minds even of those who retained from habit a mechanical belief in them, was the time to raise up all kinds of sceptical philosophy. Accordingly, France had Voltaire, and his school of negative thinkers; and England (or rather Scotland) had the profoundest negative thinker on record—David Hume; a man, the peculiarities of whose mind qualified him to detect failure of proof, and want of logical consistency, at a depth which French sceptics, with their comparatively feeble powers of analysis and abstraction, stopped far short of, and which German subtlety alone could thoroughly appreciate, or hope to rival.

If Bentham had merely continued the work of Hume, he would scarcely have been heard of in philosophy; for he was far inferior to Hume in Hume's qualities, and was in no respect fitted to excel as a metaphysician. We must not look for subtlety, or the power of recondite analysis, among his intellectual characteristics. In the former quality, few great thinkers have ever been so deficient; and to find the latter, in any considerable measure, in a mind acknowledging any kindred with his, we must have recourse to the late Mr. Mill—a man who united the great qualities of the metaphysicians of the eighteenth century with others of a different complexion, admirably qualifying him to complete and correct their work. Bentham had not these peculiar gifts: but he possessed others, not inferior, which were not possessed by any of his precursors;

which have made him a source of light to a generation which has far outgrown their influence, and, as we called him, the chief subversive thinker of an age which has long lost all that they could subvert.

To speak of him first as a merely negative philosopher—as one who refutes illogical arguments, exposes sophistry, detects contradiction and absurdity: even in that capacity, there was a wide field left vacant for him by Hume, and which he has occupied to an unprecedented extent—the field of practical abuses. This was Bentham's peculiar province—to this he was called by the whole bent of his disposition—to carry the warfare against absurdity into things practical. His was an essentially practical mind. It was by practical abuses that his mind was first turned to speculation—by the abuses of the profession which was chosen for him—that of the law. He has himself stated what particular abuse first gave that shock to his mind, the recoil of which has made the whole mountain of abuse totter: it was the custom of making the client pay for three attendances in the office of a Master in Chancery, when only one was given. The law, he found on examination, was full of such things. But were these discoveries of his? No: they were known to every lawyer who practised, to every judge who sat on the bench; and neither before nor for long after did they cause any apparent uneasiness to the consciences of these learned persons, nor hinder them from asserting, whenever occasion offered, in books, in parliament, or on the bench, that the law was the perfection of reason. During so many generations, in each of which thousands of well-educated young men were successively placed in Bentham's position and with Bentham's opportunities, he alone was found with sufficient moral sensibility and self-reliance to say to himself, that these things, however profitable they might be, were frauds, and that between them and himself there should be a gulf fixed. To this rare union of self-reliance and moral sensibility we are indebted for all that Bentham has done. Sent to Oxford by his father at the unusually early age of fifteen;

required, on admission, to declare his belief in the Thirty-nine Articles—he felt it necessary to examine them; and the examination suggested scruples, which he sought to get removed, but, instead of the satisfaction he expected, was told that it was not for boys like him to set up their judgment against the great men of the church. After a struggle, he signed; but the impression that he had done an immoral act never left him: he considered himself to have committed a falsehood; and throughout life he never relaxed in his indignant denunciations of all laws which command such falsehoods, all institutions which attach rewards to them.

By thus carrying the war of criticism and refutation, the conflict with falsehood and absurdity, into the field of practical evils, Bentham, even if he had done nothing else, would have earned an important place in the history of intellect. He carried on the warfare without intermission. To this, not only many of his most piquant chapters, but some of the most finished of his entire works, are entirely devoted—the "Defence of Usury;" the "Book of Fallacies;" and the onslaught upon Blackstone, published anonymously under the title of "A Fragment on Government," which, though a first production, and of a writer afterwards so much ridiculed for his style, excited the highest admiration no less for its composition than for its thoughts, and was attributed by turns to Lord Mansfield, to Lord Camden, and (by Dr. Johnson) to Dunning, one of the greatest masters of style among the lawyers of his day. These writings are altogether original: though of the negative school, they resemble nothing previously produced by negative philosophers; and would have sufficed to create for Bentham, among the subversive thinkers of modern Europe, a place peculiarly his own. But it is not these writings that constitute the real distinction between him and them. There was a deeper difference. It was that they were purely negative thinkers: he was positive. They only assailed error: he made it a point of conscience not to do so until he thought he could plant instead the corresponding truth. Their character was exclusively analytic: his was synthetic. They took for their starting-point the received opinion on any subject, dug round it with their logical implements, pronounced its foundations defective, and condemned it: he began *de novo,* laid his own foundations deeply and firmly, built up his own structure, and bade mankind compare the two. It was when he had solved the problem himself, or thought he had done so, that he declared all other solutions to be erroneous. Hence, what they produced will not last; it must perish, much of it has already perished, with the errors which it exploded: what he did has its own value, by which it must outlast all errors to which it is opposed. Though we may reject, as we often must, his practical conclusions, yet his premises, the collections of facts and observations from which his conclusions were drawn, remain for ever, a part of the materials of philosophy.

A place, therefore, must be assigned to Bentham among the masters of wisdom, the great teachers and permanent intellectual ornaments of the human race. He is among those who have enriched mankind with imperishable gifts; and although these do not transcend all other gifts, nor entitle him to those honors, "above all Greek, above all Roman fame," which, by a natural re-action against the neglect and contempt of the world, many of his admirers were once disposed to accumulate upon him, yet to refuse an admiring recognition of what he was, on account of what he was not, is a much worse error, and one which, pardonable in the vulgar, is no longer permitted to any cultivated and instructed mind.

If we were asked to say, in the fewest possible words, what we conceive to be Bentham's place among these great intellectual benefactors of humanity; what he was, and what he was not; what kind of service he did and did not render to truth—we should say, he was not a great philosopher; but he was a great reformer in philosophy. He brought into philosophy something which it greatly needed, and for want of which it was at a stand. It was not his doctrines which did this: it was his mode of arriving at them. He introduced into morals and politics those habits of thought, and modes of investigation, which are essential to the idea of science, and the absence of which made those departments of inquiry, as physics had been before Bacon, a field of interminable discussion, leading to no result. It was not his opinions, in short, but his method, that constituted the novelty and the value of what he did—a value beyond all price, even though we should reject the whole, as we unquestionably must a large part, of the opinions themselves.

Bentham's method may be shortly described as the method of detail; of treating wholes by separating them into their parts; abstractions, by resolving them into things; classes and generalities, by distinguishing them into the individuals of which they are made up; and breaking every question into pieces before attempting to solve it. The precise amount of originality of this process, considered as a logical conception—its degree of connection with the methods of physical science, or with the previous labors of Bacon, Hobbes, or Locke—is not an essential consideration in this place. Whatever originality there was in the method, in the subjects he applied it to, and in the rigidity with which he adhered to it, there was the greatest. Hence his interminable classifications; hence his elaborate demonstrations of the most acknowledged truths. That murder, incendiarism, robbery, are mischievous actions, he will not take for granted, without proof. Let the thing appear ever so self-evident, he will know the why and the how of it with the last degree of precision; he will distinguish all the different mischiefs of a crime, whether of the *first,* the *second,* or the *third* order; namely, 1. The evil to the sufferer, and to his personal connections; 2. The *danger* from example, and the *alarm* or painful feeling of insecurity; and, 3. The discouragement to industry and useful pursuits arising from the *alarm*, and the trouble and resources which must be expended in warding off the *danger*. After this enumeration, he will prove, from the laws of human feeling, that even the first of these evils, the sufferings of the immediate victim, will, on

the average, greatly outweigh the pleasure reaped by the offender; much more when all the other evils are taken into account. Unless this could be proved, he would account the infliction of punishment unwarrantable; and, for taking the
trouble to prove it formally, his defence is, "There are truths
which it is necessary to prove, not for their own sakes, because they are acknowledged, but that an opening may be
made for the reception of other truths which depend upon
them. It is in this manner we provide for the reception of
first principles, which, once received, prepare the way for admission of all other truths."* To which may be added, that
in this manner also do we discipline the mind for practising
the same sort of dissection upon questions more complicated
and of more doubtful issue.

It is a sound maxim, and one which all close thinkers have
felt, but which no one before Bentham ever so consistently
applied, that error lurks in generalities; that the human mind
is not capable of embracing a complex whole, until it has surveyed and catalogued the parts of which that whole is made
up; that abstractions are not realities *per se,* but an abridged
mode of expressing facts; and that the only practical mode of
dealing with them is to trace them back to the facts (whether
of experience or of consciousness) of which they are the expression. Proceeding on this principle, Bentham makes short
work with the ordinary modes of moral and political reasoning. These, it appeared to him, when hunted to their source,
for the most part terminated in *phrases*. In politics, liberty,
social order, constitution, law of nature, social compact, &c.,
were the catchwords: ethics had its analogous ones. Such
were the arguments on which the gravest questions of morality
and policy were made to turn; not reasons, but allusions to
reasons; sacramental expressions, by which a summary appeal
was made to some general sentiment of mankind, or to some
maxim in familiar use, which might be true or not, but the

* Part I., pp. 161-2, of the collected edition.

limitations of which no one had ever critically examined. And this satisfied other people, but not Bentham. He required something more than opinion as a reason for opinion. Whenever he found a *phrase* used as an argument for or against any thing, he insisted upon knowing what it meant; whether it appealed to any standard, or gave intimation of any matter of fact relevant to the question; and, if he could not find that it did either, he treated it as an attempt on the part of the disputant to impose his own individual sentiment on other people, without giving them a reason for it—a "contrivance for avoiding the obligation of appealing to any external standard, and for prevailing upon the reader to accept of the author's sentiment and opinion as a reason, and that a sufficient one, for itself." Bentham shall speak for himself on this subject. The passage is from his first systematic work, "Introduction to the Principles of Morals and Legislation;" and we could scarcely quote any thing more strongly exemplifying both the strength and weakness of his mode of philosophizing:

"It is curious enough to observe the variety of inventions men have hit upon, and the variety of phrases they have brought forward, in order to conceal from the world, and, if possible, from themselves, this very general, and therefore very pardonable, self-sufficiency.

"1. One man says he has a thing made on purpose to tell him what is right and what is wrong; and that is called a 'moral sense:' and then he goes to work at his ease, and says such a thing is right, and such a thing is wrong. Why? 'Because my moral sense tells me it is.'

"2. Another man comes, and alters the phrase; leaving out *moral,* and putting in *common* in the room of it. He then tells you that his common sense tells him what is right and wrong as surely as the other's moral sense did: meaning, by common sense, a sense of some kind or other, which, he says, is possessed by all mankind: the sense of those whose sense is not the same as the author's being struck out, as not worth taking. This contrivance does better than the other; for, a moral sense being a new thing, a man may feel about him a good while without being able to find it out: but common sense is as old as the creation; and there is no man but would be ashamed to be thought not to have as much of it as his neighbors. It has another great advantage: by appearing to share power, it lessens envy; for, when a man gets up upon this ground in order to anathematize those who differ from him, it is not by a *sic volo sic jubeo,* but by a *velitis jubeatis.*

"3. Another man comes, and says, that as to a moral sense indeed, he cannot find that he has any such thing; that, however, he has an *understanding,* which will do quite as well. This understanding, he says, is the standard of right and wrong: it tells him so and so. All good and wise men understand as he does: if other men's understandings differ in any part from his, so much the worse for them: it is a sure sign they are either defective or corrupt.

"4. Another man says that there is an eternal and immutable rule of right; that that rule of right dictates so and so: and then he begins giving you his sentiments upon any thing that comes uppermost; and these sentiments (you are to take for granted) are so many branches of the eternal rule of right.

"5. Another man, or perhaps the same man (it is no matter), says that there are certain practices conformable, and others repugnant, to the fitness of things: and then he tells you, at his leisure, what practices are conformable, and what repugnant; just as he happens to like a practice or dislike it.

"6. A great multitude of people are continually talking of the law of nature; and then they go on giving you their sentiments about what is right and what is wrong: and these sentiments, you are to understand, are so many chapters and sections of the law of nature.

"7. Instead of the phrase, law of nature, you have sometimes law of reason, right reason, natural justice, natural equity, good order. Any of them will do equally well. This latter is most used in politics. The three last are much more tolerable than the others, because they do not very explicitly claim to be any thing more than phrases: they insist but feebly upon the being looked upon as so many positive standards of themselves, and seem content to be taken, upon occasion, for phrases expressive of the conformity of the thing in question to the proper standard, whatever that may be. On most occasions, however, it will be better to say *utility:*

utility is clearer, as referring more explicitly to pain and pleasure.

"8. We have one philosopher, who says there is no harm in any thing in the world but in telling a lie; and that, if, for example, you were to murder your own father, this would only be a particular way of saying he was not your father. Of course, when this philosopher sees any thing that he does not like, he says it is a particular way of telling a lie. It is saying that the act ought to be done, or may be done, when, *in truth,* it ought not be done.

"9. The fairest and openest of them all is that sort of man who speaks out, and says, I am of the number of the elect: now God himself takes care to inform the elect what is right; and that with so good effect, that, let them strive ever so, they cannot help not only knowing it, but practising it. If, therefore, a man wants to know what is right and what is wrong, he has nothing to do but to come to me."

Few will contend that this is a perfectly fair representation of the *animus* of those who employ the various phrases so amusingly animadverted on; but that the phrases contain no argument, save what is grounded on the very feelings they are adduced to justify, is a truth which Bentham had the eminent merit of first pointing out.

It is the introduction into the philosophy of human conduct of this method of detail—of this practice of never reasoning about wholes till they have been resolved into their parts, nor about abstractions till they have been translated into realities—that constitutes the originality of Bentham in philosophy, and makes him the great reformer of the moral and political branch of it. To what he terms the "exhaustive method of classification," which is but one branch of this more general method, he himself ascribes every thing original in the systematic and elaborate work from which we have quoted. The generalities of his philosophy itself have little or no novelty: to ascribe any to the doctrine, that general utility is the foundation of morality, would imply great ignorance of the history of philosophy, of general literature, and of Bentham's own writings. He derived the idea, as he says himself, from Helvetius; and it was the doctrine no less of the religious philosophers of that age, prior to Reid and Beattie. We never saw an abler defence of the doctrine of utility than in a book written in refutation of Shaftesbury, and now little read— Brown's* "Essays on the Characteristics;" and, in Johnson's celebrated review of Soame Jenyns, the same doctrine is set forth as that both of the author and of the reviewer. In all ages of philosophy, one of its schools has been utilitarian, not only from the time of Epicurus, but long before. It was by mere accident that this opinion became connected in Bentham with his peculiar method. The utilitarian philosophers antecedent to him had no more claims to the method than their antagonists. To refer, for instance, to the Epicurean philosophy, according to the most complete view we have of the moral part of it by the most accomplished scholar of antiquity, Cicero: we ask any one who has read his philosophical writings, the "De Finibus" for instance, whether the arguments of the Epicureans do not, just as much as those of the Stoics or Platonists, consist of mere rhetorical appeals to common notions, to ἐικότα and σημεῖα instead of τεκμήρια, notions picked up, as it were, casually, and, when true at all, never so narrowly looked into as to ascertain in what sense, and under what limitations, they are true. The application of a real inductive philosophy to the problems of ethics is as unknown to the Epicurean moralists as to any of the other schools: they never take a question to pieces, and join issue on a definite point. Bentham certainly did not learn his sifting and anatomizing method from them.

This method Bentham has finally installed in philosophy; has made it, henceforth, imperative on philosophers of all schools. By it he has formed the intellects of many thinkers, who either never adopted, or have abandoned, many of his peculiar opinions. He has taught the method to men of the most opposite schools to his; he has made them perceive, that, if they do not test their doctrines by the method of detail, their adversaries

* Author of another book, which made no little sensation when it first appeared—"An Estimate of the Manners of the Times."

will. He has thus, it is not too much to say, for the first time, introduced precision of thought into moral and political philosophy. Instead of taking up their opinions by intuition, or by ratiocination from premises adopted on a mere rough view, and couched in language so vague that it is impossible to say exactly whether they are true or false, philosophers are now forced to understand one another, to break down the generality of their propositions, and join a precise issue in every dispute. This is nothing less than a revolution in philosophy. Its effect is gradually becoming evident in the writings of English thinkers of every variety of opinion, and will be felt more and more in proportion as Bentham's writings are diffused, and as the number of minds to whose formation they contribute is multiplied.

It will naturally be presumed, that, of the fruits of this great philosophical improvement, some portion at least will have been reaped by its author. Armed with such a potent instrument, and wielding it with such singleness of aim; cultivating the field of practical philosophy with such unwearied and such consistent use of a method right in itself, and not adopted by his predecessors—it cannot be but that Bentham by his own inquiries must have accomplished something considerable. And so, it will be found, he has; something not only considerable, but extraordinary; though but little compared with what he has left undone, and far short of what his sanguine and almost boyish fancy made him flatter himself that he had accomplished. His peculiar method, admirably calculated to make clear thinkers, and sure ones to the extent of their materials, has not equal efficacy for making those materials complete. It is a security for accuracy, but not for comprehensiveness; or, rather, it is a security for one sort of comprehensiveness, but not for another.

Bentham's method of laying out his subjects is admirable as a preservative against one kind of narrow and partial views. He begins by placing before himself the whole of the field of inquiry to which the particular question belongs, and divides down till he arrives at the thing he is in search of; and thus, by successively rejecting all which is *not* the thing, he gradually works out a definition of what it *is*. This, which he calls the exhaustive method, is as old as philosophy itself. Plato owes every thing to it, and does every thing by it; and the use made of it by that great man in his Dialogues, Bacon, in one of those pregnant logical hints scattered through his writings, and so much neglected by most of his pretended followers, pronounces to be the nearest approach to a true inductive method in the ancient philosophy. Bentham was probably not aware that Plato had anticipated him in the process to which he, too, declared that he owed every thing. By the practice of it, his speculations are rendered eminently systematic and consistent: no question, with him, is ever an insulated one; he sees every subject in connection with all the other subjects with which in his view it is related, and from which it requires to be distinguished; and as all that he knows, in the least degree allied to the subject, has been marshalled in an orderly manner before him, he does not, like people who use a looser method, forget and overlook a thing on one occasion to remember it on another. Hence there is probably no philosopher, of so wide a range, in whom there are so few inconsistencies. If any of the truths which he did not see had come to be seen by him, he would have remembered it everywhere and at all times, and would have adjusted his whole system to it. And this is another admirable quality which he has impressed upon the best of the minds trained in his habits of thought: when those minds open to admit new truths, they digest them as fast as they receive them.

But this system, excellent for keeping before the mind of the thinker all that he knows, does not make him know enough; it does not make a knowledge of some of the properties of a thing suffice for the whole of it, nor render a rooted habit of surveying a complex object (though ever so carefully) in only one of its aspects tantamount to the power of contemplating it in all. To give this last power, other qualities are required: whether Bentham possessed those other qualities we now have to see.

Bentham's mind, as we have already said, was eminently synthetical. He begins all his inquiries by supposing nothing to be known on the subject; and reconstructs all philosophy *ab initio,* without reference to the opinions of his predecessors. But to build either a philosophy, or any thing else, there must be materials. For the philosophy of matter, the materials are the properties of matter; for moral and political philosophy, the properties of man, and of man's position in the world. The knowledge which any inquirer possesses of these properties constitutes a limit, beyond which, as a moralist or a political philosopher, whatever be his powers of mind, he cannot reach. Nobody's synthesis can be more complete than his analysis. If, in his survey of human nature and life he has left any element out, then, wheresoever that element exerts any influence, his conclusions will fail, more or less, in their application. If he has left out many elements, and those very important, his labors may be highly valuable: he may have largely contributed to that body of partial truths, which, when completed and corrected by one another, constitute practical truth; but the applicability of his system to practice in its own proper shape will be of an exceedingly limited range.

Human nature and human life are wide subjects; and whoever would embark in an enterprise requiring a thorough knowledge of them has need both of large stores of his own, and of all aids and appliances from elsewhere. His qualifications for success will be proportional to two things—the degree in which his own nature and circumstances furnish him with a correct and complete picture of man's nature and circumstances, and his capacity of deriving light from other minds.

Bentham failed in deriving light from other minds. His writings contain few traces of the accurate knowledge of any schools of thinking but his own; and many proofs of his entire conviction, that they could teach him nothing worth knowing. For some of the most illustrious of previous thinkers, his contempt was unmeasured. In almost the only passage of the "Deontology," which from its style, and from its having before appeared in print, may be known to be Bentham's, Socrates and Plato are spoken of in terms distressing to his greatest admirers; and the incapacity to appreciate such men is a fact perfectly in unison with the general habits of Bentham's mind. He had a phrase, expressive of the view he took of all moral speculations to which his method had not been applied, or (which he considered as the same thing) not founded on a recognition of utility as the moral standard: this phrase was "vague generalities." Whatever presented itself to him in such a shape, he dismissed as unworthy of notice, or dwelt upon only to denounce as absurd. He did not heed, or rather the nature of his mind prevented it from occurring to him, that these generalities contained the whole unanalyzed experience of the human race.

Unless it can be asserted that mankind did not know any thing until logicans taught it to them; that, until the last hand has been put to a moral truth by giving it a metaphysically precise expression, all the previous rough-hewing which it has undergone by the common intellect, at the suggestion of common wants and common experience, is to go for nothing —it must be allowed, that even the originality which can, and the courage which dares, think for itself, is not a more necessary part of the philosophical character than a thoughtful regard for previous thinkers, and for the collective mind of the human race. What has been the opinion of mankind, has been the opinion of persons of all tempers and dispositions, of all partialities and prepossessions, of all varieties in position, in education, in opportunities of observation and inquiry. No one inquirer is all this: every inquirer is either young or old, rich or poor, sickly or healthy, married or unmarried, meditative or active, a poet or a logician, an ancient or a modern, a man or a woman; and, if a thinking person, has, in addition, the accidental peculiarities of his individual modes of thought. Every circumstance which gives a character to the life of a human being carries with it its peculiar biasses—its peculiar facilities for perceiving some things, and for missing or forgetting others. But, from points of view different from his, different things are perceptible; and none are more likely to have seen what he does not see than those who do not see what he sees. The general opinion of mankind is the average of the conclusions of all minds, stripped indeed of their choicest and most recondite thoughts, but freed from their twists and partialities; a net result, in which everybody's particular point of view is represented, nobody's predominant. The collective mind does not penetrate below the surface, but it sees all the surface: which profound thinkers, even by reason of their profundity, often fail to do; their intenser view of a thing in some of its aspects diverting their attention from others.

The hardiest assertor, therefore, of the freedom of private judgment; the keenest detector of the errors of his predecessors, and of the inaccuracies of current modes of thought— is the very person who most needs to fortify the weak side of his own intellect by study of the opinions of mankind in all ages and nations, and of the speculations of philosophers of the modes of thought most opposite to his own. It is there that he will find the experiences denied to himself; the remainder of the truth of which he sees but half; the truths, of which the errors he detects are commonly but the exaggerations. If, like Bentham, he brings with him an improved instrument of investigation, the greater is the probability that he will find ready prepared a rich abundance of rough ore, which was merely waiting for that instrument. A man of clear ideas errs grievously if he imagines that whatever is seen confusedly does not exist: it belongs to him, when he meets with such a thing, to dispel the mist, and fix the outlines of the vague form which is looming through it.

Bentham's contempt, then, of all other schools of thinkers;

his determination to create a philosophy wholly out of the materials furnished by his own mind, and by minds like his own —was his first disqualification as a philosopher. His second was the incompleteness of his own mind as a representative of universal human nature. In many of the most natural and strongest feelings of human nature he had no sympathy; from many of its graver experiences he was altogether cut off; and the faculty by which one mind understands a mind different from itself, and throws itself into the feelings of that other mind, was denied him by his deficiency of imagination.

With imagination in the popular sense, command of imagery and metaphorical expression, Bentham was, to a certain degree, endowed. For want, indeed, of poetical culture, the images with which his fancy supplied him were seldom beautiful; but they were quaint and humorous, or bold, forcible, and intense: passages might be quoted from him, both of playful irony and of declamatory eloquence, seldom surpassed in the writings of philosophers. The imagination, which he had not, was that to which the name is generally appropriated by the best writers of the present day; that which enables us, by a voluntary effort, to conceive the absent as if it were present, the imaginary as if it were real, and to clothe it in the feelings, which, if it were indeed real, it would bring along with it. This is the power by which one human being enters into the mind and circumstances of another. This power constitutes the poet, in so far as he does any thing but melodiously utter his own actual feelings. It constitutes the dramatist entirely. It is one of the constituents of the historian: by it we understand other times; by it Guizot interprets to us the middle ages; Nisard, in his beautiful Studies on the later Latin poets, places us in the Rome of the Cæsars; Michelet disengages the distinctive characters of the different races and generations of mankind from the facts of their history. Without it, nobody knows even his own nature, further than circumstances have actually tried it, and called it out; nor the nature of his fellow-creatures, beyond such generalizations as he may have been enabled to make from his observation of their outward conduct.

By these limits, accordingly, Bentham's knowledge of human nature is bounded. It is wholly empirical, and the empiricism of one who has had little experience. He had neither internal experience nor external: the quiet, even tenor of his life, and his healthiness of mind, conspired to exclude him from both. He never knew prosperity and adversity, passion nor satiety: he never had even the experiences which sickness gives; he lived from childhood to the age of eighty-five in boyish health. He knew no dejection, no heaviness of heart. He felt life a sore and a weary burthen. He was a boy to the last. Self-consciousness, that demon of the men of genius of our time, from Wordsworth to Byron, from Goethe to Chateaubriand, and to which this age owes so much both of its cheerful and its mournful wisdom, never was awakened in him. How much of human nature slumbered in him he knew not, neither can we know. He had never been made alive to the unseen influences which were acting on himself, nor, consequently, on his fellow-creatures. Other ages and other nations were a blank to him for purposes of instruction. He measured them but by one standard—their knowledge of facts, and their capability to take correct views of utility, and merge all other objects in it. His own lot was cast in a generation of the leanest and barrenest men whom England had yet produced; and he was an old man when a better race came in with the present century. He saw accordingly, in man, little but what the vulgarest eye can see; recognized no diversities of character but such as he who runs may read. Knowing so little of human feelings, he knew still less of the influences by which those feelings are formed: all the more subtle workings both of the mind upon itself, and of external things upon the mind, escaped him; and no one, probably, who, in a highly instructed age, ever attempted to give a rule to all human conduct, set out with a more limited conception either of the agencies by which human conduct *is,* or of those by which it *should* be, influenced.

This, then, is our idea of Bentham. He was a man both of remarkable endowments for philosophy, and of remarkable deficiencies for it; fitted beyond almost any man for drawing from his premises conclusions not only correct, but sufficiently precise and specific to be practical; but whose general conception of human nature and life furnished him with an unusually slender stock of premises. It is obvious what would be likely to be achieved by such a man; what a thinker, thus gifted and thus disqualified, could do in philosophy. He could, with close and accurate logic, hunt half-truths to their consequences and practical applications, on a scale both of greatness and of minuteness not previously exemplified; and this is the character which posterity will probably assign to Bentham.

We express our sincere and well-considered conviction when we say, that there is hardly any thing positive in Bentham's philosophy which is not true; that when his practical conclusions are erroneous, which, in our opinion, they are very often, it is not because the considerations which he urges are not rational and valid in themselves, but because some more important principle, which he did not perceive, supersedes those considerations, and turns the scale. The bad part of his writings is his resolute denial of all that he does not see, of all truths but those which he recognizes. By that alone has he exercised any bad influence upon his age; by that he has not created a school of deniers, for this is an ignorant prejudice, but put himself at the head of the school which exists always, though it does not always find a great man to give it the sanction of philosophy; thrown the mantle of intellect over the natural tendency of men in all ages to deny or disparage all feelings and mental states of which they have no consciousness in themselves.

The truths which are not Bentham's, which his philosophy takes no account of, are many and important; but his non-recognition of them does not put them out of existence: they are still with us; and it is a comparatively easy task that is reserved for us—to harmonize those truths with his. To reject his half of the truth because he overlooked the other half would be to fall into his error without having his excuse. For our own part, we have a large tolerance for one-eyed men, provided their one eye is a penetrating one: if they saw more, they probably would not see so keenly, nor so eagerly pursue one course of inquiry. Almost all rich veins of original and striking speculation have been opened by systematic half-thinkers; though, whether these new thoughts drive out others as good, or are peacefully superadded to them, depends on whether these half-thinkers are or are not followed in the same track by complete thinkers. The field of man's nature and life cannot be too much worked, or in too many directions; until every clod is turned up, the work is imperfect: no whole truth is possible but by combining the points of view of all the fractional truths, nor, therefore, until it has been fully seen what each fractional truth can do by itself.

What Bentham's fractional truths could do there is no such good means of showing as by a review of his philosophy; and such a review, though inevitably a most brief and general one, it is now necessary to attempt.

The first question in regard to any man of speculation is, What is his theory of human life? In the minds of many philosophers, whatever theory they have of this sort is latent; and it would be a revelation to themselves to have it pointed out to them in their writings as others can see it, unconsciously moulding every thing to its own likeness. But Bentham always knew his own premises, and made his reader know them: it was not his custom to leave the theoretic grounds of his practical conclusions to conjecture. Few great thinkers have afforded the means of assigning with so much certainty the exact conception which they had formed of man and of man's life.

Man is conceived by Bentham as a being susceptible of pleasures and pains, and governed in all his conduct partly by the different modifications of self-interest, and the passions commonly classed as selfish, partly by sympathies, or occasionally antipathies, towards other beings. And here Bentham's conception of human nature stops. He does not exclude religion: the prospect of divine rewards and punishments he includes under the head of "self-regarding interest;" and the devotional feeling, under that of sympathy with God. But the whole of the impelling or restraining principles, whether of this or of another world, which he recognizes, are either self-love, or love or hatred towards other sentient beings. That there might be no doubt of what he thought on the subject, he has not left us to the general evidence of his writings, but has drawn out a "Table of the Springs of Action," an express enumeration and classification of human motives, with their various names, laudatory, vituperative, and neutral; and this table, to be found in Part I. of his collected works, we recommend to the study of those who would understand his philosophy.

Man is never recognized by him as a being capable of pursuing spiritual perfection as an end; of desiring, for its own sake, the conformity of his own character to his standard of excellence, without hope of good, or fear of evil, from other source than his own inward consciousness. Even in the more limited form of conscience, this great fact in human nature escapes him. Nothing is more curious than the absence of recognition, in any of his writings, of the existence of conscience, as a thing distinct from philanthropy, from affection for God or man, and from self-interest in this world or in the next. There is a studied abstinence from any of the phrases, which, in the mouths of others, import the acknowledgment of such a fact.* If we find the words "conscience," "principle,"

---

* In a passage in the last volume of his book on Evidence, and possibly in one or two other places, the "love of justice" is spoken of as a feeling inherent in almost all mankind. It is impossible, without ex-

"moral rectitude," "moral duty," in his "Table of the Springs of Action," it is among the synonymes of the "love of reputattion;" with an intimation as to the two former phrases, that they are also sometimes synonymous with the *religious* motive, or the motive of *sympathy*. The feeling of moral approbation or disapprobation, properly so called, either towards ourselves or our fellow-creatures, he seems unaware of the existence of; and neither the word *self-respect,* nor the idea to which that word is appropriated, occurs even once, so far as our recollection serves us, in his whole writings.

Nor is it only the moral part of man's nature, in the strict sense of the term—the desire of perfection, or the feeling of an approving or of an accusing conscience—that he overlooks: he but faintly recognizes, as a fact in human nature, the pursuit of any other ideal end for its own sake. The sense of *honor* and personal dignity—that feeling of personal exaltation and degradation which acts independently of other people's opinion, or even in defiance of it; the love of *beauty,* the passion of the artist; the love of *order,* of congruity, of consistency in all things, and conformity to their end; the love of *power,* not in the limited form of power over other human beings, but abstract power, the power of making our volitions effectual; the love of *action,* the thirst for movement and activity, a principle scarcely of less influence in human life than its opposite, the love of ease—none of these powerful constituents of human nature are thought worthy of a place among the "Springs of Action;" and though there is possibly no one of them, of the existence of which an acknowledgment might not be found in some corner of Bentham's writings, no conclusions are ever founded on the acknowledgment. Man, that most complex being, is a very simple one in his eyes. Even under the head of *sympathy,* his recognition does not extend to the more complex forms of the feeling—the love of *loving,*

planations now unattainable, to ascertain what sense is to be put upon casual expressions so inconsistent with the general tenor of his philosophy.

the need of a sympathizing support, or of objects of admiration and reverence. If he thought at all of any of the deeper feelings of human nature, it was but as idiosyncrasies of taste, with which the moralist no more than the legislator had any concern, further than to prohibit such as were mischievous among the actions to which they might chance to lead. To say either that man should, or that he should not, take moral pleasure in one thing, displeasure in another, appeared to him as much an act of despotism in the moralist as in the political ruler.

It would be most unjust to Bentham to surmise (as narrow-minded and passionate adversaries are apt in such cases to do) that this picture of human nature was copied from himself; that all those constituents of humanity, which he rejected from his table of motives, were wanting in his own breast. The unusual strength of his early feelings of virtue was, as we have seen, the original cause of all his speculations; and a noble sense of morality, and especially of justice, guides and pervades them all. But having been early accustomed to keep before his mind's eye the happiness of mankind (or rather of the whole sentient world), as the only thing desirable in itself, or which rendered any thing else desirable, he confounded all disinterested feelings which he found in himself with the desire of general happiness; just as some religious writers, who loved virtue for its own sake, as much perhaps as men could do, habitually confounded their love of virtue with their fear of hell. It would have required greater subtlety than Bentham possessed to distinguish from each other feelings, which, from long habit, always acted in the same direction; and his want of imagination prevented him from reading the distinction, where it is legible enough, in the hearts of others.

Accordingly, he has not been followed in this grand oversight by any of the able men, who, from the extent of their intellectual obligations to him, have been regarded as his disciples. They may have followed him in his doctrine of utility, and his rejection of a moral sense as the test of right and wrong; but, while repudiating it as such, they have, with Hartley, acknowledged it as a fact in human nature; they have endeavored to account for it, to assign its laws: nor are they justly chargeable either with undervaluing this part of our nature, or with any disposition to throw it into the background of their speculations. If any part of the influence of this cardinal error has extended itself to them, it is circuitously, and through the effect on their minds of other parts of Bentham's doctrines.

Sympathy, the only disinterested motive which Bentham recognized, he felt the inadequacy of, except in certain limited cases, as a security for virtuous action. Personal affection, he well knew, is as liable to operate to the injury of third parties, and requires as much to be kept under government, as any other feeling whatever; and general philanthropy, considered as a motive influencing mankind in general, he estimated at its true value, when divorced from the feeling of duty —as the very weakest and most unsteady of all feelings. There remained, as a motive by which mankind are influenced, and by which they may be guided to their good, only personal interest. Accordingly, Bentham's idea of the world is that of a collection of persons pursuing each his separate interest or pleasure, and the prevention of whom from jostling one another more than is unavoidable may be attempted by hopes and fears derived from three sources—the law, religion, and public opinion. To these three powers, considered as binding human conduct, he gave the name of *sanctions*—the *political* sanction, operating by the rewards and penalties of the law; the *religious* sanction, by those expected from the Ruler of the universe; and the *popular,* which he characteristically calls also the *moral* sanction, operating through the pains and pleasures arising from the favor or disfavor of our fellow-creatures.

Such is Bentham's theory of the world. And now, in a spirit neither of apology nor of censure, but of calm appreciation, we are to inquire how far this view of human nature and life will carry any one; how much it will accomplish in morals, and how much in political and social philosophy; what it will do for the individual, and what for society.

It will do nothing for the conduct of the individual, beyond prescribing some of the more obvious dictates of worldly prudence, and outward probity and beneficence. There is no need to expatiate on the deficiencies of a system of ethics which does not pretend to aid individuals in the formation of their own character; which recognizes no such wish as that of self-culture, we may even say, no such power, as existing in human nature; and, if it did recognize, could furnish little assistance to that great duty, because it overlooks the existence of about half of the whole number of mental feelings which human beings are capable of, including all those of which the direct objects are states of their own mind.

Morality consists of two parts. One of these is self-education—the training, by the human being himself, of his affections and will. That department is a blank in Bentham's system. The other and co-equal part, the regulation of his outward actions, must be altogether halting and imperfect without the first; for how can we judge in what manner many an action will affect even the worldly interests of ourselves or others, unless we take in, as part of the question, its influence on the regulation of our or their affections and desires? A moralist on Bentham's principles may get as far as this, that he ought not to slay, burn, or steal; but what will be his qualifications for regulating the nicer shades of human behavior, or for laying down even the greater moralities as to those facts in human life which are liable to influence the depths of the character quite independently of any influence on worldly circumstances—such, for instance, as the sexual relations, or those of family in general, or any other social and sympathetic connections of an intimate kind? The moralities of these questions depend essentially on considerations which Bentham never so much as took into the account; and, when he happened to be in the right, it was always, and necessarily, on wrong or insufficient grounds.

It is fortunate for the world that Bentham's taste lay rather in the direction of jurisprudential, than of properly ethical, inquiry. Nothing expressly of the latter kind has been published under his name, except the "Deontology"—a book scarcely ever, in our experience, alluded to by any admirer of Bentham, without deep regret that it ever saw the light. We did not expect from Bentham correct systematic views of ethics, or a sound treatment of any question, the moralities of which require a profound knowledge of the human heart; but we did anticipate that the greater moral questions would have been boldly plunged into, and at least a searching criticism produced of the received opinions: we did not expect that the *petite morale* almost alone would have been treated, and that with the most pedantic minuteness, and on the *quid pro quo* principles which regulate trade. The book has not even the value which would belong to an authentic exhibition of the legitimate consequences of an erroneous line of thought; for the style proves it to have been so entirely rewritten, that it is impossible to tell how much or how little of it is Bentham's. The collected edition, now in progress, will not, it is said, include Bentham's religious writings: these, although we think most of them of exceedingly small value, are at least his; and the world has a right to whatever light they throw upon the constitution of his mind. But the omission of the "Deontology" would be an act of editorial discretion which we should deem entirely justifiable.

If Bentham's theory of life can do so little for the individual, what can it do for society?

It will enable a society which has attained a certain state of spiritual development, and the maintenance of which in that state is otherwise provided for, to prescribe the rules by which it may protect its material interests. It will do nothing (except sometimes as an instrument in the hands of a higher

doctrine) for the spiritual interests of society; nor does it
suffice of itself even for the material interests. That which
alone enables any body of human beings to exist as a society,
is national character: *that* it is which causes one nation to
succeed in what it attempts, another to fail; one nation to
understand and aspire to elevated things, another to grovel in
mean ones; which makes the greatness of one nation lasting,
and dooms another to early and rapid decay. The true teacher
of the fitting social arrangements for England, France, or
America, is the one who can point out how the English,
French, or American character can be improved, and how it
has been made what it is. A philosophy of laws and institutions, not founded on a philosophy of national character, is an
absurdity. But what could Bentham's opinion be worth on national character? How could he, whose mind contained so few
and so poor types of individual character, rise to that higher
generalization? All he can do is but to indicate means by
which, in any given state of the national mind, the material interests of society can be protected; saving the question, of
which others must judge, whether the use of those means
would have, on the national character, any injurious influence.

We have arrived, then, at a sort of estimate of what a philosophy like Bentham's can do. It can teach the means of or-
ganizing and regulating the merely *business* part of the social
arrangements. Whatever can be understood, or whatever done,
without reference to moral influences, his philosophy is equal
to: where those influences require to be taken into account,
it is at fault. He committed the mistake of supposing that the
business part of human affairs was the whole of them; all,
at least, that the legislator and the moralist had to do with.
Not that he disregarded moral influences when he perceived
them; but his want of imagination, small experience of human
feelings, and ignorance of the filiation and connection of feelings with one another, made this rarely the case.

The business part is accordingly the only province of
human affairs which Bentham has cultivated with any success;

into which he has introduced any considerable number of comprehensive and luminous practical principles. That is the field of his greatness; and there he is indeed great. He has swept away the accumulated cobwebs of centuries; he has untied knots which the efforts of the ablest thinkers, age after age, had only drawn tighter; and it is no exaggeration to say of him, that, over a great part of the field, he was the first to shed the light of reason.

We turn with pleasure from what Bentham could not do to what he did. It is an ungracious task to call a great benefactor of mankind to account for not being a greater; to insist upon the errors of a man who has originated more new truths, has given to the world more sound practical lessons, than it ever received, except in a few glorious instances, from any other individual. The unpleasing part of our work is ended. We are now to show the greatness of the man; the grasp which his intellect took of the subjects with which it was fitted to deal; the giant's task which was before him; and the hero's courage and strength with which he achieved it. Nor let that which he did be deemed of small account because its province was limited: man has but the choice to go a little way in many paths, or a great way in only one. The field of Bentham's labors was like the space between two parallel lines—narrow to excess in one direction; in another, it reached to infinity.

Bentham's speculations, as we are already aware, began with law; and in that department he accomplished his greatest triumphs. He found the philosophy of law a chaos: he left it a science. He found the practice of the law an Augean stable: he turned the river into it which is mining and sweeping away mound after mound of its rubbish.

Without joining in the exaggerated invectives against lawyers which Bentham sometimes permitted to himself, or making one portion of society alone accountable for the fault of all, we may say, that circumstances had made English lawyers in a peculiar degree, liable to the reproach of Voltaire, who defines lawyers the "conservators of ancient barbarous usages." The basis of the English law was, and still is, the feudal system. That system, like all those which existed as custom before they were established as law, possessed a certain degree of suitableness to the wants of the society among whom it grew up; that is to say, of a tribe of rude soldiers, holding a conquered people in subjection, and dividing its spoils among themselves. Advancing civilization had, however, converted this armed encampment of barbarous warriors, in the midst of enemies reduced to slavery, into an industrious, commercial, rich, and free people. The laws which were suitable to the first of these states of society could have no manner of relation to the circumstances of the second; which could not even have come into existence, unless something had been done to adapt those laws to it. But the adaptation was not the result of thought and design: it arose not from any comprehensive consideration of the new state of society and its exigencies. What was done, was done by a struggle of centuries between the old barbarism and the new civilization; between the feudal aristocracy of conquerors holding fast to the rude system they had established, and the conquered effecting their emancipation. The last was the growing power, but was never strong enough to break its bonds, though ever and anon some weak point gave way. Hence the law came to be like the costume of a full-grown man who had never put off the clothes made for him when he first went to school. Band after band had burst; and as the rent widened, then, without removing any thing except what might drop off of itself, the hole was darned, or patches of fresh law were brought from the nearest shop, and stuck on. Hence all ages of English history have given one another rendezvous in English law: their several products may be seen all together, not interfused, but heaped one upon another, as many different ages of the earth may be read in some perpendicular section of its surface; the deposits of each successive period not substituted, but superimposed on those of the preceding. And in the world of law, no less than in the physical world, every commotion and conflict of the elements has left its mark behind in some break or irregularity of the strata. Every struggle which ever rent the bosom of society is apparent in the disjointed condition of the part of the field of law which covers the spot: nay, the very traps and pitfalls which one contending party set for another are still standing; and the teeth, not of hyenas only, but of foxes and all cunning animals, are imprinted on the curious remains found in these antediluvian caves.

In the English law, as in the Roman before it, the adaptations of barbarous laws to the growth of civilized society were made chiefly by stealth. They were generally made by the courts of justice, who could not help reading the new wants of mankind in the cases between man and man which came before them; but who, having no authority to make new laws for those new wants, were obliged to do the work covertly, and evade the jealousy and opposition of an ignorant, prejudiced, and, for the most part, brutal and tyrannical legislature. Some of the most necessary of these improvements, such as the giving force of law to trusts and the breaking-up of entails, were effected in actual opposition to the strongly declared will of Parliament, whose clumsy hands, no match for the astuteness of judges, could not, after repeated trials, manage to make any law which the judges could not find a trick for rendering inoperative. The whole history of the contest about trusts may still be read in the words of a conveyance, as could the contest about entails, till the abolition of fine and recovery by a bill of the present Attorney-General; but dearly did the client pay for the cabinet of historical curiosities which he was obliged to purchase every time that he made a settlement of his estate. The result of this mode of improving social institutions was, that whatever new things were done had to be done in consistency with old forms and names; and the laws were improved with much the same effect, as if, in the improvement of agriculture, the plough could only have been introduced by making it look like a spade; or as if, when the primeval practice of ploughing by the horse's tail gave way to the innovation of harness, the tail, for form's sake, had still remained attached to the plough.

When the conflicts were over, and the mixed mass settled down into something like a fixed state, and that state a very profitable and therefore a very agreeable one to lawyers, they, following the natural tendency of the human mind, began to theorize upon it, and, in obedience to necessity, had to digest it, and give it a systematic form. It was from this thing of shreds and patches, in which the only part that approached to order or system was the early barbarous part, already more than half superseded, that English lawyers had to construct, by induction and abstraction, their philosophy of law, and without the logical habits and general intellectual cultivation which the lawyers of the Roman empire brought to a similar task. Bentham found the philosophy of law what English practising lawyers had made it—a jumble, in which *real* and *personal* property, *law* and *equity, felony, premunire, misprision,* and *misdemeanor*—words without a vestige of meaning when detached from the history of English institutions; mere tide-marks to point out the line which the sea and the shore, in their secular struggles, had adjusted as their mutual boundary—all passed for distinctions inherent in the nature of things; in which every absurdity, every lucrative abuse, had a reason found for it—a reason which only now and then even pretended to be drawn from expediency; most commonly a technical reason, one of mere form, derived from the old barbarous system. While the theory of the law was in this state, to describe what the practice of it was would require the pen of a Swift, or of Bentham himself. The whole progress of a suit at law seemed like a series of contrivances for lawyers' profit, in which the suitors were regarded as the prey; and, if the poor were not the helpless victims of every Sir Giles Overreach who could pay the price, they might thank opinion and manners for it, not the law.

It may be fancied by some people, that Bentham did an easy thing in merely calling all this absurd, and proving it to be so. But he began the contest a young man, and he had grown old before he had any followers. History will one day refuse to give credit to the intensity of the superstition which, till very lately, protected this mischievous mess from examination or doubt—passed off the charming representations of Blackstone for a just estimate of the English law, and proclaimed the shame of human reason to be the perfection of it. Glory to Bentham that he has dealt to this superstition its deathblow; that he has been the Hercules of this hydra, the St. George of this pestilent dragon! The honor is all his: nothing but his peculiar qualities could have done it. There were wanted his indefatigable perseverance; his firm self-reliance, needing no support from other men's opinion; his intensely practical turn of mind; his synthetical habits; above all, his peculiar method. Metaphysicians, armed with vague generalities, had often tried their hands at the subject, and left it no more advanced than they found it. Law is a matter of business; means and ends are the things to be considered in it, not abstractions: vagueness was not to be met by vagueness, but by definiteness and precision; details were not to be encountered with generalities, but with details. Nor could any progress be made on such a subject by merely showing that existing things were bad: it was necessary also to show how they might be made better. No great man whom we read of was qualified to do this thing, except Bentham. He has done it, once and for ever.

Into the particulars of what Bentham has done we cannot enter: many hundred pages would be required to give a tolerable abstract of it. To sum up our estimate under a few heads: First, He has expelled mysticism from the philosophy of law, and set the example of viewing laws in a practical light, as means to certain definite and precise ends. Secondly, He has cleared up the confusion and vagueness attaching to the idea of law in general, to the idea therein involved.

Thirdly, He demonstrated the necessity and practicability of *codification,* or the conversion of all law into a written and systematically arranged code; not like the Code Napoléon— a code without a single definition, requiring a constant refer- ence to anterior precedent for the meaning of its technical terms—but one containing within itself all that is necessary for its own interpretation, together with a perpetual provision for its own emendation and improvement. He has shown of what parts such a code would consist; the relation of those parts to one another; and, by his distinctions and classifica- tions, has done very much towards showing what should be, or might be, its nomenclature and arrangement. What he has left undone, he has made it comparatively easy for others to do. Fourthly, He has taken a systematic view* of the exigen- cies of society for which the civil code is intended to provide, and of the principles of human nature by which its provisions are to be tested; and this view, defective (as we have already intimated) wherever spiritual interests require to be taken into account, is excellent for the large portion of the laws of any country which are designed for the protection of material interests. Fifthly (to say nothing of the subject of punishment, for which something considerable had been done before), He found the philosophy of judicial procedure, including that of judicial establishments and of evidence, in a more wretched state than even any other part of the philosophy of law: he carried it at once almost to perfection. He left it with every one of its principles established, and little remaining to be done even in the suggestion of practical arrangements.

These assertions in behalf of Bentham may be left, without fear for the result, in the hands of those who are competent to judge of them. There are now, even in the highest seats of justice, men to whom the claims made for him will not appear extravagant. Principle after principle of those propounded by him is moreover making its way by infiltration into the un-

* See the "Principles of Civil Law," contained in Part II. of his col- lected works.

derstandings most shut against his influence, and driving nonsense and prejudice from one corner of them to another. The reform of the laws of any country, according to his principles, can only be gradual, and may be long ere it is accomplished; but the work is in progress, and both parliament and the judges are every year doing something, and often something not inconsiderable, towards the forwarding of it.

It seems proper here to take notice of an accusation sometimes made both against Bentham and against the principle of codification—as if they required one uniform suit of ready-made laws for all times and all states of society. The doctrine of codification, as the word imports, relates to the form only of the laws, not their substance: it does not concern itself with what the laws should be, but declares, that, whatever they are, they ought to be systematically arranged, and fixed down to a determinate form of words. To the accusation, so far as it affects Bentham, one of the essays in the collection of his works (then for the first time published in English) is a complete answer—that "On the Influence of Time and Place in Matters of Legislation." It may there be seen that the different exigencies of different nations with respect to law occupied his attention as systematically as any other portion of the wants which render laws necessary; with the limitations, it is true, which were set to all his speculations by the imperfections of his theory of human nature. For, taking, as we have seen, next to no account of national character, and the causes which form and maintain it, he was precluded from considering, except to a very limited extent, the laws of a country as an instrument of national culture—one of their most important aspects, and in which they must of course vary according to the degree and kind of culture already attained, as a tutor gives his pupil different lessons according to the progress already made in his education. The same laws would not have suited our wild ancestors, accustomed to rude independence, and a people of Asiatics bowed down by military despotism: the slave needs to be trained to govern himself, the savage to submit to the government of others. The same laws will not suit the English, who distrust everything which emanates from general principles, and the French, who distrust whatever does not so emanate. Very different institutions are needed to train to the perfection of their nature, or to constitute into a united nation and social polity, an essentially *subjective* people like the Germans, and an essentially *objective* people like those of Northern and Central Italy—the one affectionate and dreamy, the other passionate and worldly; the one trustful and loyal, the other calculating and suspicious; the one not practical enough, the other overmuch; the one wanting individuality, the other fellow-feeling; the one failing for want of exacting enough for itself, the other for want of conceding enough to others. Bentham was little accustomed to look at institutions in their relation to these topics. The effects of this oversight must, of course, be perceptible throughout his speculations; but we do not think the errors into which it led him very material in the greater part of civil and penal law: it is in the department of constitutional legislation that they were fundamental.

The Benthamic theory of government has made so much noise in the world of late years, it has held such a conspicuous place among Radical philosophies, and Radical modes of thinking have participated so much more largely than any others in its spirit, that many worthy persons imagine there is no other Radical philosophy extant. Leaving such people to discover their mistake as they may, we shall expend a few words in attempting to discriminate between the truth and error of this celebrated theory.

There are three great questions in government. First, To what authority is it for the good of the people that they should be subject? Secondly, How are they to be induced to obey authority? The answers to these two questions vary indefinitely, according to the degree and kind of civilization and cultivation already attained by a people, and their peculiar aptitudes for receiving more. Comes next a third question, not liable to so much variation; namely, By what means are the abuses of this authority to be checked? This third question is the only one of the three to which Bentham seriously applies himself; and he gives it the only answer it admits of—Responsibility; responsibility to persons whose interest, whose obvious and recognizable interest, accords with the end in view—good government. This being granted, it is next to be asked, In what body of persons this identity of interest with good government (that is, with the interest of the whole community) is to be found? In nothing less, says Bentham, than the numerical majority; nor, say we, even in the numerical majority itself: of no portion of the community less than all will the interest coincide, at all times and in all respects, with the interest of all. But since power given to all, by a representative government, is, in fact, given to a majority, we are obliged to fall back upon the first of our three questions; namely, Under what authority is it for the good of the people that they be placed? And if to this the answer be, Under that of a majority among themselves, Bentham's system cannot be questioned. This one assumption being made, his "Constitutional Code" is admirable. That extraordinary power which he possessed, of at once seizing comprehensive principles, and scheming out minute details, is brought into play with surpassing vigor in devising means for preventing rulers from escaping from the control of the majority; for enabling and inducing the majority to exercise that control unremittingly; and for providing them with servants of every desirable endowment, moral and intellectual, compatible with entire subservience to their will.

But *is* this fundamental doctrine of Bentham's political philosophy an universal truth? Is it, at all times and places, good for mankind to be under the absolute authority of the majority of themselves? We say, the authority; not the political authority merely, because it is chimerical to suppose that whatever has absolute power over men's bodies will not arrogate it over their minds; will not seek to control (not perhaps by legal penalties, but by the persecutions of society) opinions and feelings which depart from its standard; will not attempt to shape the education of the young by its model, and to extinguish all books, all schools, all combinations of individuals for joint action upon society, which may be attempted for the purpose of keeping alive a spirit at variance with its own. Is it, we say, the proper condition of man, in all ages and nations to be under the despotism of Public Opinion?

It is very conceivable that such a doctrine should find acceptance from some of the noblest spirits in a time of re-action against the aristocratic governments of modern Europe—governments founded on the entire sacrifice (except so far as prudence, and sometimes humane feeling, interfere) of the community generally to the self-interest and ease of a few. European reformers have been accustomed to see the numerical majority everywhere unjustly depressed, everywhere trampled upon, or at the best overlooked, by governments; nowhere possessing power enough to extort redress of their most positive grievances, provision for their mental culture, or even to prevent themselves from being taxed avowedly for the pecuniary profit of the ruling classes. To see these things, and to seek to put an end to them by means (among other things) of giving more political power to the majority, constitutes Radicalism; and it is because so many in this age have felt this wish, and have felt that the realization of it was an object worthy of men's devoting their lives to it, that such a theory of government as Bentham's has found favor with them. But, though to pass from one form of bad government to another be the ordinary fate of mankind, philosophers ought not to make themselves parties to it by sacrificing one portion of important truth to another.

The numerical majority of any society whatever, must consist of persons all standing in the same social position, and having, in the main, the same pursuits; namely, unskilled manual laborers. And we mean no disparagement to them: whatever we say to their disadvantage, we say equally of a numerical majority of shopkeepers or of squires. Where there is identity of position and pursuits, there also will be identity of partialities, passions, and prejudices; and to give to any one set of partialities, passions, and prejudices, absolute power, without counter-balance from partialities, passions, and prejudices of a different sort, is the way to render the correction of any of those imperfections hopeless; to make one narrow, mean type of human nature universal and perpetual; and to crush every influence which tends to the further improvement of man's intellectual and moral nature. There must, we know, be some paramount power in society; and that the majority should be that power is, on the whole, right, not as being just in itself but as being less unjust than any other footing on which the matter can be placed. But it is necessary that the institutions of society should make provision for keeping up, in some form or other, as a corrective to partial views, and a shelter for freedom of thought and individuality of character, a perpetual and standing opposition to the will of the majority. All countries which have long continued progressive, or been durably great, have been so because there has been an organized opposition to the ruling power, of whatever kind that power was—plebeians to patricians, clergy to kings, free-thinkers to clergy, kings to barons, commons to king and aristocracy. Almost all the greatest men who ever lived have formed part of such an opposition. Wherever some such quarrel has not been going on; wherever it has been terminated by the complete victory of one of the contending principles, and no new contest has taken the place of the old—society has either hardened into Chinese stationariness, or fallen into dissolution. A centre of resistance, round which all the moral and social elements which the ruling power views with disfavor may cluster themselves, and behind whose bulwarks they may find shelter from the attempts of that power to hunt them out of existence, is as necessary where the opinion of the majority is sovereign, as where the ruling power is a hierarchy or an aristocracy. Where no such *point d'appui* exists, there the human race will inevitably degenerate; and the question, whether the United States, for instance, will in time sink into another China (also a most commercial and industrious nation), resolves itself, to us, into the question, whether such a centre of resistance will gradually evolve itself or not.

These things being considered, we cannot think that Bentham made the most useful employment which might have been made of his great powers, when, not content with enthroning the majority as sovereign, by means of universal suffrage, without king, or house of lords, he exhausted all the resources of ingenuity in devising means for riveting the yoke of public opinion closer and closer round the necks of all public functionaries, and excluding every possibility of the exercise of the slightest or most temporary influence either by a minority, or by the functionary's own notions of right. Surely, when any power has been made the strongest power, enough has been done for it: care is thenceforth wanted rather to prevent that strongest power from swallowing up all others. Wherever all the forces of society act in one single direction, the just claims of the individual human being are in extreme peril. The power of the majority is salutary so far as it is used defensively, not offensively—as its exertion is tempered by respect for the personality of the individual, and deference to superiority of cultivated intelligence. If Bentham had employed himself in pointing out the means by which institutions fundamentally democratic might be best adapted to the preservation and strengthening of those two sentiments, he would have done something more permanently valuable, and more worthy of his great intellect. Montesquieu, with the lights of the present age, would have done it; and we are possibly destined to receive this benefit from the Montesquieu of our own times—M. de Tocqueville.

Do we, then, consider Bentham's political speculations useless? Far from it. We consider them only one-sided. He has brought out into a strong light, has cleared from a thousand confusions and misconceptions, and pointed out with admirable skill the best means of promoting, one of the ideal qualities of a perfect government—identity of interest between the trustees and the community for whom they hold their power in trust. This quality is not attainable in its ideal perfection, and must, moreover, be striven for with a perpetual eye to all other requisites: but those other requisites must still more be striven for, without losing sight of this; and, when the slightest postponement is made of it to any other end, the sacrifice, often necessary, is never unattended with evil. Bentham has pointed out how complete this sacrifice is in modern European societies; how exclusively, partial and sinister interests are the ruling power there, with only such check as is imposed by public opinion: which being thus, in the existing order of things, perpetually apparent as a source of good, he was led by natural partiality to exaggerate its intrinsic excellence. This sinister interest of rulers, Bentham hunted through all its disguises, and especially through those which hide it from the men themselves who are influenced by it. The greatest service rendered by him to the philosophy of universal human nature, is, perhaps, his illustration of what he terms "interest-begotten prejudice,"—the common tendency of man to make a duty and a virtue of following his self-interest. The idea, it is true, was far from being peculiarly Bentham's: the artifices by which we persuade ourselves that we are not yielding to our selfish inclinations when we are, had attracted the notice of all moralists, and had been probed by religious writers to a depth as much below Bentham's as their knowledge of the profundities and windings of the human heart was superior to his. But it is selfish interest in the form of class-interest, and the class-morality founded thereon, which Bentham has illustrated—the manner in which any set of persons who mix much together, and have a common interest, are apt to make that common interest their standard of virtue, and the social feelings of the members of the class are made to play into the hands of their selfish

ones; whence the union, so often exemplified in history, between the most heroic personal disinterestedness and the most
odious class-selfishness. This was one of Bentham's leading
ideas, and almost the only one by which he contributed to the
elucidation of history; much of which, except so far as this
explained it, must have been entirely inexplicable to him. The
idea was given him by Helvetius, whose book, "De l'Esprit,"
is one continued and most acute commentary on it; and together with the other great idea of Helvetius, the influence of
circumstances on character, it will make his name live by the
side of Rousseau, when most of the other French metaphysicians of the eighteenth century will be extant as such only in
literary history.

In the brief view which we have been able to give of Bentham's philosophy, it may surprise the reader that we have
said so little about the first principle of it, with which his
name is more identified than with any thing else—the "principle of utility," or, as he afterwards named it, "the greatest-
happiness principle." It is a topic on which much were to be
said, if there were room, or if it were in reality necessary for
the just estimation of Bentham. On an occasion more suitable
for a discussion of the metaphysics of morality, or on which
the elucidations necessary to make an opinion on so abstract
a subject intelligible could be conveniently given, we should
be fully prepared to state what we think on this subject. At
present, we shall only say, that while, under proper explanations, we entirely agree with Bentham in his principle, we
do not hold with him that all right thinking on the details of
morals depends on its express assertion. We think utility, or
happiness, much too complex and indefinite an end to be
sought, except through the medium of various secondary
ends, concerning which there may be, and often is, agreement among persons who differ in their ultimate standard;
and about which there does, in fact, prevail a much greater
unanimity among thinking persons than might be supposed
from their diametrical divergence on the great questions of

moral metaphysics. As mankind are much more nearly of one nature, than of one opinion about their own nature, they are more easily brought to agree in their intermediate principles—*vera illa et media axiomata,* as Bacon says—than in their first principles; and the attempt to make the bearings of actions upon the ultimate end more evident than they can be made by referring them to the intermediate ends, and to estimate their value by a direct reference to human happiness, generally terminates in attaching most importance, not to those effects which are really the greatest, but to those which can most easily be pointed to, and individually identified. Those who adopt utility as a standard can seldom apply it truly, except through the secondary principles: those who reject it, generally do no more than erect those secondary principles into first principles. It is when two or more of the secondary principles conflict, that a direct appeal to some first principle becomes necessary: and then commences the practical importance of the utilitarian controversy, which is, in other respects, a question of arrangement and logical subordination rather than of practice; important principally, in a purely scientific point of view, for the sake of the systematic unity and coherency of ethical philosophy. It is probable, however, that to the principle of utility we owe all that Bentham did; that it was necessary to him to find a first principle which he could receive as self-evident, and to which he could attach all his other doctrines as logical consequences; that to him systematic unity was an indispensable condition of his confidence in his own intellect. And there is something further to be remarked. Whether happiness be or be not the end to which morality should be referred—that it be referred to an *end* of some sort, and not left in the dominion of vague feeling, or inexplicable internal conviction; that it be made a matter of reason and calculation, and not merely of sentiment—is essential to the very idea of moral philosophy; is, in fact, what renders argument or discussion on moral questions possible. That the morality of actions depends on the consequences which they tend to produce, is the doctrine of rational persons of all schools: that the good or evil of those consequences is measured solely by pleasure or pain, is all of the doctrine of the school of utility which is peculiar to it.

In so far as Bentham's adoption of the principle of utility induced him to fix his attention upon the consequences of actions as the consideration determining their morality, so far he was indisputably in the right path; though, to go far in it without wandering, there was needed a greater knowledge of the formation of character, and of the consequences of actions upon the agent's own frame of mind, than Bentham possessed. His want of power to estimate this class of consequences, together with his want of the degree of modest deference, which, from those who have not competent experience of their own, is due to the experience of others on that part of the subject, greatly limit the value of his speculations on questions of practical ethics.

He is chargeable also with another error, which it would be improper to pass over, because nothing has tended more to place him in opposition to the common feelings of mankind, and to give to his philosophy that cold, mechanical, and ungenial air which characterizes the popular idea of a Benthamite. This error, or rather one-sidedness, belongs to him, not as a utilitarian, but as a moralist by profession, and in common with almost all professed moralists, whether religious or philosophical: it is that of treating the *moral* view of actions and characters, which is unquestionably the first and most important mode of looking at them, as if it were the sole one; whereas it is only one of three, by all of which our sentiments towards the human being may be, ought to be, and, without entirely crushing our own nature, cannot but be, materially influenced. Every human action has three aspects —its *moral* aspect, or that of its right and wrong; its *aesthetic* aspect, or that of its *beauty;* its sympathetic aspect, or that of its *lovableness.* The first addresses itself to our reason and conscience; the second, to our imagination; the third, to our human fellow-feeling. According to the first, we approve or disapprove; according to the second, we admire or despise; according to the third, we love, pity, or dislike. The morality of an action depends on its foreseeable consequences: its beauty and its lovableness, or the reverse, depend on the qualities which it is evidence of. Thus a lie is *wrong,* because its effect is to mislead, and because it tends to destroy the confidence of man in man: it is also *mean,* because it is cowardly; because it proceeds from not daring to face the consequences of telling the truth; or, at best, is evidence of want of that *power* to compass our ends by straightforward means, which is conceived as properly belonging to every person not deficient in energy or in understanding. The action of Brutus in sentencing his sons was *right,* because it was executing a law, essential to the freedom of his country, against persons of whose guilt there was no doubt; it was *admirable,* because it evinced a rare degree of patriotism, courage, and self-control: but there was nothing *lovable* in it; it affords either no presumption in regard to lovable qualities, or a presumption of their deficiency. If one of the sons had engaged in the conspiracy from affection for the other, his action would have been lovable, though neither moral nor admirable. It is not possible for any sophistry to confound these three modes of viewing an action; but it is very possible to adhere to one of them exclusively, and lose sight of the rest. Sentimentality consists in setting the last two of the three above the first: the error of moralists in general, and of Bentham, is to sink the two latter entirely. This is preeminently the case with Bentham: he both wrote and felt as if the moral standard ought not only to be paramount (which it ought), but to be alone; as if it ought to be the sole master of all our actions, and even of all our sentiments; as if either to admire or like, or despise or dislike, a person for any action which neither does good nor harm, or which does not do a good or a harm proportioned to the sentiment entertained, were an injustice and a prejudice. He carried this so far, that there were certain phrases, which, being expressive of what he considered to be this groundless liking or aversion, he could not bear to hear pronounced in his presence. Among these phrases were those of *good and bad taste*. He thought it an insolent piece of dogmatism in one person to praise or condemn another in a matter of taste; as if men's likings and dislikings, on things in themselves indifferent, were not full of the most important inferences as to every point of their character; as if a person's tastes did not show him to be wise or a fool, cultivated or ignorant, gentle or rough, sensitive or callous, generous or sordid, benevolent or selfish, conscientious or depraved.

Connected with the same topic are Bentham's peculiar opinions on poetry. Much more has been said than there is any foundation for about his contempt for the pleasures of imagination and for the fine arts. Music was throughout life his favorite amusement: painting, sculpture, and the other arts addressed to the eye, he was so far from holding in any contempt, that he occasionally recognizes them as means employable for important social ends; though his ignorance of the deeper springs of human character prevented him (as it prevents most Englishmen) from suspecting how profoundly such things enter into the moral nature of man, and into the education both of the individual and of the race. But towards poetry in the narrower sense, that which employs the language of words, he entertained no favor. Words, he thought, were perverted from their proper office when they were employed in uttering any thing but precise logical truth. He says, somewhere in his works, that, "quantity of pleasure being equal, push-pin is as good as poetry;" but this is only a paradoxical way of stating what he would equally have said of the things which he most valued and admired. Another aphorism is attributed to him, which is much more characteristic of his view of this subject: "All poetry is misrepresentation." Poetry, he thought, consisted essentially in exaggeration for effect; in proclaiming some one view of a thing very emphatically, and suppressing all the limitations and qualifications. This trait of character seems to us a curious example of what Mr. Carlyle strikingly calls "the completeness of limited men." Here is a philosopher who is happy within his narrow boundary as no man of indefinite range ever was; who flatters himself that he is so completely emancipated from the essential law of poor human intellect, by which it can only see one thing at a time well, that he can even turn round upon the imperfection, and lay a solemn interdict upon it. Did Bentham really suppose that it is in poetry only that propositions cannot be exactly true—cannot contain in themselves all the limitations and qualifications with which they require to be taken when applied to practice? We have seen how far his own prose propositions are from realizing this Utopia; and even the attempt to approach it would be incompatible, not with poetry merely, but with oratory, and popular writing of every kind. Bentham's charge is true to the fullest extent: all writing which undertakes to make men feel truths as well as see them does take up one point at a time—does seek to impress that, to drive that home; to make it sink into and color the whole mind of the reader or hearer. It is justified in doing so, if the portion of truth which it thus enforces be that which is called for by the occasion. All writing addressed to the feelings has a natural tendency to exaggeration; but Bentham should have remembered, that in this, as in many things, we must aim at too much, to be assured of doing enough.

From the same principle in Bentham came the intricate and involved style, which makes his later writings books for the student only, not the general reader. It was from his perpetually aiming at impracticable precision. Nearly all his earlier and many parts of his later writings are models, as we have already observed, of light, playful, and popular style: a

Benthamiana might be made of passages worthy of Addison or Goldsmith. But in his later years, and more advanced studies, he fell into a Latin or German structure of sentence, foreign to the genius of the English language. He could not bear, for the sake of clearness and the reader's ease, to say, as ordinary men are content to do, a little more than the truth in one sentence, and correct it in the next. The whole of the qualifying remarks which he intended to make he insisted upon embedding as parentheses in the very middle of the sentence itself; and thus, the sense being so long suspended, and attention being required to the accessory ideas before the principal idea had been properly seized, it became difficult, without some practice, to make out the train of thought. It is fortunate that so many of the most important parts of his writings are free from this defect. We regard it as a *reductio ad absurdum* of his objection to poetry. In trying to write in a manner against which the same objection should not lie, he could stop nowhere short of utter unreadableness; and, after all, attained no more accuracy than is compatible with opinions as imperfect and one-sided as those of any poet or sentimentalist breathing. Judge, then, in what state literature and philosophy would be, and what chance they would have of influencing the multitude, if his objection were allowed, and all styles of writing banished which would not stand his test.

We must here close this brief and imperfect view of Bentham and his doctrines; in which many parts of the subject have been entirely untouched, and no part done justice to, but which at least proceeds from an intimate familiarity with his writings, and is nearly the first attempt at an impartial estimate of his character as a philosopher, and of the result of his labors to the world.

After every abatement (and it has been seen whether we have made our abatements sparingly), there remains to Bentham an indisputable place among the great intellectual benefactors of mankind. His writings will long form an indispensable part of the education of the highest order of practical thinkers; and the collected edition of them ought to be in the hands of every one who would either understand his age, or take any beneficial part in the great business of it.*

* Since the first publication of this paper, Lord Brougham's brilliant series of characters has been published, including a sketch of Bentham. Lord Brougham's view of Bentham's characteristics agrees in the main points, so far as it goes, with the result of our more minute examination; but there is an imputation cast upon Bentham, of a jealous and splenetic disposition in private life, of which we feel called upon to give at once a contradiction and an explanation. It is indispensable to a correct estimate of any of Bentham's dealings with the world, to bear in mind, that, in everything except abstract speculation, he was to the last, what we have called him, essentially a boy. He had the freshness, the simplicity, the confidingness, the liveliness and activity, all the delightful qualities of boyhood, and the weaknesses which are the reverse side of those qualities—the undue importance attached to trifles, the habitual mismeasurement of the practical bearing and value of things, the readiness to be either delighted or offended on inadequate cause. These were the real sources of what was unreasonable in some of his attacks on individuals, and in particular on Lord Brougham on the subject of his law Reforms; they were no more the effect of envy or malice, or any really unamiable quality, than the freaks of a pettish child, and are scarcely a fitter subject of censure or criticism.

Coleridge

The name of Coleridge is one of the few English names of our time which are likely to be oftener pronounced, and to become symbolical of more important things, in proportion as the inward workings of the age manifest themselves more and more in outward facts. Bentham excepted, no Englishman of recent date has left his impress so deeply in the opinions and mental tendencies of those among us who attempt to enlighten their practice by philosophical meditation. If it be true, as Lord Bacon affirms, that a knowledge of the speculative opinions of the men between twenty and thirty years of age is the great source of political prophecy, the existence of Coleridge will show itself by no slight or ambiguous traces in the coming history of our country; for no one has contributed more to shape the opinions of those among its younger men, who can be said to have opinions at all.

The influence of Coleridge, like that of Bentham, extends far beyond those who share in the peculiarities of his religious or philosophical creed. He has been the great awakener in this country of the spirit of philosophy, within the bounds of traditional opinions. He has been, almost as truly as Bentham, "the great questioner of things established;" for a questioner needs not necessarily be an enemy. By Bentham, beyond all others, men have been led to ask themselves, in regard to any ancient or received opinion, Is it true? and by Coleridge, What is the meaning of it? The one took his stand *outside* the received opinion, and surveyed it as an entire stranger to it: the other looked at it from within, and endeavored to see it with the eyes of a believer in it; to discover by what apparent facts it was at first suggested, and by what appearances it has ever since been rendered continually credible—has seemed, to a succession of persons, to be a faithful interpretation of their experience. Bentham judged a proposition true or false as it accorded or not with the result of his own inquiries; and did not search very curiously into what might be meant by the proposition, when it obviously did not mean what he thought true. With Coleridge, on the contrary, the very fact that any doctrine had been believed by thoughtful men, and received by whole nations or generations of mankind, was part of the problem to be solved; was one of the phenomena to be accounted for. And, as Bentham's short and easy method of referring all to the selfish interests of aristocracies or priests or lawyers, or some other species of impostors, could not satisfy a man who saw so much farther into the complexities of the human intellect and feelings, he considered the long or extensive prevalence of any opinion as a presumption that it was not altogether a fallacy; that, to its first authors at least, it was the result of a struggle to express in words something which had a reality to them, though perhaps not to many of those who have since received the doctrine by mere tradition. The long duration of a belief, he thought, is at least proof of an adaptation in it to some portion or other of the human mind: and if, on digging down to the root, we do not find, as is generally the case, some truth, we shall find some natural want or requirement of human nature which the doctrine in question is fitted to satisfy; among which wants the instincts of selfishness and of credulity have a place, but by no means an exclusive one. From this difference in the points of view of the two philosophers, and from the too rigid adherence of each to his own, it was to be expected that Bentham should continually miss the truth which is in the traditional opinions, and Coleridge that which is out of them and at variance with them. But it was also likely that each would find, or show the way to finding, much of what the other missed.

It is hardly possible to speak of Coleridge, and his position among his contemporaries, without reverting to Bentham: they are connected by two of the closest bonds of association —resemblance and contrast. It would be difficult to find two persons of philosophic eminence more exactly the contrary of one another. Compare their modes of treatment of any subject, and you might fancy them inhabitants of different worlds. They seem to have scarcely a principle or a premise in common. Each of them sees scarcely any thing but what the other does not see. Bentham would have regarded Coleridge with a peculiar measure of the good-humored contempt with which he was accustomed to regard all modes of philosophizing different from his own. Coleridge would probably have made Bentham one of the exceptions to the enlarged and liberal appreciation which (to the credit of *his* mode of philosophizing) he extended to most thinkers of any eminence from whom he differed. But contraries, as logicians say, are but *quæ in eodem genere maxime distant*— the things which are farthest from one another in the same kind. These two agreed in being the men, who, in their age and country, did most to enforce, by precept and example, the necessity of a philosophy. They agreed in making it their occupation to recall opinions to first principles; taking no proposition for granted without examining into the grounds of it, and ascertaining that it possessed the kind and degree of evidence suitable to its nature. They agreed in recognizing that sound theory is the only foundation for sound practice; and that whoever despises theory, let him give himself what airs of wisdom he may, is self-convicted of being a quack. If a book were to be compiled containing all the best things ever said on the rule-of-thumb school of political craftsmanship, and on the insufficiency for practical purposes of what the mere practical man calls experience, it is difficult to say whether the collection would be more indebted to the writings of Bentham or of Coleridge. They agreed, too, in perceiving that the groundwork of all other philosophy must be laid in the philosophy of the mind. To lay this foundation deeply and strongly, and to raise a superstructure in accordance with it, were the objects to which their lives were devoted. They employed, indeed, for the most part, different materials; but as the materials of both were real observations, the genuine product of experience, the results will, in the end, be found, not hostile, but supplementary, to one another. Of their methods of philosophizing, the same thing may be said: they were different, yet both were legitimate logical processes. In every respect, the two men are each other's "completing counterpart:" the strong points of each correspond to the weak points of the other. Whoever could master the premises and combine the methods of both would possess the entire English philosophy of his age. Coleridge used to say that every one is born either a Platonist or an Aristotelian: it may be similarly affirmed, that every Englishman of the present day is by implication either a Benthamite or a Coleridgian; holds views of human affairs which can only be proved true on the principles either of Bentham or of Coleridge. In one respect, indeed, the parallel fails. Bentham so improved and added to the system of philosophy he adopted, that, for his successors, he may almost be accounted its founder; while Coleridge, though he has left, on the system he inculcated, such traces of himself as cannot fail to be left by any mind of original powers, was anticipated in all the essentials of his doctrine by the great Germans of the latter half of the last century, and was accompanied in it by the remarkable series of their French expositors and followers. Hence, although Coleridge is to Englishmen the type and the main source of that doctrine, he is the creator rather of the shape in which it has appeared among us than of the doctrine itself.

The time is yet far distant, when, in the estimation of Coleridge, and of his influence upon the intellect of our time, any thing like unanimity can be looked for. As a poet, Coleridge has taken his place. The healthier taste, and more intelligent canons of poetic criticism, which he was himself mainly instrumental in diffusing, have at length assigned to him his proper rank, as one among the great (and, if we look to the powers shown rather than to the amount of actual achievement, among the greatest) names in our literature. But, as a philosopher, the class of thinkers has scarcely yet arisen by whom he is to be judged. The limited philosophical public of this country is as yet too exclusively divided between those to whom Coleridge and the views which he promulgated or defended are every thing, and those to whom they are nothing. A true thinker can only be justly estimated when his thoughts have worked their way into minds formed in a different school; have been wrought and moulded into consistency with all other true and relevant thoughts; when the noisy conflict of half-truths, angrily denying one another, has subsided, and ideas which seemed mutually incompatible have been found only to require mutual limitations. This time has not yet come for Coleridge. The spirit of philosophy in England, like that of religion, is still rootedly sectarian. Conservative thinkers and Liberals, transcendentalists and admirers of Hobbes and Locke, regard each other as out of the pale of philosophical intercourse; look upon each other's speculations as vitiated by an original taint, which makes all study of them, except for purposes of attack, useless, if not mischievous. An error much the same as if Kepler had refused to profit by Ptolemy's or Tycho's observations, because those astronomers believed that the sun moved round the earth; or as if Priestley and Lavoisier, because they differed on the doctrine of phlogiston, had rejected each other's chemical experiments. It is even a still greater error than either of these. For among the truths long recognized by Continental philosophers, but which very few Englishmen have yet arrived at, one is, the importance, in the present imperfect state of mental and social science, of antagonist modes of thought; which, it will one day be felt, are as necessary to one another in speculation, as mutually checking powers are in a political constitution. A clear insight, indeed, into this necessity, is the only rational or enduring basis of philosophical tolerance; the only condition under which liberality in matters of opinion can be any thing better than a polite synonyme for indifference between one opinion and another.

All students of man and society who possess that first requisite for so difficult a study, a due sense of its difficulties, are aware that the besetting danger is not so much of embracing falsehood for truth, as of mistaking part of the truth for the whole. It might be plausibly maintained, that in almost every one of the leading controversies, past or present, in social philosophy, both sides were in the right in what they affirmed, though wrong in what they denied; and that, if either could have been made to take the other's views in addition to its own, little more would have been needed to make its doctrine correct. Take, for instance, the question, how far mankind have gained by civilization. One observer is forcibly struck by the multiplication of physical comforts; the advancement and diffusion of knowledge; the decay of superstition; the facilities of mutual intercourse; the softening of manners; the decline of war and personal conflict; the progressive limitation of the tyranny of the strong over the weak; the great works accomplished throughout the globe by the co-operation of multitudes: and he becomes that very common character, the worshipper of "our enlightened age." Another fixes his attention, not upon the value of these advantages, but upon the high price which is paid for them; the relaxation of individual energy and courage; the loss of proud and self-relying independence; the slavery of so large a portion of mankind to artificial wants; their effeminate shrinking from even the shadow of pain; the dull, unexciting monotony of their lives, and the passionless insipidity, and absence of any marked individuality, in their characters; the contrast between the narrow mechanical understanding, produced by a life spent in executing by fixed rules a fixed task, and the varied powers of the man of the woods, whose subsistence and safety depend at each instant upon his capacity of extemporarily adapting means to ends; the demoralizing effect of great inequalities in wealth and social rank; and the sufferings of the great mass of the people of civilized countries, whose wants are scarcely better provided for than those of the savage, while they are bound by a thousand fetters in lieu of the freedom and excitement which are his compensations. One who attends to these things, and to these exclusively, will be apt to infer that savage life is preferable to civilized; that the work of civilization should as far as possible be undone; and, from the premises of Rousseau, he will not improbably be led to the practical conclusions of Rousseau's disciple, Robespierre. No two thinkers can be more entirely at variance than the two we have supposed—the worshippers of civilization and of independence, of the present and of the remote past. Yet all that is positive in the opinions of either of them is true: and we see how easy it would be to choose one's path, if either half of the truth were the whole of it; and how great may be the difficulty of framing, as it is necessary to do, a set of practical maxims which combine both.

So, again, one person sees in a very strong light the need which the great mass of mankind have of being ruled over by a degree of intelligence and virtue superior to their own. He is deeply impressed with the mischief done to the uneducated and uncultivated by weaning them of all habits of reverence, appealing to them as a competent tribunal to decide the most intricate questions, and making them think themselves capable, not only of being a light to themselves, but of giving the law to their superiors in culture. He sees, further, that cultivation, to be carried beyond a certain point, requires leisure; that leisure is the natural attribute of a hereditary aristocracy; that such a body has all the means of acquiring intellectual and moral superiority: and he needs be at no loss to endow them with abundant motives to it. An aristocracy indeed, being human, are, as he cannot but see, not exempt, any more than their inferiors, from the common need of being controlled and enlightened by a still greater wisdom and goodness than their own. For this, however, his reliance is upon reverence for a Higher above them, sedulously inculcated and fostered by the course of their education. We thus see brought together all the elements of a conscientious zealot for an aristocratic government, supporting and supported by an established Christian church. There is truth, and important truth, in this thinker's premises. But there is a thinker of a very different description, in whose premises there is an equal portion of truth. This is he who says, that an average man, even an average member of an aristocracy, if he can postpone the interests of other people to his own calculations or instincts of self-interest, will do so; that all governments in all ages have done so, as far as they were permitted, and generally to a ruinous extent; and that the only possible remedy is a pure democracy, in which the people are their own governors, and can have no selfish interest in oppressing themselves.

Thus it is in regard to every important partial truth: there are always two conflicting modes of thought—one tending to give to that truth too large, the other to give it too small, a place; and the history of opinion is generally an oscillation between these extremes. From the imperfection of the human faculties, it seldom happens, that, even in the minds of eminent thinkers, each partial view of their subject passes for its worth, and none for more than its worth. But, even if this just balance exist in the mind of the wiser teacher, it will not exist in his disciples, far less in the general mind. He cannot prevent that which is new in his doctrine, and on which, being new, he is forced to insist the most strongly, from making a disproportionate impression. The impetus necessary to overcome the obstacles which resist all novelties of opinion seldom fails to carry the public mind almost as far on the contrary side of the perpendicular. Thus every excess in either direction determines a corresponding re-action; improvement consisting only in this—that the oscillation, each time, departs rather less widely from the centre, and an ever-increasing tendency is manifested to settle finally in it.

Now, the Germano-Coleridgian doctrine is, in our view of the matter, the result of such a re-action. It expresses the revolt of the human mind against the philosophy of the eighteenth century. It is ontological, because that was experimental; conservative, because that was innovative; religious, because so much of that was infidel; concrete and historical, because that was abstract and metaphysical; poetical, because that was matter-of-fact and prosaic. In every respect, it flies off in the contrary direction to its predecessor: yet, faithful to the general law of improvement last noticed, it is less extreme in its opposition, it denies less of what is true in the doctrine it wars against, than had been the case in any previous philosophic re-action; and, in particular, far less than when the philosophy of the eighteenth century triumphed, and so memorably abused its victory, over that which preceded it.

We may begin our consideration of the two systems either at one extreme or the other—with their highest philosophical generalizations, or with their practical conclusions. The former seems preferable, because it is in their highest generalities that the difference between the two systems is most familiarly known.

Every consistent scheme of philosophy requires, as its starting-point, a theory respecting the sources of human knowledge, and the objects which the human faculties are capable of taking cognizance of. The prevailing theory in the eighteenth century, on this most comprehensive of questions, was that proclaimed by Locke, and commonly attributed to Aristotle—that all knowledge consists of generalizations from experience. Of nature, or any thing whatever external to ourselves, we know, according to this theory, nothing, except the facts which present themselves to our senses, and such other facts as may, by analogy, be inferred from these. There is no knowledge *à priori;* no truths cognizable by the mind's inward light, and grounded on intuitive evidence. Sensation, and the mind's consciousness of its own acts, are not only the exclusive sources, but the sole materials, of our knowledge. From this doctrine, Coleridge, with the German philosophers since Kant (not to go farther back), and most of the English since Reid, strongly dissents. He claims for the human mind a capacity, within certain limits, of perceiving the nature and properties of "things in themselves." He distinguishes in the human intellect two faculties, which, in the technical language common to him with the Germans, he calls Understanding and Reason. The former faculty judges of phenomena, or the appearances of things, and forms generalizations from these: to the latter it belongs, by direct intuition, to perceive things, and recognize truths, not cognizable by our senses. These perceptions are not indeed innate, nor could ever have been awakened in us without experience; but they are not copies of it: experience is not their prototype; it is only the occasion by which they are irresistibly suggested. The appearances in nature excite in us, by an inherent law, ideas of those invisible things which are the causes of the visible appearances, and on whose laws those appearances depend; and we then perceive that these things must have pre-existed to render the appearances possible; just as (to use a frequent illustration of Coleridge's) we see, before we know that we have eyes: but, when once this is known to us, we perceive that eyes must have pre-existed to enable us to see. Among the truths which are thus known *à priori,* by occasion of experience, but not themselves the subjects of experience, Coleridge includes the fundamental doctrines of religion and morals, the principles of mathematics, and the ultimate laws even of physical nature; which he contends cannot be proved by experience, though they must necessarily be consistent with it, and would, if we knew them perfectly, enable us to account for all observed facts, and to predict all those which are as yet unobserved.

It is not necessary to remind any one who concerns himself with such subjects, that between the partisan of these two opposite doctrines there reigns a *bellum internecinum.* Neither side is sparing in the imputation of intellectual and moral obliquity to the perceptions, and of pernicious consequences to the creed, of its antagonists. Sensualism is the common term of abuse for the one philosophy; mysticism, for the other. The one doctrine is accused of making men beasts; the other, lunatics. It is the unaffected belief of numbers on one side of the controversy, that their adversaries are actuated by a desire to break loose from moral and religious obligation; and of numbers on the other, that their opponents are either men fit for Bedlam, or who cunningly pander to the interests of hierarchies and aristocracies by manufacturing superfine new arguments in favor of old prejudices. It is almost needless to say, that those who are freest with these mutual accusations are seldom those who are most at home in the real intricacies of the question, or who are best acquainted with the argumentative strength of the opposite side, or even of their own. But, without going to these extreme lengths, even sober men on both sides take no charitable view of the tendencies of each other's opinions.

It is affirmed that the doctrine of Locke and his followers, that all knowledge is experience generalized, leads by strict logical consequence to atheism; that Hume and other sceptics were right when they contended that it is impossible to prove a God on grounds of experience; and Coleridge (like Kant) maintains positively, that the ordinary argument for a Deity, from marks of design in the universe, or, in other words, from the resemblance of the order in nature to the effects of human skill and contrivance, is not tenable. It is further said, that the same doctrine annihilates moral obligation; reducing morality either to the blind impulses of animal sensibility, or to a calculation of prudential consequences, both equally fatal to its essence. Even science, it is affirmed, loses the character of science in this view of it, and becomes empiricism—a mere enumeration and arrangement of facts, not explaining nor accounting for them: since a fact is only then accounted for, when we are made to see in it the manifestation of laws, which, as soon as they are perceived at all, are perceived to be *necessary*. These are the charges brought by the transcendental philosophers against the school of Locke, Hartley, and Bentham. They, in their turn, allege that the transcendentalists make imagination, and not observation, the criterion of truth; that they lay down principles under which a man may enthrone his wildest dreams in the chair of philosophy, and impose them on mankind as intuitions of the pure reason: which has, in fact, been done in all ages, by all manner of mystical enthusiasts. And even if, with gross inconsistency, the private revelations of any individual Behmen or Swedenborg be disowned, or, in other words, outvoted (the only means of discrimination, which, it is contended, the theory admits of), this is still only substituting, as the test of truth, the dreams of the majority for the dreams of each individual. Whoever form a strong enough party may at any time set up the immediate perceptions of *their* reason, that is to say, any reigning prejudice, as a truth independent of experience—a truth not only requiring no proof, but to be believed in opposition to all that appears proof to the mere understanding;

nay, the more to be believed, because it cannot be put into words and into the logical form of a proposition without a contradiction in terms: for no less authority than this is claimed by some transcendentalists for their *à priori* truths. And thus a ready mode is provided, by which whoever is on the strongest side may dogmatize at his ease, and, instead of proving his propositions, may rail at all who deny them, as bereft of "the vision and the faculty divine," or blinded to its plainest revelations by a corrupt heart.

This is a very temperate statement of what is charged by these two classes of thinkers against each other. How much of either representation is correct cannot conveniently be discussed in this place. In truth, a system of consequences from an opinion, drawn by an adversary, is seldom of much worth. Disputants are rarely sufficiently masters of each other's doctrines to be good judges what is fairly deducible from them, or how a consequence which seems to flow from one part of the theory may or may not be defeated by another part. To combine the different parts of a doctrine with one another, and with all admitted truths, is not indeed a small trouble, nor one which a person is often inclined to take for other people's opinions. Enough if each does it for his own, which he has a greater interest in, and is more disposed to be just to. Were we to search among men's recorded thoughts for the choicest manifestations of human imbecility and prejudice, our specimens would be mostly taken from their opinions of the opinions of one another. Imputations of horrid consequences ought not to bias the judgment of any person capable of independent thought. Coleridge himself says (in the twenty-fifth Aphorism of his "Aids to Reflection"), "He who begins by loving Christianity better than truth will proceed by loving his own sect or church better than Christianity, and end in loving himself better than all."

As to the fundamental difference of opinion respecting the sources of our knowledge (apart from the corollaries which either party may have drawn from its own principle, or imputed to its opponent's), the question lies far too deep in the recesses of psychology for us to discuss it here. The lists having been open ever since the dawn of philosophy, it is not wonderful that the two parties should have been forced to put on their strongest armor both of attack and of defence. The question would not so long have remained a question, if the more obvious arguments on either side had been unanswerable. Each party has been able to urge in its own favor numerous and striking facts, to reconcile which with the opposite theory has required all the metaphysical resources which that theory could command. It will not be wondered at, then, that we here content ourselves with a bare statement of our opinion. It is, that the truth on this much-debated question lies with the school of Locke and of Bentham. The nature and laws of things in themselves, or of the hidden causes of the phenomena which are the objects of experience, appear to us radically inaccessible to the human faculties. We see no ground for believing that any thing can be the object of our knowledge except our experience, and what can be inferred from our experience by the analogies of experience itself; nor that there is any idea, feeling, or power, in the human mind, which, in order to account for it, requires that its origin should be referred to any other source. We are therefore at issue with Coleridge on the central idea of his philosophy; and we find no need of, and no use for, the peculiar technical terminology which he and his masters the Germans have introduced into philosophy for the double purpose of giving logical precision to doctrines which we do not admit, and of marking a relation between those abstract doctrines and many concrete experimental truths, which this language, in our judgment, serves, not to elucidate, but to disguise and obscure. Indeed, but for these peculiarities of language, it would be difficult to understand how the reproach of mysticism (by which nothing is meant in common parlance but unintelligibleness) has been fixed upon Coleridge and the Germans in the minds of many, to whom doctrines

substantially the same, when taught in a manner more superficial, and less fenced round against objections, by Reid and
Dugald Stewart, have appeared the plain dictates of "common sense," successfully asserted against the subtleties of
metaphysics.

Yet, though we think the doctrines of Coleridge and the
Germans, in the pure science of mind, erroneous, and have
no taste for their peculiar terminology, we are far from
thinking, that even in respect of this, the least valuable part
of their intellectual exertions, those philosophers have lived
in vain. The doctrines of the school of Locke stood in need of
an entire renovation: to borrow a physiological illustration
from Coleridge, they required, like certain secretions of the
human body, to be re-absorbed into the system, and secreted
afresh. In what form did that philosophy generally prevail
throughout Europe? In that of the shallowest set of doctrines,
which, perhaps, were ever passed off upon a cultivated age
as a complete psychological system—the ideology of Condil-
lac and his school; a system which affected to resolve all the
phenomena of the human mind into sensation, by a process
which essentially consisted in merely *calling* all states of
mind, however heterogeneous, by that name; a philosophy
now acknowledged to consist solely of a set of verbal generalizations, explaining nothing, distinguishing nothing, leading to nothing. That men should begin by sweeping this away
was the first sign that the age of real psychology was about to
commence. In England, the case, though different, was
scarcely better. The philosophy of Locke, as a popular doctrine, had remained nearly as it stood in his own book; which,
as its title implies, did not pretend to give an account of any
but the intellectual part of our nature; which, even within
that limited sphere, was but the commencement of a system;
and, though its errors and defects as such have been exaggerated beyond all just bounds, it did expose many vulnerable points to the searching criticism of the new school. The
least imperfect part of it, the purely logical part, had almost

dropped out of sight. With respect to those of Locke's doctrines which are properly metaphysical—however the sceptical part of them may have been followed up by others, and carried beyond the point at which he stopped—the only one of his successors who attempted and achieved any considerable improvement and extension of the analytical part, and thereby added any thing to the explanation of the human mind on Locke's principles, was Hartley. But Hartley's doctrines, so far as they are true, were so much in advance of the age, and the way had been so little prepared for them by the general tone of thinking which yet prevailed, even under the influence of Locke's writings, that the philosophic world did not deem them worthy of being attended to. Reid and Stewart were allowed to run them down uncontradicted; Brown, though a man of a kindred genius, had evidently never read them; and but for the accident of their being taken up by Priestley, who transmitted them as a kind of heirloom to his Unitarian followers, the name of Hartley might have perished, or survived only as that of a visionary physician, the author of an exploded physiological hypothesis. It perhaps required all the violence of the assaults made by Reid and the German school upon Locke's system to recall men's minds to Hartley's principles, as alone adequate to the solution, upon that system, of the peculiar difficulties which those assailants pressed upon men's attention as altogether insoluble by it. We may here notice, that Coleridge, before he adopted his later philosophical views, was an enthusiastic Hartleian; so that his abandonment of the philosophy of Locke cannot be imputed to unacquaintance with the highest form of that philosophy which had yet appeared. That he should pass through that highest form without stopping at it is itself a strong presumption that there were more difficulties in the question than Hartley had solved. That any thing has since been done to solve them, we probably owe to the revolution in opinion, of which Coleridge was one of the organs; and, even in abstract metaphysics, his writings, and those of his school of thinkers, are the richest mine from whence the opposite school can draw the materials for what has yet to be done to perfect their own theory.

If we now pass from the purely abstract to the concrete and practical doctrines of the two schools, we shall see still more clearly the necessity of the re-action, and the great service rendered to philosophy by its authors. This will be best manifested by a survey of the state of practical philosophy in Europe, as Coleridge and his compeers found it, towards the close of the last century.

The state of opinion in the latter half of the eighteenth century was by no means the same on the Continent of Europe and in our own island; and the difference was still greater in appearance than it was in reality. In the more advanced nations of the Continent, the prevailing philosophy had done its work completely: it had spread itself over every department of human knowledge; it had taken possession of the whole Continental mind; and scarcely one educated person was left who retained any allegiance to the opinions or the institutions of ancient times. In England, the native country of compromise, things had stopped far short of this; the philosophical movement had been brought to a halt in an early stage; and a peace had been patched up, by concessions on both sides, between the philosophy of the time and its traditional institutions and creeds. Hence the aberrations of the age were generally, on the Continent, at that period, the extravagances of new opinions; in England, the corruptions of old ones.

To insist upon the deficiencies of the Continental philosophy of the last century, or, as it is commonly termed, the French philosophy, is almost superfluous. That philosophy is indeed as unpopular in this country as its bitterest enemy could desire. If its faults were as well understood as they are much railed at, criticism might be considered to have finished its work. But that this is not yet the case, the nature of the imputations currently made upon the French philosophers sufficiently proves; many of these being as inconsistent with a just philosophic comprehension of their system of opinions as with charity towards the men themselves. It is not true, for example, that any of them denied moral obligation, or sought to weaken its force. So far were they from meriting this accusation, that they could not even tolerate the writers, who, like Helvetius, ascribed a selfish origin to the feelings of morality, resolving them into a sense of interest. Those writers were as much cried down among the *philosophes* themselves, and what was true and good in them (and there is much that is so) met with as little appreciation, then as now. The error of the philosophers was rather that they trusted too much to those feelings; believed them to be more deeply rooted in human nature than they are; to be not so dependent, as in fact they are, upon collateral influences. They thought them the natural and spontaneous growth of the human heart; so firmly fixed in it, that they would subsist unimpaired, nay, invigorated, when the whole system of opinions and observances with which they were habitually intertwined was violently torn away.

To tear away, was, indeed, all that these philosophers, for the most part, aimed at: they had no conception that any thing else was needful. At their millennium, superstition, priestcraft, error, and prejudice of every kind, were to be annihilated: some of them gradually added, that despotism and hereditary privileges must share the same fate; and, this accomplished, they never for a moment suspected that all the virtues and graces of humanity could fail to flourish, or that, when the noxious weeds were once rooted out, the soil would stand in any need of tillage.

In this they committed the very common error of mistaking the state of things with which they had always been familiar, for the universal and natural condition of mankind. They were accustomed to see the human race agglomerated in large nations, all (except here and there a madman or a malefactor) yielding obedience more or less strict to a set of laws prescribed by a few of their own number, and to a set of moral rules prescribed by each other's opinion; renouncing the exercise of individual will and judgment, except within the limits imposed by these laws and rules; and acquiescing in the sacrifice of their individual wishes, when the point was decided against them by lawful authority; or persevering only in hopes of altering the opinion of the ruling powers. Finding matters to be so generally in this condition, the philosophers apparently concluded that they could not possibly be in any other; and were ignorant by what a host of civilizing and restraining influences a state of things so repugnant to man's self-will, and love of independence, has been brought about, and how imperatively it demands the continuance of those influences as the condition of its own existence. The very first element of the social union, obedience to a government of some sort, has not been found so easy a thing to establish in the world. Among a timid and spiritless race, like the inhabitants of the vast plains of tropical countries, passive obedience may be of natural growth; though even there we doubt whether it has ever been found among any people with whom fatalism, or, in other words, submission to the pressure of circumstances as the decree of God, did not prevail as a religious doctrine. But the difficulty of inducing a brave and warlike race to submit their individual *arbitrium* to any common umpire has always been felt to be so great, that nothing short of supernatural power has been deemed adequate to overcome it; and such tribes have always assigned to the first institution of civil society a divine origin. So differently did those judge who knew savage man by actual experience from those who had no acquaintance with him except in the civilized state. In modern Europe itself, after the fall of the Roman Empire, to subdue the feudal anarchy, and bring the whole people of any European nation into subjection to government (although Christianity in the most concentrated

form of its influence was co-operating in the work), required thrice as many centuries as have elapsed since that
time.

Now, if these philosophers had known human nature under any other type than that of their own age, and of the
particular classes of society among whom they lived, it would
have occurred to them, that wherever this habitual submission to law and government has been firmly and durably established, and yet the vigor and manliness of character which
resisted its establishment have been in any degree preserved,
certain requisites have existed, certain conditions have been
fulfilled, of which the following may be regarded as the principal.

First, There has existed, for all who were accounted citizens—for all who were not slaves, kept down by brute force
—a system of *education,* beginning with infancy and continued through life, of which, whatever else it might include, one
main and incessant ingredient was *restraining discipline.* To
train the human being in the habit, and thence the power, of
subordinating his personal impulses and aims to what were
considered the ends of society; of adhering, against all temptation, to the course of conduct which those ends prescribed;
of controlling in himself all the feelings which were liable to
militate against those ends, and encouraging all such as
tended towards them—this was the purpose, to which every
outward motive that the authority directing the system could
command, and every inward power or principle which its
knowledge of human nature enabled it to evoke, were endeavored to be rendered instrumental. The entire civil and
military policy of the ancient commonwealths was such a system of training: in modern nations, its place has been attempted to be supplied principally by religious teaching. And
whenever and in proportion as the strictness of the restraining discipline was relaxed, the natural tendency of mankind
to anarchy re-asserted itself; the State became disorganized
from within; mutual conflict for selfish ends neutralized

the energies which were required to keep up the contest against natural causes of evil; and the nation, after a longer or briefer interval of progressive decline, became either the slave of a despotism, or the prey of a foreign invader.

The second condition of permanent political society has been found to be, the existence, in some form or other, of the feeling of allegiance, or loyalty. This feeling may vary in its objects, and is not confined to any particular form of government: but, whether in a democracy or in a monarchy, its essence is always the same; viz., that there be in the constitution of the State *something* which is settled, something permanent, and not to be called in question—something which, by general agreement, has a right to be where it is, and to be secure against disturbance, whatever else may change. This feeling may attach itself, as among the Jews (and, indeed, in most of the commonwealths of antiquity), to a common God or gods, the protectors and guardians of their State; or it may attach itself to certain persons, who are deemed to be, whether by divine appointment, by long prescription, or by the general recognition of their superior capacity and worthiness, the rightful guides and guardians of the rest; or it may attach itself to laws, to ancient liberties, or ordinances; or, finally (and this is the only shape in which the feeling is likely to exist hereafter), it may attach itself to the principles of individual freedom and political and social equality, as realized in institutions which as yet exist nowhere, or exist only in a rudimentary state. But, in all political societies which have had a durable existence, there has been some fixed point; something which men agreed in holding sacred; which, wherever freedom of discussion was a recognized principle, it was of course lawful to contest in theory, but which no one could either fear or hope to see shaken in practice; which, in short (except perhaps during some temporary crisis), was, in the common estimation, placed beyond discussion. And the necessity of this may easily be made evident. A State never is, nor, until mankind are vastly improved, can hope to be, for any long time, exempt from internal dissension; for there neither is, nor has ever been, any state of society in which collisions did not occur between the immediate interests and passions of powerful sections of the people. What, then, enables society to weather these storms, and pass through turbulent times without any permanent weakening of the securities for peaceable existence? Precisely this—that, however important the interests about which men fall out, the conflict did not affect the fundamental principles of the system of social union which happened to exist; nor threaten large portions of the community with the subversion of that on which they had built their calculations, and with which their hopes and aims had become identified. But when the questioning of these fundamental principles is, not the occasional disease or salutary medicine, but the habitual condition of the body politic, and when all the violent animosities are called forth which spring naturally from such a situation, the State is virtually in a position of civil war, and can never long remain free from it in act and fact.

The third essential condition of stability in political society is a strong and active principle of cohesion among the members of the same community or state. We need scarcely say that we do not mean nationality, in the vulgar sense of the term—a senseless antipathy to foreigners; an indifference to the general welfare of the human race, or an unjust preference of the supposed interests of our own country; a cherishing of bad peculiarities because they are national; or a refusal to adopt what has been found good by other countries. We mean a principle of sympathy, not of hostility; of union, not of separation. We mean a feeling of common interest among those who live under the same government, and are contained within the same natural or historical boundaries. We mean, that one part of the community do not consider themselves as foreigners with regard to another part; that they set a value on their connection; feel that they are one people; that their lot is cast together; that evil to any of their fellow-

countrymen is evil to themselves; and do not desire selfishly
to free themselves from their share of any common inconvenience by severing the connection. How strong this feeling
was in those ancient commonwealths which attained any durable greatness, every one knows. How happily Rome, in
spite of all her tyranny, succeeded in establishing the feeling
of a common country among the provinces of her vast and
divided empire, will appear when any one who has given
due attention to the subject shall take the trouble to point it
out.* In modern times, the countries which have had that

* We are glad to quote a striking passage from Coleridge on this very
subject. He is speaking of the misdeeds of England in Ireland; towards
which misdeeds, this Tory, as he is called (for the Tories, who neglected him in his lifetime, show no little eagerness to give themselves
the credit of his name after his death), entertained feelings scarcely
surpassed by those which are excited by the masterly exposure for
which we have recently been indebted to M. de Beaumont.

"Let us discharge," he says, "what may well be deemed a debt of
justice from every well-educated Englishman to his Roman-Catholic
fellow-subjects of the Sister Island. At least, let us ourselves understand the true cause of the evil as it now exists. To what and to whom
is the present state of Ireland mainly to be attributed? This should
be the question: and to this I answer aloud, that it is mainly attrib-
utable to those, who, during a period of little less than a whole century,
used as a substitute what Providence had given into their hand as an
opportunity; who chose to consider as superseding the most sacred duty
a code of law, which could be excused only on the plea that it enabled
them to perform it; to the sloth and improvidence, the weakness and
wickedness, of the gentry, clergy, and governors of Ireland, who per-
severed in preferring intrigue, violence, and selfish expatriation, to a
system of preventive and remedial measures, the efficacy of which had
been warranted for them alike by the whole provincial history of ancient Rome, *cui pacare subactos summa erat sapientia,* and by the
happy results of the few exceptions to the contrary scheme unhappily
pursued by their and our ancestors.

"I can imagine no work of genius that would more appropriately
decorate the dome or wall of a senate-house than an abstract of Irish
history from the landing of Strongbow to the battle of the Boyne, or
to a yet later period, embodied in intelligible emblems—an allegorical
history-piece designed in the spirit of a Reubens or a Buonarotti, and
with the wild lights, portentous shades, and saturated colors, of a

feeling in the strongest degree have been the most powerful countries—England, France, and, in proportion to their territory and resources, Holland and Switzerland; while England, in her connection with Ireland, is one of the most signal examples of the consequences of its absence. Every Italian knows why Italy is under a foreign yoke, every German knows what maintains despotism in the Austrian Empire; the evils of Spain flow as much from the absence of nationality among the Spaniards themselves as from the presence of it in their relations with foreigners; while the completest illustration of all is afforded by the republics of South America, where the parts of one and the same State adhere so slightly together, that no sooner does any province think itself aggrieved by the general government, than it proclaims itself a separate nation.

These essential requisites of civil society the French philosophers of the eighteenth century unfortunately overlooked. They found, indeed, all three—at least the first and second, and most of what nourishes and invigorates the third—already undermined by the vices of the institutions and of

---

Rembrandt, Caravaggio, and Spagnoletti. To complete the great moral and political lesson by the historic contrast, nothing more would be required than by some equally effective means to possess the mind of the spectator with the state and condition of ancient Spain at less than half a century from the final conclusion of an obstinate and almost unremitting conflict of two hundred years by Agrippa's subjugation of the Cantabrians, *omnibus Hispaniæ populis devictis et pacatis.* At the breaking-up of the empire, the West Goths conquered the country and made division of the lands. Then came eight centuries of Moorish domination. Yet so deeply had Roman wisdom impressed the fairest characters of the Roman mind, that at this very hour, if we except a comparatively insignificant portion of Arabic derivatives, the natives throughout the whole Peninsula speak a language less differing from the *Romana rustica,* or provincial Latin of the times of Lucan and Seneca, than any two of its dialects from each other. The time approaches, I trust, when our political economists may study the science of the provincial policy of the ancients in detail, under the auspices of hope, for immediate and practical purposes."—*Church and State,* p. 161.

the men that were set up as the guardians and bulwarks of them. If innovators, in their theories, disregarded the elementary principles of the social union, conservatives, in their practice, had set the first example. The existing order of things had ceased to realize those first principles: from the force of circumstances, and from the short-sighted selfishness of its administrators, it had ceased to possess the essential conditions of permanent society, and was therefore tottering to its fall. But the philosophers did not see this. Bad as the existing system was in the days of its decrepitude, according to them it was still worse when it actually did what it now only pretended to do. Instead of feeling that the effect of a bad social order, in sapping the necessary foundations of society itself, is one of the worst of its many mischiefs, the philosophers saw only, and saw with joy, that it was sapping its own foundations. In the weakening of all government, they saw only the weakening of bad government, and thought they could not better employ themselves than in finishing the task so well begun; in discrediting all that still remained of restraining discipline, because it rested on the ancient and decayed creeds against which they made war; in unsettling every thing which was still considered settled, making men doubtful of the few things of which they still felt certain; and in uprooting what little remained in the people's minds of reverence for any thing above them, of respect to any of the limits which custom and prescription had set to the indulgence of each man's fancies or inclinations, or of attachment to any of the things which belonged to them as a nation, and which made them feel their unity as such.

Much of all this was, no doubt, unavoidable, and not justly matter of blame. When the vices of all constituted authorities, added to natural causes of decay, have eaten the heart out of old institutions and beliefs, while at the same time the growth of knowledge, and the altered circumstances of the age, would have required institutions and creeds different from these, even if they had remained uncorrupt, we are far from saying that any degree of wisdom on the part of speculative thinkers could avert the political catastrophes, and the subsequent moral anarchy and unsettledness, which we have witnessed and are witnessing. Still less do we pretend that those principles and influences which we have spoken of as the conditions of the permanent existence of the social union, once lost, can ever be, or should be attempted to be, revived in connection with the same institutions or the same doctrines as before. When society requires to be rebuilt, there is no use in attempting to rebuild it on the old plan. By the union of the enlarged views and analytic powers of speculative men with the observation and contriving sagacity of men of practice, better institutions and better doctrines must be elaborated; and, until this is done, we cannot hope for much improvement in our present condition. The effort to do it in the eighteenth century would have been premature, as the attempts of the Economistes (who, of all persons then living, came nearest to it, and who were the first to form clearly the idea of a social science) sufficiently testify. The time was not ripe for doing effectually any other work than that of destruction. But the work of the day should have been so performed as not to impede that of the morrow. No one can calculate what struggles, which the cause of improvement has yet to undergo, might have been spared, if the philosophers of the eighteenth century had done any thing like justice to the past. Their mistake was, that they did not acknowledge the historical value of much which had ceased to be useful, nor saw that institutions and creeds, now effete, had rendered essential services to civilization, and still filled a place in the human mind, and in the arrangements of society, which could not without great peril be left vacant. Their mistake was, that they did not recognize, in many of the errors which they assailed, corruptions of important truths, and, in many of the institutions most cankered with abuse, necessary elements of civilized society, though in a form and vesture no longer suited to the age; and hence they involved, as far as in them lay, many great truths in a common discredit with the errors which had grown up around them. They threw away the shell, without preserving the kernel; and, attempting to new-model society without the binding forces which hold society together, met with such success as might have been anticipated.

Now, we claim, in behalf of the philosophers of the re-actionary school—of the school to which Coleridge belongs —that exactly what we blame the philosophers of the eighteenth century for not doing, they have done.

Every re-action in opinion, of course, brings into view that portion of the truth which was overlooked before. It was natural that a philosophy which anathematized all that had been going on in Europe from Constantine to Luther, or even to Voltaire, should be succeeded by another, at once a severe critic of the new tendencies of society, and an impassioned vindicator of what was good in the past. This is the easy merit of all Tory and Royalist writers. But the peculiarity of the Germano-Coleridgian school is, that they saw beyond the immediate controversy, to the fundamental principles involved in all such controversies. They were the first (except a solitary thinker here and there) who inquired, with any comprehensiveness or depth, into the inductive laws of the existence and growth of human society. They were the first to bring prominently forward the three requisites which we have enumerated as essential principles of all permanent forms of social existence; as principles, we say, and not as mere accidental advantages, inherent in the particular polity or religion which the writer happened to patronize. They were the first who pursued, philosophically and in the spirit of Baconian investigation, not only this inquiry, but others ulterior and collateral to it. They thus produced, not a piece of party advocacy, but a philosophy of society, in the only form in which it is yet possible—that of a philosophy of history; not a defence of particular ethical or religious doctrines, but a contribution, the largest made by any class of thinkers, towards the philosophy of human culture.

The brilliant light which has been thrown upon history during the last half-century has proceeded almost wholly from this school. The disrespect in which history was held by the *philosophes* is notorious: one of the soberest of them (D'Alembert, we believe) was the author of the wish, that all record whatever of past events could be blotted out. And, indeed, the ordinary mode of writing history, and the ordinary mode of drawing lessons from it, were almost sufficient to excuse this contempt. But the *philosophes* saw, as usual, what was not true, not what was. It is no wonder that they who looked on the greater part of what had been handed down from the past as sheer hinderances to man's attaining a well-being, which would otherwise be of easy attainment, should content themselves with a very superficial study of history. But the case was otherwise with those who regarded the maintenance of society at all, and especially its maintenance in a state of progressive advancement, as a very difficult task actually achieved, in however imperfect a manner, for a number of centuries, against the strongest obstacles. It was natural that they should feel a deep interest in ascertaining how this had been effected; and should be led to inquire, both what were the requisites of the permanent existence of the body politic, and what were the conditions which had rendered the preservation of these permanent requisites compatible with perpetual and progressive improvement. And hence that series of great writers and thinkers, from Herder to Michelet, by whom history, which was till then "a tale told by an idiot, full of sound and fury, signifying nothing," has been made a science of causes and effects; who, by making the facts and events of the past have a meaning and an intelligible place in the gradual evolution of humanity, have at once given history, even to the imagination, an interest like romance, and afforded the only means of predicting and guiding the future, by unfolding the agencies which have produced, and still maintain, the present.*

The same causes have naturally led the same class of thinkers to do what their predecessors never could have done for the philosophy of human culture. For the tendency of their speculations compelled them to see, in the character of the national education existing in any political society, at once the principal cause of its permanence as a society, and the chief source of its progressiveness; the former by the extent to which that education operated as a system of restraining discipline, the latter by the degree in which it called forth and invigorated the active faculties. Besides, not to have looked upon the culture of the inward man as the problem of problems would have been incompatible with the belief which many of these philosophers entertained in Christianity, and the recognition by all of them of its historical value, and the prime part which it has acted in the progress of mankind. But here too, let us not fail to observe, they rose to principles,

---

* There is something at once ridiculous and discouraging in the signs which daily meet us, of the Cimmerian darkness still prevailing in England (wherever recent foreign literature or the speculations of the Coleridgians have not penetrated) concerning the very existence of the views of general history which have been received throughout the continent of Europe for the last twenty or thirty years. A writer in "Blackwood's Magazine"—certainly not the least able publication of our day, nor this the least able writer in it— lately announced, with all the pomp and heraldry of triumphant genius, a discovery which was to disabuse the world of an universal prejudice, and create "the philosophy of Roman history." This is, that the Roman Empire perished, not from outward violence, but from inward decay; and that the barbarian conquerors were the renovators, not the destroyers, of its civilization. Why, there is not a schoolboy in France or Germany who did not possess this writer's discovery before him: the contrary opinion has receded so far into the past, that it must be rather a learned Frenchman or German who remembers that it was ever held. If the writer in "Blackwood" had read a line of Guizot (to go no further than the most obvious sources), he would probably have abstained from making himself very ridiculous, and his country, so far as depends upon him, the laughing-stock of Europe.

and did not stick in the particular case. The culture of the human being had been carried to no ordinary height, and human nature had exhibited many of its noblest manifestations, not in Christian countries only, but in the ancient world—in Athens, Sparta, Rome: nay, even barbarians, as the Germans, or still more unmitigated savages, the wild Indians, and again the Chinese, the Egyptians, the Arabs, all had their own education, their own culture—a culture which, whatever might be its tendency upon the whole, had been successful in some respect or other. Every form of polity, every condition of society, whatever else it had done, had formed its type of national character. What that type was, and how it had been made what it was, were questions which the metaphysician might overlook: the historical philosopher could not. Accordingly, the views respecting the various elements of human culture, and the causes influencing the formation of national character, which pervade the writings of the Germano-Coleridgian school, throw into the shade every thing which had been effected before, or which has been attempted simultaneously by any other school. Such views are, more than any thing else, the characteristic feature of the Goethian period of German literature; and are richly diffused through the historical and critical writings of the new French school, as well as of Coleridge and his followers.

In this long though most compressed dissertation on the Continental philosophy preceding the re-action, and on the nature of the re-action so far as directed against that philosophy, we have unavoidably been led to speak rather of the movement itself than of Coleridge's particular share in it; which, from his posteriority in date, was necessarily a subordinate one. And it would be useless, even did our limits permit, to bring together, from the scattered writings of a man who produced no systematic work, any of the fragments which he may have contributed to an edifice still incomplete, and even the general character of which we can have rendered very imperfectly intelligible to those who are not acquainted with the theory itself. Our object is to invite to the study of the original sources, not to supply the place of such a study. What was peculiar to Coleridge will be better manifested when we now proceed to review the state of popular philosophy immediately preceding him in our own island; which was different, in some material respects, from the contemporaneous Continental philosophy.

In England, the philosophical speculations of the age had not, except in a few highly metaphysical minds (whose example rather served to deter than to invite others), taken so audacious a flight, nor achieved any thing like so complete a victory over the counteracting influences, as on the Continent. There is in the English mind, both in speculation and in practice, a highly salutary shrinking from all extremes; but, as this shrinking is rather an instinct of caution than a result of insight, it is too ready to satisfy itself with any medium merely because it is a medium, and to acquiesce in a union of the disadvantages of both extremes instead of their advantages. The circumstances of the age, too, were unfavorable to decided opinions. The repose which followed the great struggles of the Reformation and the Commonwealth; the final victory over Popery and Puritanism, Jacobitism and Republicanism, and the lulling of the controversies which kept speculation and spiritual consciousness alive; the lethargy which came upon all governors and teachers, after their position in society became fixed; and the growing absorption of all classes in material interests—caused a state of mind to diffuse itself, with less of deep inward workings, and less capable of interpreting those it had, than had existed for centuries. The age seemed smitten with an incapacity of producing deep or strong feeling, such as at least could ally itself with meditative habits. There were few poets, and none of a high order; and philosophy fell mostly into the hands of men of a dry prosaic nature, who had not enough of the ma-

terials of human feeling in them to be able to imagine any of
its more complex and mysterious manifestations; all of which
they either left out of their theories, or introduced them with
such explanations as no one who had experienced the feelings could receive as adequate. An age like this, an age without earnestness, was the natural era of compromises and half-
convictions.

To make out a case for the feudal and ecclesiastical institutions of modern Europe was by no means impossible:
they had a meaning, had existed for honest ends, and an
honest theory of them might be made. But the administration
of those institutions had long ceased to accord with any
honest theory. It was impossible to justify them in principle,
except on grounds which condemned them in practice; and
grounds of which there was, at any rate, little or no recognition in the philosophy of the eighteenth century. The natural
tendency, therefore, of that philosophy, everywhere but in
England, was to seek the extinction of those institutions. In
England, it would doubtless have done the same, had it
been strong enough; but, as this was beyond its strength, an
adjustment was come to between the rival powers. What
neither party cared about, the *ends* of existing institutions,
the work that was to be done by teachers and governors, was
flung overboard. The wages of that work the teachers and
governors did care about; and those wages were secured to
them. The existing institutions in Church and State were to
be preserved inviolate, in outward semblance at least; but
were required to be, practically, as much a nullity as possible.
The Church continued to "rear her mitred front in courts and
palaces," but not, as in the days of Hildebrand or Becket, as
the champion of arts against arms, of the serf against the
seigneur, peace against war, or spiritual principles and powers
against the domination of animal force; nor even (as in the
days of Latimer and John Knox) as a body divinely commissioned to train the nation in a knowledge of God, and
obedience to his laws, whatever became of temporal prin-

cipalities and powers; and whether this end might most effectually be compassed by their assistance, or by trampling them under foot. No; but the people of England liked old things, and nobody knew how the place might be filled which the doing-away with so conspicuous an institution would leave vacant, and *quieta ne movere* was the favorite doctrine of those times: therefore, on condition of not making too much noise about religion, or taking it too much in earnest, the Church was supported, even by philosophers— as a "bulwark against fanaticism," a sedative to the religious spirit, to prevent it from disturbing the harmony of society or the tranquillity of states. The clergy of the Establishment thought they had a good bargain on these terms, and kept its conditions very faithfully.

The State, again, was no longer considered, according to the old ideal, as a concentration of the force of all the individuals of the nation in the hands of certain of its members, in order to the accomplishment of whatever could be best accomplished by systematic co-operation. It was found that the State was a bad judge of the wants of society; that it in reality cared very little for them: and when it attempted any thing beyond that police against crime, and arbitration of disputes, which are indispensable to social existence, the private sinister interest of some class or individual was usually the prompter of its proceedings. The natural inference would have been, that the constitution of the State was somehow not suited to the existing wants of society; having indeed descended, with scarcely any modifications that could be avoided, from a time when the most prominent exigencies of society were quite different. This conclusion, however, was shrunk from; and it required the peculiarities of very recent times, and the speculations of the Bentham school, to produce even any considerable tendency that way. The existing Constitution, and all the arrangements of existing society, continued to be applauded as the best possible. The celebrated theory of the three powers was got up, which made the excellence of our Constitution consist in doing less harm than would be done by any other form of government. Government altogether was regarded as a necessary evil, and was required to hide itself—to make itself as little felt as possible. The cry of the people was not, "Help us;" "Guide us;" "Do for us the things we cannot do; and instruct us, that we may do well those which we can" (and truly such requirements from such rulers would have been a bitter jest): the cry was, "Let us alone." Power to decide questions of *meum* and *tuum,* to protect society from open violence, and from some of the most dangerous modes of fraud, could not be withheld: these functions the Government was left in possession of; and to these it became the expectation of the public that it should confine itself.

Such was the prevailing tone of English belief in temporals. What was it in spirituals? Here, too, a similar system of compromise had been at work. Those who pushed their philosophical speculations to the denial of the received religious belief, whether they went to the extent of infidelity or only of heterodoxy, met with little encouragement: neither religion itself, nor the received forms of it, were at all shaken by the few attacks which were made upon them from without. The philosophy, however, of the time, made itself felt as effectually in another fashion: it pushed its way *into* religion. The *à priori* arguments for a God were first dismissed. This was indeed inevitable. The internal evidences of Christianity shared nearly the same fate: if not absolutely thrown aside, they fell into the background, and were little thought of. The doctrine of Locke, that we have no *innate* moral sense, perverted into the doctrine that we have no moral sense at all, made it appear that we had not any capacity of judging, from the doctrine itself, whether it was worthy to have come from a righteous Being. In forgetfulness of the most solemn warnings of the Author of Christianity, as well as of the apostle who was the main diffuser of it through the world, belief in his religion was left to stand upon miracles—a species of evidence, which, according to the universal belief of the early Christians themselves, was by no means peculiar to true religion; and it is melancholy to see on what frail reeds able defenders of Christianity preferred to rest, rather than upon that better evidence which alone gave to their so-called evidences any value as a collateral confirmation. In the interpretation of Christianity, the palpablest *bibliolatry* prevailed—if (with Coleridge) we may so term that superstitious worship of particular texts, which persecuted Galileo, and, in our own day, anathematized the discoveries of geology. Men whose faith in Christianity rested on the literal infallibility of the sacred volume shrank in terror from the idea that it could have been included in the scheme of Providence, that the human opinions and mental habits of the particular writers should be allowed to mix with and color their mode of conceiving and of narrating the divine transactions. Yet this slavery to the letter has not only raised every difficulty which envelops the most unimportant passage in the Bible into an objection to revelation, but has paralyzed many a well-meant effort to bring Christianity home, as a consistent scheme, to human experience, and capacities of apprehension; as if there was much of it which it was more prudent to leave *in nubibus,* lest, in the attempt to make the mind seize hold of it as a reality, some text might be found to stand in the way. It might have been expected that this idolatry of the words of Scripture would at least have saved its doctrines from being tampered with by human notions: but the contrary proved to be the effect; for the vague and sophistical mode of interpreting texts, which was necessary in order to reconcile what was manifestly irreconcilable, engendered a habit of playing fast and loose with Scripture, and finding in, or leaving out of it, whatever one pleased. Hence, while Christianity was, in theory and in intention, received and submitted to, with even "prostration of the understanding" before it, much alacrity was in fact displayed in *accommodating* it to the received philosophy, and even to the popular notions of the time. To take only one example, but so signal a one as to be *instar omnium*. If there is any one requirement of Christianity less doubtful than another, it is that of being spiritually-minded; of loving and practising good from a pure love, simply because it is good. But one of the crotchets of the philosophy of the age was, that all virtue is self-interest; and accordingly, in the text-book adopted by the Church (in one of its universities) for instruction in moral philosophy, the reason for doing good is declared to be, that God is stronger than we are, and is able to damn us if we do not. This is no exaggeration of the sentiments of Paley, and hardly even of the crudity of his language.

Thus, on the whole, England had neither the benefits, such as they were, of the new ideas, nor of the old. We were just sufficiently under the influences of each to render the other powerless. We had a Government, which we respected too much to attempt to change it, but not enough to trust it with any power, or look to it for any services that were not compelled. We had a Church, which had ceased to fulfil the honest purposes of a church, but which we made a great point of keeping up as the pretence or *simulacrum* of one. We had a highly spiritual religion (which we were instructed to obey from selfish motives), and the most mechanical and worldly notions on every other subject; and we were so much afraid of being wanting in reverence to each particular syllable of the book which contained our religion, that we let its most important meanings slip through our fingers, and entertained the most grovelling conceptions of its spirit and general purposes. This was not a state of things which could recommend itself to any earnest mind. It was sure, in no great length of time, to call forth two sorts of men: the one demanding the extinction of the institutions and creeds which had hitherto existed; the other, that they be made a reality: the one pressing the new doctrines to their utmost consequences, the other re-asserting the best meaning and purposes of the old. The first type attained its greatest height in Bentham; the last, in Coleridge.

We hold that these two sorts of men, who seem to be, and believe themselves to be, enemies, are in reality allies. The powers they wield are opposite poles of one great force of progression. What was really hateful and contemptible was the state which preceded them, and which each, in its way, has been striving now for many years to improve. Each ought to hail with rejoicing the advent of the other. But most of all ought an enlightened Radical or Liberal to rejoice over such a Conservative as Coleridge. For such a Radical must know, that the Constitution and Church of England, and the religious opinions and political maxims professed by their supporters, are not mere frauds, nor sheer nonsense; have not been got up originally, and all along maintained, for the sole purpose of picking people's pockets; without aiming at, or being found conducive to, any honest end during the whole process. Nothing, of which this is a sufficient account, would have lasted a tithe of five, eight, or ten centuries, in the most improving period and (during much of that period) the most improving nation in the world. These things, we may depend upon it, were not always without much good in them, however little of it may now be left: and reformers ought to hail the man as a brother-reformer who points out what this good is; what it is which we have a right to expect from things established; which they are bound to do for us, as the justification of their being established; so that they may be recalled to it, and compelled to do it, or the impossibility of their any longer doing it may be conclusively manifested. What is any case for reform good for, until it has passed this test? What mode is there of determining whether a thing is fit to exist, without first considering what purposes it exists for, and whether it be still capable of fulfilling them?

We have not room here to consider Coleridge's Conservative philosophy in all its aspects, or in relation to all the quarters from which objections might be raised against it.

We shall consider it with relation to Reformers, and especially to Benthamites. We would assist them to determine whether they would have to do with Conservative philosophers, or with Conservative dunces; and whether, since there are Tories, it be better that they should learn their Toryism from Lord Eldon, or even Sir Robert Peel, or from Coleridge.

Take, for instance, Coleridge's view of the grounds of a Church Establishment. His mode of treating any institution is to investigate what he terms the idea of it, or what in common parlance would be called the principle involved in it. The idea or principle of a national church, and of the Church of England in that character, is, according to him, the reservation of a portion of the land, or of a right to a portion of its produce, as a fund—for what purpose? For the worship of God? For the performance of religious ceremonies? No; for the advancement of knowledge, and the civilization and cultivation of the community. This fund he does not term "church-property," but "the nationality," or national property. He considers it as destined for "the support and maintenance of a permanent class of order, with the following duties:

"A certain smaller number were to remain at the fountainheads of the humanities, in cultivating and enlarging the knowledge already possessed, and in watching over the interests of physical and moral science; being likewise the instructors of such as constituted, or were to constitute, the remaining more numerous classes of the order. The members of this latter and far more numerous body were to be distributed throughout the country, so as not to leave even the smallest integral part or division without a resident guide, guardian, and instructor; the objects and final intention of the whole order being these—to preserve the stores and to guard the treasures of past civilization, and thus to bind the present with the past; to perfect and add to the same, and thus to connect the present with the future; but especially to diffuse through the whole community, and to every native entitled to its laws and rights, that quantity and quality of knowledge which was indispensable both for the understanding of those rights, and for the performance of the duties correspondent; finally, to secure for the nation, if not a superiority over the neighboring States, yet an equality at least, in that character of general civilization, which, equally with, or rather more than, fleets, armies, and revenue, forms the ground of its defensive and offensive power."

This organized body, set apart and endowed for the cultivation and diffusion of knowledge, is not, in Coleridge's view, necessarily a religious corporation.

"Religion may be an indispensable ally, but is not the essential constitutive end, of that national institute, which is unfortunately, at least improperly, styled the Church; a name which, in its best sense, is exclusively appropriate to the Church of Christ. . . . The *clerisy* of the nation, or national church in its primary acceptation and original intention, comprehended the learned of all denominations, the sages and professors of the law and jurisprudence, of medicine and physiology, of music, of military and civil architecture, with the mathematical as the common organ of the proceeding; in short, all the so-called liberal arts and sciences, the possession and application of which constitute the civilization of a country, as well as the theological. The last was, indeed, placed at the head of all; and of good right did it claim the precedence. But why? Because under the name of theology or divinity were contained the interpretation of languages; the conservation and tradition of past events; the momentous epochs and revolutions of the race and nation; the continuation of the records, logic, ethics, and the determination of ethical science, in application to the rights and duties of men in all their various relations, social and civil; and, lastly, the ground-knowledge, the *prima scientia,* as it was named—philosophy, or the doctrine and discipline of ideas.

"Theology formed only a part of the objects, the theologians formed only a portion of the clerks or clergy, of the national church. The theological order had precedency indeed, and deservedly; but not because its members were priests, whose office was to conciliate the invisible powers, and to superintend the interests that survive the grave; nor as being exclusively, or even principally, sacerdotal or templar, which, when it did occur, is to be considered as an accident of the age, a misgrowth of ignorance and oppression, a falsification of the constitutive principle, not a constituent part of the same. No: the theologians took the lead, because the science of theology was the root and the trunk of the knowledge of civilized man; because it gave unity and the circulating sap of life to all other sciences, by virtue of which alone they could be contemplated as forming collectively the living tree of knowledge. It had the precedency, because under the name Theology were comprised all the main aids, instruments, and materials of national education, the *nisus formativus* of the body politic, the shaping and informing spirit, which, educing or eliciting the latent man in all the natives of the soil, trains them up to be citizens of the country, free subjects of the realm. And, lastly, because to divinity belong those fundamental truths which are the common groundwork of our civil and our religious duties, not less indispensable to a right view of our temporal concerns than to a rational faith respecting our immortal well-being. Not without celestial observations can even terrestrial charts be accurately constructed."—*Church and State,* chap. v.

The nationalty, or national property, according to Coleridge, "cannot rightfully be, and without foul wrong to the nation never has been, alienated from its original purposes," from the promotion of "a continuing and progressive civilization," to the benefit of individuals, or any public purpose of merely economical or material interest. But the State may withdraw the fund from its actual holders for the better execution of its purposes. There is no sanctity attached to the means, but only to the ends. The fund is not dedicated to any particular scheme of religion, nor even to religion at all: religion has only to do with it in the character of an instrument of civilization, and in common with all the other instruments.

"I do not assert that the proceeds from the nationalty cannot be rightfully vested, except in what we now mean by clergymen and the established clergy. I have everywhere implied the contrary. . . . In relation to the national church, Christianity, or the Church of Christ, is a blessed accident, a providential boon, a grace of God. . . . As the olive-tree is said in its growth to fertilize the surrounding soil, to invigorate the roots of the vines in its immediate neighborhood, and to improve the strength and flavor of the wines; such is the relation of the Christian and the national Church. But as the olive is not the same plant with the vine, or with the elm or poplar (that is, the State) with which the vine is wedded; and as the vine, with its prop, may exist, though in less perfection, without the olive, or previously to its implantation: even so is Christianity, and *à fortiori* any particular scheme of theology derived, and supposed by its partisans to be deduced, from Christianity, no essential part of the being of the national Church, however conducive or even indispensable it may be to its well-being."—Chap. vi.

What would Sir Robert Inglis, or Sir Robert Peel, or Mr. Spooner, say to such a doctrine as this? Will they thank Coleridge for this advocacy of Toryism? What would become of the three-years' debates on the Appropriation Clause, which so disgraced this country before the face of Europe? Will the ends of practical Toryism be much served by a theory under which the Royal Society might claim a part of the church-property with as good right as the bench of bishops, if, by endowing that body like the French Institute, science could be better promoted? a theory by which the State, in the conscientious exercise of its judgment, having decided that the Church of England does not fulfil the object for which the nationalty was intended, might transfer its endowments to any other ecclesiastical body, or to any other body not ecclesiastical, which it deemed more competent to fulfil those objects; might establish any other sect, or all sects, or no sect at all, if it should deem, that, in the divided condition of religious opinion in this country, the State can no longer with advantage attempt the complete religious instruction of its people, but must for the present content itself with providing secular instruction, and such religious teaching, if any, as all can take part in; leaving each sect to apply to its own communion that which they all agree in considering as the keystone of the arch. We believe this to be the true state of affairs in Great Britain at the present time. We are far from thinking it other than a serious evil. We entirely acknowledge, that, in any person fit to be a teacher, the view he takes of religion will be intimately connected with the view he will take of all the greatest things which he has to teach. Unless the same teachers who give instruction on those other subjects are at liberty to enter freely on religion, the scheme of education will be, to a certain degree, fragmentary and incoherent. But the State at present has only the option of such an imperfect scheme, or of intrusting the whole business to perhaps the most unfit body for the exclusive charge of it that could be found among persons of any intellectual attainments; namely, the established clergy as at present trained and composed. Such a body would have no chance of being selected as the exclusive administrators of the nationalty on any foundation but that of divine right; the ground avowedly taken by the only other school of Conservative philosophy which is attempting to raise its head in this country—that of the new Oxford theologians.

Coleridge's merit in this matter consists, as it seems to us, in two things. First, that by setting in a clear light what a national-church establishment ought to be, and what, by the very fact of its existence, it must be held to pretend to be, he has pronounced the severest satire upon what in fact it is. There is some difference, truly, between Coleridge's church, in which the school-master forms the first step in the hierarchy, "who in due time, and under condition of a faithful performance of his arduous duties, should succeed to the pastorate,"* and the Church of England such as we now see. But to say the Church, and mean only the clergy, "constituted," according to Coleridge's conviction, "the first and fundamental apostasy." † He, and the thoughts which have

* P. 57.
† Literary Remains, iii. 386.

proceeded from him, have done more than would have been effected in thrice the time by Dissenters and Radicals to make the Church ashamed of the evil of her ways, and to determine that movement of improvement from within, which has begun where it ought to begin, at the universities and among the younger clergy, and which, if this sect-ridden country is ever to be really taught, must proceed, *pari passu,* with the assault carried on from without.

Secondly, We honor Coleridge for having rescued from the discredit in which the corruptions of the English Church had involved every thing connected with it, and for having vindicated against Bentham and Adam Smith and the whole eighteenth century, the principle of an endowed class, for the cultivation of learning, and for diffusing its results among the community. That such a class is likely to be behind, instead of before, the progress of knowledge, is an induction erroneously drawn from the peculiar circumstances of the last two centuries, and in contradiction to all the rest of modern history. If we have seen much of the abuses of endowments, we have not seen what this country might be made by a proper administration of them, as we trust we shall not see what it would be without them. On this subject we are entirely at one with Coleridge, and with the other great defender of endowed establishments, Dr. Chalmers; and we consider the definitive establishment of this fundamental principle to be one of the permanent benefits which political science owes to the Conservative philosophers.

Coleridge's theory of the Constitution is not less worthy of notice than his theory of the Church. The Delolme and Blackstone doctrine, the balance of the three powers, he declares he never could elicit one ray of common sense from, no more than from the balance of trade.* There is, however, according to him, an Idea of the Constitution, of which he says,

---

* The Friend, first collected edition (1818), vol. ii. p. 75.

"Because our whole history, from Alfred onwards, demonstrates the continued influence of such an idea, or ultimate aim, in the minds of our forefathers, in their characters and functions as public men, alike in what they resisted and what they claimed; in the institutions and forms of polity which they established, and with regard to those against which they more or less successfully contended; and because the result has been a progressive, though not always a direct or equable, advance in the gradual realization of the idea; and because it is actually, though (even because it is an idea) not adequately, represented in a correspondent scheme of means really existing—we speak, and have a right to speak, of the idea itself as actually existing; that is, as a principle existing in the only way in which a principle can exist—in the minds and consciences of the persons whose duties it prescribes, and whose rights it determines." * This fundamental idea "is at the same time the final criterion by which all particular frames of government must be tried: for here only can we find the great constructive principles of our representative system—those principles in the light of which it can alone be ascertained what are excrescences, symptoms of distemperature, and marks of degeneration, and what are native growths, or changes naturally attendant on the progressive development of the original germ; symptoms of immaturity, perhaps, but not of disease; or, at worst, modifications of the growth by the defective or faulty, but remediless, or only gradually remediable, qualities of the soil and surrounding elements." †

Of these principles he gives the following account:

"It is the chief of many blessings derived from the insular character and circumstances of our country, that our social institutions have formed themselves out of our proper needs and interests; that, long and fierce as the birth-struggle and growing pains have been, the antagonist powers have been of our own system, and have been allowed to work out their final balance with less disturbance from external forces than was possible in the Continental States. . . . Now, in every country of civilized men, or

* Church and State, p. 18.
† Ib., p. 19.

acknowledging the rights of property, and by means of determined boundaries and common laws united into one people or nation, the two antagonist powers or opposite interests of the State, under which all other State interests are comprised, are those of *permanence* and of *progression.*"

The interest of permanence, or the Conservative interest, he considers to be naturally connected with the land and with landed property. This doctrine, false in our opinion as an universal principle, is true of England, and of all countries where landed property is accumulated in large masses.

"On the other hand," he says, "the progression of a State in the arts and comforts of life, in the diffusion of the information and knowledge useful or necessary for all; in short, all advances in civilization, and the rights and privileges of citizens—are especially connected with, and derived from, the four classes—the mercantile, the manufacturing, the distributive, and the professional." * (We must omit the interesting historical illustrations of this maxim.) "These four last-mentioned classes I will designate by the name of the Personal Interest, as the exponent of all movable and personal possessions, including skill and acquired knowledge, the moral and intellectual stock in trade of the professional man and the artist, no less than the raw materials, and the means of elaborating, transporting, and distributing them." †

The interest of permanence, then, is provided for by a representation of the landed proprietors; that of progression, by a representation of personal property and of intellectual acquirement: and while one branch of the Legislature, the Peerage, is essentially given over to the former, he considers it a part both of the general theory, and of the actual English Constitution, that the representatives of the latter should form "the clear and effectual majority of the Lower House;" or, if not, that at least, by the added influence of

* Church and State, pp. 23-4.
† Ib., p. 29.

public opinion, they should exercise an effective preponderance there. That "the very weight intended for the effectual counterpoise of the great landholders" has, "in the course of events, been shifted into the opposite scale;" that the members for the towns "now constitute a large proportion of the political power and influence of the very class of men whose personal cupidity, and whose partial views of the landed interest at large, they were meant to keep in check"—these things he acknowledges; and only suggests a doubt, whether roads, canals, machinery, the press, and other influences favorable to the popular side, do not constitute an equivalent force to supply the deficiency.*

How much better a Parliamentary Reformer, then, is Coleridge, than Lord John Russell, or any Whig who stickles for maintaining this unconstitutional omnipotence of the landed interest! If these became the principles of Tories, we should not wait long for further reform, even in our organic institutions. It is true, Coleridge disapproved of the Reform Bill, or rather of the principle, or the no-principle, on which it was supported. He saw in it (as we may surmise) the dangers of a change amounting almost to a revolution, without any real tendency to remove those defects in the machine which alone could justify a change so extensive. And, that this is nearly a true view of the matter, all parties seem to be now agreed. The Reform Bill was not calculated materially to improve the general composition of the Legislature. The good it has done, which is considerable, consists chiefly in this, that, being so great a change, it has weakened the superstitious feeling against great changes. Any good, which is contrary to the selfish interest of the dominant class, is still only to be effected by a long and arduous struggle; but improvements, which threaten no powerful body in their social importance or in their pecuniary emoluments, are no longer resisted as they once were, because of their greatness

* Church and State, pp. 31-2.

—because of the very benefit which they promised. Witness the speedy passing of the Poor-law Amendment and the Penny-postage Acts.

Meanwhile, though Coleridge's theory is but a mere commencement, not amounting to the first lines of a political philosophy, has the age produced any other theory of government which can stand a comparison with it as to its first principles? Let us take, for example, the Benthamic theory. The principle of this may be said to be, that, since the general interest is the object of government, a complete control over the government ought to be given to those whose interest is identical with the general interest. The authors and propounders of this theory were men of extraordinary intellectual powers, and the greater part of what they meant by it is true and important. But, when considered as the foundation of a science, it would be difficult to find, among theories proceeding from philosophers, one less like a philosophical theory, or, in the works of analytical minds, any thing more entirely unanalytical. What can a philosopher make of such complex notions as "interest" and "general interest," without breaking them down into the elements of which they are composed? If by men's interest be meant what would appear such to a calculating bystander, judging what would be good for a man during his whole life, and making no account, or but little, of the gratification of his present passions—his pride, his envy, his vanity, his cupidity, his love of pleasure, his love of ease—it may be questioned, whether, in this sense, the interest of an aristocracy, and still more that of a monarch, would not be as accordant with the general interest as that of either the middle or the poorer classes; and if men's interest, in this understanding of it, usually governed their conduct, absolute monarchy would probably be the best form of government. But since men usually do what they like, often being perfectly aware that it is not for their ultimate interest, still more often that it is not for the interest of their posterity; and when they do believe that the object they are seeking is permanently good for them, almost always overrating its value—it is necessary to consider, not who are they whose permanent interest, but who are they whose immediate interests and habitual feelings, are likely to be most in accordance with the end we seek to obtain. And, as that end (the general good) is a very complex state of things—comprising as its component elements many requisites which are neither of one and the same nature, nor attainable by one and the same means—political philosophy must begin by a classification of these elements, in order to distinguish those of them which go naturally together (so that the provision made for one will suffice for the rest) from those which are ordinarily in a state of antagonism, or at least of separation, and require to be provided for apart. This preliminary classification being supposed, things would, in a perfect government, be so ordered, that, corresponding to each of the great interests of society, there would be some branch or some integral part of the governing body so constituted that it should not be merely deemed by philosophers, but actually and constantly deem itself, to have its strongest interests involved in the maintenance of that one of the ends of society which it is intended to be the guardian of. This, we say, is the thing to be aimed at—the type of perfection in a political constitution. Not that there is a possibility of making more than a limited approach to it in practice: a government must be composed out of the elements already existing in society; and the distribution of power in the constitution cannot vary much or long from the distribution of it in society itself. But wherever the circumstances of society allow any choice, wherever wisdom and contrivance are at all available, this, we conceive, is the principle of guidance; and whatever anywhere exists is imperfect and a failure, just so far as it recedes from this type.

Such a philosophy of government, we need hardly say, is in its infancy: the first step to it, the classification of the exigencies of society, has not been made. Bentham, in his

"Principles of Civil Law," has given a specimen, very useful for many other purposes, but not available, nor intended to be so, for founding a theory of representation upon it. For that particular purpose we have seen nothing comparable, as far as it goes, notwithstanding its manifest insufficiency, to Coleridge's division of the interests of society into the two antagonist interests of Permanence and Progression. The Continental philosophers have, by a different path, arrived at the same division; and this is about as far, probably, as the science of political institutions has yet reached.

In the details of Coleridge's political opinions there is much good, and much that is questionable, or worse. In political economy especially, he writes like an arrant driveller; and it would have been well for his reputation, had he never med·· dled with the subject.* But this department of knowledge can now take care of itself. On other points we meet with far-reaching remarks, and a tone of general feeling sufficient to make a Tory's hair stand on end. Thus, in the work from which we have most quoted, he calls the State policy of the last half-century "a Cyclops with one eye, and that in the back of the head;" its measures "either a series of anachronisms, or a truckling to events instead of the science that should command them." † He styles the great Commonwealthsmen "the stars of that narrow interspace of blue sky between the black clouds of the First and Second Charles's reigns." ‡ The "Literary Remains" are full of disparaging remarks on many of the heroes of Toryism and Church-of-Englandism. He sees, for instance, no difference between Whitgift and Bancroft, and Bonner and Gardiner, except

---

* Yet even on this subject he has occasionally a just thought, happily expressed; as this: "Instead of the position that all things find, it would be less equivocal and far more descriptive of the fact to say, that things are always finding their level; which might be taken as the paraphrase or ironical definition of a storm."—*Second Lay Sermon*, p. 403.
† Church and State, p. 69.
‡ Ib., p. 102.

that the last were the most consistent; that the former sinned against better knowledge: * and one of the most poignant of his writings is a character of Pitt, the very reverse of panegyrical.† As a specimen of his practical views, we have mentioned his recommendation that the parochial clergy should begin by being schoolmasters. He urges "a different division and subdivision of the kingdom," instead of "the present barbarism, which forms an obstacle to the improvement of the country, of much greater magnitude than men are generally aware." ‡ But we must confine ourselves to instances in which he has helped to bring forward great principles, either implied in the old English opinions and institutions, or at least opposed to the new tendencies.

For example: he is at issue with the *let alone* doctrine, or the theory that governments can do no better than to do nothing—a doctrine generated by the manifest selfishness and incompetence of modern European governments, but of which, as a general theory, we may now be permitted to say, that one half of it is true, and the other half false. All who are on a level with their age now readily admit that government ought not to *interdict* men from publishing their opinions, pursuing their employments, or buying and selling their goods, in whatever place or manner they deem the most advantageous. Beyond suppressing force and fraud, governments can seldom, without doing more harm than good, attempt to chain up the free agency of individuals. But does it follow from this that government cannot exercise a free agency of its own?—that it cannot beneficially employ its powers, its means of information, and its pecuniary resources (so far surpassing those of any other association or of any individual), in promoting the public welfare by a thousand means which individuals would never think

* Literary Remains, ii. 388.
† Written in the Morning Post, and now (as we rejoice to see) reprinted in Mr. Gillman's biographical memoir.
‡ Literary Remains, p. 56.

of, would have no sufficient motives to attempt, or no sufficient powers to accomplish? To confine ourselves to one,
and that a limited, view of the subject: a State ought to be
considered as a great benefit-society, or mutual-insurance
company, for helping (under the necessary regulations for
preventing abuse) that large proportion of its members who
cannot help themselves.

"Let us suppose," says Coleridge, "the negative ends of a State
already attained—namely, its own safety by means of its own
strength, and the protection of person and property for all its
members: there will then remain its positive ends—1. To make
the means of subsistence more easy to each individual. 2. To secure to each of its members the hope of bettering his own condition, or that of his children. 3. The development of those faculties
which are essential to his humanity; that is, to his rational and
moral being." *

In regard to the two former ends, he of course does not
mean that they can be accomplished merely by making laws
to that effect; or that, according to the wild doctrines now
afloat, it is the fault of the government if every one has not
enough to eat and drink. But he means that government
can do something directly, and very much indirectly, to promote even the physical comfort of the people; and that, if,
besides making a proper use of its own powers, it would
exert itself to teach the people what is in theirs, indigence
would soon disappear from the face of the earth.

Perhaps, however, the greatest service which Coleridge
has rendered to politics in his capacity of a Conservative
philosopher, though its fruits are mostly yet to come, is in
reviving the idea of a *trust* inherent in landed property. The
land, the gift of nature, the source of subsistence to all, and
the foundation of every thing that influences our physical
well-being, cannot be considered a subject of *property* in the

* Second Lay Sermon, p. 414.

same absolute sense in which men are deemed proprietors
of that in which no one has any interest but themselves—
that which they have actually called into existence by their
own bodily exertion. As Coleridge points out, such a notion
is altogether of modern growth.

"The very idea of individual or private property in our present
acceptation of the term, and according to the current notion of
the right to it, was originally confined to movable things; and
the more movable, the more susceptible of the nature of property." *

By the early institutions of Europe, property in land was
a public function, created for certain public purposes, and
held under condition of their fulfilment; and as such, we
predict, under the modifications suited to modern society, it
will again come to be considered. In this age, when every
thing is called in question, and when the foundation of private property itself needs to be argumentatively maintained
against plausible and persuasive sophisms, one may easily see
the danger of mixing up what is not really tenable with what
is; and the impossibility of maintaining an absolute right in
an individual to an unrestricted control, a *jus utendi et abu-
tendi,* over an unlimited quantity of the mere raw material
of the globe, to which every other person could originally
make out as good a natural title as himself. It will certainly
not be much longer tolerated, that agriculture should be
carried on (as Coleridge expresses it) on the same principles as those of trade; "that a gentleman should regard his
estate as a merchant his cargo, or a shopkeeper his stock;" †
that he should be allowed to deal with it as if it only existed
to yield rent to him, not food to the numbers whose hands
till it; and should have a right, and a right possessing all
the sacredness of property, to turn them out by hundreds,

* Second Lay Sermon, p. 414.
† Ib., p. 414.

and make them perish on the high road, as has been done before now by Irish landlords. We believe it will soon be thought, that a mode of property in land, which has brought things to this pass, has existed long enough.

We shall not be suspected (we hope) of recommending a general resumption of landed possessions, or the depriving any one, without compensation, of any thing which the law gives him. But we say, that, when the State allows any one to exercise ownership over more land than suffices to raise by his own labor his subsistence and that of his family, it confers on him power over other human beings—power affecting them in their most vital interests; and that no notion of private property can bar the right which the State inherently possesses, to require that the power which it has so given shall not be abused. We say also, that, by giving this direct power over so large a portion of the community, indirect power is necessarily conferred over all the remaining portion; and this, too, it is the duty of the State to place under proper control. Further, the tenure of land, the various rights connected with it, and the system on which its cultivation is carried on, are points of the utmost importance both to the economical and to the moral well-being of the whole community. And the State fails in one of its highest obligations, unless it takes these points under its particular superintendence; unless, to the full extent of its power, it takes means of providing that the manner in which land is held, the mode and degree of its division, and every other peculiarity which influences the mode of its cultivation, shall be the most favorable possible for making the best use of the land, for drawing the greatest benefit from its productive resources, for securing the happiest existence to those employed on it, and for setting the greatest number of hands free to employ their labor for the benefit of the community in other ways. We believe that these opinions will become, in no very long period, universal throughout Europe; and we gratefully bear testimony to the fact, that the first among us who has given the sanction of philosophy to so great a reform in the popular and current notions is a Conservative philosopher.

Of Coleridge as a moral and religious philosopher (the character which he presents most prominently in his principal works), there is neither room, nor would it be expedient for us, to speak more than generally. On both subjects, few men have ever combined so much earnestness with so catholic and unsectarian a spirit. "We have imprisoned," says he, "our own conceptions by the lines which we have drawn in order to exclude the conceptions of others. *J'ai trouvé que la plupart des sectes ont raison dans une bonne partie de ce qu'elles avancent, mais non pas tant en ce qu'elles nient.*" * That almost all sects, both in philosophy and religion, are right in the positive part of their tenets, though commonly wrong in the negative, is a doctrine which he professes as strongly as the eclectic school in France. Almost all errors he holds to be "truths misunderstood," "half-truths taken as the whole," though not the less, but the more, dangerous on that account.† Both the theory and practice of enlightened tolerance, in matters of opinion, might be exhibited in extracts from his writings, more copiously than in those of any other writer we know; though there are a few (and but a few) exceptions to his own practice of it. In the theory of ethics, he contends against the doctrine of general consequences, and holds, that *for man* "to obey the simple unconditional commandment of eschewing every act that implies a self-contradiction;" so to act as to "be able, without involving any contradiction, to will that the maxim of thy conduct should be the law of all intelligent beings—is the one universal and sufficient principle and guide of morality." ‡ Yet even a utilitarian can have little complaint to make of a philosopher who lays it down that "the *outward* object of virtue" is "the greatest producible sum of happiness of all men,"

---

* Biographia Literaria, ed. 1817, vol. i. p. 249.
† Literary Remains, iii. 145.
‡ The Friend, vol. i. pp. 256 and 340.

and that "happiness in its proper sense is but the continuity and sum-total of the pleasure which is allotted or happens to a man." *

But his greatest object was to bring into harmony religion and philosophy. He labored incessantly to establish, that "the Christian faith—in which," says he, "I include every article of belief and doctrine professed by the first reformers in common"—is not only divine truth, but also "the perfection of human intelligence." † All that Christianity has revealed, philosophy, according to him, can prove, though there is much which it could never have discovered: human reason, once strengthened by Christianity, can evolve all the Christian doctrines from its own sources.‡ Moreover, "if infidelity is not to overspread England as well as France," § the Scripture, and every passage of Scripture, must be submitted to this test; inasmuch as "the compatibility of a document with the conclusions of self-evident reason, and with the laws of conscience, is a condition *à priori* of any evidence adequate to the proof of its having been revealed by God;" and this, he says, is no philosophical novelty, but a principle "clearly laid down both by Moses and St. Paul." || He thus goes quite as far as the Unitarians in making man's reason and moral feelings a test of revelation; but differs *toto cœlo* from them in their rejection of its mysteries, which he regards as the highest philosophic truths; and says, that "the Christian to whom, after a long profession of Christianity, the mysteries remain as much mysteries as before, is in the same state as a schoolboy with regard to his arithmetic; to whom the *facit* at the end of the examples in his ciphering-book is the whole ground for his assuming that such and such figures amount to so and so."

* Aids to Reflection, pp. 37 and 39.
† Preface to the Aids to Reflection.
‡ Literary Remains, vol. i. p. 388.
§ Ib., iii. 263.
|| Ib., iii. p. 293.

These opinions are not likely to be popular in the religious world, and Coleridge knew it: "I quite calculate," * said he once, "on my being one day or other holden in worse repute by many Christians than the 'Unitarians' and even 'Infidels.' It must be undergone by every one who loves the truth, for its own sake, beyond all other things." For our part, we are not bound to defend him; and we must admit, that, in his attempt to arrive at theology by way of philosophy, we see much straining, and most frequently, as it appears to us, total failure. The question, however, is, not whether Coleridge's attempts are successful, but whether it is desirable or not that such attempts should be made. Whatever some religious people may think, philosophy will and must go on, ever seeking to understand whatever can be made understandable; and, whatever some philosophers may think, there is little prospect at present that philosophy will take the place of religion, or that any philosophy will be speedily received in this country, unless supposed not only to be consistent with, but even to yield collateral support to, Christianity. What is the use, then, of treating with contempt the idea of a religious philosophy? Religious philosophies are among the things to be looked for; and our main hope ought to be, that they may be such as fulfil the conditions of a philosophy—the very foremost of which is unrestricted freedom of thought. There is no philosophy possible where fear of consequences is a stronger principle than love of truth; where speculation is paralyzed, either by the belief that conclusions honestly arrived at will be punished by a just and good Being with eternal damnation, or by seeing in every text of Scripture a foregone conclusion, with which the results of inquiry must, at any expense of sophistry and self-deception, be made to quadrate.

From both these withering influences, that have so often made the acutest intellects exhibit specimens of obliquity and

* Table Talk, 2d ed. p. 91.

imbecility in their theological speculations which have made them the pity of subsequent generations, Coleridge's mind was perfectly free. Faith—the faith which is placed among religious duties—was, in his view, a state of the will and of the affections, not of the understanding. Heresy, in "the literal sense and scriptural import of the word," is, according to him, "wilful error, or belief originating in some perversion of the will." He says, therefore, that there may be orthodox heretics, since indifference to truth may as well be shown on the right side of the question as on the wrong; and denounces, in strong language, the contrary doctrine of the "pseudo-Athanasius," who "interprets catholic faith by belief," * an act of the understanding alone. The "true Lutheran doctrine," he says, is, that "neither will truth, as a mere conviction of the understanding, save, nor error condemn. To love truth sincerely is spiritually to have truth; and an error becomes a personal error, not by its aberration from logic or history, but so far as the causes of such error are in the heart, or may be traced back to some antecedent unchristian wish or habit." † "The unmistakable passions of a factionary and a schismatic, the ostentatious display, the ambitious and dishonest arts, of a sect-founder, must be superinduced on the false doctrine before the heresy makes the man a heretic." ‡

Against the other terror, so fatal to the unshackled exercise of reason on the greatest questions, the view which Coleridge took of the authority of the Scriptures was a preservative. He drew the strongest distinction between the inspiration which he owned in the various writers, and an express dictation by the Almighty of every word they wrote. "The notion of the absolute truth and divinity of every syllable of the text of the books of the Old and New Testament as we have it," he again and again asserts to be unsup-

* Literary Remains, iv. 193.
† Ib., iii. 159.
‡ Ib., p. 245.

ported by the Scripture itself; to be one of those superstitions in which "there is a heart of unbelief;" * to be, "if possible, still more extravagant" than the Papal infallibility; and declares that the very same arguments are used for both doctrines.† God, he believes, informed the minds of the writers with the truths he meant to reveal, and left the rest to their human faculties. He pleaded most earnestly, says his nephew and editor, for this liberty of criticism with respect to the Scriptures, as "the only middle path of safety and peace between a godless disregard of the unique and transcendent character of the Bible, taken generally, and that scheme of interpretation, scarcely less adverse to the pure spirit of Christian wisdom, which wildly arrays our faith in opposition to our reason, and inculcates the sacrifice of the latter to the former: for he threw up his hands in dismay at the language of some of our modern divinity on this point; as if a faith not founded on insight were aught else than a specious name for wilful positiveness! as if the Father of lights could require, or would accept, from the only one of his creatures whom he had endowed with reason, the sacrifice of fools! . . . Of the aweless doctrine, that God might, if he had so pleased, have given to man a religion which to human intelligence should not be rational, and exacted his faith in it, Coleridge's whole middle and later life was one deep and solemn denial.‡ He bewails "bibliolatry" as the pervading error of modern Protestant divinity, and the great stumbling-block of Christianity; and exclaims,§ "Oh! might I live but to utter all my meditations on this most concerning point, . . . in what sense the Bible may be called the word of God, and how and under what conditions the unity of the Spirit is translucent through the letter, which, read as the letter

* Literary Remains, iii. 229. See also pp. 254, 323; and many other passages in the 3d and 4th volumes.
† Ib., ii. 385.
‡ Preface to the 3d volume of the Literary Remains.
§ Literary Remains, iv. 6.

merely, is the word of this and that pious but fallible and im-perfect man." It is known that he did live to write down these meditations; and speculations so important will one day, it is devoutly to be hoped, be given to the world.*

Theological discussion is beyond our province; and it is not for us, in this place, to judge these sentiments of Cole-ridge: but it is clear enough that they are not the sentiments of a bigot, or of one who is to be dreaded by Liberals, lest he should illiberalize the minds of the rising generation of Tories and High-Churchmen. We think the danger is, rather, lest they should find him vastly too liberal. And yet, now, when the most orthodox divines, both in the Church and out of it, find it necessary to explain away the obvious sense of the whole first chapter of Genesis, or, failing to do that, consent to disbelieve it provisionally, on the speculation that there may hereafter be discovered a sense in which it can be be-lieved, one would think the time gone by for expecting to learn from the Bible what it never could have been intended to communicate, and to find in all its statements a literal truth, neither necessary nor conducive to what the volume itself declares to be the ends of revelation. Such, at least, was Coleridge's opinion; and, whatever influence such an opinion may have over Conservatives, it cannot do other than make them less bigots, and better philosophers.

But we must close this long essay—long in itself, though short in its relation to its subject, and to the multitude of topics involved in it. We do not pretend to have given any sufficient account of Coleridge; but we hope we may have proved to some, not previously aware of it, that there is something, both in him and in the school to which he belongs, not unworthy of their better knowledge. We may have done something to show, that a Tory philosopher cannot be wholly a Tory, but must often be a better Liberal than Liberals

* [This wish has, to a certain extent, been fulfilled by the publication of the series of letters on the Inspiration of the Scriptures, which bears the not very appropriate name of "Confessions of an Inquiring Spirit."]

themselves; while he is the natural means of rescuing from oblivion truths which Tories have forgotten, and which the prevailing schools of Liberalism never knew.

And, even if a Conservative philosophy were an absurdity, it is well calculated to drive out a hundred absurdities worse than itself. Let no one think that it is nothing to accustom people to give a reason for their opinion, be the opinion ever so untenable, the reason ever so insufficient. A person accustomed to submit his fundamental tenets to the test of reason will be more open to the dictates of reason on every other point. Not from him shall we have to apprehend the owl-like dread of light, the drudge-like aversion to change, which were the characteristics of the old unreasoning race of bigots. A man accustomed to contemplate the fair side of Toryism (the side that every attempt at a philosophy of it must bring to view), and to defend the existing system by the display of its capabilities as an engine of public good—such a man, when he comes to administer the system, will be more anxious than another person to realize those capabilities, to bring the fact a little nearer to the specious theory. "Lord, enlighten thou our enemies," should be the prayer of every true reformer; sharpen their wits, give acuteness to their perceptions, and consecutiveness and clearness to their reasoning powers. We are in danger from their folly, not from their wisdom: their weakness is what fills us with apprehension, not their strength.

For ourselves, we are not so blinded by our particular opinions as to be ignorant that in this, and in every other country of Europe, the great mass of the owners of large property, and of all the classes intimately connected with the owners of large property, are, and must be expected to be, in the main, Conservative. To suppose that so mighty a body can be without immense influence in the commonwealth, or to lay plans for effecting great changes, either spiritual or temporal, in which they are left out of the question, would be the height of absurdity. Let those who desire such changes ask themselves if they are content that these classes should be, and remain, to a man, banded against them; and what progress they expect to make, or by what means, unless a process of preparation shall be going on in the minds of these very classes, not by the impracticable method of converting them from Conservatives into Liberals, but by their being led to adopt one liberal opinion after another as a part of Conservatism itself. The first step to this is to inspire them with the desire to systematize and rationalize their own actual creed: and the feeblest attempt to do this has an intrinsic value; far more, then, one which has so much in it, both of moral goodness and true insight, as the philosophy of Coleridge.

M. de Tocqueville on
Democracy in America

It has been the rare fortune of M. de Tocqueville's book to
have achieved an easy triumph, both over the indifference of
our at once busy and indolent public to profound speculation, and over the particular obstacles which oppose the reception of speculations from a foreign, and above all from a
French, source. There is some ground for the remark often
made upon us by foreigners, that the character of our national intellect is insular. The general movement of the
European mind sweeps past us, without our being drawn
into it, or even looking sufficiently at it to discover in what
direction it is tending; and, if we had not a tolerably rapid
original movement of our own, we should long since have
been left in the distance. The French language is almost universally cultivated on this side of the Channel; a flood of
human beings perpetually ebbs and flows between London
and Paris; national prejudices and animosities are becoming

numbered among the things that were: yet the revolution which has taken place in the tendencies of French thought, which has changed the character of the higher literature of France, and almost that of the French language, seems hitherto, as far as the English public are concerned, to have taken place in vain. At a time when the prevailing tone of French speculation is one of exaggerated reaction against the doctrines of the eighteenth century, French philosophy, with us, is still synonymous with Encyclopedism. The Englishmen may almost be numbered who are aware that France has produced any great names in prose literature since Voltaire and Rousseau; and while modern history has been receiving a new aspect from the labors of men who are not only among the profoundest thinkers, but the clearest and most popular writers, of their age, even those of their works which are expressly dedicated to the history of our own country remain mostly untranslated, and in almost all cases unread.

To this general neglect, M. de Tocqueville's book forms, however, as we have already said, a brilliant exception. Its reputation was as sudden, and is as extensive, in this country as in France, and in that large part of Europe which receives its opinions from France. The progress of political dissatisfaction, and the comparisons made between the fruits of a popular constitution on one side of the Atlantic, and of a mixed government with a preponderating aristocratic element on the other, had made the working of American institutions a party question. For many years, every book of travels in America had been a party pamphlet, or had at least fallen among partisans, and been pressed into the service of one party or of the other. When, therefore, a new book, of a grave and imposing character, on Democracy in America, made its appearance even on the other side of the British Channel, it was not likely to be overlooked, or to escape an attempt to convert it to party purposes. If ever political writer had reason to believe that he had labored successfully to render his book incapable of such a use, M.

de Tocqueville was entitled to think so. But though his theories are of an impartiality without example, and his practical conclusions lean towards Radicalism, some of his phrases are susceptible of a Tory application. One of these is "the tyranny of the majority." This phrase was forthwith adopted into the Conservative dialect, and trumpeted by Sir Robert Peel in his Tamworth oration, when, as booksellers' advertisements have since frequently reminded us, he "earnestly requested the perusal" of the book by all and each of his audience. And we believe it has since been the opinion of the country gentlemen, that M. de Tocqueville is one of the pillars of Conservatism, and his book a definitive demolition of America and of Democracy. The error has done more good than the truth would perhaps have done; since the result is, that the English public now know and read the first philosophical book ever written on Democracy, as it manifests itself in modern society; a book, the essential doctrines of which it is not likely that any future speculations will subvert, to whatever degree they may modify them, while its spirit, and the general mode in which it treats its subject, constitute it the beginning of a new era in the scientific study of politics.

The importance of M. de Tocqueville's speculations is not to be estimated by the opinions which he has adopted, be these true or false. The value of his work is less in the conclusions than in the mode of arriving at them. He has applied, to the greatest question in the art and science of government, those principles, and methods of philosophizing, to which mankind are indebted for all the advances made by modern times in the other branches of the study of nature. It is not risking too much to affirm of these volumes, that they contain the first analytical inquiry into the influence of Democracy. For the first time, that phenomenon is treated of as something which, being a reality in nature, and no mere mathematical or metaphysical abstraction, manifests itself by innumerable properties, not by some one only; and must be

looked at in many aspects before it can be made the subject
even of that modest and conjectural judgment which is
alone attainable respecting a fact at once so great and so
new. Its consequences are by no means to be comprehended
in one single description, nor in one summary verdict of approval or condemnation. So complicated and endless are their
ramifications, that he who sees furthest into them will longest
hesitate before finally pronouncing whether the good or the
evil of its influence, on the whole, preponderates.

M. de Tocqueville has endeavored to ascertain and discriminate the various properties and tendencies of Democracy; the separate relations in which it stands towards the
different interests of society, and the different moral and social requisites of human nature. In the investigation, he has,
of necessity, left much undone, and must which will be better done by those who come after him, and build upon his
foundations. But he has earned the double honor of being the
first to make the attempt, and of having done more towards
the success of it than probably will ever again be done by
any one individual. His method is, as that of a philosopher
on such a subject must be, a combination of deduction with
induction: his evidences are, laws of human nature, on
the one hand; the example of America and France, and
other modern nations, so far as applicable, on the other. His
conclusions never rest on either species of evidence alone:
whatever he classes as an effect of Democracy he has both
ascertained to exist in those countries in which the state of
society is democratic, and has also succeeded in connecting
with Democracy by deductions *à priori,* tending to show
that such would naturally be its influences upon beings constituted as mankind are, and placed in a world such as we
know ours to be. If this be not the true Baconian and Newtonian method applied to society and government; if any
better, or even any other, be possible—M. de Tocqueville
would be the first to say, *candidus imperti:* if not, he is en-

titled to say to political theorists, whether calling themselves philosophers or practical men, *His utere mecum.*

That part of "Democracy in America" which was first published professes to treat of the political effects of Democracy: the second is devoted to its influence on society in the widest sense; on the relations of private life, on intellect, morals, and the habits and modes of feeling which constitute national character. The last is both a newer and a more difficult subject of inquiry than the first: there are fewer who are competent, or who will even think themselves competent, to judge M. de Tocqueville's conclusions. But, we believe, no one, in the least entitled to an opinion, will refuse to him the praise of having probed the subject to a depth which had never before been sounded; of having carried forward the controversy into a wider and a loftier region of thought; and pointed out many questions essential to the subject, which had not been before attended to—questions which he may or may not have solved, but of which, in any case, he has greatly facilitated the solution.

The comprehensiveness of M. de Tocqueville's views, and the impartiality of his feelings, have not led him into the common infirmity of those who see too many sides to a question—that of thinking them all equally important: he is able to arrive at a decided opinion. Nor has the more extensive range of considerations embraced in his Second Part affected practically the general conclusions which resulted from his First. They may be stated as follows: That Democracy, in the modern world, is inevitable; and that it is, on the whole, desirable, but desirable only under certain conditions, and those conditions capable, by human care and foresight, of being realized, but capable also of being missed. The progress and ultimate ascendency of the democratic principle has, in his eyes, the character of a law of nature. He thinks it an inevitable result of the tendencies of a progressive civilization; by which expressions he by no means intends to imply either praise or censure. No human effort, no accident even, unless one which should throw back civilization itself, can avail, in his opinion, to defeat, or even very considerably to retard, this progress. But, though the fact itself appears to him removed from human control, its salutary or baneful consequences do not. Like other great powers of nature, the tendency, though it cannot be counteracted, may be guided to good. Man cannot turn back the rivers to their source; but it rests with himself whether they shall fertilize or lay waste his fields. Left to its spontaneous course, with nothing done to prepare before it that set of circumstances under which it can exist with safety, and to fight against its worse by an apt employment of its better peculiarities, the probable effects of Democracy upon human well-being, and upon whatever is best and noblest in human character, appear to M. de Tocqueville extremely formidable. But with as much of wise effort devoted to the purpose as it is not irrational to hope for, most of what is mischievous in its tendencies may, in his opinion, be corrected, and its natural capacities of good so far strengthened and made use of as to leave no cause for regret in the old state of society, and enable the new one to be contemplated with calm contentment, if without exultation.

It is necessary to observe, that, by Democracy, M. de Tocqueville does not, in general, mean any particular form of government. He can conceive a Democracy under an absolute monarch. Nay, he entertains no small dread lest in some countries it should actually appear in that form. By Democracy, M. de Tocqueville understands equality of conditions; the absence of all aristocracy, whether constituted by political privileges, or by superiority in individual importance and social power. It is towards Democracy in this sense, towards equality between man and man, that he conceives society to be irresistibly tending. Towards Democracy in the other and more common sense, it may or may not be travelling. Equality of conditions tends naturally to produce a popular government, but not necessarily. Equality may be equal freedom or equal servitude. America is the type of the first: France, he thinks, is in danger of falling into the second. The latter country is in the condition, which, of all that civilized societies are liable to, he regards with the greatest alarm—a democratic state of society without democratic institutions. For, in democratic institutions, M. de Tocqueville sees, not an aggravation, but a corrective, of the most serious evils incident to a democratic state of society. No one is more opposed than he is to that species of democratic radicalism which would admit at once to the highest of political franchises untaught masses who have not yet been experimentally proved fit even for the lowest. But the ever-increasing intervention of the people, and of all classes of the people, in their own affairs, he regards as a cardinal maxim in the modern art of government: and he believes that the nations of civilized Europe, though not all equally advanced, are all advancing, towards a condition in which there will be no distinctions of political rights, no great or very permanent distinctions of hereditary wealth; when, as there will remain no classes nor individuals capable of making head against the government, unless all are, and are fit to be, alike citizens, all will, ere long, be equally slaves.

The opinion that there is this irresistible tendency to equality of conditions, is perhaps, of all the leading doctrines of the book, that which most stands in need of confirmation to English readers. M. de Tocqueville devotes but little space to the elucidation of it. To French readers, the historical retrospect upon which it rests is familiar; and facts known to every one establish its truth so far as relates to that country. But the the English public, who have less faith in irresistible tendencies, and who, while they require for every political theory an historical basis, are far less accustomed to link together the events of history in a connected chain, the proposition will hardly seem to be sufficiently made out. Our author's historical argument is, however, deserving of their attention:

"Let us recollect the situation of France seven hundred years ago, when the territory was divided amongst a small number of families, who were the owners of the soil, and the rulers of the inhabitants: the right of governing descended with the family inheritance from generation to generation; force was the only means by which man could act on man; and landed property was the sole source of power.

"Soon, however, the political power of the clergy was founded, and began to extend itself; the clergy opened its ranks to all classes—to the poor and the rich, the villein and the lord; equality penetrated into the government through the church; and the being, who as a serf must have vegetated in perpetual bondage, took his place as a priest in the midst of nobles, and not unfrequently above the heads of kings.

"The different relations of men became more complicated and more numerous as society gradually became more stable and more civilized. Thence the want of civil laws was felt; and the order of legal functionaries soon rose from the obscurity of their tribunals and their dusty chambers, to appear at the court of the monarch, by the side of the feudal barons in their ermine and their mail.

"Whilst the kings were ruining themselves by their great enterprises, and the nobles exhausting their resources by private wars, the lower orders were enriching themselves by commerce. The influence of money began to be perceptible in state affairs. The transactions of business opened a new road to power, and the financier rose to a station of political influence in which he was at once flattered and despised.

"Gradually the spread of mental acquirements, and the increasing taste for literature and the arts, opened chances of success to talent; knowledge became a means of government, intelligence became a social power, and the man of letters took a part in the affairs of the state.

"The value attached to the privileges of birth decreased in the exact proportion in which new paths were struck out to advancement. In the eleventh century, nobility was beyond all price; in the thirteenth, it might be purchased: it was conferred for the first time in 1270; and equality was thus introduced into the government through aristocracy itself.

"In the course of these seven hundred years, it sometimes happened, that in order to resist the authority of the crown, or to diminish the power of their rivals, the nobles granted a certain share of political rights to the people; or, more frequently, the king permitted the inferior orders to enjoy a degree of power, with the intention of lowering the aristocracy.

"As soon as land was held on any other than a feudal tenure, and personal property began in its turn to confer influence and power, every improvement which was introduced in commerce or manufactures was a fresh element of the equality of conditions. Henceforward every new discovery, every new want which grew up, and every new desire which craved satisfaction, was a step towards the universal level. The taste for luxury, the love of war, the sway of fashion, the most superficial as well as the deepest passions of the human heart, cooperated to enrich the poor and to impoverish the rich.

"From the time when the exercise of the intellect became a source of power and of wealth, it is impossible not to consider every addition to science, every fresh truth, every new idea, as a germ of power placed within the reach of the people. Poetry, eloquence, and memory, the grace of wit, the glow of imagination, the depth of thought, and all the gifts which are bestowed by Providence without respect of persons, turned to the advantage of Democracy; and, even when they were in the possession of its adversaries, they still served its cause by bringing into relief the natural greatness of man: its conquests spread, therefore, with those of civilization and knowledge; and literature became an arsenal, where the poorest and the weakest could always find weapons to their hand.

"In perusing the pages of our history, we shall scarcely meet with a single great event, in the lapse of seven hundred years, which has not turned to the advantage of equality.

"The Crusades, and the wars with the English, decimated the nobles, and divided their possessions; the erection of corporate towns introduced an element of democratic liberty into the bosom of feudal monarchy; the invention of fire-arms equalized the villein and the noble on the field of battle; printing opened the same resources to the minds of all classes; the post was established, so as to bring the same information to the door of the poor man's cottage and to the gate of the palace; and Protestantism proclaimed that all men are alike able to find the road to heaven. The discovery of America offered a thousand new paths to fortune, and placed riches and power within the reach of the adventurous and the obscure.

"If we examine what was happening in France at intervals of fifty years, beginning with the eleventh century, we shall invariably perceive that a twofold revolution has taken place in the state of society. The noble has gone down on the social ladder, and the *roturier* has gone up: the one descends as the other rises. Every half-century brings them nearer to each other.

"Nor is this phenomenon at all peculiar to France. Whithersoever we turn our eyes, we witness the same continual revolution throughout the whole of Christendom.

"Everywhere the various occurrences of national existence have turned to the advantage of Democracy: all men have aided it by their exertions. Those who have intentionally labored in its cause, and those who have served it unwittingly; those who have fought for it, and those who have declared themselves its opponents—have all been driven along in the same track; have all labored to one end, some ignorantly, and some unwillingly: all have been blind instruments in the hands of God.

"The gradual development of the equality of conditions is therefore a providential fact, and possesses all the characteristics of a divine decree: it is universal; it is durable; it constantly eludes all human interference, and all events as well as all men contribute to its progress.

"Would it be wise to imagine that a social impulse which dates from so far back can be checked by the efforts of a generation? Is it credible that the democracy which has annihilated the feudal system, and vanquished kings, will respect the *bourgeois* and the capitalist? Will it stop now that it is grown so strong, and its adversaries so weak?

"It is not necessary that God himself should speak in order to disclose to us the unquestionable signs of his will. We can discern them in the habitual course of nature, and in the invariable tendency of events.

"The Christian nations of our age seem to me to present a most alarming spectacle. The impulse which is bearing them along is so strong that it cannot be stopped; but it is not yet so rapid that it cannot be guided. Their fate is in their hands; yet a little while, and it may be so no longer."—*Introduction to the First Part.*

That such has been the actual course of events in modern history, nobody can doubt; and as truly in England as in France. Of old, every proprietor of land was sovereign over its inhabitants, while the cultivators could not call even their bodily powers their own. It was by degrees only, and in a succession of ages, that their personal emancipation was effected, and their labor became theirs to sell for whatever they could obtain for it. They became the rich men's equals in the eye of the law: but the rich had still the making of the law, and the administering of it; and the equality was at first little more than nominal. The poor, however, could now acquire property; the path was open to them to quit their own class for a higher; their rise, even to a considerable station, gradually became a common occurrence; and, to those who acquired a large fortune, the other powers and privileges of aristocracy were successively opened, until hereditary honors have become less a power in themselves than a symbol and ornament of great riches. While individuals thus continually rose from the mass, the mass itself multiplied and strengthened; the towns obtained a voice in public affairs; the many, in the aggregate, became, even in property, more and more a match for the few; and the nation became a power, distinct from the small number of individuals who once disposed even of the crown, and determined all public affairs at their pleasure. The Reformation was the dawn of the government of public opinion. Even at that early period, opinion was not formed by the higher classes exclusively; and while the publicity of all State transactions, the liberty of petition and public discussion, the press—and of late, above all, the periodical press—have rendered public opinion more and more the supreme power, the same causes have rendered the formation of it less and less dependent upon the initiative of the higher ranks. Even the direct participation of the people at large in the government, had, in various ways, been greatly extended before the political events of the last few years, when Democracy has given so signal a proof of its progress in society by the inroads it has been able to make into the political constitution; and in spite of the alarm which has been taken by the possessors of large property, who are far more generally opposed than they had been within the present generation to any additional strengthening of the popular element in the House of Commons, there is at this moment a much stronger party for a further parliamentary reform, than many good observers thought there was, twelve years ago, for that which has already taken place.

But there is a surer mode of deciding the point than any historical retrospect. Let us look at the powers which are even now at work in society itself.

To a superficial glance at the condition of our own country, nothing can seem more unlike any tendency to equality of condition. The inequalities of property are apparently greater than in any former period of history. Nearly all the land is parcelled out, in great estates, among comparatively few families; and it is not the large but the small properties which are in process of extinction. A hereditary and titled nobility, more potent by their vast possessions than by their social precedency, are constitutionally and really one of the great powers in the State. To form part of their order is that which every ambitious man aspires to, as the crowning glory of a successful career. The passion for equality, of which M. de Tocqueville speaks almost as if it were the great moral lever of modern times, is hardly known in this country, even by name. On the contrary, all ranks seem to have a passion for inequality. The hopes of every person are directed to rising in the world, not to pulling the world down to him. The greatest enemy of the political conduct of the House of Lords submits to their superiority of rank as he would to the ordinances of nature, and often thinks any amount of toil and watching repaid by a nod of recognition from one of their number.

We have put the case as strongly as it could be put by an adversary; and have stated as facts some things, which, if they have been facts, are giving visible signs that they will not always be so. If we look back even twenty years, we shall find that the popular respect for the higher classes is by no means the thing it was; and, though all who are rising wish for the continuance of advantages which they themselves hope to share, there are, among those who do not expect to rise, increasing indications that a levelling spirit is abroad; and political discontents, in whatever manner originating, show an increasing tendency to take that shape. But it is the less necessary to dwell upon these things, as we shall be satisfied with making out, in respect to the tendency to equality in England, much less than M. de Tocqueville contends for. We do not maintain, that the time is drawing near when there will be no distinction of classes: but we do contend, that the power of the higher classes, both in government and in society, is diminishing; while that of the middle and even the lower classes is increasing, and likely to increase.

The constituent elements of political importance are property, intelligence, and the power of combination. In every one of these elements, is it the higher classes, or the other portion of society, that have lately made, and are continuing to make, the most rapid advances?

Even with regard to the element of property, there cannot be room for more than a momentary doubt. The class who are rich by inheritance are so far from augmenting their fortunes, that it is much if they can be said to keep them up. A territorial aristocracy always live up to their means—generally beyond them. Our own is no exception to the rule; and as their control over the taxes becomes every day more restricted, and the liberal professions more over-crowded, they are condemned more and more to bear the burden of their own large families; which it is not easy to do, compatibly with leaving to the heir the means of keeping up, without becoming embarrassed, the old family establishments. It is a matter of notoriety how severely the difficulty of providing for younger sons is felt, even in the highest rank; and that, as a provision for daughters, alliances are now courted which would not have been endured a generation ago. The additions to the "money-power" of the higher ranks consist of the riches of the *novi homines,* who are continually aggregated to that class from among the merchants and manufacturers, and occasionally from the professions. But many of these are merely successors to the impoverished owners of the land they buy; and the fortunes of others are taken, in the way of marriage, to pay off the mortgages of older families. Even with these allowances, no doubt the number of wealthy persons is steadily on the increase; but what is this to the accumulation of capitals, and growth of incomes, in the hands of the middle class? It is that class which furnishes all the accessions to the aristocracy of wealth; and, for one who makes a large fortune, fifty acquire, without exceeding, a moderate competency, and leave their children to work, like themselves, at the laboring oar.

In point of intelligence, it can still less be affirmed that the higher classes maintain the same proportional ascendency as of old. They have shared with the rest of the world in the diffusion of information. They have improved, like all other classes, in the decorous virtues. Their humane feelings and refined tastes form, in general, a striking contrast to the coarse habits of the same class a few generations ago. But it would be difficult to point out what new idea in speculation, what invention or discovery in the practical arts, what useful institution, or what permanently valuable book, Great Britain has owed, for the last hundred years, to her hereditary aristocracy, titled or untitled;* what great public enterprise, what important national movement in religion or politics, those classes have originated, or have so much as taken in it the principal share. Considered in respect to active energies and laborious habits, to the stirring qualities which

---

* The chief exceptions, since the accession of the house of Hanover, are the chemist Cavendish in the last century, and the Earl of Rosse in the present.

fit men for playing a considerable part in the affairs of mankind, few will say that our aristocracy have not deteriorated.
It is, on the other hand, one of the commonplaces of the age,
that knowledge and intelligence are spreading, in a degree
which was formerly thought impossible, to the lower, and
down even to the lowest rank. And this is a fact, not accomplished, but in the mere dawn of its accomplishment, and
which has shown hitherto but a slight promise of its future
fruits. It is easy to scoff at the kind of intelligence which is
thus diffusing itself; but it is intelligence still. The knowledge which is power is not the highest description of knowledge only: any knowledge which gives the habit of forming
an opinion, and the capacity of expressing that opinion, constitutes a political power; and, if combined with the capacity
and habit of acting in concert, a formidable one.

It is in this last element, the power of combined action,
that the progress of the Democracy has been the most gigantic. What combination can do has been shown by an experiment, of now many years' duration, among a people the
most backward in civilization (thanks to English misgovern-
ment), between the Vistula and the Pyrenees. Even on this
side of the Irish Channel we have seen something of what
could be done by political unions, antislavery societies, and
the like; to say nothing of the less advanced, but already
powerful, organization of the working classes, the progress of
which has been suspended only by the temporary failure
arising from the manifest impracticability of its present objects. And these various associations are not the machinery
of democratic combination, but the occasional weapons which
that spirit forges as it needs them. The real political unions of
England are the newspapers. It is these which tell every person what all other persons are feeling, and in what manner
they are ready to act: it is by these that the people learn, it
may truly be said, their own wishes, and through these that
they declare them. The newspapers and the railroads are
solving the problem of bringing the Democracy of England

to vote, like that of Athens, simultaneously in one *agora;* and the same agencies are rapidly effacing those local distinctions which rendered one part of our population strangers to another, and are making us more than ever (what is the first condition of a powerful public opinion) a homogeneous people. If America has been said to prove, that, in an extensive country, a popular government may exist, England seems destined to afford the proof, that, after a certain stage in civilization, it must: for as soon as the numerically stronger have the same advantages, in means of combination and celerity of movement, as the smaller number, they are the masters; and, except by their permission, no government can any longer exist.

It may be said, doubtless, that, though the aristocratic class may be no longer in the ascendant, the power by which it is succeeded is not that of the numerical majority; that the middle class in this country is as little in danger of being outstripped by the democracy below, as of being kept down by the aristocracy above; and that there can be no difficulty for that class, aided as it would be by the rich, in making head, by its property, intelligence, and power of combination, against any possible growth of those elements of importance in the inferior classes, and in excluding the mass of mere manual laborers from any share in political rights, unless such a restricted and subordinate one as may be found compatible with the complete ascendency of property.

We are disposed partially to agree in this opinion. Universal suffrage is never likely to exist and maintain itself where the majority are *prolétaires;* and we are not unwilling to believe that a laboring class in abject poverty, like a great part of our rural population, or which expends its surplus earnings in gin or in waste, like so much of the better-paid population of the towns, may be kept politically in subjection, and that the middle classes are safe from the permanent rule of such a body, though perhaps not from its Swing outrages or Wat Tyler insurrections. But this admission leaves the fact of a tendency towards Democracy practically untouched. There is a Democracy short of pauper suffrage: the working classes themselves contain a middle as well as a lowest class. Not to meddle with the *vexata quæstio,* whether the lowest class is or is not improving in condition, it is certain that a larger and larger body of manual laborers are rising above that class, and acquiring at once decent wages and decent habits of conduct. A rapidly increasing multitude of our working people are becoming, in point of condition and habits, what the American working people are; and, if our boasted improvements are of any worth, there must be a growing tendency in society and government to make this condition of the laboring classes the general one. The nation must be most slenderly supplied with wisdom and virtue, if it cannot do something to improve its own physical condition, to say nothing of its moral. It is something gained, that well-meaning persons of all parties now at length profess to have this end in view. But in proportion as it is approached to; in proportion as the working class becomes, what all proclaim their desire that it should be, well paid, well taught, and well conducted—in the same proportion will the opinions of that class tell, according to its numbers, upon the affairs of the country. Whatever portion of the class succeeds in thus raising itself becomes a part of the ruling body; and, if the suffrage be necessary to make it so, it will not belong without the suffrage.

Meanwhile, we are satisfied if it be admitted that the government of England is progressively changing from the government of a few, to the government, not indeed of *the* many, but of many—from an aristocracy with a popular infusion, to the *régime* of the middle class. To most purposes, in the constitution of modern society, the government of a numerous middle class is Democracy. Nay, it not merely *is* Democracy, but the only Democracy of which there is yet any example: what is called universal suffrage in America arising from the fact, that America is *all* middle class; the whole people being in a condition, both as to education and pe-

cuniary means, corresponding to the middle class here. The
consequences which we would deduce from this fact will appear presently, when we examine M. de Tocqueville's view of
the moral, social, and intellectual influences of Democracy.
This cannot be done until we have briefly stated his opinions
on the purely political branch of the question. To this part
of our task we shall now proceed, with as much conciseness
as is permitted by the number and importance of the ideas,
which, holding an essential place among the grounds of his
general conclusions, have a claim not to be omitted even
from the most rapid summary.

We have already intimated, that M. de Tocqueville recognizes such a thing as a democratic state of society without
a democratic government—a state in which the people are
all equal, and subjected to one common master, who selects
indiscriminately from all of them the instruments of his government. In this sense, as he remarks, the government of the
Pacha of Egypt is a specimen of Democracy; and to this type
(with allowance for difference of civilization and manners)
he thinks that all nations are in danger of approximating, in
which the equalization of conditions has made greater progress than the spirit of liberty. Now, this he holds to be the
condition of France. The kings of France have always been
the greatest of levellers: Louis XI., Richelieu, Louis XIV.,
alike labored to break the power of the noblesse, and reduce all intermediate classes and bodies to the general level.
After them came the Revolution, bringing with it the abolition
of hereditary privileges, the emigration and dispossession of
half the great landed proprietors, and the subdivision of large
fortunes by the revolutionary law of inheritance. While the
equalization of conditions was thus rapidly reaching its extreme limits, no corresponding progress of public spirit was
taking place in the people at large. No institutions capable
of fostering an interest in the details of public affairs were
created by the Revolution: it swept away even those which
despotism had spared; and, if it admitted a portion of the

population to a voice in the government, gave it them only on the greatest but rarest occasion—the election of the great council of the State. A political act, to be done only once in a few years, and for which nothing in the daily habits of the citizen has prepared him, leaves his intellect and moral dispositions very much as it found them; and, the citizens not being encouraged to take upon themselves collectively that portion of the business of society which had been performed by the privileged classes, the central government easily drew to itself, not only the whole local administration, but much of what, in countries like ours, is performed by associations of individuals. Whether the government was revolutionary or counter-revolutionary, made no difference: under one and the other, every thing was done *for* the people, and nothing *by* the people. In France, consequently, the arbitrary power of the magistrate in detail is almost without limit. And when, of late, some attempts have been made to associate a portion of the citizens in the management of local affairs, comparatively few have been found, even among those in good circumstances (anywhere but in the large towns), who could be induced willingly to take any part in that management; who, when they had no personal object to gain, felt the public interest sufficiently their own interest not to grudge every moment which they withdrew from their occupations or pleasures to bestow upon it. With all the eagerness and violence of party contests in France, a nation more passive in the hands of any one who is uppermost does not exist. M. de Tocqueville has no faith in the virtues, nor even in the prolonged existence, of a superficial love of freedom, in the face of a practical habit of slavery; and the question, whether the French are to be a free people, depends, in his opinion, upon the possibility of creating a spirit and a habit of local self-government.

M. de Tocqueville sees the principal source and security of American freedom, not so much in the election of the President and Congress by popular suffrage, as in the administration of nearly all the business of society by the people themselves. This it is, which, according to him, keeps up the habit of attending to the public interest, not in the gross merely, or on a few momentous occasions, but in its dry and troublesome details. This, too, it is which enlightens the people; which teaches them by experience how public affairs must be carried on. The dissemination of public business as widely as possible among the people, is, in his opinion, the only means by which they can be fitted for the exercise of any share of power over the legislature, and generally also the only means by which they can be led to desire it.

For the particulars of this education of the American people by means of political institutions, we must refer to the work itself; of which it is one of the minor recommendations, that it has never been equalled even as a mere statement and explanation of the institutions of the United States. The general principle to which M. de Tocqueville has given the sanction of his authority merits more consideration than it has yet received from the professed laborers in the cause of national education. It has often been said, and requires to be repeated still oftener, that books and discourses alone are not education; that life is a problem, not a theorem; that action can only be learnt in action. A child learns to write its name only by a succession of trials; and is a man to be taught to use his mind and guide his conduct by mere precept? What can be learnt in schools is important, but not all-important. The main branch of the education of human beings is their habitual employment; which must be either their individual vocation, or some matter of general concern, in which they are called to take a part. The private money-getting operation of almost every one is more or less a mechanical routine: it brings but few of his faculties into action, while its exclusive pursuit tends to fasten his attention and interest exclusively upon himself, and upon his family as an appendage of himself; making him indifferent to the public, to the more generous objects and the nobler interests, and, in his inordinate regard for his personal comforts, selfish and cowardly. Balance these tendencies by contrary ones; give him something to do for the public, whether as a vestryman, a juryman, or an elector—and, in that degree, his ideas and feelings are taken out of this narrow circle. He becomes acquainted with more varied business, and a larger range of considerations. He is made to feel, that, besides the interests which separate him from his fellow-citizens, he has interests which connect him with them; that not only the common weal is his weal, but that it partly depends upon his exertions. Whatever might be the case in some other constitutions of society, the spirit of a commercial people will be, we are persuaded, essentially mean and slavish, wherever public spirit is not cultivated by an extensive participation of the people in the business of government in detail; nor will the desideratum of a general diffusion of intelligence among either the middle or lower classes be realized but by a corresponding dissemination of public functions, and a voice in public affairs.

Nor is this inconsistent with obtaining a considerable share of the benefits (and they are great) of what is called centralization. The principle of local self-government has been undeservedly discredited by being associated with the agitation against the new poor-law. The most active agency of a central authority in collecting and communicating information, giving advice to the local bodies, and even framing general rules for their observance, is no hindrance, but an aid, to making the local liberties an instrument of educating the people. The existence of such a central agency allows of intrusting to the people themselves, or to local bodies representative of them, many things of too great national importance to be committed unreservedly to the localities; and completes the efficacy of local self-government as a means of instruction, by accustoming the people not only to judge of particular facts, but to understand and apply, and feel practically the value of, principles. The mode of administration provided for the English poor-laws by the late act seems to us to be, in its general conception, almost theoretically perfect; and the extension of a similar mixture of central and local management to several other branches of administration, thereby combining the best fruits of popular intervention with much of the advantage of skilled supervision and traditional experience, would, we believe, be entitled to no mean rank in M. de Tocqueville's list of correctives to the inconveniences of Democracy.

In estimating the effects of democratic government as distinguished from a democratic condition of society, M. de Tocqueville assumes the state of circumstances which exists in America—a popular government in the State, combined with popular local institutions. In such a government he sees great advantages, balanced by no inconsiderable evils.

Among the advantages, one which figures in the foremost rank is that of which we have just spoken—the diffusion of intelligence; the remarkable impulse given by democratic institutions to the active faculties of that portion of the community who in other circumstances are the most ignorant, passive, and apathetic. These are characteristics of America which strike all travellers. Activity, enterprise, and a respectable amount of information, are not the qualities of a few among the American citizens, nor even of many, but of all. There is no class of persons who are the slaves of habit and routine. Every American will carry on his manufacture, or cultivate his farm, by the newest and best methods applicable to the circumstances of the case. The poorest American understands and can explain the most intricate parts of his country's institutions; can discuss her interests, internal and foreign. Much of this may justly be attributed to the universality of easy circumstances, and to the education and habits which the first settlers in America brought with them; but our author is certainly not wrong in ascribing a certain portion of it to the perpetual exercise of the faculties of every man among the people, through the universal practice of submitting all public questions to his judgment.

"It is incontestable that the people frequently conduct public business very ill; but it is impossible that the people should take a part in public business without extending the circle of their ideas, and without quitting the ordinary routine of their mental occupations. The humblest individual who is called upon to co-operate in the government of society acquires a certain degree of self-respect; and, as he possesses power, minds more enlightened than his own offer him their services. He is canvassed by a multitude of claimants who need his support; and who, seeking to deceive him in a thousand different ways, instruct him during the process. He takes a part in political undertakings which did not originate in his own conception, but which give him a general taste for such undertakings. New ameliorations are daily suggested to him in the property which he holds in common with others; and this gives him the desire of improving that property which is peculiarly his own. He is, perhaps, neither happier nor better than those who came before him; but he is better informed, and more active. I have no doubt that the democratic institutions of the United States, joined to the physical constitution of the country, are the cause (not the direct, as is so often asserted, but the indirect cause) of the prodigious commercial activity of the inhabitants. It is not engendered by the laws; but it proceeds from habits acquired through participation in making the laws.

"When the opponents of Democracy assert that a single individual performs the functions which he undertakes better than the government of the people at large, it appears to me that they are perfectly right. The government of an individual, supposing an equal degree of instruction on either side, has more constancy, more perseverance, than that of a multitude; more combination in its plans, and more perfection in its details; and is better qualified judiciously to discriminate the characters of the men it employs. If any deny this, they have never seen a democratic government, or have formed their opinion only upon a few instances. It must be conceded, that, even when local circumstances and the disposition of the people allow democratic institutions to subsist, they never display a regular and methodical system of government. Democratic liberty is far from accomplishing all the projects it undertakes with the skill of an intelligent despotism. It frequently abandons them before they have borne their fruits, or risks them when the consequences may prove dangerous; but, in the end, it produces greater results than any absolute government. It does fewer things well; but it does a greater number of things. Not what is done by a democratic government, but what is done under a democratic government by private agency, is really great. Democracy does not confer the most skilful kind of government upon the people; but it produces that which the most skilful governments are frequently unable to awaken— namely, an all-pervading and restless activity; a superabundant force; an energy which is never seen elsewhere, and which may, under favorable circumstances, beget the most amazing benefits. These are the true advantages of Democracy."—Vol. ii. chap. 6.

The other great political advantage which our author ascribes to Democracy requires less illustration, because it is more obvious, and has been oftener treated of—that the course of legislation and administration tends always in the direction of the interest of the greatest number. Although M. de Tocqueville is far from considering this quality of Democracy as the panacea in politics which it has sometimes been supposed to be, he expresses his sense of its importance, if in measured, in no undecided terms. America does not exhibit to us what we see in the best mixed constitutions—the class-interests of small minorities wielding the powers of legislation, in opposition both to the general interest and to the general opinion of the community: still less does she exhibit what has been characteristic of most representative governments, and is only gradually ceasing to characterize our own—a standing league of class-interests; a tacit compact, among the various knots of men who profit by abuses, to stand by one another in resisting reform. Nothing can subsist in America that is not recommended by arguments, which, in appearance at least, address themselves to the interest of the many. However frequently, therefore, that

interest may be mistaken, the direction of legislation towards it is maintained in the midst of the mistakes; and if a
community is so situated or so ordered that it can "support
the transitory action of bad laws, and can await without destruction the result of the *general tendency* of the laws," that
country, in the opinion of M. de Tocqueville, will prosper
more under a democratic government than under any other.
But, in aristocratic governments, the interest, or at best the
honor and glory, of the ruling class, is considered as the public interest; and all that is most valuable to the individuals
composing the subordinate classes is apt to be immolated
to that public interest with all the rigor of antique patriotism.

"The men who are intrusted with the direction of public affairs
in the United States are frequently inferior, both in point of capacity and of morality, to those whom aristocratic institutions
would raise to power; but their interest is identified and confounded with that of the majority of their fellow-citizens. They
may frequently be faithless, and frequently mistaken: but they
will never systemtatically adopt a line of conduct hostile to the
majority; and it is impossible that they should give a dangerous
or an exclusive character to the government.

"The mal-administration of a democratic magistrate is, moreover, a mere isolated fact, the effects of which do not last beyond
the short period for which he is elected. Corruption and incapacity do not act as common interests which connect men permanently with one another. A corrupt or an incapable magistrate
will not concert his measures with another magistrate, simply
because that individual is corrupt and incapable like himself;
and these two men will never unite their endeavors to promote
or screen the corruption or inaptitude of their remote posterity.
The ambition and the manœuvres of the one will serve, on the
contrary, to unmask the other. The vices of the magistrate in
democratic States are usually those of his individual character.

"But, under aristocratic governments, public men are swayed
by the interest of their order, which, if it is sometimes blended
with the interests of the majority, is frequently distinct from
them. This interest is a common and lasting bond which unites

them together. It induces them to coalesce, and combine their efforts towards attaining an end which is not always the happiness of the greatest number: and it not only connects the persons in authority with each other, but links them also to a considerable portion of the governed; since a numerous body of citizens belongs to the aristocracy, without being invested with official functions. The aristocratic magistrate, therefore, finds himself supported in his own natural tendencies by a portion of society itself, as well as by the government of which he is a member.

"The common object which connects the interest of the magistrates in aristocracies with that of a portion of their cotemporaries identifies it also with future generations of their order. They labor for ages to come, as well as for their own time. The aristocratic magistrate is thus urged towards the same point by the passions of those who surround him, by his own, and, I might almost say, by those of his posterity. Is it wonderful that he should not resist? And hence it is that the class-spirit often hurries along with it those whom it does not corrupt, and makes them unintentionally fashion society to their own particular ends, and prefashion it for their descendants."—*Ibid*.

These, then, are the advantages ascribed by our author to a democratic government. We are now to speak of its disadvantages.

According to the opinion which is prevalent among the more cultivated advocates of Democracy, one of its greatest recommendations is, that, by means of it, the wisest and worthiest are brought to the head of affairs. The people, it is said, have the strongest interest in selecting the right men. It is presumed that they will be sensible of that interest; and, subject to more or less liability of error, will, in the main, succeed in placing a high, if not the highest, degree of worth and talent in the highest situations.

M. de Tocqueville is of another opinion. He was forcibly struck with the general want of merit in the members of the American legislatures and other public functionaries. He accounts for this, not solely by the people's incapacity to discriminate merit, but partly also by their indifference to it. He thinks there is little preference for men of superior intellect; little desire to obtain their services for the public; occasionally even a jealousy of them, especially if they be also rich. They, on their part, have still less inclination to seek any such employment. Public offices are little lucrative, confer little power, and offer no guarantee of permanency. Almost any other career holds out better pecuniary prospects to a man of ability and enterprise; nor will instructed men stoop to those mean arts, and those compromises of their private opinions, to which their less distinguished competitors willingly resort. The depositaries of power, after being chosen with little regard to merit, are, partly perhaps for that very reason, frequently changed. The rapid return of elections, and even a taste for variety, M. de Tocqueville thinks, on the part of electors (a taste not unnatural wherever little regard is paid to qualifications), produces a rapid succession of new men in the legislature and in all public posts. Hence, on the one hand, great instability in the laws—every newcomer desiring to do something in the short time he has before him: while, on the other hand, there is no political *carrière;* statesmanship is not a profession. There is no body of persons educated for public business, pursuing it as their occupation, and who transmit from one to another the results of their experience. There are no traditions, no science or art of public affairs. A functionary knows little, and cares less, about the principles on which his predecessor has acted; and his successor thinks as little about his. Public transactions are therefore conducted with a reasonable share, indeed, of the common sense and common information which are general in a democratic community, but with little benefit from specific study and experience; without consistent system, long-sighted views, or persevering pursuit of distant objects.

This is likely enough to be a true picture of the American Government, but can scarcely be said to be peculiar to it. There are now few governments remaining, whether representative or absolute, of which something of the same sort might not be said. In no country where the real government resides in the minister, and where there are frequent changes of ministry, are far-sighted views of policy likely to be acted upon; whether the country be England or France, in the eighteenth century or in the nineteenth.* Crude and ill-considered legislation is the character of all governments whose laws are made, and acts of administration performed, *impromptu*—not in pursuance of a general design, but from the pressure of some present occasion; of all governments in which the ruling power is to any great extent exercised by persons not trained to government as a business. It is true, that the governments which have been celebrated for their profound policy have generally been aristocracies: but they have been very narrow aristocracies; consisting of so few members, that every member could personally participate in the business of administration. These are the governments which have a natural tendency to be administered steadily; that is, according to fixed principles. Every member of the governing body being trained to government as a profession, like other professions they respect precedent, transmit their experience from generation to generation, acquire and pre-serve a set of traditions; and, all being competent judges of each other's merits, the ablest easily rises to his proper level. The governments of ancient Rome and modern Venice were of this character; and, as all know, for ages conducted the affairs of those States with admirable constancy and skill, on fixed principles—often unworthy enough, but always emi-nently adapted to the ends of those governments. When the governing body, whether it consists of the many or of a privileged class, is so numerous, that the large majority of it do not and cannot make the practice of government the main occupation of their lives, it is impossible that there should be wisdom, foresight, and caution in the governing body it-

---

* A few sentences are here inserted from another paper by the author.

self. These qualities must be found, if found at all, not in the body, but in those whom the body trust. The opinion of a numerous ruling class is as fluctuating, as liable to be wholly given up to immediate impulses, as the opinion of the people. Witness the whole course of English history. All our laws have been made on temporary impulses. In no country has the course of legislation been less directed to any steady and consistent purpose.

In so far as it is true that there is a deficiency of remarkable merit in American public men (and our author allows that there is a large number of exceptions), the fact may perhaps admit of a less discreditable explanation. America needs very little government. She has no wars; no neighbors; no complicated international relations; no old society with its thousand abuses to reform; no half-fed and untaught millions in want of food and guidance. Society in America requires little but to be let alone. The current affairs which her government has to transact can seldom demand much more than average capacity; and it may be in the Americans a wise economy, not to pay the price of great talents when common ones will serve their purpose. We make these remarks by way of caution, not of controversy. Like many other parts of our author's doctrines, that of which we are now speaking affords work for a succession of thinkers and of accurate observers; and must, in the main, depend on future experience to confirm or refute it.

We now come to that one among the dangers of Democracy respecting which so much has been said, and which our author designates as "the despotism of the majority."

It is perhaps the greatest defect of M. de Tocqueville's book, that, from the scarcity of examples, his propositions, even when derived from observation, have the air of mere abstract speculations. He speaks of the tyranny of the majority, in general phrases; but gives hardly any instances of it, nor much information as to the mode in which it is practically exemplified. The omission was in the present instance the more excusable, as the despotism complained of was at that time, politically at least, an evil in apprehension more than in sufferance; and he was uneasy rather at the total absence of security against the tyranny of the majority, than at the frequency of its actual exertion.

Events, however, which have occurred since the publication of the first part of M. de Tocqueville's work, give indication of the shape which tyranny is most likely to assume when exercised by a majority.

It is not easy to surmise any inducements of interest, by which, in a country like America, the greater number could be led to oppress the smaller. When the majority and the minority are spoken of as conflicting interests, the rich and the poor are generally meant; but where the rich are content with being rich, and do not claim as such any political privileges, their interest and that of the poor are generally the same: complete protection to property, and freedom in the disposal of it, are alike important to both. When, indeed, the poor are so poor that they can scarcely be worse off, respect on their part for rights of property which they cannot hope to share is never safely to be calculated upon. But where all have property, either in enjoyment or in reasonable hope, and an appreciable chance of acquiring a large fortune; and where every man's way of life proceeds on the confident assurance, that, by superior exertion, he will obtain a superior reward—the importance of inviolability of property is not likely to be lost sight of. It is not affirmed of the Americans, that they make laws against the rich, or unduly press upon them in the imposition of taxes. If a laboring class, less happily circumstanced, could prematurely force themselves into influence over our own legislature, there might then be danger, not so much of violations of property, as of undue interference with contracts; unenlightened legislation for the supposed interest of the many; laws founded on mistakes in political economy. A minimum of wages, or a tax on machinery, might be attempted: as silly and as inefficacious attempts might be made to keep up wages by law as were so long made by the British Legislature to keep them down by the same means. We have no wish to see the experiment tried: but we are fully convinced that experience would correct the one error as it has corrected the other, and in the same way; namely, by complete practical failure.

It is not from the separate interests, real or imaginary, of the majority, that minorities are in danger, but from its antipathies of religion, political party, or race; and experience in America seems to confirm, what theory rendered probable, that the tyranny of the majority would not take the shape of tyrannical laws, but that of a dispensing power over all laws. The people of Massachusetts passed no law prohibiting Roman-Cathlic schools, or exempting Protestants from the penalties of incendiarism: they contented themselves with burning the Ursuline convent to the ground, aware that no jury would be found to redress the injury. In the same reliance, the people of New York and Philadelphia sacked and destroyed the houses of the Abolitionists, and the schools and churches of their black fellow-citizens; while numbers who took no share in the outrage amused themselves with the sight. The laws of Maryland still prohibit murder and burglary; but, in 1812, a Baltimore mob, after destroying the printing-office of a newspaper which had opposed the war with England, broke into the prison to which the editors had been conveyed for safety, murdered one of them, left the others for dead; and the criminals were tried and acquitted. In the same city, in 1835, a riot which lasted four days, and the foolish history of which is related in M. Chevalier's Letters, was occasioned by the fraudulent bankruptcy of the Maryland Bank. It is not so much the riots, in such instances, that are deplorable; these might have occurred in any country: it is the impossibility of obtaining aid from an executive dependent on the mob, or justice from juries which formed part of it; it is the apathetic cowardly truckling of disapproving lookers-on; almost a parallel to the passive imbecility of the people of Paris, when a handful of hired assassins perpetrated the massacres of September. For where the majority is the sole power, and a power issuing its mandates in the form of riots, it inspires a terror which the most arbitrary monarch often fails to excite. The silent sympathy of the majority may support on the scaffold the martyr of one man's tyranny; but, if we would imagine the situation of a victim of the majority itself, we must look to the annals of religious persecution for a parallel.

Yet neither ought we to forget, that even this lawless violence is not so great, because not so lasting, an evil, as tyranny through the medium of the law. A tyrannical law remains; because, so long as it is submitted to, its existence does not weaken the general authority of the laws. But, in America, tyranny will seldom use the instrument of law, because there is, in general, no permanent class to be tyrannized over. The subjects of oppression are casual objects of popular resentment, who cannot be reached by law, but only by occasional acts of lawless power; and to tolerate these, if they ever became frequent, would be consenting to live without law. Already, in the United States, the spirit of outrage has raised a spirit of resistance to outrage; of moral resistance first, as was to be wished and expected: if that fail, physical resistance will follow. The majority, like other despotic powers, will be taught, by experience, that it cannot enjoy both the advantages of civilized society, and the barbarian liberty of taking men's lives and property at its discretion. Let it once be generally understood that minorities will fight, and majorities will be shy of provoking them. The bad government of which there is any permanent danger under modern civilization is in the form of bad laws and bad tribunals: government by the *sic volo,* either of a king or a mob, belongs to past ages, and can no more exist, for long together, out of the pale of Asiatic barbarism.

The despotism, therefore, of the majority within the limits

of civil life, though a real evil, does not appear to us to be a formidable one. The tyranny which we fear, and which M. de Tocqueville principally dreads, is of another kind—a tyranny not over the body, but over the mind.

It is the complaint of M. de Tocqueville, as well as of other travellers in America, that in no country does there exist less independence of thought. In religion, indeed, the varieties of opinion which fortunately prevailed among those by whom the colonies were settled have produced a toleration in law and in fact extending to the limits of Christianity. If by ill fortune there had happened to be a religion of the majority, the case would probably have been different. On every other subject, when the opinion of the majority is made up, hardly any one, it is affirmed, dares to be of any other opinion, or at least to profess it. The statements are not clear as to the nature or amount of the inconvenience that would be suffered by any one who presumed to question a received opinion. It seems certain, however, that scarcely any person has that courage; that, when public opinion considers a question as settled, no further discussion of it takes place; and that not only nobody dares (what everybody may venture upon in Europe) to say any thing disrespectful to the public, or derogatory to its opinions, but that its wisdom and virtue are perpetually celebrated with the most servile adulation and sycophancy.

These considerations, which were much dwelt on in the author's First Part, are intimately connected with the views promulgated in his Second, respecting the influence of Democracy on intellect.

The Americans, according to M. de Tocqueville, not only profess, but carry into practice, on all subjects except the fundamental doctrines of Christianity and Christian ethics, the habit of mind which has been so often inculcated as the one sufficient security against mental slavery—the rejection of authority, and the assertion of the right of private judgment. They regard the traditions of the past merely in the light of materials, and as "a useful study for doing otherwise and better." They are not accustomed to look for guidance either to the wisdom of ancestors, or to eminent cotemporary wisdom, but require that the grounds on which they act shall be made level to their own comprehension. And, as is natural to those who govern themselves by common sense rather than by science, their cast of mind is altogether unpedantic and practical: they go straight to the end, without favor or prejudice towards any set of means; and aim at the substance of things, with something like a contempt for form.

From such habits and ways of thinking, the consequence which would be apprehended by some would be a most licentious abuse of individual independence of thought. The fact is the reverse. It is impossible, as our author truly remarks, that mankind in general should form all their opinions for themselves: an authority from which they mostly derive them may be rejected in theory; but it always exists in fact. That law above them, which older societies have found in the traditions of antiquity, or in the dogmas of priests or philosophers, the Americans find in the opinions of one another. All being nearly equal in circumstances, and all nearly alike in intelligence and knowledge, the only authority which commands an involuntary deference is that of numbers. The more perfectly each knows himself the equal of every single individual, the more insignificant and helpless he feels against the aggregate mass, and the more incredible it appears to him that the opinion of all the world can possibly be erroneous. "Faith in public opinion," says M. de Tocqueville, "becomes in such countries a species of religion, and the majority its prophet." The idea that the things which the multitude believe are still disputable is no longer kept alive by dissentient voices; the right of private judgment, by being extended to the incompetent, ceases to be exercised even by the competent; and speculation becomes possible only within the limits traced, not, as of old, by the infallibility of Aristotle, but by that of "our free and enlightened citizens," or "our free and enlightened age."

On the influence of Democracy upon the cultivation of science and art, the opinions of M. de Tocqueville are highly worthy of attention. There are many, who, partly from theoretic considerations, and partly from the marked absence in America of original efforts in literature, philosophy, or the fine arts, incline to believe that modern Democracy is fatal to them; and that, wherever its spirit spreads, they will take flight. M. de Tocqueville is not of this opinion. The example of America, as he observes, is not to the purpose; because America is, intellectually speaking, a province of England— a province in which the great occupation of the inhabitants is making money, because for that they have peculiar facilities; and are therefore, like the people of Manchester or Birmingham, for the most part contented to receive the higher branches of knowledge ready-made from the capital. In a democratic nation, which is also free, and generally educated, our author is far from thinking that there will be no public to relish or remunerate the works of science and genius. Although there will be great shifting of fortunes, and no hereditary body of wealthy persons sufficient to form a class, there will be, he thinks, from the general activity, and the absence of artificial barriers, combined with the inequality of human intelligence, a far greater number of rich individuals (*infiniment plus nombreux*) than in an aristocratic society. There will be, therefore, though not so complete a leisure, yet a leisure extending perhaps to more persons; while, from the closer contact and greater mutual intercourse between classes, the love of intellectual pleasures and occupations will spread downward very widely among those who have not the same advantages of leisure. Moreover, talents and knowledge being in a democratic society the only means of rapid improvement in fortune, they will be, in the abstract at least, by no means undervalued: whatever

measure of them any person is capable of appreciating, he
will also be desirous of possessing. Instead, therefore, of any
neglect of science and literature, the eager ambition which is
universal in such a state of society takes that direction as
well as others; and the number of those who cultivate these
pursuits becomes "immense."

It is from this fact—from the more active competition in
the products of intellect, and the more numerous public to
which they are addressed—that M. de Tocqueville deduces
the defects with which the products themselves will be
chargeable. In the multiplication of their quantity he sees the
deterioration of their quality. Distracted by so great a multitude, the public can bestow but a moment's attention on
each: they will be adapted, therefore, chiefly for striking at
the moment. Deliberate approval, and a duration beyond
the hour, become more and more difficult of attainment.
What is written for the judgment of a highly instructed few,
amidst the abundance of writings may very probably never
reach them; and their suffrage, which never gave riches, does
not now confer even glory. But the multitude of buyers affords the possibility of great pecuniary success and momentary notoriety for the work which is made up to please at
once, and to please the many. Literature thus becomes not
only a trade, but is carried on by the maxims usually adopted
by other trades which live by the number, rather than by the
quality, of their customers; that much pains need not be bestowed on commodities intended for the general market, and
that what is saved in the workmanship may be more profita-
bly expended in self-advertisement. There will thus be an
immense mass of third- and forth-rate productions, and very
few first-rate. Even the turmoil and bustle of a society in
which every one is striving to get on, is in itself, our author
observes, not favorable to meditation. "Il règne dans le sein
de ces nations un petit mouvement incommode, une sorte de
roulement incessant des hommes les uns sur les autres, qui

trouble et distrait l'esprit sans l'animer et l'élever." Not to mention that the universal tendency to action, and to rapid action, directs the taste to applications rather than principles, and hasty approximations to truth rather than scientific accuracy in it.

Passing now from the province of intellect to that of sentiments and morals, M. de Tocqueville is of opinion, that the general softening of manners, and the remarkable growth, in modern times, of humanity and philanthropy, are in great part the effect of the gradual progress of social equality. Where the different classes of mankind are divided by impassable barriers, each may have intense sympathies with his own class—more intense than it is almost possible to have with mankind in general: but those who are far below him in condition are so unlike himself, that he hardly considers them as human beings; and, if they are refractory and troublesome, will be unable to feel for them even that kindly interest which he experiences for his more unresisting domestic cattle. Our author cites a well-known passage of Madame de Sévigné's Letters in exemplification of the want of feeling exhibited even by good sort of persons towards those with whom they have no *fellow*-feeling. In America, except towards the slaves (an exception which proves the rule), he finds the sentiments of philanthropy and compassion almost universal, accompanied by a general kindness of manner, and obligingness of disposition, without much of ceremony and punctilio. As all feel that they are not above the possible need of the good-will and good offices of others, every one is ready to afford his own. The general equality penetrates also into the family relations. There is more intimacy, he thinks, than in Europe, between parents and children; but less, except in the earliest years, of paternal authority, and the filial respect which is founded on it. These, however, are among the topics which we must omit, as well as the connection which our author attempts to trace between equality of conditions and strictness of domestic morals, and some other remarks on domestic society in America, which do not appear to us to be of any considerable value.

M. de Tocqueville is of opinion, that one of the tendencies of a democratic state of society is to make every one, in a manner, retire within himself, and concentrate his interests, wishes, and pursuits within his own business and household.

The members of a democratic community are like the sands of the sea-shore, each very minute, and no one adhering to any other. There are no permanent classes, and therefore no *esprit de corps;* few hereditary fortunes, and therefore few local attachments, or outward objects consecrated by family feeling. A man feels little connection with his neighbors, little with his ancestors, little with his posterity. There are scarcely any ties to connect any two men together, except the common one of country. Now, the love of country is not, in large communities, a passion of spontaneous growth. When a man's country is his town, where his ancestors have lived for generations, of which he knows every inhabitant, and has recollections associated with every street and building; in which alone, of all places on the earth, he is not a stranger; which he is perpetually called upon to defend in the field, and in whose glory or shame he has an appreciable share, made sensible by the constant presence and rivalry of foreigners—in such a state of things, patriotism is easy. It was easy in the ancient republics, or in modern Switzerland. But, in great communities, an intense interest in public affairs is scarcely natural, except to a member of an aristocracy; who alone has so conspicuous a position, and is so personally identified with the conduct of the government, that his credit and consequence are essentially connected with the glory and power of the nation he belongs to—its glory and power (observe), not the well-being of the bulk of its inhabitants. It is difficult for an obscure person, like the citizen of a Democracy, who is in no way involved in the responsibility of public affairs, and cannot hope to exercise more than the minutest influence over them, to have the sentiment of patriotism as a living and earnest feeling. There being no intermediate objects for his attachments to fix upon, they fasten themselves on his own private affairs; and, according to national character and circumstances, it becomes his ruling passion either to improve his condition in life, or to take his ease and pleasure by the means which it already affords him.

As, therefore, the state of society becomes more democratic, it is more and more necessary to nourish patriotism by artificial means; and, of these, none are so efficacious as free institutions—a large and frequent intervention of the citizens in the management of public business. Nor does the love of country alone require this encouragement, but every feeling which connects men either by interest of sympathy with their neighbors and fellow-citizens. Popular institutions are the great means of rendering general in a people, and especially among the richer classes, the desire of being useful in their generation—useful to the public or to their neighbors, without distinction of rank—as well as courteous and unassuming in their habitual intercourse.

"When the public is supreme, there is no man who does not feel the value of public good-will, or who does not endeavor to court it by drawing to himself the esteem and affection of those amongst whom he is to live. Many of the passions which congeal and keep asunder human hearts are then obliged to retire, and hide below the surface. Pride must be dissembled; disdain does not break out; selfishness is afraid of itself. Under a free government, as most public offices are elective, the men whose elevated minds or aspiring hopes are too closely circumscribed in private life constantly feel that they cannot do without the population which surrounds them. Men learn at such times to think of their fellow-men from ambitious motives; and they frequently find it, in a manner, their interest to be forgetful of self.

"I may here be met by an objection, derived from electioneering intrigues—the meannesses of candidates, and the calumnies of their opponents. These are opportunities of animosity which occur oftener, the more frequent elections become. Such evils are doubtless great, but they are transient; whereas the benefits which attend them remain. The desire of being elected may lead some men for a time to mutual hostility; but this same desire leads all men, in the long-run, mutually to support each other; and, if it happens that an election accidentally severs two friends, the electoral system brings a multitude of citizens permanently together who would always have remained unknown to each other. Freedom engenders private animosities; but despotism gives birth to general indifference. . . .

"A brilliant achievement may win for you the favor of a people at one stroke; but to earn the love and respect of the population which surrounds you requires a long succession of little services and obscure good offices, a constant habit of kindness, and an established reputation for disinterestedness. Local freedom, then, which leads a great number of citizens to value the affections of their neighbors, and of those with whom they are in contact, perpetually draws men back to one another, in spite of the propensities which sever them; and forces them to render each other mutual assistance.

"In the United States, the more opulent citizens take great care not to stand aloof from the people: on the contrary, they constantly keep on easy terms with them; they listen to them; they speak to them every day. They know that the rich, in democracies, always stand in need of the poor; and that, in democratic times, a poor man's attachment depends more on manner than on benefits conferred. The very magnitude of such benefits, by setting the difference of conditions in a strong light, causes a secret irritation to those who reap advantage from them; but the charm of simplicity of manners is almost irresistible. . . . This truth does not penetrate at once into the minds of the rich. They generally resist it as long as the democratic revolution lasts; and they do not acknowledge it immediately after that revolution is accomplished. They are very ready to do good to the people; but they still choose to keep them at arm's-length. They think that is sufficient; but they are mistaken. They might spend fortunes thus, without warming the hearts of the population around them:

that population does not ask them for the sacrifice of their money, but of their pride.

"It would seem as if every imagination in the United States were on the stretch to invent means of increasing the wealth and satisfying the wants of the public. The best informed inhabitants of each district are incessantly using their information to discover new means of augmenting the general prosperity; and, when they have made any such discoveries, they eagerly surrender them to the mass of the people. . . .

"I have often seen Americans make great and real sacrifices to the public welfare; and I have a hundred times remarked, that, in case of need, they hardly ever fail to lend faithful support to each other. The free institutions which the inhabitants of the United States possess, and the political rights of which they make so much use, remind every citizen, and in a thousand ways, that he is a member of society. They at every instant impress upon his mind the notion, that it is the duty as well as the interest of men to make themselves useful to their fellow-creatures; and as he sees no particular reason for disliking them, since he is never either their master or their slave, his heart readily leans to the side of kindness. Men attend to the interests of the public, first by necessity, afterwards by choice: what was calculation becomes an instinct; and, by dint of working for the good of one's fellow-citizens, the habit and the taste for serving them is at length acquired.

"Many people in France consider equality of conditions as one evil, and political freedom as a second. When they are obliged to yield to the former, they strive at least to escape from the latter. But I contend, that, in order to combat the evils which equality may produce, there is only one effectual remedy; namely, political freedom."—Vol. iii. part ii. chap. 4.

With regard to the tone of moral sentiment characteristic of Democracy, M. de Tocqueville holds an opinion which we think deserves the attention of moralists. Among a class composed of persons who have been born into a distinguished position, the habitual springs of action will be very different from those of a democratic community. Speaking generally (and making abstraction both of individual peculiarities and of the influence of moral culture), it may be said of the first, that their feelings and actions will be mainly under the influence of pride; of the latter, under that of interest. Now, as, in an aristocratic society, the elevated class, though small in number, sets the fashion in opinion and feeling; even virtue will, in that state of society, seem to be most strongly recommended by arguments addressing themselves to pride; in a Democracy, by those which address themselves to self-interest. In the one, we hear chiefly of the beauty and dignity of virtue, the grandeur of self-sacrifice; in the other, of honesty the best policy, the value of character, and the common interest of every individual in the good of the whole.

Neither the one nor the other of these modes of feeling, our author is well aware, constitutes moral excellence; which must have a deeper foundation than either the calculations of self-interest, or the emotions of self-flattery. But as an auxiliary to that higher principle, and as far as possible a substitute for it when it is absent, the latter of the two, in his opinion, though the least sentimental, will stand the most wear.

"The principle of enlightened self-interest is not a lofty one; but it is clear and sure. It does not aim at mighty objects; but it attains, without impracticable efforts, all those at which it aims. As it lies within the reach of all capacities, every one can without difficulty apprehend and retain it. By its adaptation to human weaknessess, it easily obtains great dominion: nor is its dominion precarious, since it employs self-interest itself to correct self-interest; and uses, to direct the passions, the very instrument which excites them.

"The doctrine of enlightened self-interest produces no great acts of self-sacrifice; but it suggests daily small acts of self-denial. By itself it cannot suffice to make a virtuous man; but it disciplines a multitude of citizens in habits of regularity, temperance, moderation, foresight, self-command; and, if it does not at once lead men to virtue by their will, it draws them gradually in that direction by their habits. If the principle of 'interest rightly understood' were to sway the whole moral world, extraordinary virtues would doubtless be more rare; but I think that gross depravity would then also be less common. That principle, perhaps, prevents some men from rising far above the level of mankind; but a great number of others, who were falling below that level, are caught and upheld by it. Observe some few individuals, they are lowered by it: survey mankind, it is raised.

"I am not afraid to say, that the principle of enlightened self-interest appears to me the best suited of all philosophical theories to the wants of the men of our time, and that I regard it as their chief remaining security against themselves. Towards it, therefore, the minds of the moralists of our age should turn. Even should they judge it incomplete, it must nevertheless be adopted as necessary.

"No power upon earth can prevent the increasing equality of conditions from impelling the human mind to seek out what is useful, or from inclining every member of the community to concentrate his affections on himself. It must therefore be expected, that personal interest will become more than ever the principal if not the sole spring of men's actions; but it remains to be seen how each man will understand his personal interest.

"I do not think that the doctrine of self-interest, as it is professed in America, is self-evident in all its parts; but it contains a great number of truths so evident, that men, if they are but instructed, cannot fail to see them. Instruct them, then, at all hazards: for the age of implicit self-sacrifice and instinctive virtues is already flying far away from us; and the time is fast approaching, when freedom, public peace, and social order itself, will not be able to exist without instruction."—Vol. iii part ii. chap. 8.

M. de Tocqueville considers a democratic state of society as eminently tending to give the strongest impulse to the desire of physical well-being. He ascribes this not so much to the equality of conditions as to their mobility. In a country like America, every one may acquire riches: no one, at least, is artificially impeded in acquiring them, and hardly any one is born to them. Now, these are the conditions under which the passions which attach themselves to wealth, and to what

wealth can purchase, are the strongest. Those who are born
in the midst of affluence are generally more or less *blasés* to
its enjoyments. They take the comfort or luxury to which
they have always been accustomed, as they do the air they
breathe. It is not *le but de la vie,* but *une manière de vivre.*
An aristocracy, when put to the proof, has in general shown
wonderful facility in enduring the loss of riches and of physical comforts. The very pride, nourished by the elevation
which they owed to wealth, supports them under the privation of it. But to those who have chased riches laboriously
for half their lives, to lose it is the loss of all; *une vie man-
quée;* a disappointment greater than can be endured. In a
democracy, again, there is no contented poverty. No one being forced to remain poor, many who were poor daily becoming rich, and the comforts of life being apparently within
the reach of all, the desire to appropriate them descends to
the very lowest rank. Thus—

"The desire of acquiring the comforts of the world haunts the
imagination of the poor; and the dread of losing them, that of the
rich. Many scanty fortunes spring up. Those who possess them
have a sufficient share of physical gratifications to conceive a
taste for those pleasures—not enough to satisfy it. They never
procure them without exertion, and they never indulge in them
without apprehension. They are, therefore, always straining to
pursue or to retain gratifications so precious, so incomplete, and
so fugitive.

"If I inquire what passion is most natural to men who are at
once stimulated and circumscribed by the obscurity of their birth
or the mediocrity of their fortune, I can discover none more peculiarly appropriate to them than this love of physical prosperity.
The passion for physical comforts is essentially a passion of the
middle classes: with those classes it grows and spreads, and along
with them it becomes preponderant. From them it mounts into
the higher orders of society, and descends into the mass of the
people.

"I never met, in America, with any citizen so poor as not to
cast a glance of hope and longing towards the enjoyments of the

rich, or whose imagination did not indulge itself by anticipation in those good things which fate still obstinately withheld from him.

"On the other hand, I never perceived, amongst the wealthier inhabitants of the United States, that proud contempt of the indulgences of riches which is sometimes to be met with even in the most opulent and dissolute aristocracies. Most of these wealthy persons were once poor. They have felt the stimulus of privation; they have long struggled with adverse fortune; and, now that the victory is won, the passions which accompanied the contest have survived it: their minds are, as it were, intoxicated by the petty enjoyments which they have pursued for forty years.

"Not but that in the United States, as elsewhere, there are a certain number of wealthy persons, who, having come into their property by inheritance possess, without exertion, an opulence they have not earned. But even these are not less devotedly attached to the pleasures of material life. The love of physical comfort is become the predominant taste of the nation: the great current of man's passions runs in that channel, and sweeps every thing along in its course."—Vol. iii. part ii. chap. 10.

A regulated sensuality thus establishes itself—the parent of effeminacy rather than of debauchery; paying respect to the social rights of other people, and to the opinion of the world; not "leading men away in search of forbidden enjoyments, but absorbing them in the pursuit of permitted ones. This spirit is frequently combined with a species of religious morality: men wish to be as well off as they can in this world, without foregoing their chance of another."

From the preternatural stimulus given to the desire of acquiring and of enjoying wealth, by the intense competition which necessarily exists where an entire population are the competitors, arises the restlessness so characteristic of American life.

"It is strange to see with what feverish ardor the Americans pursue their own welfare; and to watch the vague dread that constantly torments them, lest they should not have chosen the shortest path which may lead to it. A native of the United States clings to this world's goods as if he were certain never to die; and is so hasty in grasping at all within his reach, that one would suppose he was constantly afraid of not living long enough to enjoy them. He clutches every thing; he holds nothing fast, but soon loosens his grasp to pursue fresh gratifications. . . .

"At first sight, there is something surprising in this strange unrest of so many happy men, uneasy in the midst of abundance. The spectacle is, however, as old as the world: the novelty is to see a whole people furnish an example of it. . . .

"When all the privileges of birth and fortune are abolished; when all professions are accessible to all, and a man's own energies may place him at the top of any one of them—an easy and unbounded career seems open to his ambition, and he will readily persuade himself that he is born to no vulgar destinies. But this is an erroneous notion, which is corrected by daily experience. The same equality which allows every citizen to conceive these lofty hopes renders all the citizens individually feeble. It circumscribes their powers on every side, while it gives freer scope to their desires. Not only are they restrained by their own weakness, but they are met at every step by immense obstacles, which they did not at first perceive. They have swept away the privileges of some of their fellow-creatures which stood in their way; but they have now to encounter the competition of all. The barrier has changed its shape rather than its place. When men are nearly alike, and all follow the same track, it is very difficult for any one individual to get on fast, and cleave a way through the homogeneous throng which surrounds and presses upon him. This constant strife between the wishes springing from the equality of conditions, and the means it supplies to satisfy them, harasses and wearies the mind."—Vol. iii. part ii. chap. 13.

And hence, according to M. de Tocqueville, while every one is devoured by ambition, hardly any one is ambitious on a large scale. Among so many competitors for but a few great prizes, none of the candidates starting from the vantage-ground of an elevated social position, very few can hope to gain those prizes, and they not until late in life. Men in general, therefore, do not look so high. A vast energy of passion in a whole community is developed and squandered in the petty pursuit of petty advancements in fortune, and the hurried snatching of petty pleasures.

To sum up our author's opinion of the dangers to which mankind are liable as they advance towards equality of condition: his fear, both in government and in intellect and morals, is not of too great liberty, but of too ready submission; not of anarchy, but of servility; not of too rapid change, but of Chinese stationariness. As Democracy advances, the opinions of mankind on most subjects of general interest will become, he believes, as compared with any former period, more rooted, and more difficult to change; and mankind are more and more in danger of losing the moral courage, and pride of independence, which make them deviate from the beaten path, either in speculation or in conduct. Even in politics, it is to be apprehended, lest, feeling their personal insignificance, and conceiving a proportionally vast idea of the importance of society at large; being jealous, moreover, of one another, but not jealous of the central power, which derives its origin from the majority, or which at least is the faithful representative of its desire to annihilate every intermediate power—they should allow that central government to assume more and more control, engross more and more of the business of society; and, on condition of making itself the organ of the general mode of feeling and thinking, should suffer it to relieve mankind from the care of their own interests, and keep them under a kind of tutelage; trampling, meanwhile, with considerable recklessness, as often as convenient, upon the rights of individuals, in the name of society and the public good.

Against these political evils, the corrective to which our author looks, is popular education, and, above all, the spirit of liberty, fostered by the extension and dissemination of political rights. Democratic institutions, therefore, are his remedy for the worst mischiefs to which a democratic state

of society is exposed. As for those to which democratic in-
situtions are themselves liable, these, he holds, society must
struggle with, and bear with so much of them as it cannot
find the means of conquering. For M. de Tocqueville is no
believer in the reality of mixed governments. There is, he
says, always and everywhere, a strongest power: in every
government, either the king, the aristocracy, or the people,
have an effective predominance, and can carry any point on
which they set their heart. "When a community really comes
to have a mixed government, that is, to be equally divided
between two adverse principles, it is either falling into a revolutionary state or into dissolution." M. de Tocqueville believes that the preponderant power which must exist everywhere is most rightly placed in the body of the people; but he
thinks it most pernicious, that this power, whether residing in
the people or elsewhere, should be "checked by no obstacles
which may retard its course, and force it to moderate its own
vehemence." The difference, in his eyes, is great between one
sort of democratic institutions and another. That form of
Democracy should be sought out and devised, and in every
way endeavored to be carried into practice, which, on the
one hand, most exercises and cultivates the intelligence and
mental activity of the majority; and, on the other, breaks the
headlong impulses of popular opinion, by delay, rigor of
forms, and adverse discussion. "The organization and the
establishment of Democracy" on these principles "is the great
political problem of our time."

And, when this problem is solved, there remains an
equally serious one—to make head against the tendency of
Democracy towards bearing down individuality, and circum-
scribing the exercise of the human faculties within narrow
limits. To sustain the higher pursuits of philosophy and art;
to vindicate and protect the unfettered exercise of reason,
and the moral freedom of the individual—these are purposes,
to which, under a Democracy, the superior spirits, and the

government so far as it is permitted, should devote their
utmost energies.

"I shall conclude by one general idea, which comprises not
only all the particular ideas which have been expressed in the
present chapter, but also most of those which it is the object of
this book to treat of.

"In the ages of aristocracy which preceded our own, there
were private persons of great power, and a social authority of
extreme weakness. The principal efforts of the men of those times
were required to strengthen, aggrandize, and secure the supreme
power; and, on the other hand, to circumscribe individual independence within narrower limits, and to subject private interests
to public. Other perils and other cares await the men of our age.
Amongst the greater part of modern nations, the government,
whatever may be its origin, its constitution, or its name, has become almost omnipotent; and private persons are falling, more
and more, into the lowest stage of weakness and dependence.

"The general character of old society was diversity: unity and
uniformity were nowhere to be met with. In modern society, all
things threaten to become so much alike, that the peculiar characteristics of each individual will be entirely lost in the uniformity of the general aspect. Our forefathers were ever prone to
make an improper use of the notion, that private rights ought to
be respected; and we are naturally prone, on the other hand,
to exaggerate the idea, that the interest of an individual ought to
bend to the interest of the many.

"The political world is metamorphosed: new remedies must
henceforth be sought for new disorders. To lay down extensive,
but distinct and immovable, limits to the action of the ruling
power; to confer certain rights on private persons, and secure to
them the undisputed enjoyment of their rights; to enable individual man to maintain whatever independence, strength, and originality he still possesses; to raise him by the side of society at
large, and uphold him in that position—these appear to me the
main objects for the legislator in the age upon which we are now
entering.

"It would seem as if the rulers of our time sought only to use

men in order to effect great things. I wish that they would try
a little more to make great men; that they would set less value
upon the work, and more upon the workmen; that they would
never forget, that a nation cannot long remain strong, when every
man belonging to it is individually weak; and that no form or
combination of social polity has yet been devised to make an
energetic people out of a community of citizens personally feeble
and pusillanimous."—Vol. iv. part iv. chap. 7.

If we were here to close this article, and leave these noble
speculations to produce their effect without further comment,
the reader, probably, would not blame us. Our recommendation is not needed in their behalf. That nothing on the whole
comparable in profundity to them had yet been written on
Democracy, will scarcely be disputed by any one who has
read even our hasty abridgment of them. We must guard, at
the same time, against attaching to these conclusions, or to
any others that can result from such inquiries, a character of
scientific certainty that can never belong to them. Democracy
is too recent a phenomenon, and of too great magnitude, for
any one who now lives to comprehend its consequences. A
few of its more immediate tendencies may be perceived or
surmised: what other tendencies, destined to overrule or to
combine with these, lie behind, there are not grounds even to
conjecture. If we revert to any similar fact in past history,
any change in human affairs approaching in greatness to what
is passing before our eyes, we shall find that no prediction
which could have been made at the time, or for many generations afterwards, would have borne any resemblance to what
has actually been the course of events. When the Greek commonwealths were crushed, and liberty in the civilized world
apparently extinguished by the Macedonian invaders; when
a rude, unlettered people of Italy stretched their conquests
and their dominion from one end to the other of the known
world; when that people in turn lost its freedom and its old
institutions, and fell under the military despotism of one of

its own citizens—what similarity is there between the effects we now know to have been produced by these causes, and any thing which the wisest person could then have anticipated from them? When the Roman Empire, containing all the art, science, literature, and industry of the world, was overrun, ravaged, and dismembered by hordes of barbarians, everybody lamented the destruction of civilization, in an event which is now admitted to have been the necessary condition of its renovation. When the Christian religion had existed but for two centuries; when the pope was only beginning to assert his ascendency—what philosopher or statesman could have foreseen the destinies of Christianity, or the part which has been acted in history by the Catholic Church? It is thus with other really great historical facts—the invention of gunpowder for instance, or of the printing-press. Even when their direct operation is as exactly measurable, because as strictly mechanical, as these were, the mere scale on which they operate gives birth to endless consequences, of a kind which would have appeared visionary to the most far-seeing contemporary wisdom.

It is not, therefore, without a deep sense of the uncertainty attaching to such predictions, that the wise would hazard an opinion as to the fate of mankind under the new democratic dispensation. But, without pretending to judge confidently of remote tendencies, those immediate ones which are already developing themselves require to be dealt with as we treat any of the other circumstances in which we are placed—by encouraging those which are salutary, and working out the means by which such as are hurtful may be counteracted. To exhort men to this, and to aid them in doing it, is the end for which M. de Tocqueville has written: and in the same spirit we will now venture to make one criticism upon him— to point out one correction, of which we think his views stand in need; and for want of which they have occasionally an air of over-subtlety and false refinement, exciting the distrust of common readers, and making the opinions themselves appear less true, and less practically important, than, it seems to us, they really are.

M. de Tocqueville, then, has, at least apparently, confounded the effects of Democracy with the effects of Civilization. He has bound up in one abstract idea the whole of the tendencies of modern commercial society, and given them one name—Democracy; thereby letting it be supposed that he ascribes to equality of conditions several of the effects naturally arising from the mere progress of national prosperity, in the form in which that progress manifests itself in modern times.

It is no doubt true, that, among the tendencies of commercial civilization, a tendency to the equalization of conditions is one, and not the least conspicuous. When a nation is advancing in prosperity; when its industry is expanding, and its capital rapidly augmenting—the number also of those who possess capital increases in at least as great a proportion; and, though the distance between the two extremes of society may not be much diminished, there is a rapid multiplication of those who occupy the intermediate positions. There may be princes at one end of the scale, and paupers at the other; but between them there will be a respectable and well-paid class of artisans, and a middle class who combine property and industry. This may be called, and is, a tendency to equalization. But this growing equality is only one of the features of progressive civilization; one of the incidental effects of the progress of industry and wealth—a most important effect, and one which, as our author shows, re-acts in a hundred ways upon the other effects; but not, therefore, to be confounded with the cause.

So far is it, indeed, from being admissible, that *mere* equality of conditions is the mainspring of those moral and social phenomena which M. de Tocqueville has characterized, that when some unusual chance exhibits to us equality of conditions by itself, severed from that commercial state of society and that progress of industry of which it is the natural concomitant, it produces few or none of the moral effects ascribed to it. Consider, for instance, the French of Lower Canada. Equality of conditions is more universal there than in the United States; for the whole people, without exception, are in easy circumstances, and there are not even that considerable number of rich individuals who are to be found in all the great towns of the American Republic. Yet, do we find in Canada that go-ahead spirit; that restless, impatient eagerness for improvement in circumstances; that mobility; that shifting and fluctuating—now up, now down, now here, now there; that absence of classes and class-spirit; that jealousy of superior attainments; that want of deference for authority and leadership; that habit of bringing things to the rule and square of each man's own understanding—which M. de Tocqueville imputes to the same cause in the United States? In all these respects, the very contrary qualities prevail. We by no means deny, that, where the other circumstances which determine these effects exist, equality of conditions has a very perceptible effect in corroborating them. We think M. de Tocqueville has shown that it has; but that it is the exclusive, or even the principal cause, we think the example of Canada goes far to disprove.

For the reverse of this experiment, we have only to look at home. Of all countries in a state of progressive commercial civilization, Great Britain is that in which the equalization of conditions has made least progress. The extremes of wealth and poverty are wider apart; and there is a more numerous body of persons, at each extreme, than in any other commercial community. From the habits of the population in regard to marriage, the poor have remained poor: from the laws which tend to keep large masses of property together, the rich have remained rich; and often, when they have lost the substance of riches, have retained its social advantages and outward trappings. Great fortunes are continually accumulated, and seldom redistributed. In this respect, therefore,

England is the most complete contrast to the United States. But in commercial prosperity, in the rapid growth of industry and wealth, she is the next after America, and not very much inferior to her. Accordingly, we appeal to all competent observers, whether, in nearly all the moral and intellectual features of American society, as represented by M. de Tocqueville, this country does not stand next to America; whether, with the single difference of our remaining respect for aristocracy, the American people, both in their good qualities and in their defects, resemble any thing so much as an exaggeration of our own middle class; whether the spirit, which is gaining more and more the ascendant with us, is not in a very great degree American; and whether all the moral elements of an American state of society are not most rapidly growing up.

For example, that entire unfixedness in the social position of individuals; that treading upon the heels of one another; that habitual dissatisfaction of each with the position he occupies, and eager desire to push himself into the next above it—has not this become, and is it not becoming more and more, an English characteristic? In England, as well as in America, it appears to foreigners, and even to Englishmen recently returned from a foreign country, as if everybody had but one wish—to improve his condition, never to enjoy it: as if no Englishman cared to cultivate either the pleasures or the virtues corresponding to his station in society, but solely to get out of it as quickly as possible; or if that cannot be done, and until it is done, to seem to have got out of it. "The hypocrisy of luxury," as M. de Tocqueville calls the maintaining an appearance beyond one's real expenditure, he considers as a democratic peculiarity. It is surely an English one. The highest class of all, indeed, is, as might be expected, comparatively exempt from these bad peculiarities. But the very existence of such a class, whose immunities and political privileges are attainable by wealth, tends to aggravate the struggle of the other classes for the possession of that passport to all other importance; and it perhaps required the example of America to prove that the "sabbathless pursuit of wealth" could be as intensely prevalent, where there were no aristocratic distinctions to tempt to it.

Again: the mobility and fluctuating nature of individual relations; the absence of permanent ties, local or personal—how often has this been commented on as one of the organic changes by which the ancient structure of English society is becoming dissolved? Without reverting to the days of clanship, or to those in which the gentry led a patriarchal life among their tenantry and neighbors, the memory of man extends to a time when the same tenants remained attached to the same landlords, the same servants to the same household. But this, with other old customs, after progressively retiring to the remote corners of our island, has nearly taken flight altogether; and it may now be said, that in all the relations of life, except those to which law and religion have given permanence, change has become the general rule, and constancy the exception.

The remainder of the tendencies which M. de Tocqueville has delineated may mostly be brought under one general agency as their immediate cause—the growing insignificance of individuals in comparison with the mass. Now, it would be difficult to show any country in which this insignificance is more marked and conspicuous than in England, or any incompatibility between that tendency and aristocratic institutions. It is not because the individuals composing the mass are all equal, but because the mass itself has grown to so immense a size, that individuals are powerless in the face of it; and because the mass, having by mechanical improvements become capable of acting simultaneously, can compel, not merely any individual, but any number of individuals, to bend before it. The House of Lords is the richest and most powerful collection of persons in Europe; yet they not only could not prevent, but were themselves compelled to pass, the Reform Bill. The daily actions of every peer and peeress are falling more and more under the yoke of *bourgeois* opinion: they feel every day a stronger necessity of showing an immaculate front to the world. When they do venture to disregard common opinion, it is in a body, and when supported by one another; whereas formerly every nobleman acted on his own notions, and dared be as eccentric as he pleased. No rank in society is now exempt from the fear of being peculiar; the unwillingness to be, or to be thought, in any respect original. Hardly anything now depends upon individuals, but all upon classes; and, among classes, mainly upon the middle class. That class is now the power in society, the arbiter of fortune and success. Ten times more money is made by supplying the wants, even the superfluous wants, of the middle, nay of the lower classes, than those of the higher. It is the middle class that now rewards even literature and art: the books by which most money is made are the cheap books; the greatest part of the profit of a picture is the profit of the engraving from it. Accordingly, all the intellectual effects which M. de Tocqueville ascribes to Democracy are taking place under the Democracy of the middle class. There is a greatly augmented number of moderate successes, fewer great literary and scientific reputations. Elementary and popular treatises are imensely multiplied; superficial information far more widely diffused: but there are fewer who devote themselves to thought for its own sake, and pursue in retirement those profounder researches, the results of which can only be appreciated by a few. Literary productions are seldom highly finished: they are got up to be read by many, and to be read but once. If the work sells for a day, the author's time and pains will be better laid out in writing a second than in improving the first. And this is not because books are no longer written for the aristocracy: they never were so. The aristocracy (saving individual exceptions) never were a reading class. It is because books are now written for a numerous, and therefore an unlearned public; no longer principally for scholars, and men of science, who have knowledge of their own, and are not imposed upon by half-knowledge; who have studied the great works of genius, and can make comparisons.*

As for the decay of authority, and diminution of respect for traditional opinions, this could not well be so far advanced among an ancient people—all whose political notions rest on an historical basis, and whose institutions themselves are built on prescription, and not on ideas of expediency, as in America, where the whole edifice of government was constructed, within the memory of man, upon abstract principles. But surely this change also is taking place as fast as could be expected under the circumstances. And even this effect, though it has a more direct connection with Democracy, has not an exclusive one. Respect for old opinions must diminish wherever science and knowledge are rapidly progressive. As the people in general become aware of the recent date of the most important physical discoveries, they are liable to form a rather contemptuous opinion of their ancestors. The mere visible fruits of scientific progress in a wealthy society, the mechanical improvements, the steam-engines, the railroads,

---

* On this account, among others, we think M. de Tocqueville right in the great importance he attaches to the study of Greek and Roman literature; not as being without faults, but as having the contrary faults to those of our own day. Not only do those literatures furnish examples of high finish and perfection in workmanship, to correct the slovenly habits of modern hasty writing; but they exhibit, in the military and agricultural commonwealths of antiquity, precisely that order of virtues in which a commercial society is apt to be deficient: and they altogether show human nature on a grander scale—with less benevolence, but more patriotism; less sentiment, but more self-control; if a lower average of virtue, more striking individual examples of it; fewer small goodnesses, but more greatness, and appreciation of greatness; more which tends to exalt the imagination, and inspire high conceptions of the capabilities of human nature. If, as every one may see, the want of affinity of these studies to the modern mind is gradually lowering them in popular estimation, this is but a confirmation of the need of them, and renders it more incumbent upon those who have the power to do their utmost towards preventing their decline.

carry the feeling of admiration for modern, and disrespect
for ancient times, down even to the wholly uneducated
classes. For that other mental characteristic which M. de
Tocqueville finds in America—a positive, matter-of-fact
spirit; a demand that all things shall be made clear to each
man's understanding; an indifference to the subtler proofs
which address themselves to more cultivated and systematically exercised intellects; for what may be called, in short,
the dogmatism of common sense—we need not look beyond
our own country. There needs no Democracy to account for
this: there needs only the habit of energetic action, without a
proportional development of the taste for speculation. Bona-
parte was one of the most remarkable examples of it; and the
diffusion of half-instruction, without any sufficient provision
made by society for sustaining the higher cultivation, tends
greatly to encourage its excess.

Nearly all those moral and social influences, therefore,
which are the subject of M. de Tocqueville's Second Part, are
shown to be in full operation in aristocratic England. What
connection they have with equality is with the growth of the
middle class, not with the annihilation of the extremes. They
are quite compatible with the existence of peers and *prolétaires;* nay, with the most abundant provision of both those
varieties of human nature. If we were sure of retaining for
ever our aristocratic institutions, society would no less have
to struggle against all these tendencies; and perhaps even
the loss of those institutions would not have so much effect
as is supposed in accelerating their triumph.

The evil is not in the preponderance of a democratic class,
but of any class. The defects which M. de Tocqueville points
out in the American, and which we see in the modern English
mind, are the ordinary ones of a commercial class. The portion of society which is predominant in America, and that
which is attaining predominance here, the American many,
and our middle class, agree in being commercial classes.
The one country is affording a complete, and the other a pro-

gressive, exemplification, that, whenever any variety of human nature becomes preponderant in a community, it imposes upon all the rest of society its own type; forcing all either to submit to it or to imitate it.

It is not in China only that a homogeneous community is naturally a stationary community. The unlikeness of one person to another is not only a principle of improvement, but would seem almost to be the only principle. It is profoundly remarked by M. Guizot, that the short duration or stunted growth of the earlier civilizations arose from this—that, in each of them, some one element of human improvement existed exclusively, or so preponderatingly as to overpower all the others; whereby the community, after accomplishing rapidly all which that one element could do, either perished for want of what it could not do, or came to a halt, and became immovable. It would be an error to suppose that such could not possibly be our fate. In the generalization which pronounces the "law of progress" to be an inherent attribute of human nature, it is forgotten, that, among the inhabitants of our earth, the European family of nations is the only one which has ever yet shown any capability of spontaneous improvement, beyond a certain low level. Let us beware of supposing that we owe this peculiarity to any superiority of nature, and not rather to combinations of circumstances, which have existed nowhere else, and may not exist for ever among ourselves. The spirit of commerce and industry is one of the greatest instruments, not only of civilization in the narrowest, but of improvement and culture in the widest, sense: to it, or to its consequences, we owe nearly all that advantageously distinguishes the present period from the middle ages. So long as other coordinate elements of improvement existed beside it, doing what it left undone, and keeping its exclusive tendencies in equipoise by an opposite order of sentiments, principles of action, and modes of thought—so long the benefits which it conferred on humanity were unqualified. But example and theory alike justify the expectation, that with its com-

plete preponderance would commence an era either of stationariness or of decline.

If, to avert this consummation, it were necessary that the
class which wields the strongest power in society should be
prevented from exercising its strength, or that those who are
powerful enough to overthrow the government should not
claim a paramount control over it, the case of civilized nations would be almost hopeless. But human affairs are not entirely governed by mechanical laws, nor men's characters
wholly and irrevocably formed by their situation in life. Economical and social changes, though among the greatest, are
not the only forces which shape the course of our species.
Ideas are not always the mere signs and effects of social circumstances: they are themselves a power in history. Let the
idea take hold of the more generous and cultivated minds,
that the most serious danger to the future prospects of mankind is in the unbalanced influence of the commercial spirit;
let the wiser and better-hearted politicians and public teachers look upon it as their most pressing duty, to protect and
strengthen whatever, in the heart of man or in his outward
life, can form a salutary check to the exclusive tendencies of
that spirit—and we should not only have individual testi-
monies against it, in all the forms of genius, from those who
have the privilege of speaking, not to their own age merely, but
to all time: there would also gradually shape itself forth a national education, which, without overlooking any other of
the requisites of human well-being, would be adapted to this
purpose in particular.

What is requisite in politics for the same end, is, not that
public opinion should not be, what it is and must be, the ruling power, but that, in order to the formation of the best public opinion, there should exist somewhere a great social support for opinions and sentiments different from those of the
mass. The shape which that support may best assume is a
question of time, place, and circumstance; but (in a commercial country, and an age, when, happily for mankind, the

military spirit is gone by) there can be no doubt about the elements which must compose it: they are, an agricultural class, a leisured class, and a learned class.

The natural tendencies of an agricultural class are in many respects the reverse of those of a manufacturing and commercial. In the first place, from their more scattered position, and less exercised activity of mind, they have usually a greater willingness to look up to, and accept of, guidance. In the next place, they are the class who have local attachments; and it is astonishing how much of character depends upon this one circumstance. If the agricultural spirit is not felt in America as a counterpoise to the commercial, it is because American agriculturists have no local attachments: they range from place to place, and are, to all intents and purposes, a commercial class. But in an old country, where the same family has long occupied the same land, the case will naturally be different. From attachment to places, follows attachment to persons who are associated with those places. Though no longer the permanent tie which it once was, the connection between tenants and landlords is one not lightly broken off—one which both parties, when they enter into it, desire and hope will be permanent. Again: with attachment to the place comes generally attachment to the occupation: a farmer seldom becomes any thing but a farmer. The rage of money-getting can scarcely, in agricultural occupations, reach any dangerous height: except where bad laws have aggravated the natural fluctuations of price, there is little room for gambling. The rewards of industry and skill are sure, but moderate: an agriculturist can rarely make a large fortune. A manufacturer or merchant, unless he can outstrip others, knows that others will outstrip him, and ruin him; while, in the irksome drudgery to which he subjects himself as a means, there is nothing agreeable to dwell on except the ultimate end. But agriculture is in itself an interesting occupation, which few wish to retire from, and which men of property and education often pursue merely for their amusement.

Men so occupied are satisfied with less gain, and are less impatient to realize it. Our town population, it has long been remarked, is becoming almost as mobile and uneasy as the American. It ought not to be so with our agriculturists: they ought to be the counterbalancing element in our national character: they should represent the type opposite to the commercial—that of moderate wishes, tranquil tastes, cultivation of the excitements and enjoyments near at hand, and compatible with their existing position.

To attain this object, how much alteration may be requisite in the system of rack-renting and tenancy at will, we cannot undertake to show in this place. It is sufficiently obvious, also, that the corn-laws must disappear; there must be no feud raging between the commercial class and that by whose influence and example its excesses are to be tempered: men are not prone to adopt the characteristics of their enemies. Nor is this all. In order that the agricultural population should count for any thing in politics, or contribute its part to the formation of the national character, it is absolutely necessary that it should be educated. And let it be remembered, that, in an agricultural people, the diffusion of information and intelligence must necessarily be artificial—the work of government, or of the superior classes. In populous towns, the mere collision of man with man, the keenness of competition, the habits of society and discussion, the easy access to reading—even the dulness of the ordinary occupations, which drives men to other excitements—produce of themselves a certain development of intelligence. The least favored class of a town population are seldom actually stupid; and have often, in some directions, a morbid keenness and acuteness. It is otherwise with the peasantry. Whatever it is desired that they should know, they must be taught; whatever intelligence is expected to grow up among them must first be implanted, and sedulously nursed.

It is not needful to go into a similar analysis of the tendencies of the other two classes—a leisured and a learned class. The capabilities which they possess for controlling the excess of the commercial spirit by a contrary spirit are at once apparent. We regard it as one of the greatest advantages of this country over America, that it possesses both these classes: and we believe that the interests of the time to come are greatly dependent upon preserving them; and upon their being rendered, as they much require to be, better and better qualified for their important functions.

If we believed that the national character of England, instead of re-acting upon the American character and raising it, was gradually assimilating itself to those points of it which the best and wisest Americans see with most uneasiness, it would be no consolation to us to think that we might possibly avoid the institutions of America; for we should have all the effects of her institutions, except those which are beneficial. The American many are not essentially a different class from our ten-pound householders; and, if the middle class are left to the mere habits and instincts of a commercial community, we shall have a "tyranny of the majority," not the less irksome because most of the tyrants may not be manual laborers. For it is a chimerical hope to overbear or outnumber the middle class: whatever modes of voting, whatever redistribution of the constituencies, are really necessary for placing the government in their hands, those, whether we like it or not, they will assuredly obtain.

The ascendency of the commercial class in modern society and politics is inevitable, and under due limitations, ought not to be regarded as an evil. That class is the most powerful; but it needs not therefore be all-powerful. Now, as ever, the great problem in government is to prevent the strongest from becoming the only power, and repress the natural tendency of the instincts and passions of the ruling body to sweep away all barriers which are capable of resisting, even for a moment, their own tendencies. Any counter-balancing power can henceforth exist only by the sufferance of the commercial class; but that it should tolerate some such limitation, we deem as important as that it should not itself be held in vassalage.

On Liberty

The grand, leading principle, towards which every argument unfolded in these pages directly converges, is the absolute and essential importance of human development in its richest diversity.—WILHELM VON HUMBOLDT: *Sphere and Duties of Government.*

To the beloved and deplored memory of her who was the inspirer, and in part the author, of all that is best in my writings—the friend and wife whose exalted sense of truth and right was my strongest incitement, and whose approbation was my chief reward—I dedicate this volume. Like all that I have written for many years, it belongs as much to her as to me; but the work as it stands has had, in a very insufficient degree, the inestimable advantage of her revision; some of the most important portions having been reserved for a more careful reëxamination, which they are now never destined to receive. Were I but capable of interpreting to the world one half the great thoughts and noble feelings which are buried in her grave, I should be the medium of a greater benefit to it, than is ever likely to arise from anything that I can write, unprompted and unassisted by her all but unrivalled wisdom.

CHAPTER 1 *Introductory*

The subject of this Essay is not the so-called Liberty of the
Will, so unfortunately opposed to the misnamed doctrine of
Philosophical Necessity; but Civil, or Social Liberty: the nature and limits of the power which can be legitimately exercised by society over the individual. A question seldom
stated, and hardly ever discussed, in general terms, but which
profoundly influences the practical controversies of the
age by its latent presence, and is likely soon to make itself
recognized as the vital question of the future. It is so far
from being new, that, in a certain sense, it has divided mankind, almost from the remotest ages, but in the stage of
progress into which the more civilized portions of the species
have now entered, it presents itself under new conditions,
and requires a different and more fundamental treatment.

The struggle between Liberty and Authority is the most
conspicuous feature in the portions of history with which we
are earliest familiar, particularly in that of Greece, Rome,
and England. But in old times this contest was between sub-

jects, or some classes of subjects, and the government. By liberty, was meant protection against the tyranny of the political rulers. The rulers were conceived (except in some of the popular governments of Greece) as in a necessarily antagonistic position to the people whom they ruled. They consisted of a governing One, or a governing tribe or caste, who derived their authority from inheritance or conquest; who, at all events, did not hold it at the pleasure of the governed, and whose supremacy men did not venture, perhaps did not desire, to contest, whatever precautions might be taken against its oppressive exercise. Their power was regarded as necessary, but also as highly dangerous; as a weapon which they would attempt to use against their subjects, no less than against external enemies. To prevent the weaker members of the community from being preyed upon by innumerable vultures, it was needful that there should be an animal of prey stronger than the rest, commissioned to keep them down. But as the king of the vultures would be no less bent upon preying on the flock than any of the minor harpies, it was indispensable to be in a perpetual attitude of defence against his beak and claws. The aim, therefore, of patriots, was to set limits to the power which the ruler should be suffered to exercise over the community; and this limitation was what they meant by liberty. It was attempted in two ways. First, by obtaining a recognition of certain immunities, called political liberties or rights, which it was to be regarded as a breach of duty in the ruler to infringe, and which, if he did infringe, specific resistance, or general rebellion, was held to be justifiable. A second, and generally a later expedient, was the establishment of constitutional checks; by which the consent of the community, or of a body of some sort supposed to represent its interests, was made a necessary condition to some of the more important acts of the governing power. To the first of these modes of limitation, the ruling power, in most European countries, was compelled, more or less, to submit. It was not so with the second; and to attain this, or when already in some degree possessed, to attain it more completely, became everywhere the principal object of the lovers of liberty. And so long as mankind were content to combat one enemy by another, and to be ruled by a master, on condition of being guaranteed more or less efficaciously against his tyranny, they did not carry their aspirations beyond this point.

A time, however, came, in the progress of human affairs, when men ceased to think it a necessity of nature that their governors should be an independent power, opposed in interest to themselves. It appeared to them much better that the various magistrates of the State should be their tenants or delegates, revocable at their pleasure. In that way alone, it seemed, could they have complete security that the powers of government would never be abused to their disadvantage. By degrees, this new demand for elective and temporary rulers became the prominent object of the exertions of the popular party, wherever any such party existed; and superseded, to a considerable extent, the previous efforts to limit the power of rulers. As the struggle proceeded for making the ruling power emanate from the periodical choice of the ruled, some persons began to think that too much importance had been attached to the limitation of the power itself. *That* (it might seem) was a resource against rulers whose interests were habitually opposed to those of the people. What was now wanted was, that the rulers should be identified with the people; that their interest and will should be the interest and will of the nation. The nation did not need to be protected against its own will. There was no fear of its tyrannizing over itself. Let the rulers be effectually responsible to it, promptly removable by it, and it could afford to trust them with power of which it could itself dictate the use to be made. Their power was but the nation's own power, concentrated, and in a form convenient for exercise. This mode of thought, or rather perhaps of feeling, was common among the last generation of European liberalism, in the Continental section of which, it still apparently predominates. Those who admit any limit to what a government may do, except in the case of such governments as they think ought not to exist, stand out as brilliant exceptions among the political thinkers of the Continent. A similar tone of sentiment might by this time have been prevalent in our own country, if the circumstances which for a time encouraged it had continued unaltered.

But, in political and philosophical theories, as well as in persons, success discloses faults and infirmities which failure might have concealed from observation. The notion, that the people have no need to limit their power over themselves, might seem axiomatic, when popular government was a thing only dreamed about, or read of as having existed at some distant period of the past. Neither was that notion necessarily disturbed by such temporary aberrations as those of the French Revolution, the worst of which were the work of an usurping few, and which, in any case, belonged, not to the permanent working of popular institutions, but to a sudden and convulsive outbreak against monarchical and aristocratic despotism. In time, however, a democratic republic came to occupy a large portion of the earth's surface, and made itself felt as one of the most powerful members of the community of nations; and elective and responsible government became subject to the observations and criticisms which wait upon a great existing fact. It was now perceived that such phrases as "self-government," and "the power of the people over themselves," do not express the true state of the case. The "people" who exercise the power, are not always the same people with those over whom it is exercised, and the "self-government" spoken of, is not the government of each by himself, but of each by all the rest. The will of the people, moreover, practically means, the will of the most numerous or the most active *part* of the people; the majority, or those who succeed in making themselves accepted as the majority: the people, consequently, *may* desire to oppress a part of their number: and precautions are as much needed against this, as against any other abuse of power. The limitation, therefore, of the power of government over individuals, loses none of its importance when the holders of power are regularly accountable to the community, that is, to the strongest party therein. This view of things, recommending itself equally to the intelligence of thinkers and to the inclination of those important classes in European society to whose real or supposed interests democracy is adverse, has had no difficulty in establishing itself; and in political speculations "the tyranny of the majority" is now generally included among the evils against which society requires to be on its guard.

Like other tyrannies, the tyranny of the majority was at first, and is still vulgarly, held in dread, chiefly as operating through the acts of the public authorities. But reflecting persons perceived that when society is itself the tyrant—society collectively, over the separate individuals who compose it— its means of tyrannizing are not restricted to the acts which it may do by the hands of its political functionaries. Society can and does execute its own mandates: and if it issues wrong mandates instead of right, or any mandates at all in things with which it ought not to meddle, it practises a social tyranny more formidable than many kinds of political oppression, since, though not usually upheld by such extreme penalties, it leaves fewer means of escape, penetrating much more deeply into the details of life, and enslaving the soul itself. Protection, therefore, against the tyranny of the magistrate is not enough; there needs protection also against the tyranny of the prevailing opinion and feeling; against the tendency of society to impose, by other means than civil penalties, its own ideas and practices as rules of conduct on those who dissent from them; to fetter the development, and, if possible, prevent the formation, of any individuality not in harmony with its ways, and compel all characters to fashion themselves upon the model of its own. There is a limit to the legitimate interference of collective opinion with individual independence; and to find that limit, and maintain it against encroachment, is as indispensable to a good condition of human affairs, as protection against political despotism.

But though this proposition is not likely to be contested in general terms, the practical question, where to place the limit—how to make the fitting adjustment between individual independence and social control—is a subject on which nearly everything remains to be done. All that makes existence valuable to any one, depends on the enforcement of restraints upon the actions of other people. Some rules of conduct, therefore, must be imposed, by law in the first place, and by opinion on many things which are not fit subjects for the operation of law. What these rules should be, is the principal question in human affairs; but if we except a few of the most obvious cases, it is one of those which least progress has been made in resolving. No two ages, and scarcely any two countries, have decided it alike; and the decision of one age or country is a wonder to another. Yet the people of any given age and country no more suspect any difficulty in it, than if it were a subject on which mankind had always been agreed. The rules which obtain among themselves appear to them self-evident and self-justifying. This all but universal illusion is one of the examples of the magical influence of custom, which is not only, as the proverb says, a second nature, but is continually mistaken for the first. The effect of custom, in preventing any misgiving respecting the rules of conduct which mankind impose on one another, is all the more complete because the subject is one on which it is not generally considered necessary that reasons should be given, either by one person to others, or by each to himself. People are accustomed to believe, and have been encouraged in the belief by some who aspire to the character of philosophers, that their feelings, on subjects of this nature, are better than reasons, and render reasons unnecessary. The practical principle which guides them to their opinions on the regulation of human conduct, is the feeling in each person's mind that everybody should be required to act as he, and those with

whom he sympathizes, would like them to act. No one, indeed, acknowledges to himself that his standard of judgment
is his own liking; but an opinion on a point of conduct, not
supported by reasons, can only count as one person's preference; and if the reasons, when given, are a mere appeal to a
similar preference felt by other people, it is still only many
people's liking instead of one. To an ordinary man, however,
his own preference, thus supported, is not only a perfectly
satisfactory reason, but the only one he generally has for any
of his notions of morality, taste, or propriety, which are not
expressly written in his religious creed; and his chief guide in
the interpretation even of that. Men's opinions, accordingly,
on what is laudable or blameable, are affected by all the
multifarious causes which influence their wishes in regard to
the conduct of others, and which are as numerous as those
which determine their wishes on any other subject. Sometimes
their reason—at other times their prejudices or superstitions: often their social affections, not seldom their antisocial
ones, their envy or jealousy, their arrogance or contemptu-
ousness: but most commonly, their desires or fears for themselves—their legitimate or illegitimate self-interest. Wherever
there is an ascendant class, a large portion of the morality of
the country emanates from its class interests, and its feelings
of class superiority. The morality between Spartans and Hel-
ots, between planters and negroes, between princes and subjects, between nobles and roturiers, between men and women,
has been for the most part the creation of these class interests
and feelings: and the sentiments thus generated, react in
turn upon the moral feelings of the members of the ascendant
class, in their relations among themselves. Where, on the
other hand, a class, formerly ascendant, has lost its ascendency, or where its ascendency is unpopular, the prevailing
moral sentiments frequently bear the impress of an impatient
dislike of superiority. Another grand determining principle
of the rules of conduct, both in act and forbearance which
have been enforced by law or opinion, has been the servility

of mankind towards the supposed preferences or aversions of their temporal masters, or of their gods. This servility, though essentially selfish, is not hypocrisy; it gives rise to perfectly genuine sentiments of abhorrence; it made men burn magicians and heretics. Among so many baser influences, the general and obvious interests of society have of course had a share, and a large one, in the direction of the moral sentiments: less, however, as a matter of reason, and on their own account, than as a consequence of the sympathies and antipathies which grew out of them: and sympathies and antipathies which had little or nothing to do with the interests of society, have made themselves felt in the establishment of moralities with quite as great force.

The likings and dislikings of society, or of some powerful portion of it, are thus the main thing which has practically determined the rules laid down for general observance, under the penalties of law or opinion. And in general, those who have been in advance of society in thought and feeling, have left this condition of things unassailed in principle, however they may have come into conflict with it in some of its details. They have occupied themselves rather in inquiring what things society ought to like or dislike, than in questioning whether its likings or dislikings should be a law to individuals. They preferred endeavoring to alter the feelings of mankind on the particular points on which they were themselves heretical, rather than make common cause in defence of freedom, with heretics generally. The only case in which the higher ground has been taken on principle and maintained with consistency, by any but an individual here and there, is that of religious belief: a case instructive in many ways, and not least so as forming a most striking instance of the fallibility of what is called the moral sense: for the *odium theologicum,* in a sincere bigot, is one of the most unequivocal cases of moral feeling. Those who first broke the yoke of what called itself the Universal Church, were in general as little willing to permit difference of religious opinion as that church itself.

But when the heat of the conflict was over, without giving a complete victory to any party, and each church or sect was reduced to limit its hopes to retaining possession of the ground it already occupied; minorities, seeing that they had no chance of becoming majorities, were under the necessity of pleading to those whom they could not convert, for permission to differ. It is accordingly on this battle-field, almost solely, that the right of the individual against society have been asserted on broad grounds of principle, and the claim of society to exercise authority over dissentients openly controverted. The great writers to whom the world owes what religious liberty it possesses, have mostly asserted freedom of conscience as an indefeasible right, and denied absolutely that a human being is accountable to others for his religious belief. Yet so natural to mankind is intolerance in whatever they really care about, that religious freedom has hardly anywhere been practically realized, except where religious indifference, which dislikes to have its peace disturbed by theological quarrels, has added its weight to the scale. In the minds of almost all religious persons, even in the most tolerant countries, the duty of toleration is admitted with tacit reserves. One person will bear with dissent in matters of church government, but not of dogma; another can tolerate everybody, short of a Papist or an Unitarian; another, every one who believes in revealed religion; a few extend their charity a little further, but stop at the belief in a God and in a future state. Wherever the sentiment of the majority is still genuine and intense, it is found to have abated little of its claim to be obeyed.

In England, from the peculiar circumstances of our political history, though the yoke of opinion is perhaps heavier, that of law is lighter, than in most other countries of Europe; and there is considerable jealousy of direct interference, by the legislative or the executive power with private conduct; not so much from any just regard for the independence of the individual, as from the still subsisting habit of looking on the government as representing an opposite interest to the public. The majority have not yet learnt to feel the power of the government their power, or its opinions their opinions. When they do so, individual liberty will probably be as much exposed to invasion from the government, as it already is from public opinion. But, as yet, there is a considerable amount of feeling ready to be called forth against any attempt of the law to control individuals in things in which they have not hitherto been accustomed to be controlled by it; and this with very little discrimination as to whether the matter is, or is not, within the legitimate sphere of legal control; insomuch that the feeling, highly salutary on the whole, is perhaps quite as often misplaced as well grounded in the particular instances of its application. There is, in fact, no recognized principle by which the propriety or impropriety of government interference is customarily tested. People decide according to their personal preferences. Some, whenever they see any good to be done, or evil to be remedied, would willingly instigate the government to undertake the business; while others prefer to bear almost any amount of social evil, rather than add one to the departments of human interests amenable to governmental control. And men range themselves on one or the other side in any particular case, according to this general direction of their sentiments; or according to the degree of interest which they feel in the particular thing which it is proposed that the government should do; or according to the belief they entertain that the government would, or would not, do it in the manner they prefer; but very rarely on account of any opinion to which they consistently adhere, as to what things are fit to be done by a government. And it seems to me that, in consequence of this absence of rule or principle, one side is at present as often wrong as the other; the interference of government is, with about equal frequency, improperly invoked and improperly condemned.

The object of this Essay is to assert one very simple principle, as entitled to govern absolutely the dealings of society with the individual in the way of compulsion and control, whether the means used be physical force in the form of legal penalties, or the moral coercion of public opinion. That principle is, that the sole end for which mankind are warranted, individually or collectively, in interfering with the liberty of action of any of their number, is self-protection. That the only purpose for which power can be rightfully exercised over any member of a civilized community, against his will, is to prevent harm to others. His own good, either physical or moral, is not a sufficient warrant. He cannot rightfully be compelled to do or forbear because it will be better for him to do so, because it will make him happier, because, in the opinions of others, to do so would be wise, or even right. There are good reasons for remonstrating with him, or reasoning with him, or persuading him, or entreating him, but not for compelling him, or visiting him with any evil, in case he do otherwise. To justify that, the conduct from which it is desired to deter him must be calculated to produce evil to some one else. The only part of the conduct of any one, for which he is amenable to society, is that which concerns others. In the part which merely concerns himself, his independence is, of right, absolute. Over himself, over his own body and mind, the individual is sovereign.

It is, perhaps, hardly necessary to say that this doctrine is meant to apply only to human beings in the maturity of their faculties. We are not speaking of children, or of young persons below the age which the law may fix as that of manhood or womanhood. Those who are still in a state to require being taken care of by others, must be protected against their own actions as well as against external injury. For the same reason, we may leave out of consideration those backward states of society in which the race itself may be considered as in its nonage. The early difficulties in the way of spontaneous progress are so great, that there is seldom any choice of means for overcoming them; and a ruler full of the spirit of improvement is warranted in the use of any expedients that will attain an end, perhaps otherwise unattainable. Despotism is a legitimate mode of government in dealing with barbarians, provided the end be their improvement, and the means justified by actually effecting that end. Liberty, as a principle, has no application to any state of things anterior to the time when mankind have become capable of being improved by free and equal discussion. Until then, there is nothing for them but implicit obedience to an Akbar or a Charlemagne, if they are so fortunate as to find one. But as soon as mankind have attained the capacity of being guided to their own improvement by conviction or persuasion (a period long since reached in all nations with whom we need here concern ourselves), compulsion, either in the direct form or in that of pains and penalties for non-compliance, is no longer admissible as a means to their own good, and justifiable only for the security of others.

It is proper to state that I forego any advantage which could be derived to my argument from the idea of abstract right, as a thing independent of utility. I regard utility as the ultimate appeal on all ethical questions; but it must be utility in the largest sense, grounded on the permanent interests of man as a progressive being. Those interests, I contend, authorize the subjection of individual spontaneity to external control, only in respect to those actions of each, which concern the interest of other people. If any one does an act hurtful to others, there is a *primâ facie* case for punishing him, by law, or, where legal penalties are not safely applicable, by general disapprobation. There are also many positive acts for the benefit of others, which he may rightfully be compelled to perform; such as, to give evidence in a court of justice; to bear his fair share in the common defence, or in any other joint work necessary to the interest of the society of which he enjoys the protection; and to perform certain acts of individual beneficence, such as saving a fellow creature's life, or interposing to protect the defenceless against ill-usage, things which whenever it is obviously a man's duty to do, he may rightfully be made responsible to society for not doing. A person may cause evil to others not only by his actions but by his inaction, and in either case he is justly accountable to them for the injury. The latter case, it is true, requires a much more cautious exercise of compulsion than the former. To make any one answerable for doing evil to others, is the rule; to make him answerable for not preventing evil, is, comparatively speaking, the exception. Yet there are many cases clear enough and grave enough to justify that exception. In all things which regard the external relations of the individual, he is *de jure* amenable to those whose interests are concerned, and if need be, to society as their protector. There are often good reasons for not holding him to the responsibility; but these reasons must arise from the special expediencies of the case: either because it is a kind of case in which he is on the whole likely to act better, when left to his own discretion, than when controlled in any way in which society have it in their power to control him; or because the attempt to exercise control would produce other evils, greater than those which it would prevent. When such reasons as these preclude the enforcement of responsibility, the conscience of the agent himself should step into the vacant judgment-seat, and protect those interests of others which have no external protection; judging himself all the more rigidly, because the case does not admit of his being made accountable to the judgment of his fellow-creatures.

But there is a sphere of action in which society, as distinguished from the individual, has, if any, only an indirect interest; comprehending all that portion of a person's life and conduct which affects only himself, or, if it also affects others, only with their free, voluntary, and undeceived consent and participation. When I say only himself, I mean directly, and in the first instance: for whatever affects himself, may affect others *through* himself; and the objection which may be grounded on this contingency, will receive consideration in the sequel. This, then, is the appropriate region of human liberty. It comprises, first, the inward domain of consciousness; demanding liberty of conscience, in the most comprehensive sense; liberty of thought and feeling; absolute freedom of opinion and sentiment on all subjects, practical or speculative, scientific, moral, or theological. The liberty of expressing and publishing opinions may seem to fall under a different principle, since it belongs to that part of the conduct of an individual which concerns other people; but, being almost of as much importance as the liberty of thought itself, and resting in great part on the same reasons, is practically inseparable from it. Secondly, the principle requires liberty of tastes and pursuits; of framing the plan of our life to suit our own character; of doing as we like, subject to such consequences as may follow; without impediment from our fellow-creatures, so long as what we do does not harm them, even though they should think our conduct foolish, perverse, or wrong. Thirdly, from this liberty of each individual, follows the liberty, within the same limits, of combination among individuals; freedom to unite, for any purpose not involving harm to others: the persons combining being supposed to be of full age, and not forced or deceived.

No society in which these liberties are not, on the whole, respected, is free, whatever may be its form of government; and none is completely free in which they do not exist absolute and unqualified. The only freedom which deserves the name, is that of pursuing our own good in our own way, so long as we do not attempt to deprive others of theirs, or impede their efforts to obtain it. Each is the proper guardian of his own health, whether bodily, or mental and spiritual. Mankind are greater gainers by suffering each other to live as seems good to themselves, than by compelling each to live as seems good to the rest.

Though this doctrine is anything but new, and, to some persons, may have the air of a truism, there is no doctrine which stands more directly opposed to the general tendency of existing opinion and practice. Society has expended fully as much effort in the attempt (according to its lights) to compel people to conform to its notions of personal, as of social excellence. The ancient commonwealths thought themselves entitled to practise, and the ancient philosophers countenanced, the regulation of every part of private conduct by public authority, on the ground that the State had a deep interest in the whole bodily and mental discipline of every one of its citizens; a mode of thinking which may have been admissible in small republics surrounded by powerful enemies, in constant peril of being subverted by foreign attack or internal commotion, and to which even a short interval of relaxed energy and self-command might so easily be fatal, that they could not afford to wait for the salutary permanent effects of freedom. In the modern world, the greater size of political communities, and above all, the separation between the spiritual and temporal authority (which placed the direction of men's consciences in other hands than those which controlled their worldly affairs), prevented so great an interference by law in the details of private life; but the engines of moral repression have been wielded more strenuously against divergence from the reigning opinion in self-regarding, than even in social matters; religion, the most powerful of the elements which have entered into the formation of moral feeling, having almost always been governed either by the ambition of a hierarchy, seeking control over every department of human conduct, or by the spirit of Puritanism. And some of those modern reformers who have placed themselves in strongest opposition to the religions of the past, have been noway behind either churches or sects in their assertion of the right of spiritual domination: M. Comte, in particular, whose social system, as unfolded in his *Traité de Politique Positive,* aims at establishing (though by moral more than by legal appliances) a despotism of society over the individual, surpassing anything contemplated in the political ideal of the most rigid disciplinarian among the ancient philosophers.

Apart from the peculiar tenets of individual thinkers, there is also in the world at large an increasing inclination to stretch unduly the powers of society over the individual, both by the force of opinion and even by that of legislation: and as the tendency of all the changes taking place in the world is to strengthen society, and diminish the power of the individual, this encroachment is not one of the evils which tend spontaneously to disappear, but, on the contrary, to grow more and more formidable. The disposition of mankind, whether as rulers or as fellow-citizens, to impose their own opinions and inclinations as a rule of conduct on others, is so energetically supported by some of the best and by some of the worst feelings incident to human nature, that it is hardly ever kept under restraint by anything but want of power; and as the power is not declining, but growing, unless a strong barrier of moral conviction can be raised against the mischief, we must expect, in the present circumstances of the world, to see it increase.

It will be convenient for the argument, if, instead of at once entering upon the general thesis, we confine ourselves in the first instance to a single branch of it, on which the principle here stated is, if not fully, yet to a certain point, recognized by the current opinions. This one branch is the Liberty of Thought: from which it is impossible to separate the cognate liberty of speaking and of writing. Although these liberties, to some considerable amount, form part of the political morality of all countries which profess religious toleration and free institutions, the grounds, both philosophical and practical, on which they rest, are perhaps not so familiar to the general mind, nor so thoroughly appreciated by many even of the leaders of opinion, as might have been expected. Those grounds, when rightly understood, are of much wider application than to only one division of the subject, and a thorough consideration of this part of the question will be found the best introduction to the remainder. Those to whom nothing which I am about to say will be new, may therefore, I hope, excuse me, if on a subject which for now three centuries has been so often discussed, I venture on one discussion more.

CHAPTER 2   *Of the Liberty of Thought and Discussion*

The time, it is to be hoped, is gone by when any defence would be necessary of the "liberty of the press" as one of the securities against corrupt or tyrannical government. No argument, we may suppose, can now be needed, against permitting a legislature or an executive, not identified in interest with the people, to prescribe opinions to them, and determine what doctrines or what arguments they shall be allowed to hear. This aspect of the question, besides, has been so often and so triumphantly enforced by preceding writers, that it needs not be specially insisted on in this place. Though the law of England, on the subject of the press, is as servile to this day as it was in the time of the Tudors, there is little danger of its being actually put in force against political discussion, except during some temporary panic, when fear of insurrection drives ministers and judges from their propriety; * and, speaking generally, it is not, in constitutional

* These words had scarcely been written, when, as if to give them an emphatic contradiction, occurred the Government Press Prosecutions of 1858. That ill-judged interference with the liberty of public discussion has not, however, induced me to alter a single word in the text, nor has it at all weakened my conviction that, moments of panic excepted, the era of pains and penalties for political discussion has, in our own country, passed away. For, in the first place, the prosecutions were not persisted in; and, in the second, they were never, properly speaking, political prosecutions. The offence charged was not that of

countries, to be apprehended, that the government, whether completely responsible to the people or not, will often attempt to control the expression of opinion, except when in doing so it makes itself the organ of the general intolerance of the public. Let us suppose, therefore, that the government is entirely at one with the people, and never thinks of exerting any power of coercion unless in agreement with what it conceives to be their voice. But I deny the right of the people to exercise such coercion, either by themselves or by their government. The power itself is illegitimate. The best government has no more title to it than the worst. It is as noxious, or more noxious, when exerted in accordance with public opinion, than when in opposition to it. If all mankind minus one, were of one opinion, and only one person were of the contrary opinion, mankind would be no more justified in silencing that one person, than he, if he had the power, would be justified in silencing mankind. Were an opinion a personal possession of no value except to the owner; if to be

---

criticizing institutions, or the acts or persons of rulers, but of circulating what was deemed an immoral doctrine, the lawfulness of Tyrannicide.

If the arguments of the present chapter are of any validity, there ought to exist the fullest liberty of professing and discussing, as a matter of ethical conviction, any doctrine, however immoral it may be considered. It would, therefore, be irrelevant and out of place to examine here, whether the doctrine of Tyrannicide deserves that title. I shall content myself with saying, that the subject has been at all times one of the open questions of morals; that the act of a private citizen in striking down a criminal, who, by raising himself above the law, has placed himself beyond the reach of legal punishment or control, has been accounted by whole nations, and by some of the best and wisest of men, not a crime, but an act of exalted virtue; and that, right or wrong, it is not of the nature of assassination, but of civil war. As such, I hold that the instigation to it, in a specific case, may be a proper subject of punishment, but only if an overt act has followed, and at least a probable connection can be established between the act and the instigation. Even then, it is not a foreign government, but the very government assailed, which alone, in the exercise of self-defence can legitimately punish attacks directed against its own existence.

obstructed in the enjoyment of it were simply a private injury, it would make some difference whether the injury was inflicted only on a few persons or on many. But the peculiar evil of silencing the expression of an opinion is, that it is robbing the human race; posterity as well as the existing generation; those who dissent from the opinion, still more than those who hold it. If the opinion is right, they are deprived of the opportunity of exchanging error for truth: if wrong, they lose, what is almost as great a benefit, the clearer perception and livelier impression of truth, produced by its collision with error.

It is necessary to consider separately these two hypotheses, each of which has a distinct branch of the argument corresponding to it. We can never be sure that the opinion we are endeavoring to stifle is a false opinion; and if we were sure, stifling it would be an evil still.

First: the opinion which it is attempted to suppress by authority may possibly be true. Those who desire to suppress it, of course deny its truth; but they are not infallible. They have no authority to decide the question for all mankind, and exclude every other person from the means of judging. To refuse a hearing to an opinion, because they are sure that it is false, is to assume that *their* certainty is the same thing as *absolute* certainty. All silencing of discussion is an assumption of infallibility. Its condemnation may be allowed to rest on this common argument, not the worse for being common.

Unfortunately for the good sense of mankind, the fact of their fallibility is far from carrying the weight in their practical judgment, which is always allowed to it in theory; for while every one well knows himself to be fallible, few think it necessary to take any precautions against their own fallibility, or admit the supposition that any opinion, of which they feel very certain, may be one of the examples of the error to which they acknowledge themselves to be liable. Absolute princes, or others who are accustomed to unlimited deference, usually feel this complete confidence in their own opinions on nearly all subjects. People more happily situated, who sometimes hear their opinions disputed, and are not wholly unused to be set right when they are wrong, place the same unbounded reliance only on such of their opinions as are shared by all who surround them, or to whom they habitually defer: for in proportion to a man's want of confidence in his own solitary judgment, does he usually repose, with implicit trust, on the infallibility of "the world" in general. And the world, to each individual, means the part of it with which he comes in contact; his party, his sect, his church, his class of society: the man may be called, by comparison, almost liberal and large-minded to whom it means anything so comprehensive as his own country or his own age. Nor is his faith in this collective authority at all shaken by his being aware that other ages, countries, sects, churches, classes, and parties have thought, and even now think, the exact reverse. He devolves upon his own world the responsibility of being in the right against the dissentient worlds of other people; and it never troubles him that mere accident has decided which of these numerous worlds is the object of his reliance, and that the same causes which make him a Churchman in London, would have made him a Buddhist or a Confucian in Pekin. Yet it is as evident in itself, as any amount of argument can make it, that ages are no more infallible than individuals; every age having held many opinions which subsequent ages have deemed not only false but absurd; and it is as certain that many opinions, now general, will be rejected by future ages, as it is that many, once general, are rejected by the present.

The objection likely to be made to this argument, would probably take some such form as the following. There is no greater assumption of infallibility in forbidding the propagation of error, than in any other thing which is done by public authority on its own judgment and responsibility. Judgment is given to men that they may use it. Because it may be used erroneously, are men to be told that they ought not to use it at all? To prohibit what they think pernicious, is not claiming exemption from error, but fulfilling the duty incumbent on them, although fallible, of acting on their conscientious conviction. If we were never to act on our opinions, because those opinions may be wrong, we should leave all our interests uncared for, and all our duties unperformed. An objection which applies to all conduct, can be no valid objection to any conduct in particular. It is the duty of governments, and of individuals, to form the truest opinions they can; to form them carefully, and never impose them upon others unless they are quite sure of being right. But when they are sure (such reasoners may say), it is not conscientiousness but cowardice to shrink from acting on their opinions, and allow doctrines which they honestly think dangerous to the welfare of mankind, either in this life or in another, to be scattered abroad without restraint, because other people, in less enlightened times, have persecuted opinions now believed to be true. Let us take care, it may be said, not to make the same mistake: but governments and nations have made mistakes in other things, which are not denied to be fit subjects for the exercise of authority: they have laid on bad taxes, made unjust wars. Ought we therefore to lay on no taxes, and, under whatever provocation, make no wars? Men, and governments, must act to the best of their ability. There is no such thing as absolute certainty, but there is assurance sufficient for the purposes of human life. We may, and must, assume our opinion to be true for the guidance of our own conduct: and it is assuming no more when we forbid bad men to pervert society by the propagation of opinions which we regard as false and pernicious.

I answer, that it is assuming very much more. There is the greatest difference between presuming an opinion to be true, because, with every opportunity for contesting it, it has not been refuted, and assuming its truth for the purpose of not permitting its refutation. Complete liberty of contradicting and disproving our opinion, is the very condition which justifies us in assuming its truth for purposes of action; and on no other terms can a being with human faculties have any rational assurance of being right.

When we consider either the history of opinion, or the ordinary conduct of human life, to what is it to be ascribed that the one and the other are no worse than they are? Not certainly to the inherent force of the human understanding; for, on any matter not self-evident, there are ninety-nine persons totally incapable of judging of it, for one who is capable; and the capacity of the hundredth person is only comparative; for the majority of the eminent men of every past generation held many opinions now known to be erroneous, and did or approved numerous things which no one will now justify. Why is it, then, that there is on the whole a preponderance among mankind of rational opinions and rational conduct? If there really is this preponderance—which there must be, unless human affairs are, and have always been, in an almost desperate state—it is owing to a quality of the human mind, the source of everything respectable in man either as an intellectual or as a moral being, namely, that his errors are corrigible. He is capable of rectifying his mistakes, by discussion and experience. Not by experience alone. There must be discussion, to show how experience is to be interpreted. Wrong opinions and practices gradually yield to fact and argument: but facts and arguments, to produce any effect on the mind, must be brought before it. Very few facts are able to tell their own story, without comments to bring out their meaning. The whole strength and value, then, of human judgment, depending on the one property, that it can be set right when it is wrong, reliance can be placed on it only when the means of setting it right are kept constantly at hand. In the case of any person whose judgment is really deserving of confidence, how has it become so? Because he has kept his mind open to criticism of his opinions and conduct. Because it has been his practice to listen to all that could be said against him; to profit by as much of it as was just, and expound to himself, and upon occasion to others, the fallacy of what was fallacious. Because he has felt, that the only way in which a human being can make some approach to knowing the whole of a subject, is by hearing what can be said about it by persons of every variety of opinion, and studying all modes in which it can be looked at by every character of mind. No wise man ever acquired his wisdom in any mode but this; nor is it in the nature of human intellect to become wise in any other manner. The steady habit of correcting and completing his own opinion by collating it with those of others, so far from causing doubt and hesitation in carrying it into practice, is the only stable foundation for a just reliance on it: for, being cognizant of all that can, at least obviously, be said against him, and having taken up his position against all gainsayers—knowing that he has sought for objections and difficulties, instead of avoiding them, and has shut out no light which can be thrown upon the subject from any quarter—he has a right to think his judgment better than that of any person, or any multitude, who have not gone through a similar process.

It is not too much to require that what the wisest of mankind, those who are best entitled to trust their own judgment, find necessary to warrant their relying on it, should be submitted to by that miscellaneous collection of a few wise and many foolish individuals, called the public. The most intolerant of churches, the Roman Catholic Church, even at the canonization of a saint, admits, and listens patiently to, a "devil's advocate." The holiest of men, it appears, cannot be admitted to posthumous honors, until all that the devil could say against him is known and weighed. If even the Newtonian philosophy were not permitted to be questioned, mankind could not feel as complete assurance of its truth as they now do. The beliefs which we have most warrant for, have no safeguard to rest on, but a standing invitation to the whole world to prove them unfounded. If the challenge is not accepted, or is accepted and the attempt fails, we are far enough from certainty still; but we have done the best that the existing state of human reason admits of; we have neglected nothing that could give the truth a chance of reaching us: if the lists are kept open, we may hope that if there be a better truth, it will be found when the human mind is capable of receiving it; and in the mean time we may rely on having attained such approach to truth, as is possible in our own day. This is the amount of certainty attainable by a fallible being, and this the sole way of attaining it.

Strange it is, that men should admit the validity of the arguments for free discussion, but object to their being "pushed to an extreme;" not seeing that unless the reasons are good for an extreme case, they are not good for any case. Strange that they should imagine that they are not assuming infallibility, when they acknowledge that there should be free discussion on all subjects which can possibly be *doubtful,* but think that some particular principle or doctrine should be forbidden to be questioned because it is *so certain,* that is, because *they are certain* that it is certain. To call any proposition certain, while there is any one who would deny its certainty if permitted, but who is not permitted, is to assume that we ourselves, and those who agree with us, are the judges of certainty, and judges without hearing the other side.

In the present age—which has been described as "destitute of faith, but terrified at scepticism,"—in which people feel sure, not so much that their opinions are true, as that they should not know what to do without them—the claims of an opinion to be protected from public attack are rested not so much on its truth, as on its importance to society. There are, it is alleged, certain beliefs, so useful, not to say indispensable to well-being, that it is as much the duty of governments to uphold those beliefs, as to protect any other of the interests of society. In a case of such necessity, and so directly in the line of their duty, something less than infallibility may, it is maintained, warrant, and even bind, governments, to act on their own opinion, confirmed by the general opinion of mankind. It is also often argued, and still oftener thought, that none but bad men would desire to weaken these salutary beliefs; and there can be nothing wrong, it is thought, in restraining bad men, and prohibiting what only such men would wish to practise. This mode of thinking makes the justification of restraints on discussion not a question of the truth of doctrines, but of their usefulness; and flatters itself by that means to escape the responsibility of claiming to be an infallible judge of opinions. But those who thus satisfy themselves, do not perceive that the assumption of infallibility is merely shifted from one point to another. The usefulness of an opinion is itself matter of opinion: as disputable, as open to discussion and requiring discussion as much, as the opinion itself. There is the same need of an infallible judge of opinions to decide an opinion to be noxious, as to decide it to be false, unless the opinion condemned has full opportunity of defending itself. And it will not do to say that the heretic may be allowed to maintain the utility or harmlessness of his opinion, though forbidden to maintain its truth. The truth of an opinion is part of its utility. If we would know whether or not it is desirable that a proposition should be believed, is it possible to exclude the consideration of whether or not it is true? In the opinion, not of bad men, but of the best men, no belief which is contrary to truth can be really useful: and can you prevent such men from urging that plea, when they are charged with culpability for denying some doctrine which they are told is useful, but which they believe to be false? Those who are on the side of received opinions, never fail to take all possible advantage of this plea; you do not find *them* handling the question of utility as if it could be completely abstracted from that of truth: on the contrary, it is, above all, because their doctrine is "the truth," that the knowledge or the belief of it is held to be so indispensable. There can be no fair discussion of the question of usefulness, when an argument so vital may be employed on one side, but not on the other. And in point of fact, when law or public feeling do not permit the truth of an opinion to be disputed, they are just as little tolerant of a denial of its usefulness. The utmost they allow is an extenuation of its absolute necessity, or of the positive guilt of rejecting it.

In order more fully to illustrate the mischief of denying a hearing to opinions because we, in our own judgment, have condemned them, it will be desirable to fix down the discussion to a concrete case; and I choose, by preference, the cases which are least favorable to me—in which the argument against freedom of opinion, both on the score of truth and on that of utility, is considered the strongest. Let the opinions impugned be the belief in a God and in a future state, or any of the commonly received doctrines of morality. To fight the battle on such ground, gives a great advantage to an unfair antagonist; since he will be sure to say (and many who have no desire to be unfair will say it internally), Are these the doctrines which you do not deem sufficiently certain to be taken under the protection of law? Is the belief in a God one of the opinions, to feel sure of which, you hold to be assuming infallibility? But I must be permitted to observe, that it is not the feeling sure of a doctrine (be it what it may) which I call an assumption of infallibility. It is the undertaking to decide that question *for others,* without allowing them to hear what can be said on the contrary side. And I denounce and reprobate this pretension not the less, if put forth on the side of my most solemn convictions. However positive any one's persuasion may be, not only of the falsity, but of the pernicious consequences—not only of the pernicious consequences, but (to adopt expressions which I altogether condemn) the immorality and impiety of an opinion; yet if, in pursuance of that private judgment, though backed by the public judgment of his country or his contemporaries, he prevents the opinion from being heard in its defence, he assumes infallibility. And so far from the assumption being less objectionable or less dangerous because the opinion is called immoral or impious, this is the case of all others in which it is most fatal. These are exactly the occasions on which the men of one generation commit those dreadful mistakes, which excite the astonishment and horror of posterity. It is among such that we find the instances memorable in history, when the arm of the law has been employed to root out the best men and the noblest doctrines; with deplorable success as to the men, though some of the doctrines have survived to be (as if in mockery) invoked, in defence of similar conduct towards those who dissent from *them,* or from their received interpretation.

Mankind can hardly be too often reminded, that there was once a man named Socrates, between whom and the legal authorities and public opinion of his time, there took place a memorable collision. Born in an age and country abounding in individual greatness, this man has been handed down to us by those who best knew both him and the age, as the most virtuous man in it; while *we* know him as the head and prototype of all subsequent teachers of virtue, the source equally of the lofty inspiration of Plato and the judicious utilitarianism of Aristotle, *"i maëstri di color che sanno,"* the two headsprings of ethical as of all other philosophy. This acknowledged master of all the eminent thinkers who have since lived—whose fame, still growing after more than two thousand years, all but outweighs the whole remainder of the names which make his native city illustrious—was put to death by his countrymen, after a judicial conviction, for impiety and immorality. Impiety, in denying the gods recognized by the State; indeed his accuser asserted (see the "Apologia") that he believed in no gods at all. Immorality, in being, by his doctrines and instructions, a "corruptor of youth." Of these charges the tribunal, there is every ground for believing, honestly found him guilty, and condemned the man who probably of all then born had deserved best of mankind, to be put to death as a criminal.

To pass from this to the only other instance of judicial in-iquity, the mention of which, after the condemnation of Soc-rates, would not be an anti-climax: the event which took place on Calvary rather more than eighteen hundred years ago. The man who left on the memory of those who witnessed his life and conversation, such an impression of his moral grandeur, that eighteen subsequent centuries have done hom-age to him as the Almighty in person, was ignominiously put to death, as what? As a blasphemer. Men did not merely mistake their benefactor; they mistook him for the exact con-trary of what he was, and treated him as that prodigy of impiety, which they themselves are now held to be, for their treatment of him. The feelings with which mankind now re-gard these lamentable transactions, especially the later of the two, render them extremely unjust in their judgment of the unhappy actors. These were, to all appearance, not bad men—not worse than men commonly are, but rather the contrary; men who possessed in a full, or somewhat more than a full measure, the religious, moral, and patriotic feel-ings of their time and people: the very kind of men who, in all times, our own included, have every chance of passing through life blameless and respected. The high-priest who rent his garments when the words were pronounced, which, according to all the ideas of his country, constituted the black-est guilt, was in all probability quite as sincere in his horror and indignation, as the generality of respectable and pious men now are in the religious and moral sentiments they profess; and most of those who now shudder at his conduct, if they had lived in his time, and been born Jews, would have acted precisely as he did. Orthodox Christians who are tempted to think that those who stoned to death the first martyrs must have been worse men than they themselves are, ought to remember that one of those persecutors was Saint Paul.

Let us add one more example, the most striking of all, if the impressiveness of an error is measured by the wisdom and virtue of him who falls into it. If ever any one, possessed of power, had grounds for thinking himself the best and most enlightened among his cotemporaries, it was the Emperor Marcus Aurelius. Absolute monarch of the whole civilized world, he preserved through life not only the most unblemished justice, but what was less to be expected from his Stoical breeding, the tenderest heart. The few failings which are attributed to him, were all on the side of indulgence: while his writings, the highest ethical product of the ancient mind, differ scarcely perceptibly, if they differ at all, from the most characteristic teachings of Christ. This man, a better Christian in all but the dogmatic sense of the word, than almost any of the ostensibly Christian sovereigns who have since reigned, persecuted Christianity. Placed at the summit of all the previous attainments of humanity, with an open, unfettered intellect, and a character which led him of himself to embody in his moral writings the Christian ideal, he yet failed to see that Christianity was to be a good and not an evil to the world, with his duties to which he was so deeply penetrated. Existing society he knew to be in a deplorable state. But such as it was, he saw, or thought he saw, that it was held together and prevented from being worse, by belief and reverence of the received divinities. As a ruler of mankind, he deemed it his duty not to suffer society to fall in pieces; and saw not how, if its existing ties were removed, any others could be formed which could again knit it together. The new religion openly aimed at dissolving these ties: unless, therefore, it was his duty to adopt that religion, it seemed to be his duty to put it down. Inasmuch then as the theology of Christianity did not appear to him true or of divine origin; inasmuch as this strange history of a crucified God was not credible to him, and a system which purported to rest entirely upon a foundation to him so wholly unbelievable, could not be foreseen by him to be that renovating agency which, after all abatements, it has in fact proved to be; the gentlest and most amiable of philosophers and rulers, under a solemn sense of duty, authorized the persecution of Christianity. To my mind this is one of the most tragical facts in all history. It is a bitter thought, how different a thing the Christianity of the world might have been, if the Christian faith had been adopted as the religion of the empire under the auspices of Marcus Aurelius instead of those of Constantine. But it would be equally unjust to him and false to truth, to deny, that no one plea which can be urged for punishing anti-Christian teaching, was wanting to Marcus Aurelius for punishing, as he did, the propagation of Christianity. No Christian more firmly believes that Atheism is false, and tends to the dissolution of society, than Marcus Aurelius believed the same things of Christianity; he who, of all men then living, might have been thought the most capable of appreciating it. Unless any one who approves of punishment for the promulgation of opinions, flatters himself that he is a wiser and better man than Marcus Aurelius—more deeply versed in the wisdom of his time, more elevated in his intellect above it—more earnest in his search for truth, or more single-minded in his devotion to it when found—let him abstain from that assumption of the joint infallibility of himself and the multitude, which the great Antoninus made with so unfortunate a result.

Aware of the impossibility of defending the use of punishment for restraining irreligious opinions, by any argument which will not justify Marcus Antoninus, the enemies of religious freedom, when hard pressed, occasionally accept this consequence, and say, with Dr. Johnson, that the persecutors of Christianity were in the right; that persecution is an ordeal through which truth ought to pass, and always passes successfully, legal penalties being, in the end, powerless against truth, though sometimes beneficially effective against mischievous errors. This is a form of the argument for religious intolerance, sufficiently remarkable not to be passed without notice.

A theory which maintains that truth may justifiably be

persecuted because persecution cannot possibly do it any harm, cannot be charged with being intentionally hostile to the reception of new truths; but we cannot commend the generosity of its dealing with the persons to whom mankind are indebted for them. To discover to the world something which deeply concerns it, and of which it was previously ignorant; to prove to it that it had been mistaken on some vital point of temporal or spiritual interest, is as important a service as a human being can render to his fellow-creatures, and in certain cases, as in those of the early Christians and of the Reformers, those who think with Dr. Johnson believe it to have been the most precious gift which could be bestowed on mankind. That the authors of such splendid benefits should be requited by martyrdom; that their reward should be to be dealt with as the vilest of criminals, is not, upon this theory, a deplorable error and misfortune, for which humanity should mourn in sackcloth and ashes, but the normal and justifiable state of things. The propounder of a new truth, according to this doctrine, should stand, as stood, in the legislation of the Locrians, the proposer of a new law, with a halter round his neck, to be instantly tightened if the public assembly did not, on hearing his reasons, then and there adopt his proposition. People who defend this mode of treating benefactors, cannot be supposed to set much value on the benefit; and I believe this view of the subject is mostly confined to the sort of persons who think that new truths may have been desirable once, but that we have had enough of them now.

But, indeed, the dictum that truth always triumphs over persecution, is one of those pleasant falsehoods which men repeat after one another till they pass into commonplaces, but which all experience refutes. History teems with instances of truth put down by persecution. If not suppressed forever, it may be thrown back for centuries. To speak only of religious opinions: the Reformation broke out at least twenty times before Luther, and was put down. Arnold of Brescia was put

down. Fra Dolcino was put down. Savonarola was put down.
The Albigeois were put down. The Vaudois were put down.
The Lollards were put down. The Hussites were put down.
Even after the era of Luther, wherever persecution was persisted in, it was successful. In Spain, Italy, Flanders, the
Austrian empire, Protestantism was rooted out; and, most
likely, would have been so in England, had Queen Mary
lived, or Queen Elizabeth died. Persecution has always succeeded, save where the heretics were too strong a party to be
effectually persecuted. No reasonable person can doubt that
Christianity might have been extirpated in the Roman empire. It spread, and became predominant, because the persecutions were only occasional, lasting but a short time, and
separated by long intervals of almost undisturbed propagandism. It is a piece of idle sentimentality that truth, merely as
truth, has any inherent power denied to error, of prevailing
against the dungeon and the stake. Men are not more
zealous for truth than they often are for error, and a sufficient application of legal or even of social penalties will
generally succeed in stopping the propagation of either. The
real advantage which truth has, consists in this, that when an
opinion is true, it may be extinguished once, twice, or many
times, but in the course of ages there will generally be found
persons to rediscover it, until some one of its reappearances
falls on a time when from favorable circumstances it escapes
persecution until it has made such head as to withstand all
subsequent attempts to suppress it.

It will be said, that we do not now put to death the in-
troducers of new opinions: we are not like our fathers who
slew the prophets, we even build sepulchres to them. It is
true we no longer put heretics to death; and the amount of
penal infliction which modern feeling would probably tolerate,
even against the most obnoxious opinions, is not sufficient to
extirpate them. But let us not flatter ourselves that we are yet
free from the stain even of legal persecution. Penalties for
opinion, or at least for its expression, still exist by law; and

their enforcement is not, even in these times, so unexampled as to make it at all incredible that they may some day be revived in full force. In the year 1857, at the summer assizes of the county of Cornwall, an unfortunate man,[*] said to be of unexceptionable conduct in all relations of life, was sentenced to twenty-one months imprisonment, for uttering, and writing on a gate, some offensive words concerning Christianity. Within a month of the same time, at the Old Bailey, two persons, on two separate occasions,[†] were rejected as jurymen, and one of them grossly insulted by the judge and by one of the counsel, because they honestly declared that they had no theological belief; and a third, a foreigner,[‡] for the same reason, was denied justice against a thief. This refusal of redress took place in virtue of the legal doctrine, that no person can be allowed to give evidence in a court of justice, who does not profess belief in a God (any god is sufficient) and in a future state; which is equivalent to declaring such persons to be outlaws, excluded from the protection of the tribunals; who may not only be robbed or assaulted with impunity, if no one but themselves, or persons of similar opinions, be present, but any one else may be robbed or assaulted with impunity, if the proof of the fact depends on their evidence. The assumption on which this is grounded, is that the oath is worthless, of a person who does not believe in a future state; a proposition which betokens much ignorance of history in those who assent to it (since it is historically true that a large proportion of infidels in all ages have been persons of distinguished integrity and honor); and would be maintained by no one who had the smallest conception how many of the persons in greatest repute with the world, both

---

[*] Thomas Pooley, Bodmin Assizes, July 31, 1857. In December following, he received a free pardon from the Crown.

[†] George Jacob Holyoake, August 17, 1857; Edward Truelove, July, 1857.

[‡] Baron de Gleichen, Marlborough Street Police Court, August 4, 1857.

for virtues and for attainments, are well known, at least to
their intimates, to be unbelievers. The rule, besides, is sui-
cidal, and cuts away its own foundation. Under pretence that
atheists must be liars, it admits the testimony of all atheists
who are willing to lie, and rejects only those who brave the
obloquy of publicly confessing a detested creed rather than
affirm a falsehood. A rule thus self-convicted of absurdity so
far as regards its professed purpose, can be kept in force
only as a badge of hatred, a relic of persecution; a persecution, too, having the peculiarity, that the qualification for undergoing it, is the being clearly proved not to deserve it. The
rule, and the theory it implies, are hardly less insulting to
believers than to infidels. For if he who does not believe in a
future state, necessarily lies, it follows that they who do believe are only prevented from lying, if prevented they are, by
the fear of hell. We will not do the authors and abettors of
the rule the injury of supposing, that the conception which
they have formed of Christian virtue is drawn from their own
consciousness.

These, indeed, are but rags and remnants of persecution,
and may be thought to be not so much an indication of the
wish to persecute, as an example of that very frequent infirmity of English minds, which makes them take a pre-
posterous pleasure in the assertion of a bad principle, when
they are no longer bad enough to desire to carry it really into
practice. But unhappily there is no security in the state of the
public mind, that the suspension of worse forms of legal persecution, which has lasted for about the space of a generation,
will continue. In this age the quiet surface of routine is as
often ruffled by attempts to resuscitate past evils, as to introduce new benefits. What is boasted of at the present time
as the revival of religion, is always, in narrow and uncultivated minds, at least as much the revival of bigotry; and
where there is the strong permanent leaven of intolerance in
the feelings of a people, which at all times abides in the
middle classes of this country, it needs but little to provoke

them into actively persecuting those whom they have never ceased to think proper objects of persecution.* For it is this —it is the opinions men entertain, and the feelings they cherish, respecting those who disown the beliefs they deem important, which makes this country not a place of mental freedom. For a long time past, the chief mischief of the legal penalties is that they strengthen the social stigma. It is that stigma which is really effective, and so effective is it, that the profession of opinions which are under the ban of society is much less common in England, than is, in many other countries, the avowal of those which incur risk of judicial punishment. In respect to all persons but those whose pecuniary circumstances make them independent of the good will of other people, opinion, on this subject, is as efficacious as law;

* Ample warning may be drawn from the large infusion of the passions of a persecutor, which mingled with the general display of the worst parts of our national character on the occasion of the Sepoy insurrection. The ravings of fanatics or charlatans from the pulpit may be unworthy of notice; but the heads of the Evangelical party have announced as their principle, for the government of Hindoos and Mahomedans, that no schools be supported by public money in which the Bible is not taught, and by necessary consequence that no public employment be given to any but real or pretended Christians. An Under-Secretary of State, in a speech delivered to his constituents on the 12th of November, 1857, is reported to have said: "Toleration of their faith" (the faith of a hundred millions of British subjects), "the superstition which they called religion, by the British Government, had had the effect of retarding the ascendency of the British name, and preventing the salutary growth of Christianity. . . . Toleration was the great corner-stone of the religious liberties of this country; but do not let them abuse that precious word toleration. As he understood it, it meant the complete liberty to all, freedom of worship, *among Christians, who worshipped upon the same foundation.* It meant toleration of all sects and denominations of *Christians who believed in the one mediation.*" I desire to call attention to the fact, that a man who has been deemed fit to fill a high office in the government of this country, under a liberal Ministry, maintains the doctrine that all who do not believe in the divinity of Christ are beyond the pale of toleration. Who, after this imbecile display can indulge the illusion that religious persecution has passed away never to return?

men might as well be imprisoned, as excluded from the means of earning their bread. Those whose bread is already secured, and who desire no favors from men in power, or from bodies of men, or from the public, have nothing to fear from the open avowal of any opinions, but to be ill-thought of and ill-spoken of, and this it ought not to require a very heroic mould to enable them to bear. There is no room for any appeal *ad misericordiam* in behalf of such persons. But though we do not now inflict so much evil on those who think differently from us, as it was formerly our custom to do, it may be that we do ourselves as much evil as ever by our treatment of them. Socrates was put to death, but the Socratic philosophy rose like the sun in heaven, and spread its illumination over the whole intellectual firmament. Christians were cast to the lions, but the Christian Church grew up a stately and spreading tree, overtopping the older and less vigorous growths, and stifling them by its shade. Our merely social intolerance, kills no one, roots out no opinions, but induces men to disguise them, or to abstain from any active effort for their diffusion. With us, heretical opinions do not perceptibly gain, or even lose, ground in each decade or generation; they never blaze out far and wide, but continue to smoulder in the narrow circles of thinking and studious persons among whom they originate, without ever lighting up the general affairs of mankind with either a true or a deceptive light. And thus is kept up a state of things very satisfactory to some minds, because, without the unpleasant process of fining or imprisoning anybody, it maintains all prevailing opinions outwardly undisturbed, while it does not absolutely interdict the exercise of reason by dissentients afflicted with the malady of thought. A convenient plan for having peace in the intellectual world, and keeping all things going on therein very much as they do already. But the price paid for this sort of intellectual pacification, is the sacrifice of the entire moral courage of the human mind. A state of things in which a large portion of the most active and inquiring intellects find it advisable to keep the genuine principles and grounds of their convictions within their own breasts, and attempt, in what they address to the public, to fit as much as they can of their own conclusions to premises which they have internally renounced, cannot send forth the open, fearless characters, and logical, consistent intellects who once adorned the thinking world. The sort of men who can be looked for under it, are either mere conformers to commonplace, or time-servers for truth whose arguments on all great subjects are meant for their hearers, and are not those which have convinced themselves. Those who avoid this alternative, do so by narrowing their thoughts and interest to things which can be spoken of without venturing within the region of principles, that is, to small practical matters, which would come right of themselves, if but the minds of mankind were strengthened and enlarged, and which will never be made effectually right until then; while that which would strengthen and enlarge men's minds, free and daring speculation on the highest subjects, is abandoned.

Those in whose eyes this reticence on the part of heretics is no evil, should consider in the first place, that in consequence of it there is never any fair and thorough discussion of heretical opinions; and that such of them as could not stand such a discussion, though they may be prevented from spreading, do not disappear. But it is not the minds of heretics that are deteriorated most, by the ban placed on all inquiry which does not end in the orthodox conclusions. The greatest harm done is to those who are not heretics, and whose whole mental development is cramped, and their reason cowed, by the fear of heresy. Who can compute what the world loses in the multitude of promising intellects combined with timid characters, who dare not follow out any bold, vigorous, independent train of thought, lest it should land them in something which would admit of being considered irreligious or immoral? Among them we may occasionally see some man of deep conscientiousness, and subtle and refined understanding, who spends a life in sophisticating with an intellect which he cannot silence, and exhausts the resources of ingenuity in attempting to reconcile the promptings of his conscience and reason with orthodoxy, which yet he does not, perhaps, to the end succeed in doing. No one can be a great thinker who does not recognize, that as a thinker it is his first duty to follow his intellect to whatever conclusions it may lead. Truth gains more even by the errors of one who, with due study and preparation, thinks for himself, than by the true opinions of those who only hold them because they do not suffer themselves to think. Not that it is solely, or chiefly, to form great thinkers, that freedom of thinking is required. On the contrary, it is as much, and even more indispensable, to enable average human beings to attain the mental stature which they are capable of. There have been, and may again be, great individual thinkers, in a general atmosphere of mental slavery. But there never has been, nor ever will be, in that atmosphere, an intellectually active people. Where any people has made a temporary approach to such a character, it has been because the dread of heterodox speculation was for a time suspended. Where there is a tacit convention that principles are not to be disputed; where the discussion of the greatest questions which can occupy humanity is considered to be closed, we cannot hope to find that generally high scale of mental activity which has made some periods of history so remarkable. Never when controversy avoided the subjects which are large and important enough to kindle enthusiasm, was the mind of a people stirred up from its foundations, and the impulse given which raised even persons of the most ordinary intellect to something of the dignity of thinking beings. Of such we have had an example in the condition of Europe during the times immediately following the Reformation; another, though limited to the Continent and to a more cultivated class, in the speculative movement of the latter half of the eighteenth century; and a third, of still briefer duration, in the intellectual fermentation of Germany during the Goethian and Fichtean period. These periods differed widely in the particular opinions which they developed; but were alike in this, that during all three the yoke of authority was broken. In each, an old mental despotism had been thrown off, and no new one had yet taken its place. The impulse given at these three periods has made Europe what it now is. Every single improvement which has taken place either in the human mind or in institutions, may be traced distinctly to one or other of them. Appearances have for some time indicated that all three impulses are well-nigh spent; and we can expect no fresh start, until we again assert our mental freedom.

Let us now pass to the second division of the argument, and dismissing the supposition that any of the received opinions may be false, let us assume them to be true, and examine into the worth of the manner in which they are likely to be held, when their truth is not freely and openly canvassed. However unwillingly a person who has a strong opinion may admit the possibility that his opinion may be false, he ought to be moved by the consideration that however true it may be, if it is not fully, frequently, and fearlessly discussed, it will be held as a dead dogma, not a living truth.

There is a class of persons (happily not quite so numerous as formerly) who think it enough if a person assents undoubtingly to what they think true, though he has no knowledge whatever of the grounds of the opinion, and could not make a tenable defence of it against the most superficial objections. Such persons, if they can once get their creed taught from authority, naturally think that no good, and some harm, comes of its being allowed to be questioned. Where their influence prevails, they make it nearly impossible for the received opinion to be rejected wisely and considerately, though it may still be rejected rashly and ignorantly; for to shut out discussion entirely is seldom possible, and when it once gets in, beliefs not grounded on conviction are apt to give way before the slightest semblance of an argument.

Waiving, however, this possibility—assuming that the true
opinion abides in the mind, but abides as a prejudice, a belief independent of, and proof against, argument—this is not
the way in which truth ought to be held by a rational being.
This is not knowing the truth. Truth, thus held, is but one
superstition the more, accidentally clinging to the words
which enunciate a truth.

If the intellect and judgment of mankind ought to be
cultivated, a thing which Protestants at least do not deny, on
what can these faculties be more appropriately exercised by
any one, than on the things which concern him so much that
it is considered necessary for him to hold opinions on them?
If the cultivation of the understanding consists in one thing
more than in another, it is surely in learning the grounds of
one's own opinions. Whatever people believe, on subjects on
which it is of the first importance to believe rightly, they
ought to be able to defend against at least the common objections. But, some one may say, "Let them be *taught* the
grounds of their opinions. It does not follow that opinions
must be merely parroted because they are never heard controverted. Persons who learn geometry do not simply commit
the theorems to memory, but understand and learn likewise
the demonstrations; and it would be absurd to say that they
remain ignorant of the grounds of geometrical truths, because
they never hear any one deny, and attempt to disprove them."
Undoubtedly: and such teaching suffices on a subject like
mathematics, where there is nothing at all to be said on the
wrong side of the question. The peculiarity of the evidence of
mathematical truths is, that all the argument is on one side.
There are no objections, and no answers to objections. But
on every subject on which difference of opinion is possible,
the truth depends on a balance to be struck between two sets
of conflicting reasons. Even in natural philosophy, there is always some other explanation possible of the same facts;
some geocentric theory instead of heliocentric, some phlogiston instead of oxygen; and it has to be shown why that

other theory cannot be the true one: and until this is shown, and until we know how it is shown, we do not understand the grounds of our opinion. But when we turn to subjects infinitely more complicated, to morals, religion, politics, social relations, and the business of life, three-fourths of the arguments for every disputed opinion consist in dispelling the appearances which favor some opinion different from it. The greatest orator, save one, of antiquity, has left it on record that he always studied his adversary's case with as great, if not with still greater, intensity than even his own. What Cicero practised as the means of forensic success, requires to be imitated by all who study any subject in order to arrive at the truth. He who knows only his own side of the case, knows little of that. His reasons may be good, and no one may have been able to refute them. But if he is equally unable to refute the reasons on the opposite side; if he does not so much as know what they are, he has no ground for preferring either opinion. The rational position for him would be suspension of judgment, and unless he contents himself with that, he is either led by authority, or adopts, like the generality of the world, the side to which he feels most inclination. Nor is it enough that he should hear the arguments of adversaries from his own teachers, presented as they state them, and accompanied by what they offer as refutations. That is not the way to do justice to the arguments, or bring them into real contact with his own mind. He must be able to hear them from persons who actually believe them; who defend them in earnest, and do their very utmost for them. He must know them in their most plausible and persuasive form; he must feel the whole force of the difficulty which the true view of the subject has to encounter and dispose of; else he will never really possess himself of the portion of truth which meets and removes that difficulty. Ninety-nine in a hundred of what are called educated men are in this condition; even of those who can argue fluently for their opinions. Their conclusion may be true, but it might be false for anything they know: they have never thrown themselves into the mental position of those who think differently from them, and considered what such persons may have to say; and consequently they do not, in any proper sense of the word, know the doctrine which they themselves profess. They do not know those parts of it which explain and justify the remainder; the considerations which show that a fact which seemingly conflicts with another is reconcilable with it, or that, of two apparently strong reasons, one and not the other ought to be preferred. All that part of the truth which turns the scale, and decides the judgment of a completely informed mind, they are strangers to; nor is it ever really known, but to those who have attended equally and impartially to both sides, and endeavored to see the reasons of both in the strongest light. So essential is this discipline to a real understanding of moral and human subjects, that if opponents of all important truths do not exist, it is indispensable to imagine them, and supply them with the strongest arguments which the most skilful devil's advocate can conjure up.

To abate the force of these considerations, an enemy of free discussion may be supposed to say, that there is no necessity for mankind in general to know and understand all that can be said against or for their opinions by philosophers and theologians. That it is not needful for common men to be able to expose all the misstatements or fallacies of an in-genious opponent. That it is enough if there is always some-body capable of answering them, so that nothing likely to mislead uninstructed persons remains unrefuted. That simple minds, having been taught the obvious grounds of the truths inculcated on them, may trust to authority for the rest, and being aware that they have neither knowledge nor talent to resolve every difficulty which can be raised, may repose in the assurance that all those which have been raised have been or can be answered, by those who are specially trained to the task.

Conceding to this view of the subject the utmost that can

be claimed for it by those most easily satisfied with the amount of understanding of truth which ought to accompany the belief of it; even so, the argument for free discussion is no way weakened. For even this doctrine acknowledges that mankind ought to have a rational assurance that all objections have been satisfactorily answered; and how are they to be answered if that which requires to be answered is not spoken? or how can the answer be known to be satisfactory, if the objectors have no opportunity of showing that it is unsatisfactory? If not the public, at least the philosophers and theologians who are to resolve the difficulties, must make themselves familiar with those difficulties in their most puzzling form; and this cannot be accomplished unless they are freely stated, and placed in the most advantageous light which they admit of. The Catholic Church has it own way of dealing with this embarrassing problem. It makes a broad separation between those who can be permitted to receive its doctrines on conviction, and those who must accept them on trust. Neither, indeed, are allowed any choice as to what they will accept; but the clergy, such at least as can be fully confided in, may admissibly and meritoriously make themselves acquainted with the arguments of opponents, in order to answer them, and may, therefore, read heretical books; the laity, not unless by special permission, hard to be obtained. This discipline recognizes a knowledge of the enemy's case as beneficial to the teachers, but finds means, consistent with this, of denying it to the rest of the world: thus giving to the élite more mental culture, though not more mental freedom, than it allows to the mass. By this device it succeeds in obtaining the kind of mental superiority which its purposes require; for though culture without freedom never made a large and liberal mind, it can make a clever *nisi prius* advocate of a cause. But in countries professing Protestantism, this resource is denied; since Protestants hold, at least in theory, that the responsibility for the choice of a religion must be borne by each for himself, and cannot be thrown off upon teachers. Besides, in the present state of the world, it is practically impossible that writings which are read by the instructed can be kept from the uninstructed. If the teachers of mankind are to be cognizant of all that they ought to know, everything must be free to be written and published without restraint.

If, however, the mischievous operation of the absence of free discussion, when the received opinions are true, were confined to leaving men ignorant of the grounds of those opinions, it might be thought that this, if an intellectual, is no moral evil, and does not affect the worth of the opinions, regarded in their influence on the character. The fact, however, is, that not only the grounds of the opinion are forgotten in the absence of discussion, but too often the meaning of the opinion itself. The words which convey it, cease to suggest ideas, or suggest only a small portion of those they were originally employed to communicate. Instead of a vivid conception and a living belief, there remain only a few phrases retained by rote; or, if any part, the shell and husk only of the meaning is retained, the finer essence being lost. The great chapter in human history which this fact occupies and fills, cannot be too earnestly studied and meditated on.

It is illustrated in the experience of almost all ethical doctrines and religious creeds. They are all full of meaning and vitality to those who originate them, and to the direct disciples of the originators. Their meaning continues to be felt in undiminished strength, and is perhaps brought out into even fuller consciousness, so long as the struggle lasts to give the doctrine or creed an ascendency over other creeds. At last it either prevails, and becomes the general opinion, or its progress stops; it keeps possession of the ground it has gained, but ceases to spread further. When either of these results has become apparent, controversy on the subject flags, and gradually dies away. The doctrine has taken its place, if not as a received opinion, as one of the admitted sects or divisions of opinion: those who hold it have generally inherited, not adopted it; and conversion from one of these doctrines to another, being now an exceptional fact, occupies little place in the thoughts of their professors. Instead of being, as at first, constantly on the alert either to defend themselves against the world, or to bring the world over to them, they have subsided into acquiescence, and neither listen, when they can help it, to arguments against their creed, nor trouble dissentients (if there be such) with arguments in its favor. From this time may usually be dated the decline in the living power of the doctrine. We often hear the teachers of all creeds lamenting the difficulty of keeping up in the minds of believers a lively apprehension of the truth which they nominally recognize, so that it may penetrate the feelings, and acquire a real mastery over the conduct. No such difficulty is complained of while the creed is still fighting for its existence: even the weaker combatants then know and feel what they are fighting for, and the difference between it and other doctrines; and in that period of every creed's existence, not a few persons may be found, who have realized its fundamental principles in all the forms of thought, have weighed and considered them in all their important bearings, and have experienced the full effect on the character, which belief in that creed ought to produce in a mind thoroughly imbued with it. But when it has come to be an hereditary creed, and to be received passively, not actively—when the mind is no longer compelled, in the same degree as at first, to exercise its vital powers on the questions which its belief presents to it, there is a progressive tendency to forget all of the belief except the formularies, or to give it a dull and torpid assent, as if accepting it on trust dispensed with the necessity of realizing it in consciousness, or testing it by personal experience; until it almost ceases to connect itself at all with the inner life of the human being. Then are seen the cases, so frequent in this age of the world as almost to form the majority, in which the creed remains as it were outside the mind, encrusting and petrifying it against all other influences addressed to the

higher parts of our nature; manifesting its power by not suffering any fresh and living conviction to get in, but itself doing
nothing for the mind or heart, except standing sentinel over
them to keep them vacant.

To what an extent doctrines intrinsically fitted to make
the deepest impression upon the mind may remain in it as
dead beliefs, without being ever realized in the imagination,
the feelings, or the understanding, is exemplified by the manner in which the majority of believers hold the doctrines of
Christianity. By Christianity I here mean what is accounted
such by all churches and sects—the maxims and precepts contained in the New Testament. These are considered sacred,
and accepted as laws, by all professing Christians. Yet it is
scarcely too much to say that not one Christian in a thousand
guides or tests his individual conduct by reference to those
laws. The standard to which he does refer it, is the custom of
his nation, his class, or his religious profession. He has thus,
on the one hand, a collection of ethical maxims, which he
believes to have been vouchsafed to him by infallible wisdom
as rules for his government; and on the other, a set of every-
day judgments and practices, which go a certain length with
some of those maxims, not so great a length with others,
stand in direct opposition to some, and are, on the whole, a
compromise between the Christian creed and the interests
and suggestions of worldly life. To the first of these standards
he gives his homage; to the other his real allegiance. All Christians believe that the blessed are the poor and humble, and
those who are ill-used by the world; that it is easier for a
camel to pass through the eye of a needle than for a rich man
to enter the kingdom of heaven; that they should judge not,
lest they be judged; that they should swear not at all; that
they should love their neighbor as themselves; that if one
take their cloak, they should give him their coat also; that
they should take no thought for the morrow; that if they
would be perfect, they should sell all that they have and give
it to the poor. They are not insincere when they say that they

believe these things. They do believe them, as people believe what they have always heard lauded and never discussed. But in the sense of that living belief which regulates conduct, they believe these doctrines just up to the point to which it is usual to act upon them. The doctrines in their integrity are serviceable to pelt adversaries with; and it is understood that they are to be put forward (when possible) as the reasons for whatever people do that they think laudable. But any one who reminded them that the maxims require an infinity of things which they never even think of doing, would gain nothing but to be classed among those very unpopular characters who affect to be better than other people. The doctrines have no hold on ordinary believers—are not a power in their minds. They have an habitual respect for the sound of them, but no feeling which spreads from the words to the things signified, and forces the mind to take *them* in, and make them conform to the formula. Whenever conduct is concerned, they look round for Mr. A and B to direct them how far to go in obeying Christ.

Now we may be well assured that the case was not thus, but far otherwise, with the early Christians. Had it been thus, Christianity never would have expanded from an obscure sect of the despised Hebrews into the religion of the Roman empire. When their enemies said, "See how these Christians love one another" (a remark not likely to be made by anybody now), they assuredly had a much livelier feeling of the meaning of their creed than they have ever had since. And to this cause, probably, it is chiefly owing that Christianity now makes so little progress in extending its domain, and after eighteen centuries, is still nearly confined to Europeans and the descendants of Europeans. Even with the strictly religious, who are much in earnest about their doctrines, and attach a greater amount of meaning to many of them than people in general, it commonly happens that the part which is thus comparatively active in their minds is that which was made by Calvin, or Knox, or some such person much nearer in character to themselves. The sayings of Christ coexist passively in their minds, producing hardly any effect beyond what is caused by mere listening to words so amiable and bland. There are many reasons, doubtless, why doctrines which are the badge of a sect retain more of their vitality than those common to all recognized sects, and why more pains are taken by teachers to keep their meaning alive; but one reason certainly is, that the peculiar doctrines are more questioned, and have to be oftener defended against open gainsayers. Both teachers and learners go to sleep at their post, as soon as there is no enemy in the field.

The same thing holds true, generally speaking, of all traditional doctrines—those of prudence and knowledge of life, as well as of morals or religion. All languages and literatures are full of general observations on life, both as to what it is, and how to conduct oneself in it; observations which everybody knows, which everybody repeats, or hears with acquiescence, which are received as truisms, yet of which most people first truly learn the meaning, when experience, generally of a painful kind, has made it a reality to them. How often, when smarting under some unforeseen misfortune or disappointment, does a person call to mind some proverb or common saying, familiar to him all his life, the meaning of which, if he had ever before felt it as he does now, would have saved him from the calamity. There are indeed reasons for this, other than the absence of discussion: there are many truths of which the full meaning *cannot* be realized, until personal experience has brought it home. But much more of the meaning even of these would have been understood and what was understood would have been far more deeply impressed on the mind, if the man had been accustomed to hear it argued *pro* and *con* by people who did understand it. The fatal tendency of mankind to leave off thinking about a thing when it is no longer doubtful, is the cause of half their errors. A contemporary author has well spoken of "the deep slumber of a decided opinion."

But what! (it may be asked) Is the absence of unanimity an indispensable condition of true knowledge? Is it necessary that some part of mankind should persist in error, to enable any to realize the truth? Does a belief cease to be real and vital as soon as it is generally received—and is a proposition never thoroughly understood and felt unless some doubt of it remains? As soon as mankind have unanimously accepted a truth, does the truth perish within them? The highest aim and best result of improved intelligence, it has hitherto been thought, is to unite mankind more and more in the acknowledgment of all important truths: and does the intelligence only last as long as it has not achieved its object? Do the fruits of conquest perish by the very completeness of the victory?

I affirm no such thing. As mankind improve, the number of doctrines which are no longer disputed or doubted will be constantly on the increase: and the well-being of mankind may almost be measured by the number and gravity of the truths which have reached the point of being uncontested. The cessation, on one question after another, of serious controversy, is one of the necessary incidents of the consolidation of opinion; a consolidation as salutary in the case of true opinions, as it is dangerous and noxious when the opinions are erroneous. But though this gradual narrowing of the bounds of diversity of opinion is necessary in both senses of the term, being at once inevitable and indispensable, we are not therefore obliged to conclude that all its consequences must be beneficial. The loss of so important an aid to the intelligent and living apprehension of a truth, as is afforded by the necessity of explaining it to, or defending it against, opponents, though not sufficient to outweigh, is no trifling drawback from, the benefit of its universal recognition. Where this advantage can no longer be had, I confess I should like to see the teachers of mankind endeavoring to provide a substitute for it; some contrivance for making the difficulties of the question as present to the learner's consciousness, as if they were pressed upon him by a dissentient champion, eager for his conversion.

But instead of seeking contrivances for this purpose, they have lost those they formerly had. The Socratic dialectics, so magnificently exemplified in the dialogues of Plato, were a contrivance of this description. They were essentially a negative discussion of the great questions of philosophy and life, directed with consummate skill to the purpose of convincing any one who had merely adopted the commonplaces of received opinion, that he did not understand the subject—that he as yet attached no definite meaning to the doctrines he professed; in order that, becoming aware of his ignorance, he might be put in the way to attain a stable belief, resting on a clear apprehension both of the meaning of doctrines and of their evidence. The school disputations of the Middle Ages had a somewhat similar object. They were intended to make sure that the pupil understood his own opinion, and (by necessary correlation) the opinion opposed to it, and could enforce the grounds of the one and confute those of the other. These last-mentioned contests had indeed the incurable defect, that the premises appealed to were taken from authority, not from reason; and, as a discipline to the mind, they were in every respect inferior to the powerful dialectics which formed the intellects of the "Socratici viri:" but the modern mind owes far more to both than it is generally willing to admit, and the present modes of education contain nothing which in the smallest degree supplies the place either of the one or of the other. A person who derives all his instruction from teachers or books, even if he escape the besetting temptation of contenting himself with cram, is under no compulsion to hear both sides; accordingly it is far from a frequent accomplishment, even among thinkers, to know both sides; and the weakest part of what everybody says in defence of his opinion, is what he intends as a reply to antagonists. It is the fashion of the present time to disparage negative logic—that which points out weaknesses in theory or errors in practice, without establishing positive truths. Such negative criticism would indeed be poor enough as an ultimate result; but as a means to attaining any positive knowledge or conviction worthy the name, it cannot be valued too highly; and until people are again systematically trained to it, there will be few great thinkers, and a low general average of intellect, in any but the mathematical and physical departments of speculation. On any other subject no one's opinions deserve the name of knowledge, except so far as he has either had forced upon him by others, or gone through of himself, the same mental process which would have been required of him in carrying on an active controversy with opponents. That, therefore, which when absent, it is so indispensable, but so difficult, to create, how worse than absurd is it to forego, when spontaneously offering itself! If there are any persons who contest a received opinion, or who will do so if law or opinion will let them, let us thank them for it, open our minds to listen to them, and rejoice that there is some one to do for us what we otherwise ought, if we have any regard for either the certainty or the vitality of our convictions, to do with much greater labor for ourselves.

It still remains to speak of one of the principal causes which make diversity of opinion advantageous, and will continue to do so until mankind shall have entered a stage of intellectual advancement which at present seems at an incalculable distance. We have hitherto considered only two possibilities: that the received opinion may be false, and some other opinion, consequently, true; or that, the received opinion being true, a conflict with the opposite error is essential to a clear apprehension and deep feeling of its truth. But there is a commoner case than either of these; when the conflicting doctrines, instead of being one true and the other false, share the truth between them; and the nonconforming opinion is needed to supply the remainder of the truth, of which the received doctrine embodies only a part. Popular opinions, on subjects not palpable to sense, are often true, but seldom or never the whole truth. They are a part of the truth; sometimes a greater, sometimes a smaller part, but exaggerated, distorted, and disjoined from the truths by which they ought to be accompanied and limited. Heretical opinions, on the other hand, are generally some of these suppressed and neglected truths, bursting the bonds which kept them down, and either seeking reconciliation with the truth contained in the common opinion, or fronting it as enemies, and setting themselves up, with similar exclusiveness, as the whole truth. The latter case is hitherto the most frequent, as, in the human mind, one-sidedness has always been the rule, and many-sidedness of exception. Hence, even in revolutions of opinion, one part of the truth usually sets while another rises. Even progress, which ought to superadd, for the most part only substitutes one partial and incomplete truth for another; improvement consisting chiefly in this, that the new fragment of truth is more wanted, more adapted to the needs of the time, than that which it displaces. Such being the partial character of prevailing opinions, even when resting on a true foundation; every opinion which embodies somewhat of the portion of truth which the common opinion omits, ought to be considered precious, with whatever amount of error and confusion that truth may be blended. No sober judge of human affairs will feel bound to be indignant because those who force on our notice truths which we should otherwise have overlooked, overlook some of those which we see. Rather, he will think that so long as popular truth is one-sided, it is more desirable than otherwise that unpopular truth should have one-sided asserters too; such being usually the most energetic, and the most likely to compel reluctant attention to the fragment of wisdom which they proclaim as if it were the whole.

Thus, in the eighteenth century, when nearly all the instructed, and all those of the uninstructed who were led by them, were lost in admiration of what is called civilization, and of the marvels of modern science, literature, and philosophy, and while greatly overrating the amount of unlikeness between the men of modern and those of ancient times, indulged the belief that the whole of the difference was in their own favor; with what a salutary shock did the paradoxes of Rousseau explode like bombshells in the midst, dislocating the compact mass of one-sided opinion, and forcing its elements to recombine in a better form and with additional ingredients. Not that the current opinions were on the whole farther from the truth than Rousseau's were; on the contrary, they were nearer to it; they contained more of positive truth, and very much less of error. Nevertheless there lay in Rousseau's doctrine, and has floated down the stream of opinion along with it, a considerable amount of exactly those truths which the popular opinion wanted; and these are the deposit which was left behind when the flood subsided. The superior worth of simplicity of life, the enervating and demoralizing effect of the trammels and hypocrisies of artificial society, are ideas which have never been entirely absent from cultivated minds since Rousseau wrote; and they will in time produce their due effect, though at present needing to be asserted as much as ever, and to be asserted by deeds, for words, on this subject, have nearly exhausted their power.

In politics, again, it is almost a commonplace, that a party of order or stability, and a party of progress or reform, are both necessary elements of a healthy state of political life; until the one or the other shall have so enlarged its mental grasp as to be a party equally of order and of progress, knowing and distinguishing what is fit to be preserved from what ought to be swept away. Each of these modes of thinking derives its utility from the deficiencies of the other; but it is in a great measure the opposition of the other that keeps each within the limits of reason and sanity. Unless opinions favorable to democracy and to aristocracy, to property and to equality, to coöperation and to competition, to luxury and to abstinence, to sociality and individuality, to liberty and discipline, and all the other standing antagonisms of practical life, are expressed with equal freedom, and enforced and defended with equal talent and energy, there is no chance of both elements obtaining their due; one scale is sure to go up, and the other down. Truth, in the great practical concerns of life, is so much a question of the reconciling and combining of opposites, that very few have minds sufficiently capacious and impartial to make the adjustment with an approach to correctness, and it has to be made by the rough process of a struggle between combatants fighting under hostile banners. On any of the great open questions just enumerated, if either of the two opinions has a better claim than the other, not merely to be tolerated, but to be encouraged and countenanced, it is the one which happens at the particular time and place to be in a minority. That is the opinion which, for the time being, represents the neglected interests, the side of human well-being which is in danger of obtaining less than its share. I am aware that there is not, in this country, any intolerance of differences of opinion on most of these topics. They are adduced to show, by admitted and multiplied examples, the universality of the fact, that only through diversity of opinion is there, in the existing state of human intellect, a chance of fair play to all sides of the truth. When there are persons to be found, who form an exception to the apparent unanimity of the world on any subject, even if the world is in the right, it is always probable that dissentients have something worth hearing to say for themselves, and that truth would lose something by their silence.

It may be objected, "But *some* received principles, especially on the highest and most vital subjects, are more than half-truths. The Christian morality, for instance, is the whole truth on that subject, and if any one teaches a morality which varies from it, he is wholly in error." As this is of all cases the most important in practice, none can be fitter to test the general maxim. But before pronouncing what Christian morality is or is not, it would be desirable to decide what is meant by Christian morality. If it means the morality of the New Testament, I wonder that any one who derives his knowledge of this from the book itself, can suppose that it was announced, or intended, as a complete doctrine of morals. The Gospel always refers to a preëxisting morality, and confines its precepts to the particulars in which that morality was to be corrected, or superseded by a wider and higher; expressing itself, moreover, in terms most general, often impossible to be interpreted literally, and possessing rather the impressiveness of poetry or eloquence than the precision of legislation. To extract from it a body of ethical doctrine, has never been possible without eking it out from the Old Testament, that is, from a system elaborate indeed, but in many respects barbarous, and intended only for a barbarous people. St. Paul, a declared enemy to this Judaical mode of interpreting the doctrine and filling up the scheme of his Master, equally assumes a preëxisting morality, namely, that of the Greeks and Romans; and his advice to Christians is in a great measure a system of accommodation to that; even to the extent of giving an apparent sanction to slavery. What is called Christian, but should rather be termed theological, morality, was not the work of Christ or the Apostles, but is of much later origin, having been gradually built up by the Catholic Church of the first five centuries, and though not implicitly adopted by moderns and Protestants, has been much less modified by them than might have been expected. For the most part, indeed, they have contented themselves with cutting off the additions which had been made to it in the Middle Ages, each sect supplying the place by fresh additions, adapted to its own character and tendencies. That mankind owe a great debt to this morality, and to its early teachers, I should be the last person to deny; but I do not scruple to say of it, that it is, in many important points, incomplete and one-sided, and that unless ideas and feelings, not sanctioned by it, had contributed to the formation of European life and character, human affairs would have been in a worse condition than they now are. Christian morality (so called) has all the characters of a reaction; it is, in great part, a protest against Paganism. Its ideal is negative rather than positive; passive rather than active; Innocence rather than Nobleness; Abstinence from Evil, rather than energetic Pursuit of Good: in its precepts (as has been well said) "thou shalt not" predominates unduly over "thou shalt." In its horror of sensuality, it made an idol of asceticism, which has been gradually compromised away into one of legality. It holds out the hope of heaven and the threat of hell, as the appointed and appropriate motives to a virtuous life: in this falling far below the best of the ancients, and doing what lies in it to give to human morality an essentially selfish character, by disconnecting each man's feelings of duty from the interests of his fellow-creatures, except so far as a self-interested inducement is offered to him for consulting them. It is essentially a doctrine of passive obedience; it inculcates submission to all authorities found established; who indeed are not to be actively obeyed when they command what religion forbids, but who are not to be resisted, far less rebelled against, for any amount of wrong to ourselves. And while, in the morality of the best Pagan nations, duty to the State holds even a disproportionate place, infringing on the just liberty of the individual; in purely Christian ethics, that grand department of duty is scarcely noticed or acknowledged. It is in the Koran, not the New Testament, that we read the maxim—"A ruler who appoints any man to an office, when there is in his dominions another man better qualified for it, sins against God and against the State." What little recognition the idea of obligation to the public obtains in modern morality, is derived from Greek and Roman sources, not from Christian; as, even in the morality of private life, whatever exists of magnanimity, high-mindedness, personal dignity, even the sense of honor, is derived from the purely human, not the religious part of our education, and never could have grown out of a standard of ethics in which the only worth, professedly recognized, is that of obedience.

I am as far as any one from pretending that these defects are necessarily inherent in the Christian ethics, in every manner in which it can be conceived, or that the many requisites of a complete moral doctrine which it does not contain, do not admit of being reconciled with it. Far less would I insinuate this of the doctrines and precepts of Christ himself. I believe that the sayings of Christ are all, that I can see any evidence of their having been intended to be; that they are irreconcilable with nothing which a comprehensive morality requires; that everything which is excellent in ethics may be brought within them, with no greater violence to their language than has been done to it by all who have attempted to deduce from them any practical system of conduct whatever. But it is quite consistent with this, to believe that they contain, and were meant to contain, only a part of the truth; that many essential elements of the highest morality are among the things which are not provided for, nor intended to be provided for in the recorded deliverances of the Founder of Christianity, and which have been entirely thrown aside in the system of ethics erected on the basis of those deliverances by the Christian Church. And this being so, I think it a great error to persist in attempting to find in the Christian doctrine that complete rule for our guidance, which its author intended it to sanction and enforce, but only partially to provide. I believe, too, that this narrow theory is becoming a grave practical evil, detracting greatly from the value of the moral training and instruction, which so many well-meaning persons are now at length exerting themselves to promote. I much fear that by attempting to form the mind and feelings on an exclusively religious type, and discarding those secular standards (as for want of a better name they may be called) which here-tofore coexisted with and supplemented the Christian ethics, receiving some of its spirit, and infusing into it some of theirs, there will result, and is even now resulting, a low, abject, servile type of character, which, submit itself as it may to what it deems the Supreme Will, is incapable of rising to or sympathizing in the conception of Supreme Goodness. I believe that other ethics than any which can be evolved from exclusively Christian sources, must exist side by side with Christian sources, must exist side by side with Christian ethics to produce the moral regeneration of mankind; and that the Christian system is no exception to the rule, that in an imperfect state of the human mind, the interests of truth require a diversity of opinions. It is not necessary that in ceasing to ignore the moral truths not contained in Christianity, men should ignore any of those which it does contain. Such prejudice, or oversight, when it occurs, is altogether an evil; but it is one from which we cannot hope to be always exempt, and must be regarded as the price paid for an inestimable good. The exclusive pretension made by a part of the truth to be the whole, must and ought to be protested against, and if a reactionary impulse should make the protestors unjust in their turn, this one-sidedness, like the other, may be lamented, but must be tolerated. If Christians would teach infidels to be just to Christianity, they should themselves be just to infidelity. It can do truth no service to blink the fact, known to all who have the most ordinary acquaintance with literary history, that a large portion of the noblest and most valuable moral teaching has been the work, not only of men who did not know, but of men who knew and rejected, the Christian faith.

I do not pretend that the most unlimited use of the freedom of enunciating all possible opinions would put an end to the evils of religious or philosophical sectarianism. Every truth which men of narrow capacity are in earnest about, is sure to be asserted, inculcated, and in many ways even acted on, as if no other truth existed in the world, or at all events none that could limit or qualify the first. I acknowledge that the tendency of all opinions to become sectarian is not cured by the freest discussion, but is often heightened and exacerbated thereby; the truth which ought to have been, but was not, seen, being rejected all the more violently because proclaimed by persons regarded as opponents. But it is not on the impassioned partisan, it is on the calmer and more disinterested by-stander, that this collision of opinions works its salutary effect. Not the violent conflict between parts of the truth, but the quiet suppression of half of it, is the formidable evil: there is always hope when people are forced to listen to both sides; it is when they attend only to one that errors harden into prejudices, and truth itself ceases to have the effect of truth, by being exaggerated into falsehood. And since there are few mental attributes more rare than that judicial faculty which can sit in intelligent judgment between two sides of a question, of which only one is represented by an advocate before it, truth has no chance but in proportion as every side of it, every opinion which embodies any fraction of the truth, not only finds advocates, but is so advocated as to be listened to.

We have now recognized the necessity to the mental well-being of mankind (on which all their other well-being depends) of freedom of opinion, and freedom of the expression of opinion, on four distinct grounds; which we will now briefly recapitulate.

First, if any opinion is compelled to silence, that opinion may, for aught we can certainly know, be true. To deny this is to assume our own infallibility.

Secondly, though the silenced opinion be an error, it may, and very commonly does, contain a portion of truth; and since the general or prevailing opinion on any subject is rarely or never the whole truth, it is only by the collision of adverse opinions that the remainder of the truth has any chance of being supplied.

Thirdly, even if the received opinion be not only true, but the whole truth; unless it is suffered to be, and actually is, vigorously and earnestly contested, it will, by most of those who receive it, be held in the manner of a prejudice, with little comprehension or feeling of its rational grounds. And not only this, but, fourthly, the meaning of the doctrine itself will be in danger of being lost, or enfeebled, and deprived of its vital effect on the character and conduct: the dogma becoming a mere formal profession, inefficacious for good, but cumbering the ground, and preventing the growth of any real and heartfelt conviction from reason or personal experience.

Before quitting the subject of freedom of opinion, it is fit to take some notice of those who say, that the free expression of all opinions should be permitted, on condition that the manner be temperate, and do not pass the bounds of fair discussion. Much might be said on the impossibility of fixing where these supposed bounds are to be placed; for if the test be offence to those whose opinion is attacked, I think experience testifies that this offence is given whenever the attack is telling and powerful, and that every opponent who pushes them hard, and whom they find it difficult to answer, appears to them, if he shows any strong feeling on the subject, an intemperate opponent. But this, though an important consideration in a practical point of view, merges in a more fundamental objection. Undoubtedly the manner of asserting an opinion, even though it be a true one, may be very objectionable, and may justly incur severe censure. But the principal offences of the kind are such as it is mostly impossible, unless by accidental self-betrayal, to bring home to conviction. The gravest of them is, to argue sophistically, to suppress facts or arguments, to misstate the elements of the case, or misrepresent the opposite opinion. But all this, even to the most aggravated degree, is so continually done in perfect good faith, by persons who are not considered, and in many other respects may not deserve to be considered, ignorant or incompetent, that it is rarely possible on adequate grounds conscientiously to stamp the misrepresentation as morally culpable; and still less could law presume to interfere with this kind of controversial misconduct. With regard to what is commonly meant by intemperate discussion, namely, invective, sarcasm, personality, and the like, the denunciation of these weapons would deserve more sympathy if it were ever proposed to interdict them equally to both sides; but it is only desired to restrain the employment of them against the prevailing opinion: against the unprevailing they may not only be used without general disapproval, but will be likely to obtain for him who uses them the praise of honest zeal and righteous indignation. Yet whatever mischief arises from their use, is greatest when they are employed against the comparatively defenceless; and whatever unfair advantage can be derived by any opinion from this mode of asserting it, accrues almost exclusively to received opinions. The worst offence of this kind which can be committed by a polemic, is to stigmatize those who hold the contrary opinion as bad and immoral men. To calumny of this sort, those who hold any unpopular opinion are peculiarly exposed, because they are in general few and uninfluential, and nobody but themselves feels much interest in seeing justice done them; but this weapon is, from the nature of the case, denied to those who attack a prevailing opinion: they can neither use it with safety to themselves, nor, if they could, would it do anything but recoil on their own cause. In general, opinions contrary to those commonly received can only obtain a hearing by studied moderation of language, and the most cautious avoidance of unnecessary offence, from which they hardly ever deviate even in a slight degree without losing ground: while unmeasured vituperation employed on the side of the prevailing opinion, really does deter people from professing contrary opinions, and from listening to those who profess them. For the interest, therefore, of truth and justice, it is far more important to restrain this employment of vituperative language than the other; and, for example, if it were necessary to choose, there would be much more need to discourage offensive attacks on infidelity, than on religion. It is, however, obvious that law and authority have no business with restraining either, while opinion ought, in every instance, to determine its verdict by the circumstances of the individual case; condemning every one, on whichever side of the argument he places himself, in whose mode of advocacy either want of candor, or malignity, bigotry, or intolerance of feeling manifest themselves; but not inferring these vices from the side which a person takes, though it be the contrary side of the question to our own: and giving merited honor to every one, whatever opinion he may hold, who has calmness to see and honesty to state what his opponents and their opinions really are, exaggerating nothing to their discredit, keeping nothing back which tells, or can be supposed to tell, in their favor. This is the real morality of public discussion; and if often violated, I am happy to think that there are many controversialists who to a great extent observe it, and a still greater number who conscientiously strive towards it.

CHAPTER 3 *Of Individuality, As One of the Elements of Well-Being*

Such being the reasons which make it imperative that human beings should be free to form opinions, and to express their opinions without reserve; and such the baneful consequences to the intellectual, and through that to the moral nature of man, unless this liberty is either conceded, or asserted in spite of prohibition; let us next examine whether the same reasons do not require that men should be free to act upon their opinions—to carry these out in their lives, without hindrance, either physical or moral, from their fellow-men, so long as it is at their own risk and peril. This last proviso is of course indispensable. No one pretends that actions should be as free as opinions. On the contrary, even opinions lose their immunity, when the circumstances in which they are expressed are such as to constitute their expression a positive instigation to some mischievous act. An opinion that corn-dealers are starvers of the poor, or that private property is robbery, ought to be unmolested when simply circulated through the press, but may justly incur punishment when delivered orally to an excited mob assembled before the house of a corn-dealer, or when handed about among the same mob in the form of a placard. Acts, of whatever kind, which, without justifiable cause, do harm to others, may be, and in the more important cases absolutely require to be, controlled by the unfavorable sentiments, and, when needful, by the active interference of mankind. The liberty of the individual must be thus far limited; he must not make himself a nuisance to other people. But if he refrains from molesting others in what concerns them, and merely acts according to his own inclination and judgment in things which concern himself, the same reasons which show that opinion should be free, prove also that he should be allowed, without molestation, to carry his opinions into practice at his own cost. That mankind are not infallible; that their truths, for the most part, are only half-truths; that unity of opinion, unless resulting from the fullest and freest comparison of opposite opinions, is not desirable, and diversity not an evil, but a good, until mankind are much more capable than at present of recognizing all sides of the truth, are principles applicable to men's modes of action, not less than to their opinions. As it is useful that while mankind are imperfect there should be different opinions, so is it that there should be different experiments of living; that free scope should be given to varieties of character, short of injury to others; and that the worth of different modes of life should be proved practically, when any one thinks fit to try them. It is desirable, in short, that in things which do not primarily concern others, individuality should assert itself. Where, not the person's own character, but the traditions or customs of other people are the rule of conduct, there is wanting one of the principal ingredients of human happiness, and quite the chief ingredient of individual and social progress.

In maintaining this principle, the greatest difficulty to be encountered does not lie in the appreciation of means towards an acknowledged end, but in the indifference of persons in general to the end itself. If it were felt that the free development of individuality is one of the leading essentials of well-being; that it is not only a coördinate element with all that is designated by the terms civilization, instruction, education, culture, but is itself a necessary part and condition of all those things; there would be no danger that liberty should be undervalued, and the adjustment of the boundaries between it and social control would present no extraordinary difficulty. But the evil is, that individual spontaneity is hardly recognized by the common modes of thinking, as having any intrinsic worth, or deserving any regard on its own account. The majority, being satisfied with the ways of mankind as they now are (for it is they who make them what they are), cannot comprehend why those ways should not be good enough for everybody; and what is more, spontaneity forms no part of the ideal of the majority of moral and social reformers, but is rather looked on with jealousy, as a troublesome and perhaps rebellious obstruction to the general acceptance of what these reformers, in their own judgment, think would be best for mankind. Few persons, out of Germany, even comprehend the meaning of the doctrine which Wilhelm von Humboldt, so eminent both as a *savant* and as a politician, made the text of a treatise—that "the end of man, or that which is prescribed by the eternal or immutable dictates of reason, and not suggested by vague and transient desires, is the highest and most harmonious development of his powers to a complete and consistent whole;" that, therefore, the object "towards which every human being must ceaselessly direct his efforts, and on which especially those who design to influence their fellow-men must ever keep their eyes, is the individuality of power and development;" that for this there are two requisites, "freedom, and a variety of situations;" and that from the union of these arise "individual vigor and manifold diversity," which combine themselves in "originality." *

Little, however, as people are accustomed to a doctrine like that of Von Humboldt, and surprising as it may be to them to find so high a value attached to individuality, the question, one must nevertheless think, can only be one of degree. No one's idea of excellence in conduct is that people should do absolutely nothing but copy one another. No one would assert that people ought not to put into their mode of life, and into the conduct of their concerns, any impress whatever of their own judgment, or of their own individual character. On the other hand, it would be absurd to pretend that people ought to live as if nothing whatever had been known in the world before they came into it; as if experience had as yet done nothing towards showing that one mode of existence, or of conduct, is preferable to another. Nobody denies that people should be so taught and trained in youth, as to know and benefit by the ascertained results of human experience. But it is the privilege and proper condition of a human being, arrived at the maturity of his faculties, to use and interpret experience in his own way. It is for him to find out what part of recorded experience is properly applicable to his own circumstances and character. The traditions and customs of other people are, to a certain ex-

* *The Sphere and Duties of Government,* from the German of Baron Wilhelm von Humboldt, pp. 11-13.

tent, evidence of what their experience has taught *them;* presumptive evidence, and as such, have a claim to his deference: but, in the first place, their experience may be too narrow; or they may not have interpreted it rightly. Secondly, their interpretation of experience may be correct, but unsuitable to him. Customs are made for customary circumstances, and customary characters: and his circumstances or his character may be uncustomary. Thirdly, though the customs be both good as customs, and suitable to him, yet to conform to custom, merely *as* custom, does not educate or develop in him any of the qualities which are the distinctive endowment of a human being. The human faculties of perception, judgment, discriminative feeling, mental activity, and even moral preference, are exercised only in making a choice. He who does anything because it is the custom, makes no choice. He gains no practice either in discerning or in desiring what is best. The mental and moral, like the muscular powers, are improved only by being used. The faculties are called into no exercise by doing a thing merely because others do it, no more than by believing a thing only because others believe it. If the grounds of an opinion are not conclusive to the person's own reason, his reason cannot be strengthened, but is likely to be weakened by his adopting it: and if the inducements to an act are not such as are consentaneous to his own feelings and character (where affection, or the rights of others, are not concerned), it is so much done towards rendering his feelings and character inert and torpid, instead of active and energetic.

He who lets the world, or his own portion of it, choose his plan of life for him, has no need of any other faculty than the ape-like one of imitation. He who chooses his plan for himself, employs all his faculties. He must use observation to see, reasoning and judgment to foresee, activity to gather materials for decision, discrimination to decide, and when he has decided, firmness and self-control to hold to his deliberate decision. And these qualities he requires and exercises exactly in proportion as the part of his conduct which he determines according to his own judgment and feelings is a large one. It is possible that he might be guided in some good path, and kept out of harm's way, without any of these things. But what will be his comparative worth as a human being? It really is of importance, not only what men do, but also what manner of men they are that do it. Among the works of man, which human life is rightly employed in perfecting and beautifying, the first in importance surely is man himself. Supposing it were possible to get houses built, corn grown, battles fought, causes tried, and even churches erected and prayers said, by machinery—by automatons in human form—it would be a considerable loss to exchange for these automatons even the men and women who at present inhabit the more civilized parts of the world, and who assuredly are but starved specimens of what nature can and will produce. Human nature is not a machine to be built after a model, and set to do exactly the work prescribed for it, but a tree, which requires to grow and develop itself on all sides, according to the tendency of the inward forces which make it a living thing.

It will probably be conceded that it is desirable people should exercise their understandings, and that an intelligent following of custom, or even occasionally an intelligent deviation from custom, is better than a blind and simply mechanical adhesion to it. To a certain extent it is admitted, that our understanding should be our own: but there is not the same willingness to admit that our desires and impulses should be our own likewise; or that to possess impulses of our own, and of any strength, is anything but a peril and a snare. Yet desires and impulses are as much a part of a perfect human being, as beliefs and restraints: and strong impulses are only perilous when not properly balanced; when one set of aims and inclinations is developed into strength, while others, which ought to coexist with them, remain weak and inactive. It is not because men's desires are strong that they act ill;

it is because their consciences are weak. There is no natural connection between strong impulses and a weak conscience. The natural connection is the other way. To say that one person's desires and feelings are stronger and more various than those of another, is merely to say that he has more of the raw material of human nature, and is therefore capable, perhaps of more evil, but certainly of more good. Strong impulses are but another name for energy. Energy may be turned to bad uses; but more good may always be made of an energetic nature, than of an indolent and impassive one. Those who have most natural feeling, are always those whose cultivated feelings may be made the strongest. The same strong susceptibilities which make the personal impulses vivid and powerful, are also the source from whence are generated the most passionate love of virtue, and the sternest self-control. It is through the cultivation of these, that society both does its duty and protects its interests: not by rejecting the stuff of which heroes are made, because it knows not how to make them. A person whose desires and impulses are his own—are the expression of his own nature, as it has been developed and modified by his own culture—is said to have a character. One whose desires and impulses are not his own, has no character, no more than a steam-engine has a character. If, in addition to being his own, his impulses are strong, and are under the government of a strong will, he has an energetic character. Whoever thinks that individuality of desires and impulses should not be encouraged to unfold itself, must maintain that society has no need of strong natures —is not the better for containing many persons who have much character—and that a high general average of energy is not desirable.

In some early states of society, these forces might be, and were, too much ahead of the power which society then possessed of disciplining and controlling them. There has been a time when the element of spontaneity and individuality was in excess, and the social principle had a hard struggle with it.

The difficulty then was, to induce men of strong bodies or minds to pay obedience to any rules which required them to control their impulses. To overcome this difficulty, law and discipline, like the Popes struggling against the Emperors, asserted a power over the whole man, claiming to control all his life in order to control his character—which society had not found any other sufficient means of binding. But society has now fairly got the better of individuality; and the danger which threatens human nature is not the excess, but the deficiency, of personal impulses and preferences. Things are vastly changed, since the passions of those who were strong by station or by personal endowment were in a state of habitual rebellion against laws and ordinances, and required to be rigorously chained up to enable the persons within their reach to enjoy any particle of security. In our times, from the highest class of society down to the lowest, every one lives as under the eye of a hostile and dreaded censorship. Not only in what concerns others, but in what concerns only themselves, the individual, or the family, do not ask themselves— what do I prefer? or, what would suit my character and disposition? or, what would allow the best and highest in me to have fair play, and enable it to grow and thrive? They ask themselves, what is suitable to my position? what is usually done by persons of my station and pecuniary circumstances? or (worse still) what is usually done by persons of a station and circumstances superior to mine? I do not mean that they choose what is customary, in preference to what suits their own inclination. It does not occur to them to have any inclination, except for what is customary. Thus the mind itself is bowed to the yoke: even in what people do for pleasure, conformity is the first thing thought of; they like in crowds; they exercise choice only among things commonly done: peculiarity of taste, eccentricity of conduct, are shunned equally with crimes: until by dint of not following their own nature, they have no nature to follow: their human capacities are withered and starved: they become incapable of any strong wishes or native pleasures, and are generally without either opinions or feelings of home growth, or properly their own. Now is this, or is it not, the desirable condition of human nature?

It is so, on the Calvinistic theory. According to that, the one great offence of man is Self-will. All the good of which humanity is capable, is comprised in Obedience. You have no choice; thus you must do, and no otherwise: "whatever is not a duty is a sin." Human nature being radically corrupt, there is no redemption for any one until human nature is killed within him. To one holding this theory of life, crushing out any of the human faculties, capacities, and susceptibilities, is no evil: man needs no capacity, but that of surrendering himself to the will of God: and if he uses any of his faculties for any other purpose but to do that supposed will more effectually, he is better without them. That is the theory of Calvinism; and it is held, in a mitigated form, by many who do not consider themselves Calvinists; the mitigation consisting in giving a less ascetic interpretation to the alleged will of God; asserting it to be his will that mankind should gratify some of their inclinations; of course not in the manner they themselves prefer, but in the way of obedience, that is, in a way prescribed to them by authority; and, therefore, by the necessary conditions of the case, the same for all.

In some such insidious form there is at present a strong tendency to this narrow theory of life, and to the pinched and hidebound type of human character which it patronizes. Many persons, no doubt, sincerely think that human beings thus cramped and dwarfed, are as their Maker designed them to be; just as many have thought that trees are a much finer thing when clipped into pollards, or cut out into figures of animals, than as nature made them. But if it be any part of religion to believe that man was made by a good Being, it is more consistent with that faith to believe, that this Being gave all human faculties that they might be cultivated and unfolded, not rooted out and consumed, and that he takes delight in every nearer approach made by his creatures to the ideal conception embodied in them, every increase in any of their capabilities of comprehension, of action, or of enjoyment. There is a different type of human excellence from the Calvinistic; a conception of humanity as having its nature bestowed on it for other purposes than merely to be abnegated. "Pagan self-assertion" is one of the elements of human worth, as well as "Christian self-denial." * There is a Greek ideal of self-development, which the Platonic and Christian ideal of self-government blends with, but does not supersede. It may be better to be a John Knox than an Alcibiades, but it is better to be a Pericles than either; nor would a Pericles, if we had one in these days, be without anything good which belonged to John Knox.

It is not by wearing down into uniformity all that is individual in themselves, but by cultivating it and calling it forth, within the limits imposed by the rights and interests of others, that human beings become a noble and beautiful object of contemplation; and as the works partake the character of those who do them, by the same process human life also becomes rich, diversified, and animating, furnishing more abundant ailment to high thoughts and elevating feelings, and strengthening the tie which binds every individual to the race, by making the race infinitely better worth belonging to. In proportion to the development of his individuality, each person becomes more valuable to himself, and is therefore capable of being more valuable to others. There is a greater fulness of life about his own existence, and when there is more life in the units there is more in the mass which is composed of them. As much compression as is necessary to prevent the stronger specimens of human nature from encroaching on the rights of others, cannot be dispensed with; but for this there is ample compensation even in the point of view of human development. The means of development

* Sterling's *Essays.*

which the individual loses by being prevented from gratifying his inclinations to the injury of others, are chiefly obtained at the expense of the development of other people. And even to himself there is a full equivalent in the better development of the social part of his nature, rendered possible by the restraint put upon the selfish part. To be held to rigid rules of justice for the sake of others, develops the feelings and capacities which have the good of others for their object. But to be restrained in things not affecting their good, by their mere displeasure, develops nothing valuable, except such force of character as may unfold itself in resisting the restraint. If acquiesced in, it dulls and blunts the whole nature. To give any fair play to the nature of each, it is essential that different persons should be allowed to lead different lives. In proportion as this latitude has been exercised in any age, has that age been noteworthy to posterity. Even despotism does not produce its worst effects, so long as Individuality exists under it; and whatever crushes individuality is despotism, by whatever name it may be called, and whether it professes to be enforcing the will of God or the injunctions of men.

Having said that Individuality is the same thing with development, and that it is only the cultivation of individuality which produces, or can produce, well-developed human beings, I might here close the argument: for what more or better can be said of any condition of human affairs, than that it brings human beings themselves nearer to the best thing they can be? or what worse can be said of any obstruction to good, than that it prevents this? Doubtless, however, these considerations will not suffice to convince those who most need convincing; and it is necessary further to show, that these developed human beings are of some use to the underdeveloped—to point out to those who do not desire liberty, and would not avail themselves of it, that they may be in some intelligible manner rewarded for allowing other people to make use of it without hindrance.

In the first place, then, I would suggest that they might possibly learn something from them. It will not be denied by anybody, that originality is a valuable element in human affairs. There is always need of persons not only to discover new truths, and point out when what were once truths are true no longer, but also to commence new practices, and set the example of more enlightened conduct, and better taste and sense in human life. This cannot well be gainsaid by anybody who does not believe that the world has already attained perfection in all its ways and practices. It is true that this benefit is not capable of being rendered by everybody alike: there are but few persons, in comparison with the whole of mankind, whose experiments, if adopted by others, would be likely to be any improvement on established practice. But these few are the salt of the earth; without them, human life would become a stagnant pool. Not only is it they who introduce good things which did not before exist; it is they who keep the life in those which already existed. If there were nothing new to be done, would human intellect cease to be necessary? Would it be a reason why those who do the old things should forget why they are done, and do them like cattle, not like human beings? There is only too great a tendency in the best beliefs and practices to degenerate into the mechanical; and unless there were a succession of persons whose ever-recurring originality prevents the grounds of those beliefs and practices from becoming merely traditional, such dead matter would not resist the smallest shock from anything really alive, and there would be no reason why civilization should not die out, as in the Byzantine Empire. Persons of genius, it is true, are, and are always likely to be, a small minority; but in order to have them, it is necessary to preserve the soil in which they grow. Genius can only breathe freely in an *atmosphere* of freedom. Persons of genius are, *ex vi termini, more* individual than any other people—less capable, consequently, of fitting themselves, without hurtful compression, into any of the small number of moulds which society provides in order to save its members the trouble of forming their own character. If from timidity they consent to be forced into one of these moulds, and to let all that part of themselves which cannot expand under the pressure remain unexpanded, society will be little the better for their genius. If they are of a strong character, and break their fetters, they become a mark for the society which has not succeeded in reducing them to commonplace, to point at with solemn warning as "wild," "erratic," and the like; much as if one should complain of the Niagara river for not flowing smoothly between its banks like a Dutch canal.

I insist thus emphatically on the importance of genius, and the necessity of allowing it to unfold itself freely both in thought and in practice, being well aware that no one will deny the position in theory, but knowing also that almost every one, in reality, is totally indifferent to it. People think genius a fine thing if it enables a man to write an exciting poem, or paint a picture. But in its true sense, that of originality in thought and action, though no one says that it is not a thing to be admired, nearly all, at heart, think that they can do very well without it. Unhappily this is too natural to be wondered at. Originality is the one thing which unoriginal minds cannot feel the use of. They cannot see what it is to do for them: how should they? If they could see what it would do for them, it would not be originality. The first service which originality has to render them, is that of opening their eyes: which being once fully done, they would have a chance of being themselves original. Meanwhile, recollecting that nothing was ever yet done which some one was not the first to do, and that all good things which exist are the fruits of originality, let them be modest enough to believe that there is something still left for it to accomplish, and assure themselves that they are more in need of originality, the less they are conscious of the want.

In sober truth, whatever homage may be professed, or even paid, to real or supposed mental superiority, the general tendency of things throughout the world is to render mediocrity the ascendant power among mankind. In ancient history, in the Middle Ages, and in a diminishing degree through the long transition from feudality to the present time, the individual was a power in himself; and if he had either great talents or a high social position, he was a considerable power. At present individuals are lost in the crowd. In politics it is almost a triviality to say that public opinion now rules the world. The only power deserving the name is that of masses, and of governments while they make themselves the organ of the tendencies and instincts of masses. This is as true in the moral and social relations of private life as in public transactions. Those whose opinions go by the name of public opinion, are not always the same sort of public: in America, they are the whole white population; in England, chiefly the middle class. But they are always a mass, that is to say, collective mediocrity. And what is a still greater novelty, the mass do not now take their opinions from dignitaries in Church or State, from ostensible leaders, or from books. Their thinking is done for them by men much like themselves, addressing them or speaking in their name, on the spur of the moment, through the newspapers. I am not complaining of all this. I do not assert that anything better is compatible, as a general rule, with the present low state of the human mind. But that does not hinder the government of mediocrity from being mediocre government. No government by a democracy or a numerous aristocracy, either in its political acts or in the opinions, qualities, and tone of mind which it fosters, ever did or could rise above mediocrity, except in so far as the sovereign Many have let themselves be guided (which in their best times they always have done) by the counsels and influence of a more highly gifted and instructed One or Few. The initiation of all wise or noble things, comes and must come from individuals; generally at first from some one individual. The honor and glory of the average man is that he is capable of following that initiative; that he can respond internally to wise and noble things, and be led to them with his eyes open. I am not countenancing the sort of "hero-worship" which applauds the strong man of genius for forcibly seizing on the government of the world and making it do his bidding in spite of itself. All he can claim is, freedom to point out the way. The power of compelling others into it, is not only inconsistent with the freedom and development of all the rest, but corrupting to the strong man himself. It does seem, however, that when the opinions of masses of merely average men are everywhere become or becoming the dominant power, the counterpoise and corrective to that tendency would be, the more and more pronounced individuality of those who stand on the higher eminences of thought. It is in these circumstances most especially, that exceptional individuals, instead of being deterred, should be encouraged in acting differently from the mass. In other times there was no advantage in their doing so, unless they acted not only differently, but better. In this age the mere example of nonconformity, the mere refusal to bend the knee to custom, is itself a service. Precisely because the tyranny of opinion is such as to make eccentricity a reproach, it is desirable, in order to break through that tyranny, that people should be eccentric. Eccentricity has always abounded when and where strength of character has abounded; and the amount of eccentricity in a society has generally been proportional to the amount of genius, mental vigor, and moral courage which it contained. That so few now dare to be eccentric, marks the chief danger of the time.

I have said that it is important to give the freest scope possible to uncustomary things, in order that it may in time appear which of these are fit to be converted into customs. But independence of action, and disregard of custom are not solely deserving of encouragement for the chance they afford that better modes of action, and customs more worthy of general adoption, may be struck out; nor is it only persons of decided mental superiority who have a just claim to carry on their lives in their own way. There is no reason that all human existences should be constructed on some one, or some small number of patterns. If a person possesses any tolerable amount of common sense and experience, his own mode of laying out his existence is the best, not because it is the best in itself, but because it is his own mode. Human beings are not like sheep; and even sheep are not undistinguishably alike. A man cannot get a coat or a pair of boots to fit him, unless they are either made to his measure, or he has a whole warehouseful to choose from: and is it easier to fit him with a life than with a coat, or are human beings more like one another in their whole physical and spiritual conformation than in the shape of their feet? If it were only that people have diversities of taste, that is reason enough for not attempting to shape them all after one model. But different persons also require different conditions for their spiritual development; and can no more exist healthily in the same moral, than all the variety of plants can in the same physical, atmosphere and climate. The same things which are helps to one person towards the cultivation of his higher nature, are hindrances to another. The same mode of life is a healthy excitement to one, keeping all his faculties of action and enjoyment in their best order, while to another it is a distracting burden, which suspends or crushes all internal life. Such are the differences among human beings in their sources of pleasure, their susceptibilities of pain, and the operation on them of different physical and moral agencies, that unless there is a corresponding diversity in their modes of life, they neither obtain their fair share of happiness, nor grow up to the mental, moral, and æsthetic stature of which their nature is capable. Why then should tolerance, as far as the public sentiment is concerned, extend only to tastes and modes of life which extort acquiescence by the multitude of their adherents? Nowhere (except in some monastic institutions) is diversity of taste entirely unrecognized; a person may without blame, either like or dislike rowing, or smoking, or music, or athletic exercises, or chess, or cards, or study, because both those who like each of these things, and those who dislike them, are too numerous to be put down. But the man, and still more the woman, who can be accused either of doing "what nobody does," or of not doing "what everybody does," is the subject of as much depreciatory remark as if he or she had committed some grave moral delinquency. Persons require to possess a title, or some other badge of rank, or the consideration of people of rank, to be able to indulge somewhat in the luxury of doing as they like without detriment to their estimation. To indulge somewhat, I repeat: for whoever allow themselves much of that indulgence, incur the risk of something worse than disparaging speeches—they are in peril of a commission *de lunatico,* and of having their property taken from them and given to their relations.*

* There is something both contemptible and frightful in the sort of evidence on which, of late years, any person can be judicially declared unfit for the management of his affairs; and after his death, his disposal of his property can be set aside, if there is enough of it to pay the expenses of litigation—which are charged on the property itself. All the minute details of his daily life are pried into, and whatever is found which, seen through the medium of the perceiving and describing faculties of the lowest of the low, bears an appearance unlike absolute commonplace, is laid before the jury as evidence of insanity, and often with success; the jurors being little, if at all, less vulgar and ignorant than the witnesses; while the judges, with that extraordinary want of knowledge of human nature and life which continually astonishes us in English lawyers, often help to mislead them. These trials speak volumes as to the state of feeling and opinion among the vulgar with regard to human liberty. So far from setting any value on individuality—so far from respecting the rights of each individual to act, in things indifferent, as seems good to his own judgment and inclinations, judges and juries cannot even conceive that a person in a state of sanity can desire such freedom. In former days, when it was proposed to burn atheists, charitable people used to suggest putting them in a madhouse instead: it would be nothing surprising now-a-days were we to see this done, and the doers applauding themselves, because, instead of persecuting for religion, they had adopted so hu-

There is one characteristic of the present direction of public opinion, peculiarly calculated to make it intolerant of any marked demonstration of individuality. The general average of mankind are not only moderate in intellect, but also moderate in inclinations: they have no tastes or wishes strong enough to incline them to do anything unusual, and they consequently do not understand those who have, and class all such with the wild and intemperate whom they are accustomed to look down upon. Now, in addition to this fact which is general, we have only to suppose that a strong movement has set in towards the improvement of morals, and it is evident what we have to expect. In these days such a movement has set in; much has actually been effected in the way of increased regularity of conduct, and discouragement of excesses; and there is a philanthropic spirit abroad, for the exercise of which there is no more inviting field than the moral and prudential improvement of our fellow-creatures. These tendencies of the times cause the public to be more disposed than at most former periods to prescribe general rules of conduct, and endeavor to make every one conform to the approved standard. And that standard, express or tacit, is to desire nothing strongly. Its idea of character is to be without any marked character; to maim by compression, like a Chinese lady's foot, every part of human nature which stands out prominently, and tends to make the person markedly dissimilar in outline to commonplace humanity.

As is usually the case with ideals which exclude one half of what is desirable, the present standard of approbation produces only an inferior imitation of the other half. Instead of great energies guided by vigorous reason, and strong feelings strongly controlled by a conscientious will, its result is weak feelings and weak energies, which therefore can be kept in outward conformity to rule without any strength

mane and Christian a mode of treating these unfortunates, not without a silent satisfaction at their having thereby obtained their deserts.

either of will or of reason. Already energetic characters on any large scale are becoming merely traditional. There is now scarcely any outlet for energy in this country except business. The energy expended in that may still be regarded as considerable. What little is left from that employment, is expended on some hobby; which may be a useful, even a philanthropic hobby, but is always some one thing, and generally a thing of small dimensions. The greatness of England is now all collective: individually small, we only appear capable of anything great by our habit of combining; and with this our moral and religious philanthropists are perfectly contented. But it was men of another stamp than this that made England what it has been; and men of another stamp will be needed to prevent its decline.

The despotism of custom is everywhere the standing hindrance to human advancement, being in unceasing antagonism to that disposition to aim at something better than customary, which is called, according to circumstances, the spirit of liberty, or that of progress or improvement. The spirit of improvement is not always a spirit of liberty, for it may aim at forcing improvements on an unwilling people; and the spirit of liberty, in so far as it resists such attempts, may ally itself locally and temporarily with the opponents of improvement; but the only unfailing and permanent source of improvement is liberty, since by it there are as many possible independent centres of improvement as there are individuals. The progressive principle, however, in either shape, whether as the love of liberty or of improvement, is antagonistic to the sway of Custom, involving at least emancipation from that yoke; and the contest between the two constitutes the chief interest of the history of mankind. The greater part of the world has, properly speaking, no history, because the despotism of Custom is complete. This is the case over the whole East. Custom is there, in all things, the final appeal; justice and right mean conformity to custom; the argument of custom no one, unless some tyrant intoxicated with power, thinks of resisting. And we see the result. Those nations must once have had originality; they did not start out of the ground populous, lettered, and versed in many of the arts of life; they made themselves all this, and were then the greatest and most powerful nations in the world. What are they now? The subjects or dependents of tribes whose forefathers wandered in the forests when theirs had magnificent palaces and gorgeous temples, but over whom custom exercised only a divided rule with liberty and progress. A people, it appears, may be progressive for a certain length of time, and then stop: when does it stop? When it ceases to possess individuality. If a similar change should befall the nations of Europe, it will not be in exactly the same shape: the despotism of custom with which these nations are threatened is not precisely stationariness. It proscribes singularity, but it does not preclude change, provided all change together. We have discarded the fixed costumes of our forefathers; every one must still dress like other people, but the fashion may change once or twice a year. We thus take care that when there is change, it shall be for change's sake, and not from any idea of beauty or convenience; for the same idea of beauty or convenience would not strike all the world at the same moment, and be simultaneously thrown aside by all at another moment. But we are progressive as well as changeable: we continually make new inventions in mechanical things, and keep them until they are again superseded by better; we are eager for improvement in politics, in education, even in morals, though in this last our idea of improvement chiefly consists in persuading or forcing other people to be as good as ourselves. It is not progress that we object to; on the contrary, we flatter ourselves that we are the most progressive people who ever lived. It is individuality that we war against: we should think we had done wonders if we had made ourselves all alike; forgetting that the unlikeness of one person to another is generally the first thing which draws the attention of either to the imperfection of his own type, and the superiority of another, or the possibility, by combining the advantages of both, of producing something better than either. We have a warning example in China—a nation of much talent, and, in some respects, even wisdom, owing to the rare good fortune of having been provided at an early period with a particularly good set of customs, the work, in some measure, of men to whom even the most enlightened European must accord, under certain limitations, the title of sages and philosophers. They are remarkable, too, in the excellence of their apparatus for impressing, as far as possible, the best wisdom they possess upon every mind in the community, and securing that those who have appropriated most of it shall occupy the posts of honor and power. Surely the people who did this have discovered the secret of human progressiveness, and must have kept themselves steadily at the head of the movement of the world. On the contrary, they have become stationary—have remained so for thousands of years; and if they are ever to be farther improved, it must be by foreigners. They have succeeded beyond all hope in what English philanthropists are so industriously working at—in making a people all alike, all governing their thoughts and conduct by the same maxims and rules; and these are the fruits. The modern *régime* of public opinion is, in an unorganized form, what the Chinese educational and political systems are in an organized; and unless individuality shall be able successfully to assert itself against this yoke, Europe, notwithstanding its noble antecedents and its professed Christianity, will tend to become another China.

What is it that has hitherto preserved Europe from this lot? What has made the European family of nations an improving, instead of a stationary portion of mankind? Not any superior excellence in them, which when it exists, exists as the effect, not as the cause; but their remarkable diversity of character and culture. Individuals, classes, nations, have been extremely unlike one another: they have struck out a great variety of paths, each leading to something valuable;

and although at every period those who travelled in different paths have been intolerant of one another, and each would have thought it an excellent thing if all the rest could have been compelled to travel his road, their attempts to thwart each other's development have rarely had any permanent success, and each has in time endured to receive the good which the others have offered. Europe is, in my judgment, wholly indebted to this plurality of paths for its progressive and many-sided development. But it already begins to possess this benefit in a considerably less degree. It is decidedly advancing towards the Chinese ideal of making all people alike. M. de Tocqueville, in his last important work, remarks how much more the Frenchmen of the present day resemble one another, than did those even of the last generation. The same remark might be made of Englishmen in a far greater degree. In a passage already quoted from Wilhelm von Humboldt, he points out two things as necessary conditions of human development, because necessary to render people unlike one another; namely, freedom, and variety of situations. The second of these two conditions is in this country every day diminishing. The circumstances which surround different classes and individuals, and shape their characters, are daily becoming more assimilated. Formerly, different ranks, different neighborhoods, different trades and professions, lived in what might be called different worlds; at present, to a great degree in the same. Comparatively speaking, they now read the same things, listen to the same things, see the same things, go to the same places, have their hopes and fears directed to the same objects, have the same rights and liberties, and the same means of asserting them. Great as are the differences of position which remain, they are nothing to those which have ceased. And the assimilation is still proceeding. All the political changes of the age promote it, since they all tend to raise the low and to lower the high. Every extension of education promotes it, because education brings people under common influences, and gives them access to the general stock of facts and sentiments. Improvements in the means of communication promote it, by bringing the inhabitants of distant places into personal contact, and keeping up a rapid flow of changes of residence between one place and another. The increase of commerce and manufactures promotes it, by diffusing more widely the advantages of easy circumstances, and opening all objects of ambition, even the highest, to general competition, whereby the desire of rising becomes no longer the character of a particular class, but of all classes. A more powerful agency than even all these, in bringing about a general similarity among mankind, is the complete establishment, in this and other free countries, of the ascendency of public opinion in the State. As the various social eminences which enabled persons entrenched on them to disregard the opinion of the multitude gradually become levelled; as the very idea of resisting the will of the public, when it is positively known that they have a will, disappears more and more from the minds of practical politicians; there ceases to be any social support for non-conformity—any substantive power in society, which, itself opposed to the ascendancy of numbers, is interested in taking under its protection opinions and tendencies at variance with those of the public.

The combination of all these causes forms so great a mass of influences hostile to Individuality, that it is not easy to see how it can stand its ground. It will do so with increasing difficulty, unless the intelligent part of the public can be made to feel its value—to see that it is good there should be differences, even though not for the better, even though, as it may appear to them, some should be for the worse. If the claims of Individuality are ever to be asserted, the time is now, while much is still wanting to complete the enforced assimilation. It is only in the earlier stages that any stand can be successfully made against the encroachment. The demand that all other people shall resemble ourselves, grows by what it feeds on. If resistance waits till life is reduced *nearly* to one uniform type, all deviations from that type will come to be considered impious, immoral, even monstrous and contrary to nature. Mankind speedily become unable to conceive diversity, when they have been for some time unaccustomed to see it.

CHAPTER 4 *Of the Limits to the Authority of Society Over the Individual*

What, then, is the rightful limit to the sovereignty of the individual over himself? Where does the authority of society begin? How much of human life should be assigned to individuality, and how much to society?

Each will receive its proper share, if each has that which more particularly concerns it. To individuality should belong the part of life in which it is chiefly the individual that is interested; to society, the part which chiefly interests society.

Though society is not founded on a contract, and though no good purpose is answered by inventing a contract in order to deduce social obligations from it, every one who receives the protection of society owes a return for the benefit, and the fact of living in society renders it indispensable that each should be bound to observe a certain line of conduct towards the rest. This conduct consists, first, in not injuring the interests of one another; or rather certain interests, which, either by express legal provision or by tacit understanding, ought to be considered as rights; and secondly, in each person's bearing his share (to be fixed on some equitable principle) of the labors and sacrifices incurred for defending the society or its members from injury and molestation. These conditions society is justified in enforcing, at all costs to those who endeavor to withhold fulfilment. Nor is this all that society may do. The acts of an individual may be hurtful to others, or wanting in due consideration for their welfare, without going the length of violating any of their constituted rights. The offender may then be justly punished by opinion, though not by law. As soon as any part of a person's conduct affects prejudicially the interests of others, society has jurisdiction over it, and the question whether the general welfare will or will not be promoted by interfering with it, becomes open to discussion. But there is no room for entertaining any such question when a person's conduct affects the interests of no persons besides himself, or needs not affect them unless they like (all the persons concerned being of full age, and the ordinary amount of understanding). In all such cases there should be perfect freedom, legal and social, to do the action and stand the consequences.

It would be a great misunderstanding of this doctrine, to suppose that it is one of selfish indifference, which pretends that human beings have no business with each other's conduct in life, and that they should not concern themselves about the well-doing or well-being of one another, unless their own interest is involved. Instead of any diminution, there is need of a great increase of disinterested exertion to promote the good of others. But disinterested benevolence can find other instruments to persuade people to their good, than whips and scourges, either of the literal or the metaphorical sort. I am the last person to undervalue the self-regarding virtues; they are only second in importance, if even second, to the social. It is equally the business of education to cultivate both. But even education works by conviction and persuasion as well as by compulsion, and it is by the former only that, when the period of education is past, the self-regarding virtues should be inculcated. Human beings owe to each other help to distinguish the better from the worse, and encouragement to choose the former and avoid the latter.

They should be forever stimulating each other to increased exercise of their higher faculties, and increased direction of their feelings and aims towards wise instead of foolish, elevating instead of degrading, objects and contemplations. But neither one person, nor any number of persons, is warranted in saying to another human creature of ripe years, that he shall not do with his life for his own benefit what he chooses to do with it. He is the person most interested in his own well-being: the interest which any other person, except in cases of strong personal attachment, can have in it, is trifling, compared with that which he himself has; the interest which society has in him individually (except as to his conduct to others) is fractional, and altogether indirect: while, with respect to his own feelings and circumstances, the most ordinary man or woman has means of knowledge immeasurably surpassing those that can be possessed by anyone else. The interference of society to overrule his judgment and purposes in what only regards himself, must be grounded on general presumptions; which may be altogether wrong, and even if right, are as likely as not to be misapplied to individual cases, by persons no better acquainted with the circumstances of such cases than those are who look at them merely from without. In this department, therefore, of human affairs, Individuality has its proper field of action. In the conduct of human beings towards one another, it is necessary that general rules should for the most part be observed, in order that people may know what they have to expect; but in each person's own concerns, his individual spontaneity is entitled to free exercise. Considerations to aid his judgment, exhortations to strengthen his will, may be offered to him, even obtruded on him, by others; but he, himself, is the final judge. All errors which he is likely to commit against advice and warning, are far outweighed by the evil of allowing others to constrain him to what they deem his good.

I do not mean that the feelings with which a person is regarded by others, ought not to be in any way affected by his self-regarding qualities or deficiencies. This is neither possible nor desirable. If he is eminent in any of the qualities which conduce to his own good, he is, so far, a proper object of admiration. He is so much the nearer to the ideal perfection of human nature. If he is grossly deficient in those qualities, a sentiment the opposite of admiration will follow. There is a degree of folly, and a degree of what may be called (though the phrase is not unobjectionable) lowness or depravation of taste, which, though it cannot justify doing harm to the person who manifests it, renders him necessarily and properly a subject of distaste, or, in extreme cases, even of contempt: a person could not have the opposite qualities in due strength without entertaining these feelings. Though doing no wrong to anyone, a person may so act as to compel us to judge him, and feel to him, as a fool, or as a being of an inferior order: and since this judgment and feeling are a fact which he would prefer to avoid, it is doing him a service to warn him of it beforehand, as of any other disagreeable consequence to which he exposes himself. It would be well, indeed, if this good office were much more freely rendered than the common notions of politeness at present permit, and if one person could honestly point out to another that he thinks him in fault, without being considered unmannerly or presuming. We have a right, also, in various ways, to act upon our unfavorable opinion of any one, not to the oppression of his individuality, but in the exercise of ours. We are not bound, for example, to seek his society; we have a right to avoid it (though not to parade the avoidance), for we have a right to choose the society most acceptable to us. We have a right, and it may be our duty to caution others against him, if we think his example or conversation likely to have a pernicious effect on those with whom he associates. We may give others a preference over him in optional good offices, except those which tend to his improvement. In these various modes a person may suffer very severe penalties at the hands of others, for faults which directly concern only himself; but he suffers these penalties only in so far as they are the natural, and, as it were, the spontaneous consequences of the faults themselves, not because they are purposely inflicted on him for the sake of punishment. A person who shows rashness, obstinacy, self-conceit—who cannot live within moderate means—who cannot restrain himself from hurtful indulgences—who pursues animal pleasures at the expense of those of feeling and intellect—must expect to be lowered in the opinion of others, and to have a less share of their favorable sentiments, but of this he has no right to complain, unless he has merited their favor by special excellence in his social relations, and has thus established a title to their good offices, which is not affected by his demerits towards himself.

What I contend for is, that the inconveniences which are strictly inseparable from the unfavorable judgment of others, are the only ones to which a person should ever be subjected for that portion of his conduct and character which concerns his own good, but which does not affect the interests of others in their relations with him. Acts injurious to others require a totally different treatment. Encroachment on their rights; infliction on them of any loss or damage not justified by his own rights; falsehood or duplicity in dealing with them; unfair or ungenerous use of advantages over them; even selfish abstinence from defending them against injury—these are fit objects of moral reprobation, and, in grave cases, of moral retribution and punishment. And not only these acts, but the dispositions which lead to them, are properly immoral, and fit subjects of disapprobation which may rise to abhorrence. Cruelty of disposition; malice and ill-nature; that most anti-social and odious of all passions, envy; dissimulation and insincerity; irascibility on insufficient cause, and resentment disproportioned to the provocation; the love of domineering over others; the desire to engross more than one's share of advantages (the πλεονεξία of the Greeks); the pride which derives gratification from the abasement of others; the egotism which thinks self and its concerns more important than everything else, and decides all doubtful questions in his own favor—these are moral vices, and constitute a bad and odious moral character: unlike the self-regarding faults previously mentioned, which are not properly immoralities, and to whatever pitch they may be carried, do not constitute wickedness. They may be proofs of any amount of folly, or want of personal dignity and self-respect; but they are only a subject of moral reprobation when they involve a breach of duty to others, for whose sake the individual is bound to have care for himself. What are called duties to ourselves are not socially obligatory, unless circumstances render them at the same time duties to others. The term duty to oneself, when it means anything more than prudence, means self-respect or self-development; and for none of these is any one accountable to his fellow-creatures, because for none of them is it for the good of mankind that he be held accountable to them.

The distinction between the loss of consideration which a person may rightly incur by defect of prudence or of personal dignity, and the reprobation which is due to him for an offence against the rights of others, is not a merely nominal distinction. It makes a vast difference both in our feelings and in our conduct towards him, whether he displeases us in things in which we think we have a right to control him, or in things in which we know that we have not. If he displeases us, we may express our distaste, and we may stand aloof from a person as well as from a thing that displeases us; but we shall not therefore feel called on to make his life uncomfortable. We shall reflect that he already bears, or will bear, the whole penalty of his error; if he spoils his life by mismanagement, we shall not, for that reason, desire to spoil it still further: instead of wishing to punish him, we shall rather endeavor to alleviate his punishment, by showing him how he may avoid or cure the evils his conduct tends to bring upon him. He may be to us an object of pity, perhaps of dislike, but not of anger or resentment; we shall not treat him like an enemy of society: the worst we shall think ourselves justified in doing is leaving him to himself, if we do not interfere benevolently by showing interest or concern for him. It is far otherwise if he has infringed the rules necessary for the protection of his fellow-creatures, individually or collectively. The evil consequences of his acts do not then fall on himself, but on others; and society, as the protector of all its members, must retaliate on him; must inflict pain on him for the express purpose of punishment, and must take care that it be sufficiently severe. In the one case, he is an offender at our bar, and we are called on not only to sit in judgment on him, but, in one shape or another, to execute our own sentence: in the other case, it is not our part to inflict any suffering on him, except what may incidentally follow from our using the same liberty in the regulation of our own affairs, which we allow to him in his.

The distinction here pointed out between the part of a person's life which concerns only himself, and that which concerns others, many persons will refuse to admit. How (it may be asked) can any part of the conduct of a member of society be a matter of indifference to the other members? No person is an entirely isolated being; it is impossible for a person to do anything seriously or permanently hurtful to himself, without mischief reaching at least to his near connections, and often far beyond them. If he injures his property, he does harm to those who directly or indirectly derived support from it, and usually diminishes, by a greater or less amount, the general resources of the community. If he deteriorates his bodily or mental faculties, he not only brings evil upon all who depended on him for any portion of their happiness, but disqualifies himself for rendering the services which he owes to his fellow-creatures generally; perhaps becomes a burden on their affection or benevolence; and if such conduct were very frequent, hardly any offence that is committed would detract more from the general sum of good. Finally, if by his vices or follies a person does no direct harm to others, he is nevertheless (it may be said) injurious by his example; and ought to be compelled to control himself, for the sake of those whom the sight or knowledge of his conduct might corrupt or mislead.

And even (it will be added) if the consequences of misconduct could be confined to the vicious or thoughtless individual, ought society to abandon to their own guidance those who are manifestly unfit for it? If protection against themselves is confessedly due to children and persons under age, is not society equally bound to afford it to persons of mature years who are equally incapable of self-government? If gambling, or drunkenness, or incontinence, or idleness, or uncleanliness, are as injurious to happiness, and as great a hindrance to improvement, as many or most of the acts prohibited by law, why (it may be asked) should not law, so far as is consistent with practicability and social convenience, endeavor to repress these also? And as a supplement to the unavoidable imperfections of law, ought not opinion at least to organize a powerful police against these vices, and visit rigidly with social penalties those who are known to practise them? There is no question here (it may be said) about restricting individuality, or impeding the trial of new and original experiments in living. The only things it is sought to prevent are things which have been tried and condemned from the beginning of the world until now; things which experience has shown not to be useful or suitable to any person's individuality. There must be some length of time and amount of experience, after which a moral or prudential truth may be regarded as established: and it is merely desired to prevent generation after generation from falling over the same precipice which has been fatal to their predecessors.

I fully admit that the mischief which a person does to himself, may seriously affect, both through their sympathies and their interests, those nearly connected with him, and in a minor degree, society at large. When, by conduct of this sort, a person is led to violate a distinct and assignable obligation to any other person or persons, the case is taken out of the self-

regarding class, and becomes amenable to moral disapprobation in the proper sense of the term. If, for example, a
man, through intemperance or extravagance, becomes unable to pay his debts, or, having undertaken the moral responsibility of a family, becomes from the same cause incapable of supporting or educating them, he is deservedly
reprobated, and might be justly punished; but it is for the
breach of duty to his family or creditors, not for the extravagance. If the resources which ought to have been devoted to
them, had been diverted from them for the most prudent in-
vestment, the moral culpability would have been the same.
George Barnwell murdered his uncle to get money for his
mistress, but if he had done it to set himself up in business,
he would equally have been hanged. Again, in the frequent
case of a man who causes grief to his family by addiction to
bad habits, he deserves reproach for his unkindness or in-
gratitude; but so he may for cultivating habits not in themselves vicious, if they are painful to those with whom he
passes his life, or who from personal ties are dependent on
him for their comfort. Whoever fails in the consideration
generally due to the interests and feelings of others, not being
compelled by some more imperative duty, or justified by allowable self-preference, is a subject of moral disapprobation
for that failure, but not for the cause of it, nor for the errors,
merely personal to himself, which may have remotely led to
it. In like manner, when a person disables himself, by conduct purely self-regarding, from the performance of some
definite duty incumbent on him to the public, he is guilty of a
social offence. No person ought to be punished simply for being drunk; but a soldier or a policeman should be punished
for being drunk on duty. Whenever, in short, there is a definite damage, or a definite risk of damage, either to an individual or to the public, the case is taken out of the province
of liberty, and placed in that of morality or law.

But with regard to the merely contingent, or, as it may be
called, constructive injury which a person causes to society,

by conduct which neither violates any specific duty to the public, nor occasions perceptible hurt to any assignable individual except himself; the inconvenience is one which society can afford to bear, for the sake of the greater good of human freedom. If grown persons are to be punished for not taking proper care of themselves, I would rather it were for their own sake, than under pretence of preventing them from impairing their capacity of rendering to society benefits which society does not pretend it has a right to exact. But I cannot consent to argue the point as if society had no means of bringing its weaker members up to its ordinary standard of rational conduct, except waiting till they do something irrational, and then punishing them, legally or morally, for it. Society has had absolute power over them during all the early portion of their existence: it has had the whole period of childhood and nonage in which to try whether it could make them capable of rational conduct in life. The existing generation is master both of the training and the entire circumstances of the generation to come; it cannot indeed make them perfectly wise and good, because it is itself so lamentably deficient in goodness and wisdom; and its best efforts are not always, in individual cases, its most successful ones; but it is perfectly well able to make the rising generation, as a whole, as good as, and a little better than, itself. If society lets any considerable number of its members grow up mere children, incapable of being acted on by rational consideration of distant motives, society has itself to blame for the consequences. Armed not only with all the powers of education, but with the ascendency which the authority of a received opinion always exercises over the minds who are least fitted to judge for themselves; and aided by the *natural* penalties which cannot be prevented from falling on those who incur the distaste or the contempt of those who know them; let not society pretend that it needs, besides all this, the power to issue commands and enforce obedience in the personal concerns of individuals, in which, on all principles of justice and policy, the decision ought to rest with those who are to abide the consequences. Nor is there anything which tends more to discredit and frustrate the better means of influencing conduct, than a resort to the worse. If there be among those whom it is attempted to coerce into prudence or temperance, any of the material of which vigorous and independent characters are made, they will infallibly rebel against the yoke. No such person will ever feel that others have a right to control him in his concerns, such as they have to prevent him from injuring them in theirs; and it easily comes to be considered a mark of spirit and courage to fly in the face of such usurped authority, and do with ostentation the exact opposite of what it enjoins; as in the fashion of grossness which succeeded, in the time of Charles II., to the fanatical moral intolerance of the Puritans. With respect to what is said of the necessity of protecting society from the bad example set to others by the vicious or the self-indulgent; it is true that bad example may have a pernicious effect, especially the example of doing wrong to others with impunity to the wrongdoer. But we are now speaking of conduct which, while it does no wrong to others, is supposed to do great harm to the agent himself: and I do not see how those who believe this, can think otherwise than that the example, on the whole, must be more salutary than hurtful, since, if it displays the misconduct, it displays also the painful or degrading consequences which, if the conduct is justly censured, must be supposed to be in all or most cases attendant on it.

But the strongest of all the arguments against the interference of the public with purely personal conduct, is that when it does interfere, the odds are that it interferes wrongly, and in the wrong place. On questions of social morality, of duty to others, the opinion of the public, that is, of an overruling majority, though often wrong, is likely to be still oftener right; because on such questions they are only required to judge of their own interests; of the manner in which some

mode of conduct, if allowed to be practised, would affect
themselves. But the opinion of a similar majority, imposed as
a law on the minority, on questions of self-regarding conduct,
is quite as likely to be wrong as right; for in these cases
public opinion means, at the best, some people's opinion of
what is good or bad for other people; while very often it does
not even mean that; the public, with the most perfect indifference, passing over the pleasure or convenience of those
whose conduct they censure, and considering only their own
preference. There are many who consider as an injury to
themselves any conduct which they have a distaste for, and
resent it as an outrage to their feelings; as a religious bigot,
when charged with disregarding the religious feelings of others, has been known to retort that they disregard his feelings,
by persisting in their abominable worship or creed. But there
is no parity between the feeling of a person for his own
opinion, and the feeling of another who is offended at his
holding it; no more than between the desire of a thief to take
a purse, and the desire of the right owner to keep it. And a
person's taste is as much his own peculiar concern as his
opinion or his purse. It is easy for any one to imagine an
ideal public, which leaves the freedom and choice of individuals in all uncertain matters undisturbed, and only requires
them to abstain from modes of conduct which universal experience has condemned. But where has there been seen a
public which set any such limit to its censorship? or when
does the public trouble itself about universal experience? In
its interferences with personal conduct it is seldom thinking
of anything but the enormity of acting or feeling differently
from itself; and this standard of judgment, thinly disguised,
is held up to mankind as the dictate of religion and philosophy, by nine tenths of all moralists and speculative writers.
These teach that things are right because they are right; because we feel them to be so. They tell us to search in our
own minds and hearts for laws of conduct binding on ourselves and on all others. What can the poor public do but

apply these instructions, and make their own personal feelings of good and evil, if they are tolerably unanimous in them, obligatory on all the world?

The evil here pointed out is not one which exists only in theory; and it may perhaps be expected that I should specify the instances in which the public of this age and country improperly invests its own preferences with the character of moral laws. I am not writing an essay on the aberrations of existing moral feeling. That is too weighty a subject to be discussed parenthetically, and by way of illustration. Yet examples are necessary, to show that the principle I maintain is of serious and practical moment, and that I am not endeavoring to erect a barrier against imaginary evils. And it is not difficult to show, by abundant instances, that to extend the bounds of what may be called moral police, until it encroaches on the most unquestionably legitimate liberty of the individual, is one of the most universal of all human propensities.

As a first instance, consider the antipathies which men cherish on no better grounds than that persons whose religious opinions are different from theirs, do not practise their religious observances, especially their religious abstinences. To cite a rather trivial example, nothing in the creed or practice of Christians does more to envenom the hatred of Mahomedans against them, than the fact of their eating pork. There are few acts which Christians and Europeans regard with more unaffected disgust, than Mussulmans regard this particular mode of satisfying hunger. It is, in the first place, an offence against their religion; but this circumstance by no means explains either the degree or the kind of their repugnance; for wine also is forbidden by their religion, and to partake of it is by all Mussulmans accounted wrong, but not disgusting. Their aversion to the flesh of the "unclean beast" is, on the contrary, of that peculiar character, resembling an instinctive antipathy, which the idea of uncleanness, when once it thoroughly sinks into the feelings, seems always to excite even in those whose personal habits are anything but scrupulously cleanly, and of which the sentiment of religious impurity, so intense in the Hindoos, is a remarkable example. Suppose now that in a people, of whom the majority were Mussulmans, that majority should insist upon not permitting pork to be eaten within the limits of the country. This would be nothing new in Mahomedan countries.* Would it be a legitimate exercise of the moral authority of public opinion? and if not, why not? The practice is really revolting to such a public. They also sincerely think that it is forbidden and abhorred by the Deity. Neither could the prohibition be censured as religious persecution. It might be religious in its origin, but it would not be persecution for religion, since nobody's religion makes it a duty to eat pork. The only tenable ground of condemnation would be, that with the personal tastes and self-regarding concerns of individuals the public has no business to interfere.

To come somewhat nearer home: the majority of Spaniards consider it a gross impiety, offensive in the highest degree to the Supreme Being, to worship him in any other manner than the Roman Catholic; and no other public worship is lawful on Spanish soil. The people of all Southern Europe look upon a married clergy as not only irreligious, but unchaste, indecent, gross, disgusting. What do Protestants think of these perfectly sincere feelings, and of the

---

* The case of the Bombay Parsees is a curious instance in point. When this industrious and enterprising tribe, the descendants of the Persian fire-worshippers, flying from their native country before the Caliphs, arrived in Western India, they were admitted to toleration by the Hindoo sovereigns, on condition of not eating beef. When those regions afterwards fell under the dominion of Mahomedan conquerors, the Parsees obtained from them a continuance of indulgence, on condition of refraining from pork. What was at first obedience to authority became a second nature, and the Parsees to this day abstain both from beef and pork. Though not required by their religion, the double abstinence has had time to grow into a custom of their tribe; and custom, in the East, is a religion.

attempt to enforce them against non-Catholics? Yet, if mankind are justified in interfering with each other's liberty in
things which do not concern the interests of others, on what
principle is it possible consistently to exclude these cases? or
who can blame people for desiring to suppress what they
regard as a scandal in the sight of God and man? No stronger
case can be shown for prohibiting anything which is regarded
as a personal immorality, than is made out for suppressing
these practices in the eyes of those who regard them as im-
pieties; and unless we are willing to adopt the logic of persecutors, and to say that we may persecute others because
we are right, and that they must not persecute us because
they are wrong, we must be aware of admitting a principle
of which we should resent as a gross injustice the application
to ourselves.

The preceding instances may be objected to, although un-
reasonably, as drawn from contingencies impossible among
us: opinion, in this country, not being likely to enforce abstinence from meats, or to interfere with people for wor-
shipping, and for either marrying or not marrying, according to their creed or inclination. The next example, however,
shall be taken from an interference with liberty which we
have by no means passed all danger of. Wherever the puritans have been sufficiently powerful, as in New England,
and in Great Britain at the time of the Commonwealth,
they have endeavored, with considerable success, to put
down all public, and nearly all private, amusements: especially music, dancing, public games, or other assemblages for
purposes of diversion, and the theatre. There are still in this
country large bodies of persons by whose notions of morality
and religion these recreations are condemned; and those persons belonging chiefly to the middle class, who are the ascendant power in the present social and political condition
of the kingdom, it is by no means impossible that persons of
these sentiments may at some time or other command a
majority in Parliament. How will the remaining portion of

the community like to have the amusements that shall be permitted to them regulated by the religious and moral sentiments of the stricter Calvinists and Methodists? Would they not, with considerable peremptoriness, desire these intrusively pious members of society to mind their own business? This is precisely what should be said to every government and every public, who have the pretension that no person shall enjoy any pleasure which they think wrong. But if the principle of the pretension be admitted, no one can reasonably object to its being acted on in the sense of the majority, or other preponderating power in the country; and all persons must be ready to conform to the idea of a Christian commonwealth, as understood by the early settlers in New England, if a religious profession similar to theirs should ever succeed in regaining its lost ground, as religions supposed to be declining have so often been known to do.

To imagine another contingency, perhaps more likely to be realized than the one last mentioned. There is confessedly a strong tendency in the modern world towards a democratic constitution of society, accompanied or not by popular political institutions. It is affirmed that in the country where this tendency is most completely realized—where both society and the government are most democratic—the United States—the feeling of the majority, to whom any appearance of a more showy or costly style of living than they can hope to rival is disagreeable, operates as a tolerably effectual sumptuary law, and that in many parts of the Union it is really difficult for a person possessing a very large income, to find any mode of spending it, which will not incur popular disapprobation. Though such statements as these are doubtless much exaggerated as a representation of existing facts, the state of things they describe is not only a conceivable and possible, but a probable result of democratic feeling, combined with the notion that the public has a right to a veto on the manner in which individuals shall spend their incomes. We have only further to suppose a considerable diffusion of Socialist opinions, and it may become infamous in the eyes of the majority to possess more property than some very small amount, or any income not earned by manual labor. Opinions similar in principle to these, already prevail widely among the artisan class, and weigh oppressively on those who are amenable to the opinion chiefly of that class, namely, its own members. It is known that the bad workmen who form the majority of the operatives in many branches of industry, are decidedly of opinion that bad workmen ought to receive the same wages as good, and that no one ought to be allowed, through piecework or otherwise, to earn by superior skill or industry more than others can without it. And they employ a moral police, which occasionally becomes a physical one, to deter skilful workmen from receiving, and employers from giving, a larger remuneration for a more useful service. If the public have any jurisdiction over private concerns, I cannot see that these people are in fault, or that any individual's particular public can be blamed for asserting the same authority over his individual conduct, which the general public asserts over people in general.

But, without dwelling upon supposititious cases, there are, in our own day, gross usurpations upon the liberty of private life actually practised, and still greater ones threatened with some expectation of success, and opinions proposed which assert an unlimited right in the public not only to prohibit by law everything which it thinks wrong, but in order to get at what it thinks wrong, to prohibit any number of things which it admits to be innocent.

Under the name of preventing intemperance, the people of one English colony, and of nearly half the United States, have been interdicted by law from making any use whatever of fermented drinks, except for medical purposes: for prohibition of their sale is in fact, as it is intended to be, prohibition of their use. And though the impracticability of executing the law has caused its repeal in several of the States which had adopted it, including the one from which it de-

rives its name, an attempt has notwithstanding been commenced, and is prosecuted with considerable zeal by many
of the professed philanthropists, to agitate for a similar law
in this country. The association, or "Alliance" as it terms itself, which has been formed for this purpose, has acquired
some notoriety through the publicity given to a correspondence between its Secretary and one of the very few English
public men who hold that a politician's opinions ought to be
founded on principles. Lord Stanley's share in this correspondence is calculated to strengthen the hopes already built
on him, by those who know how rare such qualities as are
manifested in some of his public appearances, unhappily are
among those who figure in political life. The organ of the
Alliance, who would "deeply deplore the recognition of
any principle which could be wrested to justify bigotry and
persecution," undertakes to point out the "broad and impassable barrier" which divides such principles from those of
the association. "All matters relating to thought, opinion, conscience, appear to me," he says, "to be without the sphere of
legislation; all pertaining to social act, habit, relation, subject
only to a discretionary power vested in the State itself, and
not in the individual, to be within it." No mention is made of
a third class, different from either of these, viz., acts and
habits which are not social, but individual; although it is to
this class, surely, that the act of drinking fermented liquors
belongs. Selling fermented liquors, however, is trading, and
trading is a social act. But the infringement complained of is
not on the liberty of the seller, but on that of the buyer and
consumer; since the State might just as well forbid him to
drink wine, as purposely make it impossible for him to obtain it. The Secretary, however, says, "I claim, as a citizen, a
right to legislate whenever my social rights are invaded by
the social act of another." And now for the definition of these
"social rights." "If anything invades my social rights, certainly the traffic in strong drink does. It destroys my primary
right of security, by constantly creating and stimulating social

disorder. It invades my right of equality, by deriving a profit from the creation of a misery, I am taxed to support. It impedes my right to free moral and intellectual development, by surrounding my path with dangers, and by weakening and demoralizing society, from which I have a right to claim mutual aid and intercourse." A theory of "social rights," the like of which probably never before found its way into distinct language—being nothing short of this—that it is the absolute social right of every individual, that every other individual shall act in every respect exactly as he ought; that whosoever fails thereof in the smallest particular, violates my social right, and entitles me to demand from the legislature the removal of the grievance. So monstrous a principle is far more dangerous than any single interference with liberty; there is no violation of liberty which it would not justify; it acknowledges no right to any freedom whatever, except perhaps to that of holding opinions in secret, without ever disclosing them: for the moment an opinion which I consider noxious, passes any one's lips, it invades all the "social rights" attributed to me by the Alliance. The doctrine ascribes to all mankind a vested interest in each other's moral, intellectual, and even physical perfection, to be defined by each claimant according to his own standard.

Another important example of illegitimate interference with the rightful liberty of the individual, not simply threatened, but long since carried into triumphant effect, is Sabbatarian legislation. Without doubt, abstinence on one day in the week, so far as the exigencies of life permit, from the usual daily occupation, though in no respect religiously binding on any except Jews, is a highly beneficial custom. And inasmuch as this custom cannot be observed without a general consent to that effect among the industrious classes, therefore, in so far as some persons by working may impose the same necessity on others, it may be allowable and right that the law should guarantee to each, the observance by others of the custom, by suspending the greater operations of industry on a particular day. But this justification, grounded on the direct interest which others have in each individual's observance of the practice, does not apply to the self-chosen occupations in which a person may think fit to employ his leisure; nor does it hold good, in the smallest degree, for legal restrictions on amusements. It is true that the amusement of some is the day's work of others; but the pleasure, not to say the useful recreation, of many, is worth the labor of a few, provided the occupation is freely chosen, and can be freely resigned. The operatives are perfectly right in thinking that if all worked on Sunday seven days' work would have to be given for six days' wages: but so long as the great mass of employments are suspended, the small number who for the enjoyment of others must still work, obtain a proportional increase of earnings; and they are not obliged to follow those occupations, if they prefer leisure to emolument. If a further remedy is sought, it might be found in the establishment by custom of a holiday on some other day of the week for those particular classes of persons. The only ground, therefore, on which restrictions on Sunday amusements can be defended, must be that they are religiously wrong; a motive of legislation which never can be too earnestly protested again. "Deorum injuriæ Diis curæ." It remains to be proved that society or any of its officers holds a commission from on high to avenge any supposed offence to Omnipotence, which is not also a wrong to our fellow-creatures. The notion that it is one man's duty that another should be religious, was the foundation of all the religious persecutions ever perpetrated, and if admitted, would fully justify them. Though the feeling which breaks out in the repeated attempts to stop railway travelling on Sunday, in the resistance to the opening of Museums, and the like, has not the cruelty of the old persecutors, the state of mind indicated by it is fundamentally the same. It is a determination not to tolerate others in doing what is permitted by their religion, because it is not permitted by the persecutor's religion. It is a belief that God not only abominates the act of the misbeliever, but will not hold us guiltless if we leave him unmolested.

I cannot refrain from adding to these examples of the little account commonly made of human liberty, the language of downright persecution which breaks out from the press of this country, whenever it feels called on to notice the remarkable phenomenon of Mormonism. Much might be said on the unexpected and instructive fact, that an alleged new revelation, and a religion founded on it, the product of palpable imposture, not even supported by the *prestige* of extraordinary qualities in its founder, is believed by hundreds of thousands, and has been made the foundation of a society, in the age of newspapers, railways, and the electric telegraph. What here concerns us is, that this religion, like other and better religions, has its martyrs; that its prophet and founder was, for his teaching, put to death by a mob; that others of its adherents lost their lives by the same lawless violence; that they were forcibly expelled, in a body, from the country in which they first grew up; while, now that they have been chased into a solitary recess in the midst of a desert, many in this country openly declare that it would be right (only that it is not convenient) to send an expedition against them, and compel them by force to conform to the opinions of other people. The article of the Mormonite doctrine which is the chief provocative to the antipathy which thus breaks through the ordinary restraints of religious tolerance, is its sanction of polygamy; which, though permitted to Mahomedans, and Hindoos, and Chinese, seems to excite unquenchable animosity when practised by persons who speak English, and profess to be a kind of Christians. No one has a deeper disapprobation than I have of this Mormon institution; both for other reasons, and because, far from being in any way countenanced by the principle of liberty, it is a direct infraction of that principle, being a mere riveting of the chains of one half of the community, and an emancipation of the other from reciprocity of obligation towards them. Still, it must be remembered that this relation is as much voluntary on the part of the women concerned in it, and who may be deemed the sufferers by it, as is the case with any other form of the marriage institution; and however surprising this fact may appear, it has its explanation in the common ideas and customs of the world, which teaching women to think marriage the one thing needful, make it intelligible that many a woman should prefer being one of several wives, to not being a wife at all. Other countries are not asked to recognize such unions, or release any portion of their inhabitants from their own laws on the score of Mormonite opinions. But when the dissentients have conceded to the hostile sentiments of others, far more than could justly be demanded; when they have left the countries to which their doctrines were unacceptable, and established themselves in a remote corner of the earth, which they have been the first to render habitable to human beings; it is difficult to see on what principles but those of tyranny they can be prevented from living there under what laws they please, provided they commit no aggression on other nations, and allow perfect freedom of departure to those who are dissatisfied with their ways. A recent writer, in some respects of considerable merit, proposes (to use his own words) not a crusade, but a *civilizade,* against this polygamous community, to put an end to what seems to him a retrograde step in civilization. It also appears so to me, but I am not aware that any community has a right to force another to be civilized. So long as the sufferers by the bad law do not invoke assistance from other communities, I cannot admit that persons entirely unconnected with them ought to step in and require that a condition of things with which all who are directly interested appear to be satisfied, should be put an end to because it is a scandal to persons some thousands of miles distant, who have no part or concern in it. Let them send missionaries, if they please, to preach against it; and let them, by any fair means (of which silencing the teachers is not one), oppose the progress of similar doctrines among their own people. If civilization has got the better of barbarism when barbarism had the world to itself, it is too much to profess to be afraid lest barbarism, after having been fairly got under, should revive and conquer civilization. A civilization that can thus succumb to its vanquished enemy must first have become so degenerate, that neither its appointed priests and teachers, nor anybody else, has the capacity, or will take the trouble, to stand up for it. If this be so, the sooner such a civilization receives notice to quit, the better. It can only go on from bad to worse, until destroyed and regenerated (like the Western Empire) by energetic barbarians.

CHAPTER 5 *Applications*

The principles asserted in these pages must be more generally admitted as the basis for discussion of details, before a consistent application of them to all the various departments of government and morals can be attempted with any prospect of advantage. The few observations I propose to make on questions of detail, are designed to illustrate the principles, rather than to follow them out to their consequences. I offer, not so much applications, as specimens of application; which may serve to bring into greater clearness the meaning and limits of the two maxims which together form the entire doctrine of this Essay, and to assist the judgment in holding the balance between them, in the cases where it appears doubtful which of them is applicable to the case.

The maxims are, first, that the individual is not accountable to society for his actions, in so far as these concern the interests of no person but himself. Advice, instruction, persuasion, and avoidance by other people, if thought necessary by them for their own good, are the only measures by which society can justifiably express its dislike or disapprobation of his conduct. Secondly, that for such actions as are prejudicial to the interests of others, the individual is accountable, and may be subjected either to social or to legal punishments, if society is of opinion that the one or the other is requisite for its protection.

In the first place, it must by no means be supposed, because damage, or probability of damage, to the interests of others, can alone justify the interference of society, that therefore it always does justify such interference. In many cases, an individual, in pursuing a legitimate object, necessarily and therefore legitimately causes pain or loss to others, or intercepts a good which they had a reasonable hope of obtaining. Such oppositions of interest between individuals often arise from bad social institutions, but are unavoidable while those institutions last; and some would be unavoidable under any institutions. Whoever succeeds in an overcrowded profession, or in a competitive examination; whoever is preferred to another in any contest for an object which both desire, reaps benefit from the loss of others, from their wasted exertion and their disappointment. But it is, by common admission, better for the general interest of mankind, that persons should pursue their objects undeterred by this sort of consequences. In other words, society admits no right, either legal or moral, in the disappointed competitors, to immunity from this kind of suffering; and feels called on to interfere, only when means of success have been employed which it is contrary to the general interest to permit—namely, fraud or treachery, and force.

Again, trade is a social act. Whoever undertakes to sell any description of goods to the public, does what affects the interest of other persons, and of society in general; and thus his conduct, in principle, comes within the jurisdiction of society: accordingly, it was once held to be the duty of governments, in all cases which were considered of importance, to fix prices, and regulate the processes of manufacture. But it is now recognized, though not till after a long struggle, that both the cheapness and the good quality of commodities are most effectually provided for by leaving the producers and sellers perfectly free, under the sole check of equal freedom to the buyers for supplying themselves elsewhere. This is the so-called doctrine of Free Trade, which rests on grounds different from, though equally solid with, the principle of individual liberty asserted in this Essay. Restrictions on trade, or on production for purposes of trade, are indeed restraints; and all restraint, *quâ* restraint, is an evil: but the restraints in question affect only that part of conduct which society is competent to restrain, and are wrong solely because they do not really produce the results which it is desired to produce by them. As the principle of individual liberty is not involved in the doctrine of Free Trade, so neither is it in most of the questions which arise respecting the limits of that doctrine: as for example, what amount of public control is admissible for the prevention of fraud by adulteration; how far sanitary precautions, or arrangements to protect work-people employed in dangerous occupations, should be enforced on employers. Such questions involve considerations of liberty, only in so far as leaving people to themselves is always better, *cæteris paribus,* than controlling them: but that they may be legitimately controlled for these ends, is in principle undeniable. On the other hand, there are questions relating to interference with trade, which are essentially questions of liberty; such as the Maine Law, already touched upon; the prohibition of the importation of opium into China; the restriction of the sale of poisons; all cases, in short, where the object of the interference is to make it impossible or difficult to obtain a particular commodity. These interferences are objectionable, not as infringements on the liberty of the producer or seller, but on that of the buyer.

One of these examples, that of the sale of poisons, opens a new question; the proper limits of what may be called the functions of police; how far liberty may legitimately be invaded for the prevention of crime, or of accident. It is one of the undisputed functions of government to take precautions against crime before it has been committed, as well as to detect and punish it afterwards. The preventive function of government, however, is far more liable to be abused, to the prejudice of liberty, than the punitory function; for there is hardly any part of the legitimate freedom of action of a human being which would not admit of being represented, and fairly too, as increasing the facilities for some form or other of delinquency. Nevertheless, if a public authority, or even a private person, sees any one evidently preparing to commit a crime, they are not bound to look on inactive until the crime is committed, but may interfere to prevent it. If poisons were never bought or used for any purpose except the commission of murder, it would be right to prohibit their manufacture and sale. They may, however, be wanted not only for innocent but for useful purposes, and restrictions cannot be imposed in the one case without operating in the other. Again, it is a proper office of public authority to guard against accidents. If either a public officer or any one else saw a person attempting to cross a bridge which had been ascertained to be unsafe, and there were no time to warn him of his danger, they might seize him and turn him back, without any real infringement of his liberty; for liberty consists in doing what one desires, and he does not desire to fall into the river. Nevertheless, when there is not a certainty, but only a danger of mischief, no one but the person himself can judge of the sufficiency of the motive which may prompt him to incur the risk: in this case, therefore (unless he is a child, or delirious, or in some state of excitement or absorption incompatible with the full use of the reflecting faculty), he ought, I conceive, to be only warned of the danger; not forcibly prevented from exposing himself to it. Similar considerations, applied to such a question as the sale of poisons, may enable us to decide which among the possible modes of regulation are or are not contrary to principle. Such a precaution, for example, as that of labelling the drug with some word expressive of its dangerous character, may be enforced without violation of liberty: the buyer cannot wish not to know that the thing he possesses has poisonous qualities. But to require in all cases the certificate of a medical practitioner, would make it sometimes impossible, always expensive, to obtain the article for legitimate uses. The only mode apparent to me, in which difficulties may be thrown in the way of crime committed through this means, without any infringement, worth taking into account, upon the liberty of those who desire the poisonous substance for other purposes, consists in providing what, in the apt language of Bentham, is called "preappointed evidence." This provision is familiar to every one in the case of contracts. It is usual and right that the law, when a contract is entered into, should require as the condition of its enforcing performance, that certain formalities should be observed, such as signatures, attestation of witnesses, and the like, in order that in case of subsequent dispute, there may be evidence to prove that the contract was really entered into, and that there was nothing in the circumstances to render it legally invalid: the effect being, to throw great obstacles in the way of fictitious contracts, or contracts made in circumstances which, if known, would destroy their validity. Precautions of a similar nature might be enforced in the sale of articles adapted to be instruments of crime. The seller, for example, might be required to enter in a register the exact time of the transaction, the name and address of the buyer, the precise quality and quantity sold; to ask the purpose for which it was wanted, and record the answer he received. When there was no medical prescription, the presence of some third person might be required, to bring home the fact to the purchaser, in case there should afterwards be reason to believe that the article had been applied to criminal purposes. Such regulations would in general be no material impediment to obtaining the article, but a very considerable one to making an improper use of it without detection.

The right inherent in society, to ward off crimes against itself by antecedent precautions, suggests the obvious limitations to the maxim, that purely self-regarding misconduct cannot properly be meddled with in the way of prevention or punishment. Drunkenness, for example, in ordinary cases, is not a fit subject for legislative interference; but I should deem it perfectly legitimate that a person, who had once been convicted of any act of violence to others under the influence of drink, should be placed under a special legal restriction, personal to himself; that if he were afterwards found drunk, he should be liable to a penalty, and that if when in that state he committed another offence, the punishment to which he would be liable for that other offence should be increased in severity. The making himself drunk, in a person whom drunkenness excites to do harm to others, is a crime against others. So, again, idleness, except in a person receiving support from the public, or except when it constitutes a breach on contract, cannot without tyranny be made a subject of legal punishment; but if either from idleness or from any other avoidable cause, a man fails to perform his legal duties to others, as for instance to support his children, it is no tyranny to force him to fulfil that obligation, by compulsory labor, if no other means are available.

Again, there are many acts which, being directly injurious only to the agents themselves, ought not to be legally interdicted, but which, if done publicly, are a violation of good manners, and coming thus within the category of offences against others, may rightfully be prohibited. Of this kind are offences against decency; on which it is unnecessary to dwell, the rather as they are only connected indirectly with our subject, the objection to publicity being equally strong in the case of many actions not in themselves condemnable, nor supposed to be so.

There is another question to which an answer must be found, consistent with the principles which have been laid down. In cases of personal conduct supposed to be blameable, but which respect for liberty precludes society from preventing or punishing, because the evil directly resulting falls wholly on the agent; what the agent is free to do, ought other persons to be equally free to counsel or instigate? This question is not free from difficulty. The case of a person who solicits another to do an act, is not strictly a case of self-regarding conduct. To give advice or offer inducements to any one, is a social act, and may therefore, like actions in general which affect others, be supposed amenable to social control. But a little reflection corrects the first impression, by showing that if the case is not strictly within the definition of individual liberty, yet the reasons on which the principle of individual liberty is grounded, are applicable to it. If people must be allowed, in whatever concerns only themselves, to act as seems best to themselves at their own peril, they must equally be free to consult with one another about what is fit to be so done; to exchange opinions, and give and receive suggestions. Whatever it is permitted to do, it must be permitted to advise to do. The question is doubtful, only when the instigator derives a personal benefit from his advice; when he makes it his occupation, for subsistence or pecuniary gain, to promote what society and the State consider to be an evil. Then, indeed, a new element of complication is introduced; namely, the existence of classes of persons with an interest opposed to what is considered as the public weal, and whose mode of living is grounded on the counteraction of it. Ought this to be interfered with, or not? Fornication, for example, must be tolerated, and so must gambling; but should a person be free to be a pimp, or to keep a gambling-house? The case is one of those which lie on the exact boundary line between two principles, and it is not at once apparent to which of the two it properly belongs. There are arguments on both sides. On the side of toleration it may be said, that the fact of following anything as an occupation, and living or profiting by the practice of it, cannot make that criminal which would otherwise be admissible; that the act should either be consistently permitted or consistently prohibited; that if the principles which we have hitherto defended are true, society has no business, *as* society, to decide anything to be wrong which concerns only the individual; that it cannot go beyond dissuasion, and that one person should be as free to persuade, as another to dissuade. In opposition to this it may be contended, that although the public, or the State, are not warranted in authoritatively deciding, for purposes of repression or punishment, that such or such conduct affecting only the interests of the individual is good or bad, they are fully justified in assuming, if they regard it as bad, that its being so or not is at least a disputable question: That, this being supposed, they cannot be acting wrongly in endeavoring to exclude the influence of solicitations which are not disinterested, of instigators who cannot possibly be impartial—who have a direct personal interest on one side, and that side the one which the State believes to be wrong, and who confessedly promote it for personal objects only. There can surely, it may be urged, be nothing lost, no sacrifice of good, by so ordering matters that persons shall make their election, either wisely or foolishly, on their own prompting, as free as possible from the arts of persons who stimulate their inclinations for interested purposes of their own. Thus (it may be said) though the statutes respecting unlawful games are utterly indefensible—though all persons should be free to gamble in their own or each other's houses, or in any place of meeting established by their own subscriptions, and open only to the members and their visitors—yet public gambling-houses should not be permitted. It is true that the prohibition is never effectual, and that whatever amount of tyrannical power is given to the police, gambling-houses can always be maintained under other pretences but they may be compelled to conduct their operations with a certain degree of secrecy and mystery, so that nobody knows anything about them but those who seek them; and more than this, society ought not to aim at. There is considerable force in these arguments. I will not venture to decide whether they are sufficient to justify the moral anomaly of punishing the accessary, when the principal is (and must be) allowed to go free; of fining or imprisoning the procurer, but not the fornicator, the gambling-house keeper, but not the gambler. Still less ought the common operations of buying and selling to be interfered with on analogous grounds. Almost every article which is bought and sold may be used in excess, and the sellers have a pecuniary interest in encouraging that excess; but no argument can be founded on this, in favor, for instance, of the Maine Law; because the class of dealers in strong drinks, though interested in their abuse, are indispensably required for the sake of their legitimate use. The interest, however, of these dealers in promoting intemperance is a real evil, and justifies the State in imposing restrictions and requiring guarantees which but for that justification would be infringements of legitimate liberty.

A further question is, whether the State, while it permits, should nevertheless indirectly discourage conduct which it deems contrary to the best interests of the agent; whether, for example, it should take measures to render the means of drunkenness more costly, or add to the difficulty of procuring them, by limiting the number of the places of sale. On this as on most other practical questions, many distinctions require to be made. To tax stimulants for the sole purpose of making them more difficult to be obtained, is a measure differing only in degree from their entire prohibition; and would be justifiable only if that were justifiable. Every increase of cost is a prohibition, to those whose means do not come up to the augmented price; and to those who do, it is a penalty laid on them for gratifying a particular taste. Their choice of pleasures, and their mode of expending their income, after satisfying their legal and moral obligations to the State and to individuals, are their own concern, and must rest with their own judgment. These considerations may seem at first sight to condemn the selection of stimulants as special subjects of taxation for purposes of revenue. But it must be remembered that taxation for fiscal purposes is absolutely inevitable; that in most countries it is necessary that a considerable part of that taxation should be indirect; that the State, therefore, cannot help imposing penalties, which to some persons may be prohibitory, on the use of some articles of consumption. It is hence the duty of the State to consider, in the imposition of taxes, what commodities the consumers can best spare; and *à fortiori,* to select in preference those of which it deems the use, beyond a very moderate quantity, to be positively injurious. Taxation, therefore, of stimulants, up to the point which produces the largest amount of revenue (supposing that the State needs all the revenue which it yields) is not only admissible, but to be approved of.

The question of making the sale of these commodities a more or less exclusive privilege, must be answered differently, according to the purposes to which the restriction is intended to be subservient. All places of public resort require the restraint of a police, and places of this kind peculiarly, because offences against society are especially apt to originate there. It is, therefore, fit to confine the power of selling these commodities (at least for consumption on the spot) to persons of known or vouched-for respectability of conduct; to make such regulations respecting hours of opening and closing as may be requisite for public surveillance, and to withdraw the license if breaches of the peace repeatedly take place through the connivance or incapacity of the keeper of the house, or if it becomes a rendezvous for concocting and preparing offences against the law. Any further restriction I do not conceive to be, in principle, justifiable. The limitation in number, for instance, of beer and spirit-houses, for the express purpose of rendering them more difficult of access, and diminishing the occasions of temptation, not only exposes all to an inconvenience because there are some by whom the facility would be abused, but is suited only to a state of society in which the laboring classes are avowedly treated as children or savages, and placed under an education of restraint, to fit them for future admission to the privileges of freedom. This is not the principle on which the laboring classes are professedly governed in any free country; and no person who sets due value on freedom will give his adhesion to their being so governed, unless after all efforts have been exhausted to educate them for freedom and govern them as freemen, and it has been definitely proved that they can only be governed as children. The bare statement of the alternative shows the absurdity of supposing that such efforts have been made in any case which needs be considered here. It is only because the institutions of this country are a mass of inconsistencies, that things find admittance into our practice which belong to the system of despotic, or what is called paternal, government, while the general freedom of our institutions precludes the exercise of the amount of control necessary to render the restraint of any real efficacy as a moral education.

It was pointed out in an early part of this Essay, that the liberty of the individual, in things wherein the individual is alone concerned, implies a corresponding liberty in any number of individuals to regulate by mutual agreement such things as regard them jointly, and regard no persons but themselves. This question presents no difficulty, so long as the will of all the persons implicated remains unaltered; but since that will may change, it is often necessary, even in things in which they alone are concerned, that they should enter into engagements with one another; and when they do, it is fit, as a general rule, that those engagements should be kept. Yet in the laws, probably, of every country, this general rule has some exceptions. Not only persons are not held to engagements which violate the rights of third parties, but it is sometimes considered a sufficient reason for releasing them from an engagement, that it is injurious to themselves. In this and most other civilized countries, for example, an engagement by which a person should sell himself, or allow himself to be sold, as a slave, would be null and void; neither enforced by law nor by opinion. The ground for thus limiting his power of voluntarily disposing of his own lot in life, is apparent, and is very clearly seen in this extreme case. The reason for not interfering, unless for the sake of others, with a person's voluntary acts, is consideration for his liberty. His voluntary choice is evidence that what he so chooses is desirable, or at the least endurable, to him, and his good is on the whole best provided for by allowing him to take his own means of pursuing it. But by selling himself for a slave, he abdicates his liberty; he foregoes any future use of it, beyond that single act. He therefore defeats, in his own case, the very purpose which is the justification of allowing him to dispose of himself. He is no longer free; but is thenceforth in a position which has no longer the presumption in its favor, that would be afforded by his voluntarily remaining in it. The principle of freedom cannot require that he should be free not to be free. It is not freedom, to be allowed to alienate his freedom. These reasons, the force of which is so conspicuous in this peculiar case, are evidently of far wider application; yet a limit is everywhere set to them by the necessities of life, which continually require, not indeed that we should resign our freedom, but that we should consent to this and the other limitation of it. The principle, however, which demands uncontrolled freedom of action in all that concerns only the agents themselves, requires that those who have become bound to one another, in things which concern no third party, should be able to release one another from the engagement: and even without such voluntary release, there are perhaps no contracts or engagements, except those that relate to money or money's worth, of which one can venture to say that there ought to be no liberty whatever of retractation. Baron Wilhelm von Humboldt, in the excellent Essay from which I have already quoted, states it as his conviction, that engagements which involve personal relations or services, should never be legally binding beyond a limited duration of time; and that the most important of these engagements, marriage, having the peculiarity that its objects are frustrated unless the feelings of both the parties are in harmony with it, should require nothing more than the declared will of either party to dissolve it. This subject is too important, and too complicated, to be discussed in a parenthesis, and I touch on it only so far as is necessary for purposes of illustration. If the conciseness and generality of Baron Humboldt's dissertation had not obliged him in this instance to content himself with enunciating his conclusion without discussing the premises, he would doubtless have recognized that the question cannot be decided on grounds so simple as those to which he confines himself. When a person, either by express promise or by conduct, has encouraged another to rely upon his continuing to act in a certain way—to build expectations and calculations, and stake any part of his plan of life upon that supposition, a new series of moral obligations arises on his part towards that person, which may possibly be overruled, but cannot be ignored. And again, if the relation between two contracting parties has been followed by consequences to others; if it has placed third parties in any peculiar position, or, as in the case of marriage, has even called third parties into existence, obligations arise on the part of both the contracting parties towards those third persons, the fulfilment of which, or at all events the mode of fulfilment, must be greatly affected by the continuance or disruption of the relation between the original parties to the contract. It does not follow, nor can I admit, that these obligations extend to requiring

the fulfilment of the contract at all costs to the happiness of
the reluctant party; but they are a necessary element in the
question; and even if, as Von Humboldt maintains, they
ought to make no difference in the *legal* freedom of the parties to release themselves from the engagement (and I also
hold that they ought not to make *much* difference), they
necessarily make a great difference in the *moral* freedom. A
person is bound to take all these circumstances into account,
before resolving on a step which may affect such important
interests of others; and if he does not allow proper weight to
those interests, he is morally responsible for the wrong. I
have made these obvious remarks for the better illustration of
the general principle of liberty, and not because they are at
all needed on the particular question, which, on the contrary,
is usually discussed as if the interest of children was everything, and that of grown persons nothing.

I have already observed that, owing to the absence of any
recognized general principles, liberty is often granted where it
should be withheld, as well as withheld where it should be
granted; and one of the cases in which, in the modern European world, the sentiment of liberty is the strongest, is a
case where, in my view, it is altogether misplaced. A person
should be free to do as he likes in his own concerns; but he
ought not to be free to do as he likes in acting for another
under the pretext that the affairs of another are his own
affairs. The State, while it respects the liberty of each in
what specially regards himself, is bound to maintain a vig-
ilant control over his exercise of any power which it allows
him to possess over others. This obligation is almost entirely disregarded in the case of the family relations, a case,
in its direct influence on human happiness, more important
than all others taken together. The almost despotic power of
husbands over wives needs not be enlarged upon here, because nothing more is needed for the complete removal of
the evil, than that wives should have the same rights, and
should receive the protection of law in the same manner, as

all other persons; and because, on this subject, the defenders of established injustice do not avail themselves of the plea of liberty, but stand forth openly as the champions of power. It is in the case of children, that misapplied notions of liberty are a real obstacle to the fulfilment by the State of its duties. One would almost think that a man's children were supposed to be literally, and not metaphorically, a part of himself, so jealous is opinion of the smallest interference of law with his absolute and exclusive control over them; more jealous than of almost any interference with his own freedom of action: so much less do the generality of mankind value liberty than power. Consider, for example, the case of education. Is it not almost a self-evident axiom, that the State should require and compel the education, up to a certain standard, of every human being who is born its citizen? Yet who is there that is not afraid to recognize and assert this truth? Hardly any one indeed will deny that it is one of the most sacred duties of the parents (or, as law and usage now stand, the father), after summoning a human being into the world, to give to that being an education fitting him to perform his part well in life towards others and towards himself. But while this is unanimously declared to be the father's duty, scarcely anybody, in this country, will bear to hear of obliging him to perform it. Instead of his being required to make any exertion or sacrifice for securing education to the child, it is left to his choice to accept it or not when it is provided gratis! It still remains unrecognized, that to bring a child into existence without a fair prospect of being able, not only to provide food for its body, but instruction and training for its mind, is a moral crime, both against the unfortunate offspring and against society; and that if the parent does not fulfil this obligation, the State ought to see it fulfilled at the charge, as far as possible, of the parent.

Were the duty of enforcing universal education once admitted, there would be an end to the difficulties about what the State should teach, and how it should teach, which now convert the subject into a mere battle-field for sects and parties, causing the time and labor which should have been spent in educating, to be wasted in quarrelling about education. If the government would make up its mind to *require* for every child a good education, it might save itself the trouble of *providing* one. It might leave to parents to obtain the education where and how they pleased, and content itself with helping to pay the school fees of the poorer classes of children, and defraying the entire school expenses of those who have no one else to pay for them. The objections which are urged with reason against State education, do not apply to the enforcement of education by the State, but to the State's taking upon itself to direct that education: which is a totally different thing. That the whole or any large part of the education of the people should be in State hands, I go as far as any one in deprecating. All that has been said of the importance of individuality of character, and diversity in opinions and modes of conduct, involves, as of the same unspeakable importance, diversity of education. A general State education is a mere contrivance for moulding people to be exactly like one another: and as the mould in which it casts them is that which pleases the predominant power in the government, whether this be a monarch, a priesthood, an aristocracy, or the majority of the existing generation, in proportion as it is efficient and successful, it establishes a despotism over the mind, leading by natural tendency to one over the body. An education established and controlled by the State, should only exist, if it exist at all, as one among many competing experiments, carried on for the purpose of example and stimulus, to keep the others up to a certain standard of excellence. Unless, indeed, when society in general is in so backward a state that it could not or would not provide for itself any proper institutions of education, unless the government undertook the task; then, indeed, the government may, as the less of two great evils, take upon itself the business of schools and universities, as it may that of joint-stock companies, when private enterprise, in a shape fitted for undertaking great works of industry does not exist in the country. But in general, if the country contains a sufficient number of persons qualified to provide education under government auspices, the same persons would be able and willing to give an equally good education on the voluntary principle, under the assurance of remuneration afforded by a law rendering education compulsory, combined with State aid to those unable to defray the expense.

The instrument for enforcing the law could be no other than public examinations, extending to all children, and beginning at an early age. An age might be fixed at which every child must be examined, to ascertain if he (or she) is able to read. If a child proves unable, the father, unless he has some sufficient ground of excuse, might be subjected to a moderate fine, to be worked out, if necessary, by his labor, and the child might be put to school at his expense. Once in every year the examination should be renewed, with a gradually extending range of subjects, so as to make the universal acquisition, and what is more, retention, of a certain minimum of general knowledge, virtually compulsory. Beyond that minimum, there should be voluntary examinations on all subjects, at which all who come up to a certain standard of proficiency might claim a certificate. To prevent the State from exercising through these arrangements, an improper influence over opinion, the knowledge required for passing an examination (beyond the merely instrumental parts of knowledge, such as languages and their use) should, even in the higher class of examinations, be confined to facts and positive science exclusively. The examinations on religion, politics, or other disputed topics, should not turn on the truth or falsehood of opinions, but on the matter of fact that such and such an opinion is held, on such grounds, by such authors, or schools, or churches. Under this system, the rising generation would be no worse off in regard to all disputed truths, than they are at present; they would be brought up either churchmen or dissenters as they now are, the State merely taking care that they should be instructed churchmen, or instructed dissenters. There would be nothing to hinder them from being taught religion, if their parents chose, at the same schools where they were taught other things. All attempts by the State to bias the conclusions of its citizens on disputed subjects, are evil; but it may very properly offer to ascertain and certify that a person possesses the knowledge, requisite to make his conclusions, on any given subject, worth attending to. A student of philosophy would be the better for being able to stand an examination both in Locke and in Kant, whichever of the two he takes up with, or even if with neither: and there is no reasonable objection to examining an atheist in the evidences of Christianity, provided he is not required to profess a belief in them. The examinations, however, in the higher branches of knowledge should, I conceive, be entirely voluntary. It would be giving too dangerous a power to governments, were they allowed to exclude any one from professions, even from the profession of teacher, for alleged deficiency of qualifications: and I think, with Wilhelm von Humboldt, that degrees, or other public certificates of scientific or professional acquirements, should be given to all who present themselves for examination, and stand the test; but that such certificates should confer no advantage over competitors, other than the weight which may be attached to their testimony by public opinion.

It is not in the matter of education only, that misplaced notions of liberty prevent moral obligations on the part of parents from being recognized, and legal obligations from being imposed, where there are the strongest grounds for the former always, and in many cases for the latter also. The fact itself, of causing the existence of a human being, is one of the most responsible actions in the range of human life. To undertake this responsibility—to bestow a life which may be either a curse or a blessing—unless the being on whom it is to be bestowed will have at least the ordinary chances of a desirable existence, is a crime against that being. And in a country either over-peopled, or threatened with being so, to produce children, beyond a very small number, with the effect of reducing the reward of labor by their competition, is a serious offence against all who live by the remuneration of their labor. The laws which, in many countries on the Continent, forbid marriage unless the parties can show that they have the means of supporting a family, do not exceed the legitimate powers of the State: and whether such laws be expedient or not (a question mainly dependent on local circumstances and feelings), they are not objectionable as violations of liberty. Such laws are interferences of the State to prohibit a mischievous act—an act injurious to others, which ought to be a subject of reprobation, and social stigma, even when it is not deemed expedient to superadd legal punishment. Yet the current ideas of liberty, which bend so easily to real infringements of the freedom of the individual, in things which concern only himself, would repel the attempt to put any restraint upon his inclinations when the consequence of their indulgence is a life, or lives, of wretchedness and depravity to the offspring, with manifold evils to those sufficiently within reach to be in any way affected by their actions. When we compare the strange respect of mankind for liberty, with their strange want of respect for it, we might imagine that a man had an indispensable right to do harm to others, and no right at all to please himself without giving pain to any one.

I have reserved for the last place a large class of questions respecting the limits of government interference, which, though closely connected with the subject of this Essay, do not, in strictness, belong to it. These are cases in which the reasons against interference do not turn upon the principle of liberty: the question is not about restraining the actions of individuals, but about helping them: it is asked whether the government should do, or cause to be done, something for their benefit, instead of leaving it to be done by themselves, individually, or in voluntary combination.

The objections to government interference, when it is not such as to involve infringement of liberty, may be of three kinds.

The first is, when the thing to be done is likely to be better done by individuals than by the government. Speaking generally, there is no one so fit to conduct any business, or to determine how or by whom it shall be conducted, as those who are personally interested in it. This principle condemns the interferences, once so common, of the legislature, or the officers of government, with the ordinary processes of industry. But this part of the subject has been sufficiently enlarged upon by political economists, and is not particularly related to the principles of this Essay.

The second objection is more nearly allied to our subject. In many cases, though individuals may not do the particular thing so well, on the average, as the officers of government, it is nevertheless desirable that it should be done by them, rather than by the government, as a means to their own mental education—a mode of strengthening their active faculties, exercising their judgment, and giving them a familiar knowledge of the subjects with which they are thus left to deal. This is a principal, though not the sole, recommendation of jury trial (in cases not political); of free and popular local and municipal institutions; of the conduct of industrial and philanthropic enterprises by voluntary associations. These are not questions of liberty, and are connected with that subject only by remote tendencies; but they are questions of development. It belongs to a different occasion from the present to dwell on these things as parts of national education; as being, in truth, the peculiar training of a citizen, the practical part of the political education of a free people, taking them out of the narrow circle of personal and family selfishness, and accustoming them to the comprehension of joint interests, the management of joint concerns—habituating them to act from public or semi-public motives, and guide their conduct by aims which unite instead of isolating them from one another. Without these habits and powers, a free constitution can neither be worked nor preserved, as is exemplified by the too-often transitory nature of political freedom in countries where it does not rest upon a sufficient basis of local liberties. The management of purely local business by the localities, and of the great enterprises of industry by the union of those who voluntarily supply the pecuniary means, is further recommended by all the advantages which have been set forth in this Essay as belonging to individuality of development, and diversity of modes of action. Government operations tend to be everywhere alike. With individuals and voluntary associations, on the contrary, there are varied experiments, and endless diversity of experience. What the State can usefully do, is to make itself a central depository, and active circulator and diffuser, of the experience resulting from many trials. Its business is to enable each experimentalist to benefit by the experiments of others, instead of tolerating no experiments but its own.

The third, and most cogent reason for restricting the interference of government, is the great evil of adding unnecessarily to its power. Every function superadded to those already exercised by the government, causes its influence over hopes and fears to be more widely diffused, and converts, more and more, the active and ambitious part of the public into hangers-on of the government, or of some party which aims at becoming the government. If the roads, the railways, the banks, the insurance offices, the great joint-stock companies, the universities, and the public charities, were all of them branches of the government; if, in addition, the municipal corporations and local boards, with all that now devolves on them, became departments of the central administration; if the employés of all these different enterprises were appointed and paid by the government, and looked to the government for every rise in life; not all the freedom of the press and popular constitution of the legislature would make this or any other country free otherwise than in name. And the evil would be greater, the more efficiently and scientifically the administrative machinery was constructed—the more skilful the arrangements for obtaining the best qualified hands and heads with which to work it. In England it has of late been proposed that all the members of the civil service of government should be selected by competitive examination, to obtain for those employments the most intelligent and instructed persons procurable; and much has been said and written for and against this proposal. One of the arguments most insisted on by its opponents, is that the occupation of a permanent official servant of the State does not hold out sufficient prospects of emolument and importance to attract the highest talents, which will always be able to find a more inviting career in the professions, or in the service of companies and other public bodies. One would not have been surprised if this argument had been used by the friends of the proposition, as an answer to its principal difficulty. Coming from the opponents it is strange enough. What is urged as an objection is the safety-valve of the proposed system. If indeed all the high talent of the country *could* be drawn into the service of the government, a proposal tending to bring about that result might well inspire uneasiness. If every part of the business of society which required organized concert, or large and comprehensive views, were in the hands of the government, and if government offices were universally filled by the ablest men, all the enlarged culture and practised intelligence in the country, except the purely speculative, would be concentrated in a numerous bureaucracy, to whom alone the rest of the community would look for all things: the multitude for direction and dictation in all they had to do; the able and aspiring for personal advancement. To be admitted into the ranks of this bureaucracy, and when admitted, to rise therein, would be the sole objects of ambition. Under this régime, not only is the outside public ill-qualified, for want of practical experience, to criticize or check the mode of operation of the bureaucracy, but even if the accidents of despotic or the natural working of popular institutions occasionally raise to the summit a ruler or rulers of reforming inclinations, no reform can be effected which is contrary to the interest of the bureaucracy. Such is the melancholy condition of the Russian empire, as is shown in the accounts of those who have had sufficient opportunity of observation. The Czar himself is powerless against the bureaucratic body; he can send any one of them to Siberia, but he cannot govern without them, or against their will. On every decree of his they have a tacit veto, by merely refraining from carrying it into effect. In countries of more advanced civilization and of a more insurrectionary spirit, the public, accustomed to expect everything to be done for them by the State, or at least to do nothing for themselves without asking from the State not only leave to do it, but even how it is to be done, naturally hold the State responsible for all evil which befalls them, and when the evil exceeds their amount of patience, they rise against the government and make what is called a revolution; whereupon somebody else, with or without legitimate authority from the nation, vaults into the seat, issues his orders to the bureaucracy, and everything goes on much as it did before; the bureaucracy being unchanged, and nobody else being capable of taking their place.

A very different spectacle is exhibited among a people accustomed to transact their own business. In France, a large part of the people having been engaged in military service, many of whom have held at least the rank of non-commissioned officers, there are in every popular insurrection several persons competent to take the lead, and improvise some tolerable plan of action. What the French are in military affairs, the Americans are in every kind of civil business; let them be left without a government, every body of Americans is able to improvise one, and to carry on that or any other public business with a sufficient amount of intelligence, order, and decision. This is what every free people ought to be: and a people capable of this is certain to be free; it will never let itself be enslaved by any man or body of men because these are able to seize and pull the reins of the central administration. No bureaucracy can hope to make such a people as this do or undergo anything that they do not like. But where everything is done through the bureaucracy, nothing to which the bureaucracy is really adverse can be done at all. The constitution of such countries is an organization of the experience and practical ability of the nation, into a disciplined body for the purpose of governing the rest; and the more perfect that organization is in itself, the more successful in drawing to itself and educating for itself the persons of greatest capacity from all ranks of the community, the more complete is the bondage of all, the members of the bureaucracy included. For the governors are as much the slaves of their organization and discipline, as the governed are of the governors. A Chinese mandarin is as much the tool and creature of a despotism as the humblest cultivator. An individual Jesuit is to the utmost degree of abasement the slave of his order, though the order itself exists for the collective power and importance of its members.

It is not, also, to be forgotten, that the absorption of all the principal ability of the country into the governing body is fatal, sooner or later, to the mental activity and progressiveness of the body itself. Banded together as they are—working a system which, like all systems, necessarily proceeds in a great measure by fixed rules—the official body are under the constant temptation of sinking into indolent routine, or, if they now and then desert that mill-horse round, of rushing into some half-examined crudity which has struck the fancy of some leading member of the corps: and the sole check to these closely allied, though seemingly opposite, tendencies, the only stimulus which can keep the ability of the body itself up to a high standard, is liability to the watchful criticism of equal ability outside the body. It is indispensable, therefore, that the means should exist, independently of the government, of forming such ability, and furnishing it with the opportunities and experience necessary for a correct judgment of great practical affairs. If we would possess permanently a skilful and efficient body of functionaries—above all, a body able to originate and willing to adopt improvements; if we would not have our bureaucracy degenerate into a pedantocracy, this body must not engross all the occupations which form and cultivate the faculties required for the government of mankind.

To determine the point at which evils, so formidable to human freedom and advancement, begin, or rather at which they begin to predominate over the benefits attending the collective application of the force of society, under its recognized chiefs, for the removal of the obstacles which stand in the way of its well-being, to secure as much of the advantages of centralized power and intelligence, as can be had without turning into governmental channels too great a proportion of the general activity, is one of the most difficult and complicated questions in the art of government. It is, in a great measure, a question of detail, in which many and various considerations must be kept in view, and no absolute rule can be laid down. But I believe that the practical principle in which safety resides, the ideal to be kept in view, the standard by which to test all arrangements intended for overcoming the difficulty, may be conveyed in these words: the greatest dissemination of power consistent with efficiency; but the greatest possible centralization of information, and diffusion of it from the centre. Thus, in municipal administration, there would be, as in the New England States, a very minute division among separate officers, chosen by the localities, of all business which is not better left to the persons directly interested; but besides this, there would be, in each department of local affairs, a central superintendence, forming a branch of the general government. The organ of this superintendence would concentrate, as in a focus, the variety of information and experience derived from the conduct of that branch of public business in all the localities, from everything analogous which is done in foreign countries, and from the general principles of political science. This central organ should have a right to know all that is done, and its special duty should be that of making the knowledge acquired in one place available for others. Emancipated from the petty prejudices and narrow views of a locality by its elevated position and comprehensive sphere of observation, its advice would naturally carry much authority; but its actual power, as a permanent institution, should, I conceive, be limited to compelling the local officers to obey the laws laid down for their guidance. In all things not provided for by general rules, those officers should be left to their own judgment, under responsibility to their constituents. For the violation of rules, they should be responsible to law, and the rules themselves should be laid down by the legislature; the central administrative authority only watching over their execution, and if they were not properly carried into effect, appealing, according to the nature of the case, to the tribunal to enforce the law, or to the constituencies to dismiss the functionaries who had not executed it according to its spirit. Such, in its general conception, is the central superintendence which the Poor Law Board is intended to exercise over the administrators of the Poor Rate throughout the country. Whatever powers the Board exercises beyond this limit, were right and necessary in that peculiar case, for the cure of rooted habits of mal-administration in matters deeply affecting not the localities merely, but the whole community; since no locality has a moral right to make itself by mismanagement a nest of pauperism, necessarily overflowing into other localities, and impairing the moral and physical condition of the whole laboring community. The powers of administrative coercion and subordinate legislation possessed by the Poor Law Board (but which, owing to the state of opinion on the subject, are very scantily exercised by them), though perfectly justifiable in a case of a first-rate national interest, would be wholly out of place in the superintendence of interests purely local. But a central organ of information and instruction for all the localities, would be equally valuable in all departments of administration. A government cannot have too much of the kind of activity which does not impede, but aids and stimulates, individual exertion and development. The mischief begins when, instead of calling forth the activity and powers of individuals and bodies, it substitutes its own activity for theirs; when, instead of informing, advising, and, upon occasion, denouncing, it makes them work in fetters or bids them stand aside and does their work instead of them. The worth of a State, in the long run, is the worth of the individuals composing it; and a State which postpones the interests of *their* mental expansion and elevation, to a little more of administrative skill, or that semblance of it which practice gives, in the details of business; a State which dwarfs its men, in order that they may be more docile instruments in its hands even for beneficial purposes, will find that with small men no great thing can really be accomplished; and that the perfection of machinery to which it has sacrificed everything, will in the end avail it nothing, for want of the vital power which, in order that the machine might work more smoothly, it has preferred to banish.

by the Poor Law Board (but which, owing to the state of opinion on the subject, are very seldom exercised by them: though perhaps giving rise in a case of a first-rate national interest...

Utilitarianism

CHAPTER 1 *General Remarks*

There are few circumstances, among those which make up the present condition of human knowledge, more unlike what might have been expected, or more significant of the backward state in which speculation on the most important subjects still lingers, than the little progress which has been made in the decision of the controversy respecting the criterion of right and wrong. From the dawn of philosophy, the question concerning the *summum bonum,* or, what is the same thing, concerning the foundation of morality, has been accounted the main problem in speculative thought, has occupied the most gifted intellects, and divided them into sects and schools, carrying on a vigorous warfare against one another. And, after more than two thousand years, the same discussions continue, philosophers are still ranged under the same contending banners, and neither thinkers nor mankind at large seem nearer to being unanimous on the subject than when the youth Socrates listened to the old Protagoras, and asserted (if Plato's dialogue be grounded on a real conversation) the theory of utilitarianism against the popular morality of the so-called sophist.

It is true, that similar confusion and uncertainty, and in some cases similar discordance, exist respecting the first principles of all the sciences, not excepting that which is deemed the most certain of them—mathematics; without much impairing, generally indeed without impairing at all, the trustworthiness of the conclusions of those sciences. An apparent anomaly, the explanation of which is, that the detailed doctrines of a science are not usually deduced from, nor depend for their evidence upon, what are called its first principles. Were it not so, there would be no science more precarious, or whose conclusions were more insufficiently made out, than algebra; which derives none of its certainty from what are commonly taught to learners as its elements; since these, as laid down by some of its most eminent teachers, are as full of fictions as English law, and of mysteries as theology. The truths which are ultimately accepted as the first principles of a science are really the last results of metaphysical analysis, practised on the elementary notions with which the science is conversant; and their relation to the science is not that of foundations to an edifice, but of roots to a tree, which may perform their office equally well though they be never dug down to and exposed to light. But, though in science the particular truths precede the general theory, the contrary might be expected to be the case with a practical art, such as morals or legislation. All action is for the sake of some end; and rules of action, it seems natural to suppose, must take their whole character and color from the end to which they are subservient. When we engage in a pursuit, a clear and precise conception of what we are pursuing would seem to be the first thing we need, instead of the last we are to look forward to. A test of right and wrong must be the means, one would think, of ascertaining what is right or wrong, and not a consequence of having already ascertained it.

The difficulty is not avoided by having recourse to the

popular theory of a natural faculty, a sense or instinct, informing us of right and wrong. For, besides that the existence of such a moral instinct is itself one of the matters in dispute, those believers in it who have any pretensions to philosophy have been obliged to abandon the idea that it discerns what is right or wrong in the particular case in hand, as our other senses discern the sight or sound actually present. Our moral faculty, according to all those of its interpreters who are entitled to the name of thinkers, supplies us only with the general principles of moral judgments: it is a branch of our reason, not of our sensitive faculty; and must be looked to for the abstract doctrines of morality, not for perception of it in the concrete. The intuitive, no less than what may be termed the inductive, school of ethics, insists on the necessity of general laws. They both agree that the morality of an individual action is not a question of direct perception, but of the application of a law to an individual case. They recognize also, to a great extent, the same moral laws, but differ as to their evidence, and the source from which they derive their authority. According to the one opinion, the principles of morals are evident *à priori;* requiring nothing to command assent, except that the meaning of the terms be understood. According to the other doctrine, right and wrong, as well as truth and falsehood, are questions of observation and experience. But both hold equally, that morality must be deduced from principles; and the intuitive school affirm, as strongly as the inductive, that there is a science of morals. Yet they seldom attempt to make out a list of the *à priori* principles which are to serve as the premises of the science; still more rarely do they make any effort to reduce those various principles to one first principle, or common ground of obligation. They either assume the ordinary precepts of morals as of *à priori* authority, or they lay down as the common groundwork of those maxims some generality much less obviously authoritative than the maxims themselves, and which has never succeeded in gaining popular acceptance. Yet, to sup-

port their pretensions, there ought either to be some one
fundamental principle or law at the root of all morality; or,
if there be several, there should be a determinate order of
precedence among them; and the one principle, or the rule
for deciding between the various principles when they conflict, ought to be self-evident.

To inquire how far the bad effects of this deficiency have
been mitigated in practice, or to what extent the moral beliefs of mankind have been vitiated or made uncertain by
the absence of any distinct recognition of an ultimate standard, would imply a complete survey and criticism of past and
present ethical doctrine. It would, however, be easy to show
that whatever steadiness or consistency these moral beliefs
have attained has been mainly due to the tacit influence of a
standard not recognized. Although the non-existence of an
acknowledged first principle has made ethics not so much a
guide as a consecration of men's actual sentiments, still, as
men's sentiments, both of favor and of aversion, are greatly
influenced by what they suppose to be the effects of things
upon their happiness, the principle of utility, or, as Bentham
latterly called it, the greatest-happiness principle, has had a
large share in forming the moral doctrines even of those who
most scornfully reject its authority. Nor is there any school of
thought which refuses to admit that the influence of actions
on happiness is a most material and even predominant consideration in many of the details of morals, however unwilling to acknowledge it as the fundamental principle of morality
and the source of moral obligation. I might go much further, and say, that, to all those *à priori* moralists who deem it
necessary to argue at all, utilitarian arguments are indispensable. It is not my present purpose to criticise these thinkers;
but I cannot help referring, for illustration, to a systematic
treatise by one of the most illustrious of them—the "Metaphysics of Ethics," by Kant. This remarkable man, whose
system of thought will long remain one of the landmarks in
the history of philosophical speculation, does, in the treatise

in question, lay down an universal first principle as the origin and ground of moral obligation. It is this: "So act, that the rule on which thou actest would admit of being adopted as a law by all rational beings." But, when he begins to deduce from this precept any of the actual duties of morality, he fails, almost grotesquely, to show that there would be any contradiction, any logical (not to say physical) impossibility, in the adoption by all rational beings of the most outrageously immoral rules of conduct. All he shows is, that the *consequences* of their universal adoption would be such as no one would choose to incur.

On the present occasion, I shall, without further discussion of the other theories, attempt to contribute something towards the understanding and appreciation of the Utilitarian or Happiness theory, and towards such proof as it is susceptible of. It is evident that this cannot be proof in the ordinary and popular meaning of the term. Questions of ultimate ends are not amenable to direct proof. Whatever can be proved to be good, must be so by being shown to be a means to something admitted to be good without proof. The medical art is proved to be good by its conducing to health; but how is it possible to prove that health is good? The art of music is good, for the reason, among others, that it produces pleasure; but what proof is it possible to give that pleasure is good? If, then, it is asserted that there is a comprehensive formula, including all things which are in themselves good, and that whatever else is good is not so as an end, but as a mean, the formula may be accepted or rejected, but is not a subject of what is commonly understood by proof. We are not, however, to infer that its acceptance or rejection must depend on blind impulse or arbitrary choice. There is a larger meaning of the word "proof," in which this question is as amenable to it as any other of the disputed questions of philosophy. The subject is within the cognizance of the rational faculty, and neither does that faculty deal with it solely in the way of intuition. Considerations may be presented capable of determining the intellect either to give or withhold its assent to the doctrine; and this is equivalent to proof.

We shall examine presently of what nature are these considerations; in what manner they apply to the case; and what rational grounds, therefore, can be given for accepting or rejecting the utilitarian formula. But it is a preliminary condition of rational acceptance or rejection, that the formula should be correctly understood. I believe that the very imperfect notion ordinarily formed of its meaning is the chief obstacle which impedes its reception; and that, could it be cleared even from only the grosser misconceptions, the question would be greatly simplified, and a large proportion of its difficulties removed. Before, therefore, I attempt to enter into the philosophical grounds which can be given for assenting to the utilitarian standard, I shall offer some illustrations of the doctrine itself, with the view of showing more clearly what it is, distinguishing it from what it is not, and disposing of such of the practical objections to it as either originate in, or are closely connected with, mistaken interpretations of its meaning. Having thus prepared the ground, I shall afterwards endeavor to throw such light as I can upon the question, considered as one of philosophical theory.

CHAPTER 2   *What Utilitarianism Is*

A passing remark is all that needs be given to the ignorant blunder of supposing that those who stand up for utility, as the test of right and wrong, use the term in that restricted and merely colloquial sense in which utility is opposed to pleasure. An apology is due to the philosophical opponents of utilitarianism for even the momentary appearance of confounding them with any one capable of so absurd a misconception; which is the more extraordinary, inasmuch as the contrary accusation, of referring every thing to pleasure, and that, too, in its grossest form, is another of the common charges against utilitarianism: and, as has been pointedly remarked by an able writer, the same sort of persons, and often the very same persons, denounce the theory "as impracticably dry when the word 'utility' precedes the word 'pleasure,' and as too practicably voluptuous when the word 'pleasure' precedes the word 'utility.'" Those who know any thing about the matter are aware, that every writer, from Epicurus to Bentham, who maintained the theory of utility, meant by it, not something to be contradistinguished from pleasure, but pleasure itself, together with exemption from pain; and, instead of opposing the useful to the agreeable or the ornamental, have always declared that the useful means these, among other things. Yet the common herd, including the herd of writers, not only in newspapers and periodicals, but in books of weight and pretension, are perpetually falling into this shallow mistake. Having caught up the word "utilitarian," while knowing nothing whatever about it but its sound, they habitually express by it the rejection or the neglect of pleasure in some of its forms; of beauty, of ornament, or of amusement. Nor is the term thus ignorantly misapplied solely in disparagement, but occasionally in compliment; as though it implied superiority to frivolity and the mere pleasures of the moment. And this perverted use is the only one in which the word is popularly known, and the one from which the new generation are acquiring their sole notion of its meaning. Those who introduced the word, but who had for many years discontinued it as a distinctive appellation, may well feel themselves called upon to resume it, if by doing so they can hope to contribute any thing towards rescuing it from this utter degradation.*

The creed which accepts, as the foundation of morals, Utility, or the Greatest-happiness Principle, holds that actions are right in proportion as they tend to promote happiness, wrong as they tend to produce the reverse of happiness. By happiness is intended pleasure and the absence of pain; by unhappiness, pain and the privation of pleasure. To give a clear view of the moral standard set up by the theory, much more requires to be said; in particular, what things it includes in the ideas of pain and pleasure, and to what extent this is left an open question. But these supplementary explanations do not affect the theory of life on which this theory of morality is grounded—namely, that pleasure, and freedom from pain, are the only things desirable as ends; and that all desirable things (which are as numerous in the utilitarian as in any other scheme) are desirable either for the pleasure inherent in themselves, or as means to the promotion of pleasure and the prevention of pain.

Now, such a theory of life excites in many minds, and among them in some of the most estimable in feeling and purpose, inveterate dislike. To suppose that life has (as they express it) no higher end than pleasure—no better and nobler object of desire and pursuit—they designate as utterly mean and grovelling; as a doctrine worthy only of swine, to whom the followers of Epicurus were, at a very early period, contemptuously likened: and modern holders of the doctrine are

---

* The author of this essay has reason for believing himself to be the first person who brought the word "utilitarian" into use. He did not invent it, but adopted it from a passing expression in Mr. Galt's Annals of the Parish. After using it as a designation for several years, he and others abandoned it from a growing dislike to any thing resembling a badge or watchword of sectarian distinction. But as a name for one single opinion, not a set of opinions—to denote the recognition of utility as a standard, not any particular way of applying it—the term supplies a want in the language, and offers, in many cases, a convenient mode of avoiding tiresome circumlocution.

occasionally made the subject of equally polite comparisons by its German, French, and English assailants.

When thus attacked, the Epicureans have always answered, that it is not they, but their accusers, who represent human nature in a degrading light, since the accusation supposes human beings to be capable of no pleasures except those of which swine are capable. If this supposition were true, the charge could not be gainsaid, but would then be no longer an imputation; for, if the sources of pleasure were precisely the same to human beings and to swine, the rule of life which is good enough for the one would be good enough for the other. The comparison of the Epicurean life to that of beasts is felt as degrading, precisely because a beast's pleasures do not satisfy a human being's conceptions of happiness. Human beings have faculties more elevated than the animal appetites; and, when once made conscious of them, do not regard any thing as happiness which does not include their gratification. I do not, indeed, consider the Epicureans to have been by any means faultless in drawing out their scheme of consequences from the utilitarian principle. To do this in any sufficient manner, many Stoic as well as Christian elements require to be included. But there is no known Epicurean theory of life which does not assign to the pleasures of the intellect, of the feelings and imagination, and of the moral sentiments, a much higher value as pleasures than to those of mere sensation. It must be admitted, however, that utilitarian writers in general have placed the superiority of mental over bodily pleasures chiefly in the greater permanency, safety, uncostliness, &c., of the former—that is, in their circumstantial advantages rather than in their intrinsic nature. And, on all these points, utilitarians have fully proved their case; but they might have taken the other, and, as it may be called, higher ground, with entire consistency. It is quite compatible with the principle of utility to recognize the fact, that some *kinds* of pleasure are more desirable and more valuable than others. It would be absurd, that while, in

lecture

estimating all other things, quality is considered as well as quantity, the estimation of pleasures should be supposed to depend on quantity alone.

If I am asked what I mean by difference of quality in pleasures, or what makes one pleasure more valuable than another, merely as a pleasure, except its being greater in amount, there is but one possible answer. Of two pleasures, if there be one to which all or almost all who have experience of both give a decided preference, irrespective of any feeling of moral obligation to prefer it, that is the more desirable pleasure. If one of the two is, by those who are competently acquainted with both, placed so far above the other that they prefer it, even though knowing it to be attended with a greater amount of discontent, and would not resign it for any quantity of the other pleasure which their nature is capable of, we are justified in ascribing to the preferred enjoyment a superiority in quality, so far outweighing quantity, as to render it, in comparison, of small account.

Now, it is an unquestionable fact, that those who are equally acquainted with and equally capable of appreciating and enjoying both do give a most marked preference to the manner of existence which employs their higher faculties. Few human creatures would consent to be changed into any of the lower animals, for a promise of the fullest allowance of a beast's pleasures: no intelligent human being would consent to be a fool, no instructed person would be an ignoramus, no person of feeling and conscience would be selfish and base, even though they should be persuaded that the fool, the dunce, or the rascal is better satisfied with his lot than they are with theirs. They would not resign what they possess more than he for the most complete satisfaction of all the desires which they have in common with him. If they ever fancy they would, it is only in cases of unhappiness so extreme, that, to escape from it, they would exchange their lot for almost any other, however undesirable in their own eyes. A being of higher faculties requires more to make him happy, is capable probably of more acute suffering, and certainly accessible to it at more points, than one of an inferior type; but, in spite of these liabilities, he can never really wish to sink into what he feels to be a lower grade of existence. We may give what explanation we please of this unwillingness; we may attribute it to pride, a name which is given indiscriminately to some of the most and to some of the least estimable feelings of which mankind are capable; we may refer it to the love of liberty and personal independence—an appeal to which was with the Stoics one of the most effective means for the inculcation of it; to the love of power, or to the love of excitement, both of which do really enter into and contribute to it: but its most appropriate appellation is a sense of dignity, which all human beings possess in one form or other, and in some, though by no means in exact, proportion to their higher faculties, and which is so essential a part of the happiness of those in whom it is strong, that nothing which conflicts with it could be, otherwise than momentarily, an object of desire to them. Whoever supposes that this preference takes place at a sacrifice of happiness; that the superior being, in any thing like equal circumstances, is not happier than the inferior—confounds the two very different ideas of happiness and content. It is indisputable, that the being whose capacities of enjoyment are low has the greatest chance of having them fully satisfied; and a highly endowed being will always feel that any happiness which he can look for, as the world is constituted, is imperfect. But he can learn to bear its imperfections, if they are at all bearable; and they will not make him envy the being who is indeed unconscious of the imperfections, but only because he feels not at all the good which those imperfections qualify. It is better to be a human being dissatisfied, than a pig satisfied; better to be Socrates dissatisfied, than a fool satisfied. And if the fool or the pig are of a different opinion, it is because they only know their own side of the question. The other party to the comparison knows both sides.

It may be objected, that many who are capable of the higher pleasures, occasionally, under the influence of temptation, postpone them to the lower. But this is quite compatible with a full appreciation of the intrinsic superiority of the higher. Men often, from infirmity of character, make their election for the nearer good, though they know it to be the less valuable, and this no less when the choice is between two bodily pleasures than when it is between bodily and mental. They pursue sensual indulgences to the injury of health, though perfectly aware that health is the greater good. It may be further objected, that many who begin with youthful enthusiasm for every thing noble, as they advance in years sink into indolence and selfishness. But I do not believe that those who undergo this very common change voluntarily choose the lower description of pleasures in preference to the higher. I believe, that, before they devote themselves exclusively to the one, they have already become incapable of the other. Capacity for the nobler feelings is in most natures a very tender plant, easily killed, not only by hostile influences, but by mere want of sustenance; and, in the majority of young persons, it speedily dies away if the occupations to which their position in life has devoted them, and the society into which it has thrown them, are not favorable to keeping that higher capacity in exercise. Men lose their high aspirations as they lose their intellectual tastes, because they have not time or opportunity for indulging them; and they addict themselves to inferior pleasures, not because they deliberately prefer them, but because they are either the only ones to which they have access, or the only ones which they are any longer capable of enjoying. It may be questioned, whether any one, who has remained equally susceptible to both classes of pleasures, ever knowingly and calmly preferred the lower; though many in all ages have broken down in an ineffectual attempt to combine both.

From this verdict of the only competent judges, I apprehend there can be no appeal. On a question, which is the best worth having of two pleasures, or which of two modes of existence is the most grateful to the feelings, apart from its moral attributes and from its consequences, the judgment of those who are qualified by knowledge of both, or, if they differ, that of the majority among them, must be admitted as final. And there needs be the less hesitation to accept this judgment respecting the quality of pleasures, since there is no other tribunal to be referred to even on the question of quantity. What means are there of determining which is the acutest of two pains, or the intensest of two pleasurable sensations, except the general suffrage of those who are familiar with both? Neither pains nor pleasures are homogeneous, and pain is always heterogeneous with pleasure. What is there to decide whether a particular pleasure is worth purchasing at the cost of a particular pain, except the feelings and judgment of the experienced? When, therefore, those feelings and judgment declare the pleasures derived from the higher faculties to be preferable *in kind,* apart from the question of intensity, to those of which the animal nature, disjoined from the higher faculties, is susceptible, they are entitled on this subject to the same regard.

I have dwelt on this point, as being a necessary part of a perfectly just conception of Utility or Happiness, considered as the directive rule of human conduct. But it is by no means an indispensable condition to the acceptance of the utilitarian standard; for that standard is not the agent's own greatest happiness, but the greatest amount of happiness altogether: and, if it may possibly be doubted whether a noble character is always the happier for its nobleness, there can be no doubt that it makes other people happier, and that the world in general is immensely a gainer by it. Utilitarianism, therefore, could only attain its end by the general cultivation of nobleness of character, even if each individual were only benefited by the nobleness of others, and his own, so far as happiness

universal hedon-ism

is concerned, were a sheer deduction from the benefit. But the bare enunciation of such an absurdity as this last renders refutation superfluous.

According to the Greatest-happiness Principle, as above explained, the ultimate end, with reference to and for the sake of which all other things are desirable (whether we are considering our own good or that of other people), is an existence exempt as far as possible from pain, and as rich as possible in enjoyments, both in point of quantity and quality; the test of quality, and the rule for measuring it against quantity, being the preference felt by those, who in their opportunities of experience, to which must be added their habits of self-consciousness and self-observation, are best furnished with the means of comparison. This, being, according to the utilitarian opinion, the end of human action, is necessarily also the standard of morality: which may accordingly be defined, the rules and precepts for human conduct, by the observance of which an existence such as has been described might be, to the greatest extent possible, secured to all mankind; and not to them only, but, so far as the nature of things admits, to the whole sentient creation.

Against this doctrine, however, arises another class of objectors, who say that happiness, in any form, cannot be the rational purpose of human life and action; because, in the first place, it is unattainable: and they contemptuously ask, What right hast thou to be happy? a question which Mr. Carlyle clinches by the addition, What right, a short time ago, hadst thou even *to be?* Next, they say that men can do *without* happiness; that all noble human beings have felt this, and could not have become noble but by learning the lesson of Entsagen, or renunciation; which lesson, thoroughly learnt and submitted to, they affirm to be the beginning and necessary condition of all virtue.

The first of these objections would go to the root of the matter, were it well founded; for, if no happiness is to be had at all by human beings, the attainment of it cannot be the end of morality, or of any rational conduct. Though, even in that case, something might still be said for the utilitarian theory; since utility includes not solely the pursuit of happiness, but the prevention or mitigation of unhappiness: and, if the former aim be chimerical, there will be all the greater scope and more imperative need for the latter, so long at least as mankind think fit to live, and do not take refuge in the simultaneous act of suicide recommended under certain conditions by Novalis. When, however, it is thus positively asserted to be impossible that human life should be happy, the assertion, if not something like a verbal quibble, is at least an exaggeration. If by happiness be meant a continuity of highly pleasurable excitement, it is evident enough that this is impossible. A state of exalted pleasure lasts only moments, or in some cases, and with some intermissions, hours or days; and is the occasional brilliant flash of enjoyment, not its permanent and steady flame. Of this the philosophers who have taught that happiness is the end of life were as fully aware as those who taunt them. The happiness which they meant was not a life of rapture, but moments of such, in an existence made up of few and transitory pains, many and various pleasures, with a decided predominance of the active over the passive, and having, as the foundation of the whole, not to expect more from life than it is capable of bestowing. A life thus composed, to those who have been fortunate enough to obtain it, has always appeared worthy of the name of "happiness." And such an existence is even now the lot of many, during some considerable portion of their lives. The present wretched education and wretched social arrangements are the only real hindrance to its being attainable by almost all.

The objectors, perhaps, may doubt whether human beings, if taught to consider happiness as the end of life, would be satisfied with such a moderate share of it. But great numbers of mankind have been satisfied with much less. The main constituents of a satisfied life appear to be two, either of which by itself is often found sufficient for the purpose—tranquillity and excitement. With much tranquillity, many find that they can be content with very little pleasure; with much excitement, many can reconcile themselves to a considerable quantity of pain. There is assuredly no inherent impossibility in enabling even the mass of mankind to unite both; since the two are so far from being incompatible, that they are in natural alliance; the prolongation of either being a preparation for, and exciting a wish for, the other. It is only those in whom indolence amounts to a vice, that do not desire excitement after an interval of repose; it is only those in whom the need of excitement is a disease, that feel the tranquillity which follows excitement dull and insipid, instead of pleasurable in direct proportion to the excitement which preceded it. When people who are tolerably fortunate in their outward lot do not find in life sufficient enjoyment to make it valuable to them, the cause generally is, caring for nobody but themselves. To those who have neither public nor private affections, the excitements of life are much curtailed, and, in any case, dwindle in value as the time approaches when all selfish interests must be terminated by death; while those who leave after them objects of personal affection, and especially those who have also cultivated a fellow-feeling with the collective interests of mankind, retain as lively an interest in life on the eve of death as in the vigor of youth and health. Next to selfishness, the principal cause which makes life unsatisfactory is want of mental cultivation. A cultivated mind—I do not mean that of a philosopher, but any mind to which the fountains of knowledge have been opened, and which has been taught, in any tolerable degree, to exercise its faculties—finds sources of inexhaustible interest in all that surrounds it; in the objects of nature, the achievements of art, the imaginations of poetry, the incidents of history, the ways of mankind past and present, and their prospects in the future. It is possible, indeed, to become indifferent to all this, and that, too, without having exhausted a thousandth part of it; but only when one has had from the beginning no moral or human interest in these things, and has sought in them only the gratification of curiosity.

Now, there is absolutely no reason in the nature of things why an amount of mental culture sufficient to give an intelligent interest in these objects of contemplation should not be the inheritance of every one born in a civilized country. As little is there an inherent necessity that any human being should be a selfish egotist, devoid of every feeling or care but those which centre in his own miserable individuality. Something far superior to this is sufficiently common even now to give ample earnest of what the human species may be made. Genuine private affections, and a sincere interest in the public good, are possible, though in unequal degrees, to every rightly brought up human being. In a world in which there is so much to interest, so much to enjoy, and so much also to correct and improve, every one who has this moderate amount of moral and intellectual requisites is capable of an existence which may be called enviable; and unless such a person, through bad laws, or subjection to the will of others, is denied the liberty to use the sources of happiness within his reach, he will not fail to find this enviable existence, if he escape the positive evils of life, the great sources of physical and mental suffering—such as indigence, disease, and the unkindness, worthlessness, or premature loss, of objects of affection. The main stress of the problem lies, therefore, in the contest with these calamities, from which it is a rare good fortune entirely to escape; which, as things now are, cannot be obviated, and often cannot be, in any material degree, mitigated. Yet no one, whose opinion deserves a moment's consideration, can doubt that most of the great positive evils of the world are in themselves removable, and will, if human affairs continue to improve, be in the end reduced within narrow limits. Poverty, in any sense implying suffering, may be completely extinguished by the wisdom of society, combined with the good sense and providence of individuals.

Even that most intractable of enemies, disease, may be indefinitely reduced in dimensions by good physical and moral education, and proper control of noxious influences; while the progress of science holds out a promise for the future of still more direct conquests over this detestable foe. And every advance in that direction relieves us from some, not only of the chances which cut short our own lives, but, what concerns us still more, which deprive us of those in whom our happiness is wrapped up. As for vicissitudes of fortune, and other disappointments connected with worldly circumstances, these are principally the effect either of gross imprudence, of ill-regulated desires, or of bad or imperfect social institutions. All the grand sources, in short, of human suffering, are in a great degree, many of them almost entirely, conquerable by human care and effort: and though their removal is grievously slow; though a long succession of generations will perish in the breach before the conquest is completed, and this world becomes all that, if will and knowledge were not wanting, it might easily be made—yet every mind sufficiently intelligent and generous to bear a part, however small and unconspicuous, in the endeavor, will draw a noble enjoyment from the contest itself, which he would not, for any bribe in the form of selfish indulgence, consent to be without.

And this leads to the true estimation of what is said by the objectors concerning the possibility and the obligation of learning to do without happiness. Unquestionably, it is possible to do without happiness: it is done involuntarily by nineteen-twentieths of mankind, even in those parts of our present world which are least deep in barbarism; and it often has to be done voluntarily by the hero or the martyr, for the sake of something which he prizes more than his individual happiness. But this something—what is it, unless the happiness of others, or some of the requisites of happiness? It is noble to be capable of resigning entirely one's own portion of happiness, or chances of it: but, after all, this self-sacrifice must be for some end; it is not its own end; and if we are told that its end is not happiness, but virtue, which is better than happiness, I ask, Would the sacrifice be made if the hero or martyr did not believe that it would earn for others immunity from similar sacrifices? Would it be made if he thought that his renunciation of happiness for himself would produce no fruit for any of his fellow-creatures but to make their lot like his, and place them also in the condition of persons who have renounced happiness? All honor to those who can abnegate for themselves the personal enjoyment of life, when by such renunciation they contribute worthily to increase the amount of happiness in the world; but he who does it, or professes to do it, for any other purpose, is no more deserving of admiration than the ascetic mounted on his pillar. He may be an inspiriting proof of what men *can* do, but assuredly not an example of what they *should*.

Though it is only in a very imperfect state of the world's arrangements that any one can best serve the happiness of others by the absolute sacrifice of his own, yet, so long as the world is in that imperfect state, I fully acknowledge that the readiness to make such a sacrifice is the highest virtue which can be found in man. I will add, that in this condition of the world, paradoxical as the assertion may be, the conscious ability to do without happiness gives the best prospect of realizing such happiness as is attainable. For nothing except that consciousness can raise a person above the chances of life, by making him feel, that, let fate and fortune do their worst, they have not power to subdue him; which, once felt, frees him from excess of anxiety concerning the evils of life, and enables him, like many a Stoic in the worst times of the Roman Empire, to cultivate in tranquillity the sources of satisfaction accessible to him, without concerning himself about the uncertainty of their duration, any more than about their inevitable end.

Meanwhile, let utilitarians never cease to claim the morality of self-devotion as a possession which belongs by as good a right to them as either to the Stoic or to the Transcendentalist. The utilitarian morality does recognize in human beings the power of sacrificing their own greatest good for the good of others. It only refuses to admit that the sacrifice is itself a good. [A sacrifice which does not increase, or tend to increase, the sum total of happiness, it considers as wasted. The only self-renunciation which it applauds is devotion to the happiness, or to some of the means of happiness, of others, either of mankind collectively, or of individuals within the limits imposed by the collective interests of mankind.]

I must again repeat, what the assailants of utilitarianism seldom have the justice to acknowledge, that the happiness which forms the utilitarian standard of what is right in conduct is not the agent's own happiness, but that of all concerned; as, between his own happiness and that of others, utilitarianism requires him to be as strictly impartial as a disinterested and benevolent spectator. In the golden rule of Jesus of Nazareth, we read the complete spirit of the ethics of utility. To do as you would be done by, and to love your neighbor as yourself, constitute the ideal perfection of utilitarian morality. As the means of making the nearest approach to this ideal, utility would enjoin, first, that laws and social arrangements should place the happiness or (as, speaking practically, it may be called) the interest of every individual as nearly as possible in harmony with the interest of the whole; and, secondly, that education and opinion, which have so vast a power over human character, should so use that power as to establish in the mind of every individual an indissoluble association between his own happiness and the good of the whole—especially between his own happiness, and the practice of such modes of conduct, negative and positive, as regard for the universal happiness prescribes— so that not only he may be unable to conceive the possibility of happiness to himself, consistently with conduct opposed to the general good, but also that a direct impulse to promote the general good may be in every individual one of the habitual motives of action, and the sentiments connected therewith may fill a large and prominent place in every human being's sentient existence. If the impugners of the utilitarian morality represented it to their own minds in this its true character, I know not what recommendation possessed by any other morality they could possibly affirm to be wanting to it; what more beautiful or more exalted developments of human nature any other ethical system can be supposed to foster; or what springs of action, not accessible to the utilitarian, such systems rely on for giving effect to their mandates.

The objectors to utilitarianism cannot always be charged with representing it in a discreditable light. On the contrary, those among them who entertain any thing like a just idea of its disinterested character sometimes find fault with its standard as being too high for humanity. They say it is exacting too much to require that people shall always act from the inducement of promoting the general interests of society. But this is to mistake the very meaning of a standard of morals, and confound the rule of action with the motive of it. It is the business of ethics to tell us what are our duties, or by what test we may know them; but no system of ethics requires that the sole motive of all we do shall be a feeling of duty; on the contrary, ninety-nine hundredths of all our actions are done from other motives, and rightly so done, if the rule of duty does not condemn them. It is the more unjust to utilitarianism that this particular misapprehension should be made a ground of objection to it, inasmuch as utilitarian moralists have gone beyond almost all others in affirming that the motive has nothing to do with the morality of the action, though much with the worth of the agent. He who saves a fellow-creature from drowning does what is morally right, whether his motive be duty, or the hope of being paid for his trouble: he who betrays the friend that trusts him is guilty of a crime, even if his object be to serve another friend to whom he is under greater obligations. But to speak only of actions done from the motive of duty, and in direct obedience to principle: it is a misapprehension of the utilitarian mode of thought to conceive it as implying that people should fix their minds upon so wide a generality as the world or society at large. The great majority of good actions are intended, not for the benefit of the world, but for that of individuals, of which the good of the world is made up; and the thoughts of the most virtuous man need not on these occasions travel beyond the particular persons concerned, except so far as is necessary to assure himself, that, in benefiting them, he is not violating the rights—that is, the legitimate and authorized expectations—of any one else. The multiplication of happiness is, according to the utilitarian ethics, the object of virtue: the occasions on which any person (except one in a thousand) has it in his power to do this on an extended scale—in other words, to be a public benefactor—are but exceptional; and on these occasions alone is he called on to consider public utility: in every other case, private utility, the interest or happiness of some few persons, is all he has to attend to. Those alone, the influence of whose actions extends to society in general, need concern themselves habitually about so large an object. In the case of abstinences indeed—of things which people forbear to do from moral considerations, though the consequences in the particular case might be beneficial—it would be unworthy of an intelligent agent not to be consciously aware that the action is of a class, which, if practised generally, would be generally injurious, and that this is the ground of the obligation to abstain from it. The amount of regard for the public interest implied in this recognition is no greater than is demanded by every system of morals; for they all enjoin to abstain from whatever is manifestly pernicious to society.

The same considerations dispose of another reproach against the doctrine of utility, founded on a still grosser misconception of the purpose of a standard of morality, and of the very meaning of the words "right" and "wrong." It is often affirmed, that utilitarianism renders men cold and unsympathizing; that it chills their moral feelings towards individuals; that it makes them regard only the dry and hard consideration of the consequences of actions, not taking into their moral estimate the qualities from which those actions emanate. If the assertion means that they do not allow their judgment respecting the rightness or wrongness of an action to be influenced by their opinion of the qualities of the person who does it, this is a complaint, not against utilitarianism, but against having any standard of morality at all: for certainly no known ethical standard decides an action to be good or bad because it is done by a good or a bad man; still less because done by an amiable, a brave, or a benevolent man, or the contrary. These considerations are relevant, not to the estimation of actions, but of persons; and there is nothing in the utilitarian theory inconsistent with the fact, that there are other things which interest us in persons besides the rightness and wrongness of their actions. The Stoics indeed, with the paradoxical misuse of language which was part of their system, and by which they strove to raise themselves above all concern about any thing but virtue, were fond of saying, that he who has that, has every thing; that he, and only he, is rich, is beautiful, is a king. But no claim of this description is made for the virtuous man by the utilitarian doctrine. Utilitarians are quite aware that there are other desirable possessions and qualities besides virtue, and are perfectly willing to allow to all of them their full worth. They are also aware that a right action does not necessarily indicate a virtuous character; and that actions which are blamable often proceed from qualities entitled to praise. When this is apparent in any particular case, it modifies their estimation, not certainly of the act, but of the agent. I grant that they are, notwithstanding, of opinion, that, in the long-run, the best proof of a good character is good actions; and resolutely refuse to consider any mental disposition as good, of which the predominant tendency is to produce bad conduct. This makes them unpopular with many people: but it is an unpopularity which they must share with every one who regards the distinction between right and wrong in a serious light; and the reproach is not one which a conscientious utilitarian need be anxious to repel.

If no more be meant by the objection than that many utilitarians look on the morality of actions, as measured by the utilitarian standards, with too exclusive a regard, and do not lay sufficient stress upon the other beauties of character which go towards making a human being lovable or admirable, this may be admitted. Utilitarians who have cultivated their moral feelings, but not their sympathies nor their artistic perceptions, do fall into this mistake; and so do all other moralists under the same conditions. What can be said in excuse for other moralists is equally available for them; namely, that, if there is to be any error, it is better that it should be on that side. As a matter of fact, we may affirm that among utilitarians, as among adherents of other systems, there is every imaginable degree of rigidity and of laxity in the application of their standard: some are even puritanically rigorous, while others are as indulgent as can possibly be desired by sinner or by sentimentalist. But, on the whole, a doctrine which brings prominently forward the interest that mankind have in the repression and prevention of conduct which violates the moral law, is likely to be inferior to no other in turning the sanctions of opinion against such violations. It is true, the question, What does violate the moral law? is one on which those who recognize different standards of morality are likely now and then to differ. But difference of opinion on moral questions was not first introduced into the world by utilitarianism; while that doctrine does supply, if not always an easy, at all events a tangible and intelligible, mode of deciding such differences.

It may not be superfluous to notice a few more of the common misapprehensions of utilitarian ethics, even those which are so obvious and gross that it might appear impossible for any person of candor and intelligence to fall into them; since persons even of considerable mental endowments often give themselves so little trouble to understand the bearings of any opinion against which they entertain a prejudice, and men are in general so little conscious of this voluntary ignorance as a defect, that the vulgarest misunderstandings of ethical doctrines are continually met with in the deliberate writings of persons of the greatest pretensions both to high principle and to philosophy. We not uncommonly hear the doctrine of utility inveighed against as a *godless* doctrine. If it be necessary to say any thing at all against so mere an assumption, we may say that the question depends upon what idea we have formed of the moral character of the Deity. If it be a true belief, that God desires, above all things, the happiness of his creatures, and that this was his purpose in their creation, utility is not only not a godless doctrine, but more profoundly religious than any other. If it be meant that utilitarianism does not recognize the revealed will of God as the supreme law of morals, I answer, that an utilitarian, who believes in the perfect goodness and wisdom of God, necessarily believes that whatever God has thought fit to reveal on the subject of morals must fulfil the requirements of utility in a supreme degree. But others besides utilitarians have been of opinion, that the Christian revelation was intended, and is fitted, to inform the hearts and minds of mankind with a spirit which should enable them to find for themselves what is right, and incline them to do it when found, rather than to tell them, except in a very general way, what it is; and that we need a doctrine of ethics, carefully followed out, to *interpret* to us the will of God. Whether this opinion is correct or not, it is superfluous here to discuss; since whatever aid religion, either natural or revealed, can afford to ethical investigation, is as open to the utilitarian moralist as to any other. He can use it as the testimony of God to the usefulness or hurtfulness of any given course of action, by as good a right as others can use it for the indication of a transcendental law, having no connection with usefulness or with happiness.

Again: Utility is often summarily stigmatized as an immoral doctrine by giving it the name of Expediency, and, taking advantage of the popular use of that term, to contrast it with Principle. But the Expedient, in the sense in which it is opposed to the Right, generally means that which is expedient for the particular interest of the agent himself; as when a minister sacrifices the interests of his country to keep himself in place. When it means any thing better than this, it means that which is expedient for some immediate object, some temporary purpose, but which violates a rule whose observance is expedient in a much higher degree. The Expedient, in this sense, instead of being the same thing with the useful, is a branch of the hurtful. Thus it would often be expedient, for the purpose of getting over some momentary embarrassment, or attaining some object immediately useful to ourselves or others, to tell a lie. But inasmuch as the cultivation in ourselves of a sensitive feeling on the subject of veracity is one of the most useful, and the enfeeblement of that feeling one of the most hurtful, things to which our conduct can be instrumental; and inasmuch as any, even unintentional, deviation from truth does that much towards weakening the trustworthiness of human assertion, which is not only the principal support of all present social well-being, but the insufficiency of which does more than any one thing that can be named to keep back civilization, virtue, every thing on which human happiness on the largest scale depends—we feel that the violation, for a present advantage, of a rule of such transcendent expediency, is not expedient; and that he, who, for the sake of a convenience to himself or to some other individual, does what depends on him to deprive mankind of the good, and inflict upon them the evil, involved in the greater or less reliance which they can place in each other's word, acts the part of one of their worst enemies. Yet that even this rule, sacred as it is, admits of possible exceptions, is acknowledged by all moralists; the chief of which is, when the withholding of some fact (as of information from a malefactor, or of bad news from a person dangerously ill) would save an individual (especially an individual other than one's self) from great and unmerited evil, and when the withholding can only be effected by denial. But in order that the exception may not extend itself beyond the need, and may have the least possible effect in weakening reliance on veracity, it ought to be recognized, and, if possible, its limits defined; and, if the principle of utility is good for any thing, it must be good for weighing these conflicting utilities against one another, and marking out the region within which one or the other preponderates.

Again: defenders of utility often find themselves called upon to reply to such objections as this—that there is not time, previous to action, for calculating and weighing the effects of any line of conduct on the general happiness. This is exactly as if any one were to say that it is impossible to guide our conduct by Christianity, because there is not time, on every occasion on which any thing has to be done, to read through the Old and New Testaments. The answer to the objection is, that there has been ample time; namely, the whole past duration of the human species. During all that time, mankind have been learning by experience the tendencies of actions, on which experience all the prudence as well as all the morality of life are dependent. People talk as if the commencement of this course of experience had hitherto been put off, and as if, at the moment when some man feels tempted to meddle with the property or life of another, he had to begin considering for the first time whether murder and theft are injurious to human happiness. Even then, I do not think that he would find the question very puzzling; but, at all events, the matter is now done to his hand. It is truly a whimsical supposition, that, if mankind were agreed in considering utility to be the test of morality, they would remain without any agreement as to what *is* useful, and would take no measures for having their notions on the subject taught to the young, and enforced by law and opinion. There

is no difficulty in proving any ethical standard whatever to
work ill, if we suppose universal idiocy to be conjoined with
it: but, on any hypothesis short of that, mankind must by this
time have acquired positive beliefs as to the effects of some
actions on their happiness; and the beliefs which have thus
come down are the rules of morality for the multitude, and
for the philosopher, until he has succeeded in finding better.
That philosophers might easily do this, even now, on many
subjects; that the received code of ethics is by no means of
divine right; and that mankind have still much to learn as
to the effects of actions on the general happiness—I admit,
or, rather, earnestly maintain. The corollaries from the principle of utility, like the precepts of every practical art, admit
of indefinite improvement; and, in a progressive state of the
human mind, their improvement is perpetually going on. But
to consider the rules of morality as improvable is one thing;
to pass over the intermediate generalizations entirely, and
endeavor to test each individual action directly by the first
principle, is another. It is a strange notion, that the acknowledgment of a first principle is inconsistent with the admission
of secondary ones. To inform a traveller respecting the place
of his ultimate destination is not to forbid the use of landmarks and direction-posts on the way. The proposition that
happiness is the end and aim of morality does not mean that
no road ought to be laid down to that goal, or that persons
going thither should not be advised to take one direction
rather than another. Men really ought to leave off talking a
kind of nonsense on this subject which they would neither
talk nor listen to on other matters of practical concernment.
Nobody argues that the art of navigation is not founded on
astronomy, because sailors cannot wait to calculate the "Nau-
tical Almanac." Being rational creatures, they go to sea with
it ready calculated; and all rational creatures go out upon the
sea of life with their minds made up on the common questions of right and wrong, as well as on many of the far more
difficult questions of wise and foolish. And this, as long as

foresight is a human quality, it is to be presumed they will continue to do. Whatever we adopt as the fundamental principle of morality, we require subordinate principles to apply it by: the impossibility of doing without them, being common to all systems, can afford no argument against any one in particular; but gravely to argue as if no such secondary principles could be had, and as if mankind had remained till now, and always must remain, without drawing any general conclusions from the experience of human life, is as high a pitch, I think, as absurdity has ever reached in philosophical controversy.

The remainder of the stock arguments against utilitarianism mostly consist in laying to its charge the common infirmities of human nature, and the general difficulties which embarrass conscientious persons in shaping their course through life. We are told that an utilitarian will be apt to make his own particular case an exception to moral rules; and, when under temptation, will see an utility in the breach of a rule greater than he will see in its observance. But is utility the only creed which is able to furnish us with excuses for evil-doing, and means of cheating our own conscience? They are afforded in abundance by all doctrines which recognize as a fact in morals the existence of conflicting considerations; which all doctrines do that have been believed by sane persons. It is not the fault of any creed, but of the complicated nature of human affairs, that rules of conduct cannot be so framed as to require no exceptions, and that hardly any kind of action can safely be laid down as either always obligatory or always condemnable. There is no ethical creed which does not temper the rigidity of its laws by giving a certain latitude, under the moral responsibility of the agent, for accommodation to peculiarities of circumstances; and under every creed, at the opening thus made, self-deception and dishonest casuistry get in. There exists no moral system under which there do not arise unequivocal cases of conflicting obligation. These are the real difficulties;

the knotty points both in the theory of ethics, and in the conscientious guidance of personal conduct. They are overcome practically with greater or with less success according to the intellect and virtue of the individual; but it can hardly be pretended that any one will be the less qualified for dealing with them, from possessing an ultimate standard to which conflicting rights and duties can be referred. If utility is the ultimate source of moral obligations, utility may be invoked to decide between them when their demands are incompatible. Though the application of the standard may be difficult, it is better than none at all: while in other systems, the moral laws all claiming independent authority, there is no common umpire entitled to interfere between them; their claims to precedence one over another rest on little better than sophistry; and unless determined, as they generally are, by the unacknowledged influence of considerations of utility, afford a free scope for the action of personal desires and partialities. We must remember that only in these cases of conflict between secondary principles is it requisite that first principles should be appealed to. There is no case of moral obligation in which some secondary principle is not involved; and, if only one, there can seldom be any real doubt which one it is, in the mind of any person by whom the principle itself is recognized.

CHAPTER 3   *Of the Ultimate Sanction of the Principle of Utility*

The question is often asked, and properly so, in regard to any supposed moral standard, What is its sanction? what are the motives to obey it? or, more specifically, what is the source of its obligation? whence does it derive its binding force? It is a necessary part of moral philosophy to provide the answer to this question; which, though frequently assuming the shape of an objection to the utilitarian morality, as if it had some special applicability to that above others, really arises in regard to all standards. It arises, in fact, whenever a person is called on to *adopt* a standard, or refer morality to any basis on which he has not been accustomed to rest it. For the customary morality, that which education and opinion have consecrated, is the only one which presents itself to the mind with the feeling of being *in itself* obligatory: and, when a person is asked to believe that this morality *derives* its obligation from some general principle round which custom has not thrown the same halo, the assertion is to him a paradox; the supposed corollaries seem to have a more binding force than the original theorem; the superstructure seems to stand better without than with what is represented as its foundation. He says to himself, "I feel that I am bound not to rob or murder, betray or deceive; but why am I bound to promote the general happiness? If my own happiness lies in something else, why may I not give that the preference?"

If the view adopted by the utilitarian philosophy of the nature of the moral sense be correct, this difficulty will always present itself, until the influences which form moral character have taken the same hold of the principle which they have taken of some of the consequences; until, by the improvement of education, the feeling of unity with our fellow-creatures shall be (what it cannot be denied that Christ intended it to be) as deeply rooted in our character, and, to our own consciousness, as completely a part of our nature, as the horror of crime is in an ordinarily well brought up young person. In the mean time, however, the difficulty has no peculiar application to the doctrine of utility, but is inherent in every attempt to analyze morality, and reduce it to principles; which, unless the principle is already in men's minds invested with as much sacredness as any of its applications, always seems to divest them of a part of their sanctity.

The principle of utility either has, or there is no reason why it might not have, all the sanctions which belong to any other system of morals. Those sanctions are either external or internal. Of the external sanctions it is not necessary to speak at any length. They are, the hope of favor and the fear of displeasure from our fellow-creatures, or from the Ruler of the universe, along with whatever we may have of sympathy or affection for them; or of love and awe of him, inclining us to do his will independently of selfish consequences. There is evidently no reason why all these motives for observance should not attach themselves to the utilitarian morality as completely and as powerfully as to any other. Indeed, those of them which refer to our fellow-creatures are sure to do so, in proportion to the amount of general intelligence: for, whether there be any other ground of moral obligation than the general happiness or not, men do desire happiness; and, however imperfect may be their own practice, they desire and commend all conduct in others towards themselves by which they think their happiness is promoted. With regard to the religious motive, if men believe, as most profess to do, in the goodness of God, those who think that conduciveness to the general happiness is the essence, or even only the criterion, of good, must necessarily believe that it is also that which God approves. The whole force, therefore, of external reward and punishment, whether physical or moral, and whether proceeding from God or from our fellow-men, together with all that the capacities of human nature admit of disinterested devotion to either, become available to enforce the utilitarian morality, in proportion as that morality is recognized; and the more powerfully, the more the appliances of education and general cultivation are bent to the purpose.

So far as to external sanctions. The internal sanction of duty, whatever our standard of duty may be, is one and the same—a feeling in our own mind; a pain, more or less intense, attendant on violation of duty, which, in properly cultivated moral natures, rises in the more serious cases into shrinking from it as an impossibility. This feeling, when disinterested, and connecting itself with the pure idea of duty, and not with some particular form of it, or with any of the merely accessory circumstances, is the essence of Conscience: though in that complex phenomenon, as it actually exists, the simple fact is, in general, all incrusted over with collateral associations, derived from sympathy, from love, and still more from fear; from all the forms of religious feeling; from the recollections of childhood, and of all our past life; from self-esteem, desire of the esteem of others, and occasionally even self-abasement. This extreme complication is, I apprehend, the origin of the sort of mystical character, which, by a tendency of the human mind of which there are many other examples, is apt to be attributed to the idea of moral obligation, and which leads people to believe that the idea cannot possibly attach itself to any other objects than those which, by a supposed mysterious law, are found in our present experience to excite it. Its binding force, however, consists in the existence of a mass of feeling which must be broken through in order to do what violates our standard of right; and which, if we do nevertheless violate that standard, will probably have to be encountered afterwards in the form of remorse. Whatever theory we have of the nature or origin of conscience, this is what essentially constitutes it.

The ultimate sanction, therefore, of all morality (external motives apart) being a subjective feeling in our own minds, I see nothing embarrassing, to those whose standard is utility, in the question, What is the sanction of that particular standard? We may answer, The same as of all other moral standards—the conscientious feelings of mankind. Undoubtedly this sanction has no binding efficacy on those who do not possess the feelings it appeals to; but neither will these persons be more obedient to any other moral principle than to the utilitarian one. On them, morality of any kind has no hold but through the external sanctions. Meanwhile the feelings exist—a fact in human nature, the reality of which, and the great power with which they are capable of acting on those in whom they have been duly cultivated, are proved by experience. No reason has ever been shown why they may not be cultivated to as great intensity in connection with the utilitarian as with any other rule of morals.

There is, I am aware, a disposition to believe that a person who sees in moral obligation a transcendental fact, an objective reality belonging to the province of "things in themselves," is likely to be more obedient to it than one who believes it to be entirely subjective, having its seat in human consciousness only. But, whatever a person's opinion may be on this point of ontology, the force he is really urged by is his own subjective feeling, and is exactly measured by its strength. No one's belief that Duty is an objective reality is stronger than the belief that God is so; yet the belief in God, apart from the expectation of actual reward and punishment, only operates on conduct through, and in proportion to, the subjective religious feeling. The sanction, so far as it is disinterested, is always in the mind itself: and the notion, therefore, of the transcendental moralists must be, that this sanction will not exist *in* the mind, unless it is believed to have its root out of the mind; and that if a person is able to say to himself, "This which is restraining me, and which is called my conscience, is only a feeling in my own mind," he may possibly draw the conclusion, that, when the feeling ceases, the obligation ceases; and that, if he find the feeling inconvenient, he may disregard it, and endeavor to get rid of it. But is this danger confined to the utilitarian morality? Does the belief that moral obligation has its seat outside the mind make the feeling of it too strong to be got rid of? The fact is so far otherwise, that all moralists admit and lament the ease with which, in the generality of minds, conscience can be silenced or stifled. The question, Need I obey my conscience?

is quite as often put to themselves by persons who never heard of the principle of utility as by its adherents. Those whose conscientious feelings are so weak as to allow of their asking this question, if they answer it affirmatively, will not do so because they believe in the transcendental theory, but because of the external sanctions.

It is not necessary, for the present purpose, to decide whether the feeling of duty is innate or implanted. Assuming it to be innate, it is an open question to what objects it naturally attaches itself; for the philosophic supporters of that theory are now agreed that the intuitive perception is of principles of morality, and not of the details. If there be any thing innate in the matter, I see no reason why the feeling which is innate should not be that of regard to the pleasures and pains of others. If there is any principle of morals which is intuitively obligatory, I should say it must be that. If so, the intuitive ethics would coincide with the utilitarian, and there would be no further quarrel between them. Even as it is, the intuitive moralists, though they believe that there are other intuitive moral obligations, do already believe this to be one; for they unanimously hold that a large *portion* of morality turns upon the consideration due to the interests of our fellow-creatures. Therefore, if the belief in the transcendental origin of moral obligation gives any additional efficacy to the internal sanction, it appears to me that the utilitarian principle has already the benefit of it.

On the other hand, if, as is my own belief, the moral feelings are not innate, but acquired, they are not for that reason the less natural. It is natural to man to speak, to reason, to build cities, to cultivate the ground, though these are acquired faculties. The moral feelings are not indeed a part of our nature, in the sense of being in any perceptible degree present in all of us; but this, unhappily, is a fact admitted by those who believe the most strenuously in their transcendental origin. Like the other acquired capacities above referred to, the moral faculty, if not a part of our nature, is a natural outgrowth from it; capable like them, in a certain small degree, of springing up spontaneously, and susceptible of being brought by cultivation to a high degree of development. Unhappily, it is also susceptible, by a sufficient use of the external sanctions and of the force of early impressions, of being cultivated in almost any direction; so that there is hardly any thing so absurd or so mischievous that it may not, by means of these influences, be made to act on the human mind with all the authority of conscience. To doubt that the same potency might be given by the same means to the principle of utility, even if it had no foundation in human nature, would be flying in the face of all experience.

But moral associations which are wholly of artificial creation, when intellectual culture goes on, yield by degrees to the dissolving force of analysis: and if the feeling of duty, when associated with utility, would appear equally arbitrary; if there were no leading department of our nature, no powerful class of sentiments, with which that association would harmonize, which would make us feel it congenial, and incline us not only to foster it in others (for which we have abundant interested motives), but also to cherish it in ourselves; if there were not, in short, a natural basis of sentiment for utilitarian morality—it might well happen that this association also, even after it had been implanted by education, might be analyzed away.

But there *is* this basis of powerful natural sentiment; and this it is, which, when once the general happiness is recognized as the ethical standard, will constitute the strength of the utilitarian morality. This firm foundation is that of the social feelings of mankind; the desire to be in unity with our fellow-creatures, which is already a powerful principle in human nature, and happily one of those which tend to become stronger, even without express inculcation from the influences of advancing civilization. The social state is at once so natural, so necessary, and so habitual to man, that except in some unusual circumstances, or by an effort of voluntary abstraction, he never conceives himself otherwise than as a member of a body; and this association is riveted more and more as mankind are further removed from the state of savage independence. Any condition, therefore, which is essential to a state of society, becomes more and more an inseparable part of every person's conception of the state of things which he is born into, and which is the destiny of a human being. Now, society between human beings, except in the relation of master and slave, is manifestly impossible on any other footing than that the interests of all are to be consulted. Society between equals can only exist on the understanding that the interests of all are to be regarded equally. And since, in all states of civilization, every person except an absolute monarch has equals, every one is obliged to live on these terms with somebody; and, in every age, some advance is made towards a state in which it will be impossible to live permanently on other terms with anybody. In this way, people grow up unable to conceive as possible to them a state of total disregard of other people's interests. They are under a necessity of conceiving themselves as at least abstaining from all the grosser injuries, and (if only for their own protection) living in a state of constant protest against them. They are also familiar with the fact of co-operating with others, and proposing to themselves a collective, not an individual, interest as the aim (at least for the time being) of their actions. So long as they are co-operating, their ends are identified with those of others: there is at least a temporary feeling that the interests of others are their own interests. Not only does all strengthening of social ties, and all healthy growth of society, give to each individual a stronger personal interest in practically consulting the welfare of others: it also leads him to identify his *feelings* more and more with their good, or at least with an ever greater degree of practical consideration for it. He comes, as though instinctively, to be conscious of himself as a being who *of course* pays regard to others. The good of others becomes to him a thing naturally and

necessarily to be attended to, like any of the physical conditions of our existence. Now, whatever amount of this feeling
a person has, he is urged by the strongest motives, both of
interest and of sympathy, to demonstrate it, and, to the utmost of his power, encourage it in others; and, even if he has
none of it himself, he is as greatly interested as any one else
that others should have it. Consequently, the smallest germs
of the feeling are laid hold of and nourished by the contagion
of sympathy and the influences of education, and a complete
web of corroborative association is woven round it by the
powerful agency of the external sanctions. This mode of conceiving ourselves and human life, as civilization goes on, is
felt to be more and more natural. Every step in political improvement renders it more so, by removing the sources of opposition of interest, and levelling those inequalities of legal
privilege between individuals or classes, owing to which there
are large portions of mankind whose happiness it is still practicable to disregard. In an improving state of the human
mind, the influences are constantly on the increase which
tend to generate in each individual a feeling of unity with all
the rest, which, if perfect, would make him never think of or
desire any beneficial condition for himself, in the benefits of
which they are not included. If we now suppose this feeling
of unity to be taught as a religion, and the whole force of
education, of institutions, and of opinion, directed, as it once
was in the case of religion, to make every person grow up
from infancy surrounded on all sides both by the profession
and the practice of it, I think that no one who can realize this
conception will feel any misgiving about the sufficiency of the
ultimate sanction for the Happiness morality. To any ethical
student who finds the realization difficult, I recommend, as a
means of facilitating it, the second of M. Comte's two principal works, the "Traité de Politique Positive." I entertain
the strongest objections to the system of politics and morals
set forth in that treatise: but I think it has superabundantly
shown the possibility of giving to the service of humanity,

even without the aid of belief in a Providence, both the psychological power and the social efficacy of a religion; making it take hold of human life, and color all thought, feeling, and action, in a manner of which the greatest ascendency ever exercised by any religion may be but a type and foretaste, and of which the danger is, not that it should be insufficient, but that it should be so excessive as to interfere unduly with human freedom and individuality.

Neither is it necessary to the feeling which constitutes the binding force of the utilitarian morality on those who recognize it, to wait for those social influences which would make its obligation felt by mankind at large. In the comparatively early state of human advancement in which we now live, a person cannot indeed feel that entireness of sympathy with all others which would make any real discordance in the general direction of their conduct in life impossible; but already a person in whom the social feeling is at all developed cannot bring himself to think of the rest of his fellow-creatures as struggling rivals with him for the means of happiness, whom he must desire to see defeated in their object in order that he may succeed in his. The deeply rooted conception which every individual even now has of himself as a social being tends to make him feel it one of his natural wants, that there should be harmony between his feelings and aims and those of his fellow-creatures. If differences of opinion and of mental culture make it impossible for him to share many of their actual feelings—perhaps make him denounce and defy those feelings—he still needs to be conscious that his real aim and theirs do not conflict; that he is not opposing himself to what they really wish for—namely, their own good—but is, on the contrary, promoting it. This feeling in most individuals is much inferior in strength to their selfish feelings, and is often wanting altogether. But, to those who have it, it possesses all the characters of a natural feeling. It does not present itself to their minds as a superstition of education, or a law despotically imposed by the power of society, but as an attribute which it would not be well for them to be without. This conviction is the ultimate sanction of the greatest-happiness morality. This it is which makes any mind of well-developed feelings work with, and not against, the outward motives to care for others, afforded by what I have called the external sanctions; and when those sanctions are wanting, or act in an opposite direction, constitutes in itself a powerful internal binding force, in proportion to the sensitiveness and thoughtfulness of the character: since few but those whose mind is a moral blank could bear to lay out their course of life on the plan of paying no regard to others, except so far as their own private interest compels.

CHAPTER 4 *Of What Sort of Proof the Principle of Utility Is Susceptible*

It has already been remarked, that questions of ultimate ends do not admit of proof, in the ordinary acceptation of the term. To be incapable of proof by reasoning is common to all first principles; to the first premises of our knowledge, as well as to those of our conduct. But the former, being matters of fact, may be the subject of a direct appeal to the faculties which judge of fact; namely, our senses, and our internal consciousness. Can an appeal be made to the same faculties on questions of practical ends? Or by what other faculty is cognizance taken of them?

Questions about ends are, in other words, questions what things are desirable. The utilitarian doctrine is, that happiness is desirable, and the only thing desirable, as an end; all other things being only desirable as means to that end. What ought to be required of this doctrine—what conditions is it requisite that the doctrine should fulfil—to make good its claim to be believed?

The only proof capable of being given that an object is visible, is that people actually see it: the only proof that a sound is audible, is that people hear it: and so of the other sources of our experience. In like manner, I apprehend, the sole evidence it is possible to produce that any thing is desirable, is that people do actually desire it. If the end which the utilitarian doctrine proposes to itself were not, in theory and in practice, acknowledged to be an end, nothing could ever convince any person that it was so. No reason can be given why the general happiness is desirable, except that each person, so far as he believes it to be attainable, desires his own happiness. This, however, being a fact, we have not only all the proof which the case admits of, but all which it is possible to require, that happiness is a good; that each person's happiness is a good to that person; and the general happiness, therefore, a good to the aggregate of all persons. Happiness has made out its title as *one* of the ends of conduct, and consequently one of the criteria of morality.

But it has not, by this alone, proved itself to be the sole criterion. To do that, it would seem, by the same rule, necessary to show, not only that people desire happiness, but that they never desire any thing else. Now, it is palpable that they do desire things, which, in common language, are decidedly distinguished from happiness. They desire, for example, virtue and the absence of vice, no less really than pleasure and the absence of pain. The desire of virtue is not as universal, but it is as authentic a fact, as the desire of happiness; and hence the opponents of the utilitarian standard deem that they have a right to infer that there are other ends of human action besides happiness, and that happiness is not the standard of approbation and disapprobation.

But does the utilitarian doctrine deny that people desire virtue, or maintain that virtue is not a thing to be desired?

The very reverse. It maintains not only that virtue is to be desired, but that it is to be desired disinterestedly, for itself. Whatever may be the opinion of utilitarian moralists as to the original conditions by which virtue is made virtue; however they may believe (as they do) that actions and dispositions are only virtuous because they promote another end than virtue—yet this being granted, and it having been decided, from considerations of this description, what *is* virtuous, they not only place virtue at the very head of the things which are good as means to the ultimate end, but they also recognize, as a psychological fact, the possibility of its being, to the individual, a good in itself, without looking to any end beyond it; and hold that the mind is not in a right state, not in a state conformable to utility, not in the state most conducive to the general happiness, unless it does love virtue in this manner—as a thing desirable in itself, even although, in the individual instance, it should not produce those other desirable consequences which it tends to produce, and on account of which it is held to be virtue. This opinion is not, in the smallest degree, a departure from the Happiness principle. The ingredients of happiness are very various, and each of them is desirable in itself, and not merely when considered as swelling an aggregate. The principle of utility does not mean that any given pleasure—as music, for instance—or any given exemption from pain—as, for example, health—are to be looked upon as means to a collective something termed happiness, and to be desired on that account. They are desired and desirable in and for themselves: besides being means, they are a part of the end. Virtue, according to the utilitarian doctrine, is not naturally and originally part of the end, but it is capable of becoming so, and, in those who love it disinterestedly, it has become so, and is desired and cherished, not as a means to happiness, but as a part of their happiness.

To illustrate this farther: we may remember that virtue is not the only thing, originally a means, and which, if it were not a means to any thing else, would be and remain indifferent, but which, by association with what it is a means to, comes to be desired for itself, and that, too, with the utmost intensity. What, for example, shall we say of the love of money? There is nothing originally more desirable about money than about any heap of glittering pebbles. Its worth is solely that of the things which it will buy: the desires for other things than itself, which it is a means of gratifying. Yet the love of money is not only one of the strongest moving forces of human life, but money is, in many cases, desired in and for itself: the desire to possess it is often stronger than the desire to use it, and goes on increasing when all the desires which point to ends beyond it, to be compassed by it, are falling off. It may, then, be said truly, that money is desired, not for the sake of an end, but as part of the end. From being a means to happiness, it has come to be itself a principal ingredient of the individual's conception of happiness. The same may be said of the majority of the great objects of human life—power, for example, or fame; except that to each of these there is a certain amount of immediate pleasure annexed, which has at least the semblance of being naturally inherent in them: a thing which cannot be said of money. Still, however, the strongest natural attraction, both of power and of fame, is the immense aid they give to the attainment of our other wishes; and it is the strong association thus generated between them and all our objects of desire which gives to the direct desire of them the intensity it often assumes, so as in some characters to surpass in strength all other desires. In these cases, the means have become a part of the end, and a more important part of it than any of the things which they are means to. What was once desired as an instrument for the attainment of happiness has come to be desired for its own sake. In being desired for its own sake, it is, however, desired as *part* of happiness. The person is made, or thinks he would be made, happy by its mere possession, and is made unhappy by failure to obtain it. The desire of it is not a different thing from the desire of happiness, any more than the love of music or the desire of health. They are included in happiness. They are some of the elements of which the desire of happiness is made up. Happiness is not an abstract idea, but a concrete whole; and these are some of its parts. And the utilitarian standard sanctions and approves their being so. Life would be a poor thing, very ill provided with sources of happiness, if there were not this provision of nature, by which things originally indifferent, but conducive to, or otherwise associated with, the satisfaction of our primitive desires, become in themselves sources of pleasure more valuable than the primitive pleasures, both in permanency, in the space of human existence that they are capable of covering, and even in intensity.

Virtue, according to the utilitarian conception, is a good of this description. There was no original desire of it, or motive to it, save its conduciveness to pleasure, and especially to protection from pain. But, through the association thus formed, it may be felt a good in itself, and desired as such with as great intensity as any other good; and with this difference between it and the love of money, of power, or of fame —that all of these may, and often do, render the individual noxious to the other members of the society to which he belongs, whereas there is nothing which makes him so much a blessing to them as the cultivation of the disinterested love of virtue. And consequently the utilitarian standard, while it tolerates and approves those other acquired desires, up to the point beyond which they would be more injurious to the general happiness than promotive of it, enjoins and requires the cultivation of the love of virtue up to the greatest strength possible, as being above all things important to the general happiness.

It results from the preceding considerations, that there is in reality nothing desired except happiness. Whatever is desired otherwise than as a means to some end beyond itself, and ultimately to happiness, is desired as itself a part of happiness, and is not desired for itself until it has become so.

Those who desire virtue for its own sake, desire it either because the consciousness of it is a pleasure, or because the consciousness of being without it is a pain, or for both reasons united: as in truth the pleasure and pain seldom exist separately, but almost always together; the same person feeling pleasure in the degree of virtue attained, and pain in not having attained more. If one of these gave him no pleasure, and the other no pain, he would not love or desire virtue, or would desire it only for the other benefits which it might produce to himself or to persons whom he cared for.

We have now, then, an answer to the question, of what sort of proof the principle of utility is susceptible. If the opinion which I have now stated is psychologically true; if human nature is so constituted as to desire nothing which is not either a part of happiness or a means of happiness—we can have no other proof, and we require no other, that these are the only things desirable. If so, happiness is the sole end of human action, and the promotion of it the test by which to judge of all human conduct; from whence it necessarily follows that it must be the criterion of morality, since a part is included in the whole.

And, now, to decide whether this is really so; whether mankind do desire nothing for itself but that which is a pleasure to them, or of which the absence is a pain—we have evidently arrived at a question of fact and experience, dependent, like all similar questions, upon evidence. It can only be determined by practised self-consciousness and self-observation, assisted by observation of others. I believe that these sources of evidence, impartially consulted, will declare that desiring a thing and finding it pleasant, aversion to it and thinking of it as painful, are phenomena entirely inseparable, or rather two parts of the same phenomenon—in strictness of language, two different modes of naming the same psychological fact; that to think of an object as desirable (unless for the sake of its consequences), and to think of it as pleasant, are one and the same thing; and that to desire any thing,

Mill's aim is to found a science ethics based on exp. Just as he has founded a logic founded on exp. He rejects ... oorlness...

except in proportion as the idea of it is pleasant, is a physical and metaphysical impossibility.

So obvious does this appear to me, that I expect it will hardly be disputed: and the objection made will be, not that desire can possibly be directed to any thing ultimately except pleasure, and exemption from pain, but that the will is a different thing from desire; that a person of confirmed virtue, or any other person whose purposes are fixed, carries out his purposes without any thought of the pleasure he has in contemplating them, or expects to derive from their fulfilment; and persists in acting on them, even though these pleasures are much diminished by changes in his character, or decay of his passive sensibilities, or are outweighed by the pains which the pursuit of the purposes may bring upon him. All this I fully admit, and have stated it elsewhere as positively and emphatically as any one. Will, the active phenomenon, is a different thing from desire, the state of passive sensibility, and, though originally an offshoot from it, may in time take root, and detach itself from the parent stock; so much so, that in the case of an habitual purpose, instead of willing the thing because we desire it, we often desire it only because we will it. This, however, is but an instance of that familiar fact, the power of habit, and is nowise confined to the case of virtuous actions. Many indifferent things, which men originally did from a motive of some sort, they continue to do from habit. Sometimes this is done unconsciously, the consciousness coming only after the action; at other times with conscious volition, but volition which has become habitual, and is put in operation by the force of habit, in opposition, perhaps, to the deliberate preference, as often happens with those who have contracted habits of vicious or hurtful indulgence. Third and last comes the case in which the habitual act of will in the individual instance is not in contradiction to the general intention prevailing at other times, but in fulfilment of it; as in the case of the person of confirmed virtue, and of all who pursue deliberately and consistently any determinate end. The distinction between will and desire, thus understood, is an authentic and highly important psychological fact; but the fact consists solely in this—that will, like all other parts of our constitution, is amenable to habit, and that we may will from habit what we no longer desire for itself, or desire only because we will it. It is not the less true, that will, in the beginning, is entirely produced by desire; including in that term the repelling influence of pain, as well as the attractive one of pleasure. Let us take into consideration no longer the person who has a confirmed will to do right, but him in whom that virtuous will is still feeble, conquerable by temptation, and not to be fully relied on: by what means can it be strengthened? How can the will to be virtuous, where it does not exist in sufficient force, be implanted or awakened? Only by making the person *desire* virtue; by making him think of it in a pleasurable light, or of its absence in a painful one. It is by associating the doing right with pleasure, or the doing wrong with pain, or by eliciting and impressing and bringing home to the person's experience the pleasure naturally involved in the one or the pain in the other, that it is possible to call forth that will to be virtuous, which, when confirmed, acts without any thought of either pleasure or pain. Will is the child of desire, and passes out of the domination of its parent only to come under that of habit. That which is the result of habit affords no presumption of being intrinsically good; and there would be no reason for wishing that the purpose of virtue should become independent of pleasure and pain, were it not that the influence of the pleasurable and painful associations which prompt to virtue is not sufficiently to be depended on for unerring constancy of action until it has acquired the support of habit. Both in feeling and in conduct, habit is the only thing which imparts certainty; and it is because of the importance to others of being able to rely absolutely on one's feelings and conduct, and to one's self of being able to rely on one's own, that the will to do right ought to be cultivated into this habitual independence.

In other words, this state of the will is a means to good, not intrinsically a good; and does not contradict the doctrine, that nothing is a good to human beings but in so far as it is either itself pleasurable, or a means of attaining pleasure or averting pain.

But, if this doctrine be true, the principle of utility is proved. Whether it is so or not, must now be left to the consideration of the thoughtful reader.

CHAPTER 5 *On the Connection Between Justice and Utility*

In all ages of speculation, one of the strongest obstacles to the reception of the doctrine, that Utility or Happiness is the criterion of right and wrong, has been drawn from the idea of Justice. The powerful sentiment and apparently clear perception which that word recalls, with a rapidity and certainty resembling an instinct, have seemed to the majority of thinkers to point to an inherent quality in things; to show that the Just must have an existence in nature as something absolute, generically distinct from every variety of the Expedient, and, in idea, opposed to it, though (as is commonly acknowledged) never, in the long-run, disjoined from it in fact.

In the case of this, as of our other moral sentiments, there is no necessary connection between the question of its origin and that of its binding force. That a feeling is bestowed on us by nature does not necessarily legitimate all its promptings. The feeling of justice might be a peculiar instinct, and might yet require, like our other instincts, to be controlled and enlightened by a higher reason. If we have intellectual instincts leading us to judge in a particular way, as well as animal instincts that prompt us to act in a particular way, there is no necessity that the former should be more infallible in their sphere than the latter in theirs: it may as well happen that wrong judgments are occasionally suggested by those, as wrong actions by these. But though it is one thing to believe that we have natural feelings of justice, and another to acknowledge them as an ultimate criterion of conduct, these two opinions are very closely connected in point of fact. Mankind are always predisposed to believe that any subjective feeling, not otherwise accounted for, is a revelation of some objective reality. Our present object is to determine whether the reality, to which the feeling of justice corresponds, is one which needs any such special revelation; whether the justice or injustice of an action is a thing intrinsically peculiar, and distinct from all its other qualities, or only a combination of certain of those qualities, presented under a peculiar aspect. For the purpose of this inquiry, it is practically important to consider, whether the feeling itself, of justice and injustice, is *sui generis* like our sensations of color and taste, or a derivative feeling, formed by a combination of others. And this it is the more essential to examine, as people are in general willing enough to allow, that, objectively, the dictates of Justice coincide with a part of the field of General Expediency; but inasmuch as the subjective mental feeling of Justice is different from that which commonly attaches to simple expediency, and, except in the extreme cases of the latter, is far more imperative in its demands, people find it difficult to see, in Justice, only a particular kind or branch of general utility, and think that its superior binding force requires a totally different origin.

To throw light upon this question, it is necessary to attempt to ascertain what is the distinguishing character of justice, or of injustice; what is the quality, or whether there is any quality, attributed in common to all modes of conduct designated as unjust (for justice, like many other moral attributes, is best defined by its opposite), and distinguishing them from such modes of conduct as are disapproved, but without having that particular epithet of disapprobation applied to them. If, in every thing which men are accustomed to characterize as just or unjust, some one common attribute, or collection of attributes, is always present, we may judge whether this particular attribute, or combination of attributes, would be capable of gathering round it a sentiment of that peculiar character and intensity by virtue of the general laws of our emotional constitution; or whether the sentiment is inexplicable, and requires to be regarded as a special provision of nature. If we find the former to be the case, we shall, in resolving this question, have resolved also the main problem; if the latter, we shall have to seek for some other mode of investigating it.

To find the common attributes of a variety of objects, it is necessary to begin by surveying the objects themselves in the concrete. Let us therefore advert successively to the various modes of action, and arrangements of human affairs, which are classed, by universal or widely spread opinion, as Just or as Unjust. The things well known to excite the sentiments associated with those names are of a very multifarious character. I shall pass them rapidly in review, without studying any particular arrangement.

In the first place, it is mostly considered unjust to deprive any one of his personal liberty, his property, or any other thing which belongs to him by law. Here, therefore, is one instance of the application of the terms Just and Unjust in a perfectly definite sense; namely, that it is just to respect, unjust to violate, the *legal rights* of any one. But this judgment admits of several exceptions, arising from the other forms in which the notions of justice and injustice present themselves. For example: the person who suffers the deprivation may (as the phrase is) have *forfeited* the rights which he is so deprived of; a case to which we shall return presently. But also—

Secondly, The legal rights of which he is deprived may be rights which *ought* not to have belonged to him: in other words, the law which confers on him these rights may be a bad law. When it is so, or when (which is the same thing for our purpose) it is supposed to be so, opinions will differ as to the justice or injustice of infringing it. Some maintain that no law, however bad, ought to be disobeyed by an individual citizen; that his opposition to it, if shown at all, should only be shown in endeavoring to get it altered by competent authority. This opinion (which condemns many of the most illustrious benefactors of mankind, and would often protect pernicious institutions against the only weapons, which, in the state of things existing at the time, have any chance of succeeding against them) is defended, by those who hold it, on grounds of expediency; principally on that of the importance, to the common interest of mankind, of maintaining inviolate the sentiment of submission to law. Other persons, again, hold the directly contrary opinion, that any law, judged to be bad, may blamelessly be disobeyed, even though it be not judged to be unjust, but only inexpedient; while others would confine the license of disobedience to the case of unjust laws. But, again, some say that all laws which are inexpedient are unjust, since every law imposes some restriction on the natural liberty of mankind; which restriction is an injustice, unless legitimated by tending to their good. Among these diversities of opinion, it seems to be universally admitted that there may be unjust laws, and that law, consequently, is not the ultimate criterion of justice, but may give to one person a benefit, or impose on another an evil, which justice condemns. When, however, a law is thought to be unjust, it seems always to be regarded as being so in the same way in which a breach of law is unjust—namely, by infringing somebody's right; which, as it cannot in this case be a legal right, receives a different appellation, and is called a moral right. We may say, therefore, that a second case of injustice consists in taking or withholding from any person that to which he has a *moral right*.

Thirdly, It is universally considered just, that each person should obtain that (whether good or evil) which he *deserves;* and unjust, that he should obtain a good, or be made to undergo an evil, which he does not deserve. This is, perhaps, the clearest and most emphatic form in which the idea of justice is conceived by the general mind. As it involves the notion of desert, the question arises, What constitutes desert? Speaking in a general way, a person is understood to deserve good if he does right; evil, if he does wrong: and, in a more particular sense, to deserve good from those to whom he does or has done good, and evil from those to whom he does or has done evil. The precept of returning good for evil has never been regarded as a case of the fulfilment of justice, but as one in which the claims of justice are waived, in obedience to other considerations.

Fourthly, It is confessedly unjust to *break faith* with any one; to violate an engagement, either express or implied; or disappoint expectations raised by our own conduct, at least if we have raised those expectations knowingly and voluntarily. Like the other obligations of justice already spoken of, this one is not regarded as absolute, but as capable of being overruled by a stronger obligation of justice on the other side, or by such conduct on the part of the person concerned as is deemed to absolve us from our obligation to him, and to constitute a *forfeiture* of the benefit which he has been led to expect.

Fifthly, It is, by universal admission, inconsistent with justice to be *partial;* to show favor or preference to one person over another in matters to which favor and preference do not properly apply. Impartiality, however, does not seem to be regarded as a duty in itself, but rather as instrumental to some other duty; for it is admitted that favor and preference are not always censurable, and indeed the cases in which they are condemned are rather the exception than the rule. A person would be more likely to be blamed than applauded for giving his family or friends no superiority in good offices over strangers, when he could do so without violating any other duty; and no one thinks it unjust to seek one person in preference to another as a friend, connection, or companion. Impartiality, where rights are concerned, is of course obligatory; but this is involved in the more general obligation of giving to every one his right. A tribunal, for example, must be impartial, because it is bound to award, without regard to any other consideration, a disputed object to the one of two parties who has the right to it. There are other cases in which impartiality means, being solely influenced by desert; as with those who, in the capacity of judges, preceptors, or parents, administer reward and punishment as such. There are cases, again, in which it means being solely influenced by consideration for the public interest; as in making a selection among candidates for a government employment. Impartiality, in short, as an obligation of justice, may be said to mean being exclusively influenced by the considerations which it is supposed ought to influence the particular case in hand, and resisting the solicitation of any motives which prompt to conduct different from what those considerations would dictate.

Nearly allied to the idea of impartiality is that of *equality;* which often enters as a component part both into the conception of justice and into the practice of it, and, in the eyes of many persons, constitutes its essence. But, in this still more than in any other case, the notion of justice varies in different persons, and always conforms in its variations to their notion of utility. Each person maintains that equality is the dictate of justice, except where he thinks that expediency requires inequality. The justice of giving equal protection to the rights of all is maintained by those who support the most outrageous inequality in the rights themselves. Even in slave countries, it is theoretically admitted that the rights of the slave, such as they are, ought to be as sacred as those of the master, and that a tribunal which fails to enforce them with equal strictness is wanting in justice; while, at the same time, institutions which leave to the slave scarcely any rights to enforce are not deemed unjust, because they are not deemed inexpedient. Those who think that utility requires distinctions of rank do not consider it unjust that riches and social privileges should be unequally dispensed; but those who think this inequality inexpedient think it unjust also. Whoever thinks that government is necessary sees no injustice in as much inequality as is constituted by giving to the magistrate powers not granted to other people. Even among those who hold levelling doctrines, there are as many questions of justice as there are differences of opinion about expediency. Some Communists consider it unjust that the produce of the labor of the community should be shared on any other principle than that of exact equality; others think it just that those should receive most whose wants are greatest; while others hold that those who work harder, or who produce more, or whose services are more valuable to the community, may justly claim a larger quota in the division of the produce. And the sense of natural justice may be plausibly appealed to in behalf of every one of these opinions.

Among so many diverse applications of the term Justice, which yet is not regarded as ambiguous, it is a matter of some difficulty to seize the mental link which holds them together, and on which the moral sentiment adhering to the term essentially depends. Perhaps, in this embarrassment, some help may be derived from the history of the word, as indicated by its etymology.

In most, if not in all languages, the etymology of the word which corresponds to Just points distinctly to an origin connected with the ordinances of law. *Justum* is a form of *jussum*—that which has been ordered. Δίκαιον comes directly from δίκη, a suit at law. *Recht,* from which came *right* and *righteous,* is synonymous with law. The courts of justice, the administration of justice, are the courts and the administration of law. *La justice,* in French, is the established term for judicature. I am not committing the fallacy imputed with some show of truth to Horne Tooke, of assuming that a word must still continue to mean what it originally meant. Etymology is slight evidence of what the idea now signified is, but the very best evidence of how it sprang up. There can, I think, be no doubt that the *idée mère,* the primitive element, in the formation of the notion of justice, was conformity to law. It constituted the entire idea among the Hebrews up to the birth of Christianity; as might be expected in the case of a people whose laws attempted to embrace all subjects on which precepts were required, and who believed those laws to be a direct emanation from the Supreme Being. But other nations, and in particular the Greeks and Romans, who knew that their laws had been made originally, and still continued to be made, by men, were not afraid to admit that those men might make bad laws; might do, by law, the same things, and from the same motives, which, if done by individuals without the sanction of law, would be called unjust. And hence the sentiment of injustice came to be attached, not to all violations of law, but only to violations of such laws as *ought* to exist, including such as ought to exist, but do not; and to laws themselves, if supposed to be contrary to what ought to be law. In this manner, the idea of law and of its injunctions was still predominant in the notion of justice, even when the laws actually in force ceased to be accepted as the standard of it.

It is true that mankind consider the idea of justice and its obligations as applicable to many things which neither are, nor is it desired that they should be, regulated by law. Nobody desires that laws should interfere with the whole detail of private life; yet every one allows, that, in all daily conduct, a person may and does show himself to be either just or unjust. But, even here, the idea of the breach of what ought to be law still lingers in a modified shape. It would always give us pleasure, and chime in with our feelings of fitness, that acts which we deem unjust should be punished, though we do not always think it expedient that this should be done by the tribunals. We forego that gratification on account of incidental inconveniences. We should be glad to see just conduct enforced, and injustice repressed, even in the minutest details, if we were not with reason afraid of trusting the magistrate with so unlimited an amount of power over individuals. When we think that a person is bound in justice to do a thing, it is an ordinary form of language to say, that he ought to be compelled to do it. We should be gratified to see the obligation enforced by anybody who had the power. If we see that its enforcement by law would be inexpedient, we lament the impossibility, we consider the impunity given to injustice as an evil, and strive to make amends for it by bringing a strong expression of our own and the public disapprobation to bear upon the offender. Thus the idea of legal constraint is still the generating idea of the notion of justice, though undergoing several transformations before that notion, as it exists in an advanced state of society, becomes complete.

The above is, I think, a true account, as far as it goes, of the origin and progressive growth of the idea of justice. But we must observe, that it contains, as yet, nothing to distinguish that obligation from moral obligation in general. For the truth is, that the idea of penal sanction, which is the essence of law, enters not only into the conception of injustice, but into that of any kind of wrong. We do not call any thing wrong, unless we mean to imply that a person ought to be punished in some way or other for doing it; if not by law, by the opinion of his fellow-creatures; if not by opinion, by the reproaches of his own conscience. This seems the real turning-point of the distinction between morality and simple expediency. It is a part of the notion of Duty in every one of its forms, that a person may rightfully be compelled to fulfil it. Duty is a thing which may be *exacted* from a person, as one exacts a debt. Unless we think that it may be exacted from him, we do not call it his duty. Reasons of prudence, or the interest of other people, may militate against actually exacting it; but the person himself, it is clearly understood, would not be entitled to complain. There are other things, on the contrary, which we wish that people should do, which we like or admire them for doing, perhaps dislike or despise them for not doing, but yet admit that they are not bound to do: it is not a case of moral obligation: we do not blame them; that is, we do not think that they are proper objects of punishment. How we come by these ideas of deserving and not deserving punishment, will appear, perhaps, in the sequel: but I think there is no doubt that this distinction lies at the bottom of the notions of right and wrong; that we call any conduct wrong, or employ instead some other term of dislike or disparagement, according as we think that the person ought, or ought not, to be punished for it; and we say it would be right to do so and so, or merely that it would be desirable or laudable, according as we would wish to see the person whom it concerns compelled, or only persuaded and exhorted, to act in that manner.*

This, therefore, being the characteristic difference which marks off, not justice, but morality in general, from the remaining provinces of Expediency and Worthiness, the character is still to be sought which distinguishes justice from other branches of morality. Now, it is known that ethical writers divide moral duties into two classes, denoted by the ill-chosen expressions, duties of perfect and of imperfect obligation: the latter being those in which, though the act is obligatory, the particular occasions of performing it are left to our choice; as in the case of charity or beneficence, which we are indeed bound to practise, but not towards any definite

---

* See this point enforced and illustrated by Professor Bain, in an admirable chapter (entitled "The Ethical Emotions, or the Moral Sense") of the second of the two treatises composing his elaborate and profound work on the Mind.

person, nor at any prescribed time. In the more precise language of philosophic jurists, duties of perfect obligation are those duties in virtue of which a correlative *right* resides in some person or persons: duties of imperfect obligation are those moral obligations which do not give birth to any right. I think it will be found that this distinction exactly coincides with that which exists between justice and the other obligations of morality. In our survey of the various popular acceptations of justice, the term appeared generally to involve the idea of a personal right—a claim on the part of one or more individuals, like that which the law gives when it confers a proprietary or other legal right. Whether the injustice consists in depriving a person of a possession, or in breaking faith with him, or in treating him worse than he deserves, or worse than other people who have no greater claims, in each case the supposition implies two things—a wrong done, and some assignable person who is wronged. Injustice may also be done by treating a person better than others; but the wrong in this case is to his competitors, who are also assignable persons. It seems to me that this feature in the case —a right in some person, correlative to the moral obligation —constitutes the specific difference between justice, and generosity or beneficence. Justice implies something which it is not only right to do, and wrong not to do, but which some individual person can claim from us as his moral right. No one has a moral right to our generosity or beneficence, because we are not morally bound to practise those virtues towards any given individual. And it will be found, with respect to this as to every correct definition, that the instances which seem to conflict with it are those which most confirm it; for if a moralist attempts, as some have done, to make out that mankind generally, though not any given individual, have a right to all the good we can do them, he at once, by that thesis, includes generosity and beneficence within the category of justice. He is obliged to say that our utmost exertions are *due* to our fellow-creatures, thus assimilating them to a debt;

or that nothing less can be a sufficient *return* for what society does for us, thus classing the case as one of gratitude; both of which are acknowledged cases of justice. Wherever there is a right, the case is one of justice, and not of the virtue of beneficence; and whoever does not place the distinction between justice and morality in general where we have now placed it will be found to make no distinction between them at all, but to merge all morality in justice.

Having thus endeavored to determine the distinctive elements which enter into the composition of the idea of justice, we are ready to enter on the inquiry, whether the feeling which accompanies the idea is attached to it by a special dispensation of nature, or whether it could have grown up by any known laws out of the idea itself; and, in particular, whether it can have originated in considerations of general expediency.

I conceive that the sentiment itself does not arise from any thing which would commonly or correctly be termed an idea of expediency; but that, though the sentiment does not, whatever is moral in it does.

We have seen that the two essential ingredients in the sentiment of justice are the desire to punish a person who has done harm, and the knowledge or belief that there is some definite individual or individuals to whom harm has been done.

Now, it appears to me that the desire to punish a person who has done harm to some individual is a spontaneous outgrowth from two sentiments, both in the highest degree natural, and which either are or resemble instincts—the impulse of self-defence, and the feeling of sympathy.

It is natural to resent, and to repel or retaliate, any harm done or attempted against ourselves, or against those with whom we sympathize. The origin of this sentiment it is not necessary here to discuss. Whether it be an instinct, or a result of intelligence, it is, we know, common to all animal nature; for every animal tries to hurt those who have hurt, or who it thinks are about to hurt, itself or its young. Human beings, on this point, only differ from other animals in two particulars: first, in being capable of sympathizing, not solely with their offspring, or, like some of the more noble animals, with some superior animal who is kind to them, but with all human, and even with all sentient beings; secondly, in having a more developed intelligence, which gives a wider range to the whole of their sentiments, whether self-regarding or sympathetic. By virtue of his superior intelligence, even apart from his superior range of sympathy, a human being is capable of apprehending a community of interest between himself and the human society of which he forms a part, such that any conduct which threatens the security of the society generally is threatening to his own, and calls forth his instinct (if instinct it be) of self-defence. The same superiority of intelligence, joined to the power of sympathizing with human beings generally, enables him to attach himself to the collective idea of his tribe, his country, or mankind, in such a manner that any act hurtful to them raises his instinct of sympathy, and urges him to resistance.

The sentiment of justice, in that one of its elements which consists of the desire to punish, is thus, I conceive, the natural feeling of retaliation, or vengeance, rendered by intellect and sympathy applicable to those injuries—that is, to those hurts—which wound us through, or in common with, society at large. This sentiment in itself has nothing moral in it: what is moral is, the exclusive subordination of it to the social sympathies, so as to wait on and obey their call. For the natural feeling would make us resent indiscriminately whatever any one does that is disagreeable to us; but, when moralized by the social feeling, it only acts in the directions conformable to the general good: just persons resenting a hurt to society, though not otherwise a hurt to themselves, and not resenting a hurt to themselves, however painful, un-

less it be of the kind which society has a common interest
with them in the repression of.

It is no objection against this doctrine to say, that, when
we feel our sentiment of justice outraged, we are not thinking
of society at large, or of any collective interest, but only of the
individual case. It is common enough, certainly, though the
reverse of commendable, to feel resentment merely because
we have suffered pain; but a person whose resentment is
really a moral feeling—that is, who considers whether an act
is blamable before he allows himself to resent it—such a
person, though he may not say expressly to himself that he
is standing up for the interest of society, certainly does feel
that he is asserting a rule which is for the benefit of others
as well as for his own. If he is not feeling this; if he is regarding the act solely as it affects him individually—he is not
consciously just; he is not concerning himself about the justice of his actions. This is admitted even by anti-utilitarian
moralists. When Kant (as before remarked) propounds as
the fundamental principle of morals, "So act that thy rule of
conduct might be adopted as a law by all rational beings," he
virtually acknowledges that the interest of mankind collectively, or at least of mankind indiscriminately, must be in the
mind of the agent when conscientiously deciding on the
morality of the act. Otherwise he uses words without a meaning; for that a rule even of utter selfishness could not *possibly*
be adopted by all rational beings—that there is any insuperable obstacle in the nature of things to its adoption—cannot be even plausibly maintained. To give any meaning to
Kant's principle, the sense put upon it must be, that we ought
to shape our conduct by a rule which all rational beings might
adopt *with benefit to their collective interest.*

To recapitulate: the idea of justice supposes two things—
a rule of conduct, and a sentiment which sanctions the rule.
The first must be supposed common to all mankind, and intended for their good: the other (the sentiment) is a desire

that punishment may be suffered by those who infringe the rule. There is involved, in addition, the conception of some definite person who suffers by the infringement; whose rights (to use the expression appropriated to the case) are violated by it. And the sentiment of justice appears to me to be, the animal desire to repel or retaliate a hurt or damage to one's self, or to those with whom one sympathizes, widened so as to include all persons, by the human capacity of enlarged sympathy, and the human conception of intelligent self-interest. From the latter elements, the feeling derives its morality; from the former, its peculiar impressiveness and energy of self-assertion.

I have, throughout, treated the idea of a *right* residing in the injured person, and violated by the injury, not as a separate element in the composition of the idea and sentiment, but as one of the forms in which the other two elements clothe themselves. These elements are, a hurt to some assignable person or persons on the one hand, and a demand for punishment on the other. An examination of our own minds, I think, will show that these two things include all that we mean when we speak of violation of a right. When we call any thing a person's right, we mean that he has a valid claim on society to protect him in the possession of it, either by the force of law, or by that of education and opinion. If he has what we consider a sufficient claim, on whatever account, to have something guaranteed to him by society, we say that he has a right to it. If we desire to prove that any thing does not belong to him by right, we think this done as soon as it is admitted that society ought not to take measures for securing it to him, but should leave him to chance, or to his own exertions. Thus a person is said to have a right to what he can earn in fair professional competition, because society ought not to allow any other person to hinder him from endeavoring to earn in that manner as much as he can. But he has not a right to three hundred a year, though he may happen to be earning it, because society is not called on to provide that he shall earn that sum. On the contrary, if he owns ten thousand pounds three-per-cent stock, he *has* a right to three hundred a year, because society has come under an obligation to provide him with an income of that amount.

To have a right, then, is, I conceive, to have something which society ought to defend me in the possession of. If the objector goes on to ask why it ought, I can give him no other reason than general utility. If that expression does not seem to convey a sufficient feeling of the strength of the obligation, nor to account for the peculiar energy of the feeling, it is because there goes to the composition of the sentiment, not a rational only, but also an animal element—the thirst for retaliation; and this thirst derives its intensity, as well as its moral justification, from the extraordinarily important and impressive kind of utility which is concerned. The interest involved is that of security; to every one's feelings, the most vital of all interests. All other earthly benefits are needed by one person, not needed by another; and many of them can, if necessary, be cheerfully foregone, or replaced by something else. But security no human being can possibly do without: on it we depend for all our immunity from evil, and for the whole value of all and every good, beyond the passing moment; since nothing but the gratification of the instant could be of any worth to us if we could be deprived of everything the next instant by whoever was momentarily stronger than ourselves. Now, this most indispensable of all necessaries, after physical nutriment, cannot be had, unless the machinery for providing it is kept unintermittedly in active play. Our notion, therefore, of the claim we have on our fellow-creatures to join in making safe for us the very groundwork of our existence, gathers feelings around it so much more intense than those concerned in any of the more common cases of utility, that the difference in degree (as is often the case in psychology) becomes a real difference in kind. The claim assumes that character of absoluteness, that apparent infinity, and incommensurability with all other considerations, which constitute the distinction between the feeling of right and wrong and that of ordinary expediency and inexpediency. The feelings concerned are so powerful, and we count so positively on finding a responsive feeling in others (all being alike interested), that *ought* and *should* grow into *must,* and recognized indispensability becomes a moral necessity, analogous to physical, and often not inferior to it in binding force.

If the preceding analysis, or something resembling it, be not the correct account of the notion of justice; if justice be totally independent of utility, and be a standard *per se,* which the mind can recognize by simple introspection of itself—it is hard to understand why that internal oracle is so ambiguous, and why so many things appear either just or unjust, according to the light in which they are regarded.

We are continually informed that Utility is an uncertain standard, which every different person interprets differently; and that there is no safety but in the immutable, ineffaceable, and unmistakable dictates of Justice, which carry their evidence in themselves, and are independent of the fluctuations of opinion. One would suppose from this, that, on questions of justice, there could be no controversy; that, if we take that for our rule, its application to any given case could leave us in as little doubt as a mathematical demonstration. So far is this from being the fact, that there is as much difference of opinion and as much discussion about what is just as about what is useful to society. Not only have different nations and individuals different notions of justice, but, in the mind of one and the same individual, justice is not some one rule, principle, or maxim, but many, which do not always coincide in their dictates, and, in choosing between which, he is guided either by some extraneous standard, or by his own personal predilections.

For instance: there are some who say that it is unjust to

punish any one for the sake of example to others; that punishment is just, only when intended for the good of the sufferer himself. Others maintain the extreme reverse; contending that to punish persons who have attained years of discretion, for their own benefit, is despotism and injustice; since, if the matter at issue is solely their own good, no one has a right to control their own judgment of it; but that they may justly be punished to prevent evil to others, this being the exercise of the legitimate right of self-defence. Mr. Owen, again, affirms that it is unjust to punish at all; for the criminal did not make his own character: his education, and the circumstances which surrounded him, have made him a criminal; and for these he is not responsible. All these opinions are extremely plausible; and so long as the question is argued as one of justice simply, without going down to the principles which lie under justice, and are the source of its authority, I am unable to see how any of these reasoners can be refuted. For, in truth, every one of the three builds upon rules of justice confessedly true. The first appeals to the acknowledged injustice of singling out an individual, and making him a sacrifice, without his consent, for other people's benefit. The second relies on the acknowledged justice of self-defence, and the admitted injustice of forcing one person to conform to another's notions of what constitutes his good. The Owenite invokes the admitted principle, that it is unjust to punish any one for what he cannot help. Each is triumphant so long as he is not compelled to take into consideration any other maxims of justice than the one he has selected; but, as soon as their several maxims are brought face to face, each disputant seems to have exactly as much to say for himself as the others. No one of them can carry out his own notion of justice without trampling upon another equally binding. These are difficulties; they have always been felt to be such; and many devices have been invented to turn rather than to overcome them. As a refuge from the last of the three, men imagined what they called the "freedom of the will;" fancying that they could not justify punishing a man whose will is in a thoroughly hateful state, unless it be supposed to have come into that state through no influence of anterior circumstances. To escape from the other difficulties, a favorite contrivance has been the fiction of a contract, whereby at some unknown period all the members of society engaged to obey the laws, and consented to be punished for any disobedience to them; thereby giving to their legislators the right, which it is assumed they would not otherwise have had, of punishing them, either for their own good or for that of society. This happy thought was considered to get rid of the whole difficulty, and to legitimate the infliction of punishment, in virtue of another received maxim of justice, *Volenti non fit injuria,* "That is not unjust which is done with the consent of the person who is supposed to be hurt by it." I need hardly remark, that, even if the consent were not a mere fiction, this maxim is not superior in authority to the others which it is brought in to supersede. It is, on the contrary, an instructive specimen of the loose and irregular manner in which supposed principles of justice grow up. This particular one evidently came into use as a help to the coarse exigencies of courts of law, which are sometimes obliged to be content with very uncertain presumptions, on account of the greater evils which would often arise from any attempt on their part to cut finer. But even courts of law are not able to adhere consistently to the maxim; for they allow voluntary engagements to be set aside on the ground of fraud, and sometimes on that of mere mistake or misinformation.

Again: when the legitimacy of inflicting punishment is admitted, how many conflicting conceptions of justice come to light in discussing the proper apportionment of punishments to offences! No rule on the subject recommends itself so strongly to the primitive and spontaneous sentiment of justice, as the *lex talionis,* "An eye for an eye, and a tooth for a tooth." Though this principle of the Jewish and of the

Mahometan law has been generally abandoned in Europe as a practical maxim, there is, I suspect, in most minds, a secret hankering after it; and, when retribution accidentally falls on an offender in that precise shape, the general feeling of satisfaction evinced bears witness how natural is the sentiment to which this repayment in kind is acceptable. With many, the test of justice in penal infliction is that the punishment should be proportioned to the offence—meaning that it should be exactly measured by the moral guilt of the culprit (whatever be their standard for measuring moral guilt); the consideration, what amount of punishment is necessary to deter from the offence, having nothing to do with the question of justice, in their estimation: while there are others to whom that consideration is all in all; who maintain that it is not just, at least for man, to inflict on a fellow-creature, whatever may be his offences, any amount of suffering beyond the least that will suffice to prevent him from repeating, and others from imitating, his misconduct.

To take another example from a subject already once referred to. In a co-operative industrial association, is it just or not that talent or skill should give a title to superior remuneration? On the negative side of the question it is argued, that whoever does the best he can deserves equally well, and ought not in justice to be put in a position of inferiority for no fault of his own; that superior abilities have already advantages more than enough, in the admiration they excite, the personal influence they command, and the internal sources of satisfaction attending them, without adding to these a superior share of the world's goods; and that society is bound in justice rather to make compensation to the less favored, for this unmerited inequality of advantages, than to aggravate it. On the contrary side it is contended, that society receives more from the more efficient laborer; that, his services being more useful, society owes him a larger return for them; that a greater share of the joint result is actually his work, and not to allow his claim to it is a kind of robbery; that, if he is only to receive as much as others, he can only be justly required to produce as much, and to give a smaller amount of time and exertion, proportioned to his superior efficiency. Who shall decide between these appeals to conflicting principles of justice? Justice has in this case two sides to it, which it is impossible to bring into harmony; and the two disputants have chosen opposite sides: the one looks to what it is just that the individual should receive; the other, to what it is just that the community should give. Each, from his own point of view, is unanswerable; and any choice between them, on grounds of justice, must be perfectly arbitrary. Social utility alone can decide the preference.

How many, again, and how irreconcilable, are the standards of justice to which reference is made in discussing the repartition of taxation! One opinion is, that payment to the State should be in numerical proportion to pecuniary means. Others think that justice dictates what they term "graduated taxation,"—taking a higher percentage from those who have more to spare. In point of natural justice, a strong case might be made for disregarding means altogether, and taking the same absolute sum (whenever it could be got) from every one; as the subscribers to a mess, or to a club, all pay the same sum for the same privileges, whether they can all equally afford it or not. Since the protection (it might be said) of law and government is afforded to and is equally required by all, there is no injustice in making all buy it at the same price. It is reckoned justice, not injustice, that a dealer should charge to all customers the same price for the same article; not a price varying according to their means of payment. This doctrine, as applied to taxation, finds no advocates, because it conflicts so strongly with man's feelings of humanity and of social expediency; but the principle of justice which it invokes is as true and as binding as those which can be appealed to against it. Accordingly, it exerts a tacit influence on the line of defence employed for other modes of assessing taxation. People feel obliged to argue that the State does more for the rich than for the poor, as a justification for its taking more from them: though this is in reality not true; for the rich would be far better able to protect themselves, in the absence of law or government, than the poor, and indeed would probably be successful in converting the poor into their slaves. Others, again, so far defer to the same conception of justice as to maintain that all should pay an equal capitation-tax for the protection of their persons (these being of equal value to all), and an unequal tax for the protection of their property, which is unequal. To this others reply, that the all of one man is as valuable to him as the all of another. From these confusions, there is no other mode of extrication than the utilitarian.

Is, then, the difference between the Just and the Expedient a merely imaginary distinction? Have mankind been under a delusion in thinking that justice is a more sacred thing than policy, and that the latter ought only to be listened to after the former has been satisfied? By no means. The exposition we have given of the nature and origin of the sentiment recognizes a real distinction; and no one of those who profess the most sublime contempt for the consequences of actions as an element in their morality attaches more importance to the distinction that I do. While I dispute the pretensions of any theory which sets up an imaginary standard of justice not grounded on utility, I account the justice which is grounded on utility to be the chief part, and incomparably the most sacred and binding part, of all morality. Justice is a name for certain classes of moral rules which concern the essentials of human well-being more nearly, and are therefore of more absolute obligation, than any other rules for the guidance of life; and the notion which we have found to be of the essence of the idea of justice, that of a right residing in an individual, implies and testifies to this more binding obligation.

The moral rules which forbid mankind to hurt one another

(in which we must never forget to include wrongful interference with each other's freedom) are more vital to human
well-being than any maxims, however important, which only
point out the best mode of managing some department of human affairs. They have also the peculiarity, that they are the
main element in determining the whole of the social feelings
of mankind. It is their observance which alone preserves
peace among human beings: if obedience to them were not
the rule, and disobedience the exception, every one would see
in every one else an enemy, against whom he must be perpetually guarding himself. What is hardly less important,
these are the precepts which mankind have the strongest
and the most direct inducements for impressing upon one
another. By merely giving to each other prudential instruction or exhortation, they may gain, or think they gain,
nothing; in inculcating on each other the duty of positive
beneficence, they have an unmistakable interest, but far less
in degree: a person may possibly not need the benefits of
others; but he always needs that they should not do him hurt.
Thus the moralities which protect every individual from being harmed by others, either directly or by being hindered in
his freedom of pursuing his own good, are at once those
which he himself has most at heart, and those which he has
the strongest interest in publishing and enforcing by word and
deed. It is by a person's observance of these, that his fitness
to exist as one of the fellowship of human beings is tested
and decided; for on that depends his being a nuisance or not
to those with whom he is in contact. Now, it is these moralities, primarily, which compose the obligations of justice. The
most marked cases of injustice, and those which give the tone
to the feeling of repugnance which characterizes the sentiment, are acts of wrongful aggression, or wrongful exercise of
power over some one; the next are those which consist in
wrongfully withholding from him something which is his due:
in both cases inflicting on him a positive hurt, either in the
form of direct suffering, or of the privation of some good

which he had reasonable ground, either of a physical or of a social kind, for counting upon.

The same powerful motives which command the observance of these primary moralities enjoin the punishment of those who violate them; and as the impulses of self-defence, of defence of others, and of vengeance, are all called forth against such persons, retribution, or evil for evil, becomes closely connected with the sentiment of justice, and is universally included in the idea. Good for good is also one of the dictates of justice; and this, though its social utility is evident, and though it carries with it a natural human feeling, has not at first sight that obvious connection with hurt or injury, which, existing in the most elementary cases of just and unjust, is the source of the characteristic intensity of the sentiment. But the connection, though less obvious, is not less real. He who accepts benefits, and denies a return of them when needed, inflicts a real hurt, by disappointing one of the most natural and reasonable of expectations, and one which he must at least tacitly have encouraged, otherwise the benefits would seldom have been conferred. The important rank, among human evils and wrongs, of the disappointment of expectation, is shown in the fact, that it constitutes the principal criminality of two such highly immoral acts as a breach of friendship and a breach of promise. Few hurts which human beings can sustain are greater, and none wound more, than when that on which they habitually and with full assurance relied fails them in the hour of need; and few wrongs are greater than this mere withholding of good: none excite more resentment, either in the person suffering, or in a sympathizing spectator. The principle, therefore, of giving to each what they deserve—that is, good for good, as well as evil for evil—is not only included within the idea of Justice as we have defined it, but is a proper object of that intensity of sentiment which places the Just, in human estimation, above the simply Expedient.

Most of the maxims of justice current in the world, and

commonly appealed to in its transactions, are simply instrumental to carrying into effect the principles of justice which
we have now spoken of. That a person is only responsible for
what he has done voluntarily, or could voluntarily have
avoided; that it is unjust to condemn any person unheard;
that the punishment ought to be proportioned to the offence,
and the like—are maxims intended to prevent the just principle of evil for evil from being perverted to the infliction of
evil without that justification. The greater part of these common maxims have come into use from the practice of courts
of justice, which have been naturally led to a more complete recognition and elaboration than was likely to suggest
itself to others, of the rules necessary to enable them to fulfil
their double function, of inflicting punishment when due, and
of awarding to each person his right.

That first of judicial virtues, impartiality, is an obligation
of justice, partly for the reason last mentioned, as being a
necessary condition of the fulfilment of the other obligations
of justice. But this is not the only source of the exalted rank,
among human obligations, of those maxims of equality and
impartiality, which, both in popular estimation and in that of
the most enlightened, are included among the precepts of
justice. In one point of view, they may be considered as corollaries from the principles already laid down. If it is a duty
to do to each according to his deserts, returning good for
good as well as repressing evil by evil, it necessarily follows
that we should treat all equally well (when no higher duty
forbids) who have deserved equally well of *us;* and that society should treat all equally well who have deserved equally
well of *it*—that is, who have deserved equally well absolutely. This is the highest abstract standard of social and distributive justice, towards which all institutions, and the efforts
of all virtuous citizens, should be made in the utmost possible degree to converge. But this great moral duty rests upon
a still deeper foundation; being a direct emanation from the
first principle of morals, and not a mere logical corollary

from secondary or derivative doctrines. It is involved in the very meaning of Utility, or the Greatest-happiness Principle. That principle is a mere form of words without rational signification, unless one person's happiness, supposed equal in degree (with the proper allowance made for kind), is counted for exactly as much as another's. Those conditions being supplied, Bentham's dictum, "Everybody to count for one, nobody for more than one," might be written under the principle of utility as an explanatory commentary.* The

* This implication, in the first principle of the utilitarian scheme of perfect impartiality between persons, is regarded by Mr. Herbert Spencer (in his "Social Statics") as a disproof of the pretensions of utility to be a sufficient guide to right; since (he says) the principle of utility presupposes the anterior principle, that everybody has an equal right to happiness. It may be more correctly described as supposing that equal amounts of happiness are equally desirable, whether felt by the same or by different persons. This, however, is not a *pre*-supposition; not a premise needful to support the principle of utility, but the very principle itself: for what is the principle of utility, if it be not that "happiness" and "desirable" are synonymous terms? If there is any anterior principle implied, it can be no other than this—that the truths of arithmetic are applicable to the valuation of happiness, as of all other measurable quantities.

[Mr. Herbert Spencer, in a private communication on the subject of the preceding note, objects to being considered an opponent of Utilitarianism, and states that he regards happiness as the ultimate end of morality; but deems that end only partially attainable by empirical generalizations from the observed results of conduct, and completely attainable only by deducing, from the laws of life and the conditions of existence, what kinds of action necessarily tend to produce happiness, and what kinds to produce unhappiness. With the exception of the word "necessarily," I have no dissent to express from this doctrine; and (omitting that word) I am not aware that any modern advocate of utilitarianism is of a different opinion. Bentham certainly, to whom, in the "Social Statics," Mr. Spencer particularly referred, is, least of all writers, chargeable with unwillingness to deduce the effect of actions on happiness from the laws of human nature and the universal conditions of human life. The common charge against him is of relying too exclusively upon such deductions, and declining altogether to be bound by the generalizations from specific experience which Mr. Spencer thinks that utilitarians generally con-

equal claim of everybody to happiness, in the estimation of the moralist and the legislator, involves an equal claim to all the means of happiness, except in so far as the inevitable conditions of human life, and the general interest, in which that of every individual is included, set limits to the maxim; and those limits ought to be strictly construed. As every other maxim of justice, so this, is by no means applied or held applicable universally: on the contrary, as I have already remarked, it bends to every person's ideas of social expediency. But, in whatever case it is deemed applicable at all, it is held to be the dictate of justice. All persons are deemed to have a *right* to equality of treatment, except when some recognized social expediency requires the reverse. And hence all social inequalities, which have ceased to be considered expedient, assume the character, not of simple inexpediency, but of injustice, and appear so tyrannical, that people are apt to wonder how they ever could have been tolerated; forgetful that they themselves perhaps tolerate other inequalities under an equally mistaken notion of expediency, the correction of which would make that which they approve seem quite as monstrous as what they have at last learnt to condemn. The entire history of social improvement has been a series of transitions, by which one custom or institution after another, from being a supposed primary necessity of social existence, has passed into the rank of an universally stigmatized injustice and tyranny. So it has been with the distinctions of slaves and freemen, nobles and serfs, patricians and plebeians; and so it will be, and in part already is, with the aristocracies of color, race, and sex.

It appears, from what has been said, that justice is a name

fine themselves to. My own opinion (and, as I collect, Mr. Spencer's) is, that in ethics, as in all other branches of scientific study, the consilience of the results of both these processes, each corroborating and verifying the other, is requisite to give to any general proposition the kind and degree of evidence which constitutes scientific proof.]

for certain moral requirements, which, regarded collectively, stand higher in the scale of social utility, and are therefore of more paramount obligation, than any others; though particular cases may occur in which some other social duty is so important as to overrule any one of the general maxims of justice. Thus, to save a life, it may not only be allowable, but a duty, to steal, or take by force, the necessary food or medicine, or to kidnap, and compel to officiate, the only qualified medical practitioner. In such cases, as we do not call any thing justice which is not a virtue, we usually say, not that justice must give way to some other moral principle, but that what is just in ordinary cases is, by reason of that other principle, not just in the particular case. By this useful accommodation of language, the character of indefeasibility attributed to justice is kept up, and we are saved from the necessity of maintaining that there can be laudable injustice.

The considerations which have now been adduced, resolve, I conceive, the only real difficulty in the utilitarian theory of morals. It has always been evident that all cases of justice are also cases of expediency: the difference is in the peculiar sentiment which attaches to the former, as contradistinguished from the latter. If this characteristic sentiment has been sufficiently accounted for; if there is no necessity to assume for it any peculiarity of origin; if it is simply the natural feeling of resentment, moralized by being made co-extensive with the demands of social good; and if this feeling not only does but ought to exist in all the classes of cases to which the idea of justice corresponds—that idea no longer presents itself as a stumbling-block to the utilitarian ethics. Justice remains the appropriate name for certain social utilities which are vastly more important, and therefore more absolute and imperative, than any others are as a class (though not more so than others may be in particular cases), and which therefore ought to be, as well as naturally are, guarded by a sentiment not only different in degree, but also in kind; distinguished from the milder feeling which attaches to the mere idea of promoting human pleasure or convenience, at once by the more definite nature of its commands, and by the sterner character of its sanctions.

from Considerations on
Representative Government

CHAPTER 3 *That the Ideally Best Form of Government Is Representative Government*

It has long (perhaps throughout the entire duration of British freedom) been a common form of speech, that if a good despot could be insured, despotic monarchy would be the best form of government. I look upon this as a radical and most pernicious misconception of what good government is, which, until it can be got rid of, will fatally vitiate all our speculations on government.

The supposition is, that absolute power, in the hands of an eminent individual, would insure a virtuous and intelligent performance of all the duties of government. Good laws would be established and enforced, bad laws would be reformed; the best men would be placed in all situations of trust; justice would be as well administered, the public burdens would be as light and as judiciously imposed, every branch of administration would be as purely and as intelligently conducted as the circumstances of the country and its degree of intellectual and moral cultivation would admit. I am willing, for the sake of the argument, to concede all this, but I must point out how great the concession is, how much more is needed to produce even an approximation to these results than is conveyed in the simple expression, a good despot. Their realization would in fact imply, not merely a good monarch, but an all-seeing one. He must be at all times informed correctly, in considerable detail, of the conduct and working of every branch of administration, in every district of the country, and must be able, in the twenty-four hours per day, which are all that is granted to a king as to the humblest laborer, to give an effective share of attention and superintendence to all parts of this vast field; or he must at least be capable of discerning and choosing out, from among the mass of his subjects, not only a large abundance of honest and able men, fit to conduct every branch of public administration under supervision and control, but also the small number of men of eminent virtues and talents who can be trusted not only to do without that supervision, but to exercise it themselves over others. So extraordinary are the faculties and energies required for performing this task in any supportable manner, that the good despot whom we are supposing can hardly be imagined as consenting to undertake it unless as a refuge from intolerable evils, and a transitional preparation for something beyond. But the argument can do without even this immense item in the account. Suppose the difficulty vanished. What should we then have? One man of superhuman mental activity managing the entire affairs of a mentally passive people. Their passivity is implied in the very idea of absolute power. The nation as a whole, and every individual composing it, are without any potential voice in their own destiny. They exercise no will in respect to their collective interests. All is decided for them by a will not their own, which it is legally a crime for them to disobey. What sort of human beings can be formed under such a regimen? What development can either their thinking or their active faculties attain under it? On matters of pure theory they might perhaps be allowed to speculate, so long as their speculations either did not approach politics, or had not the remotest connection with its practice. On practical affairs they could at most be only suffered to suggest; and even under the most moderate of despots, none but persons of already admitted or reputed superiority could hope that their suggestions would be known to, much less regarded by, those who had the management of affairs. A person must have a very unusual taste for intellectual exercise in and for itself who will put himself to the trouble of thought when it is to have no outward effect, or qualify himself for functions which he has no chance of being allowed to exercise. The only sufficient incitement to mental exertion, in any but a few minds in a generation, is the prospect of some practical use to be made of its results. It does not follow that the nation will be wholly destitute of intellectual power. The common business of life, which must necessarily be performed by each individual or family for themselves, will call forth some amount of intelligence and practical ability within a certain narrow range of ideas. There may be a select class of *savants* who cultivate science with a view to its physical uses or for the pleasure of the pursuit. There will be a bureaucracy, and persons in training for the bureaucracy, who will be taught at least some empirical maxims of government and public administration. There may be, and often has been, a systematic organization of the best mental power in the country in some special direction (commonly military) to promote the grandeur of the despot. But the public at large remain without information and without interest on all the greater matters of practice; or, if they have any knowledge of them, it is but a *dilettante* knowledge, like that which people have of the mechanical arts who have never handled a tool. Nor is it only in their intelligence that they suffer. Their moral capacities are equally stunted. Wherever the sphere of action of human beings is artificially circumscribed, their sentiments are narrowed and dwarfed in the same proportion. The food of feeling is action; even domestic affection lives upon voluntary good offices. Let a person have nothing to do for his country, and he will not care for it. It has been said of old that in a despotism there is at most but one patriot, the despot himself; and the saying rests on a just appreciation of the effects of absolute subjection even to a good and wise master. Religion remains; and here, at least, it may be thought, is an agency that may be relied on for lifting men's eyes and minds above the dust at their feet. But religion, even supposing it to escape perversion for the purposes of despotism, ceases in these circumstances to be a social concern, and narrows into a personal affair between an individual and his Maker, in which the issue at stake is but his private salvation. Religion in this shape is quite consistent with the most selfish and contracted egoism, and identifies the votary as little in feeling with the rest of his kind as sensuality itself.

A good despotism means a government in which, so far as depends on the despot, there is no positive oppression by officers of state, but in which all the collective interests of the people are managed for them, all the thinking that has relation to collective interests done for them, and in which their minds are formed by, and consenting to, this abdication of their own energies. Leaving things to the government, like leaving them to Providence, is synonymous with caring nothing about them, and accepting their results, when disagreeable, as visitations of Nature. With the exception, therefore, of a few studious men who take an intellectual interest in speculation for its own sake, the intelligence and sentiments of the whole people are given up to the material interests, and when these are provided for, to the amusement and ornamentation of private life. But to say this is to say, if the whole testimony of history is worth any thing, that the era of national decline has arrived; that is, if the nation had ever attained any thing to decline from. If it has never risen above the condition of an Oriental people, in that condition it continues to stagnate; but if, like Greece or Rome, it had realized any thing higher, through the energy, patriotism, and enlargement of mind, which, as national qualities, are the fruits solely of freedom, it relapses in a few generations into the Oriental state. And that state does not mean stupid tranquillity,with security against change for the worse; it often means being overrun, conquered, and reduced to domestic slavery either by a stronger despot, or by the nearest barbarous people who retain along with their savage rudeness the energies of freedom.

Such are not merely the natural tendencies, but the inherent necessities of despotic government, from which there is no outlet, unless is so far as the despotism consents not to be despotism; in so far as the supposed good despot abstains from exercising his power, and, though holding it in reserve, allows the general business of government to go on as if the people really governed themselves. However little probable it may be, we may imagine a despot observing many of the rules and restraints of constitutional government. He might allow such freedom of the press and of discussion as would enable a public opinion to form and express itself on national affairs. He might suffer local interests to be managed, without the interference of authority, by the people themselves. He might even surround himself with a council or councils of government, freely chosen by the whole or some portion of the nation, retaining in his own hands the power of taxation, and the supreme legislative as well as executive authority. Were he to act thus, and so far abdicate as a despot, he would do away with a considerable part of the evils characteristic of despotism. Political activity and capacity for public affairs would no longer be prevented from growing up in the body of the nation, and a public opinion would form itself, not the mere echo of the government. But such improvement would be the beginning of new difficulties. This public opinion, independent of the monarch's dictation, must be either with him or against him; if not the one, it will be the other. All governments must displease many persons, and these having now regular organs, and being able to express their sentiments, opinions adverse to the measures of government would often be expressed. What is the monarch to do when these unfavorable opinions happen to be in the majority? Is he to alter his course? Is he to defer to the nation? If so, he is no longer a despot, but a constitutional king; an organ or first minister of the people, distinguished only by being irremovable. If not, he must either put down opposition by his despotic power, or there will arise a permanent antagonism between the people and one man, which can have but one possible ending. Not even a religious principle of passive obedience and "right divine" would long ward off the natural consequences of such a position. The monarch would have to succumb, and conform to the conditions of constitutional royalty, or give place to some one who would. The despotism, being thus chiefly nominal, would possess few of the advantages supposed to belong to absolute monarchy, while it would realize in a very imperfect degree those of a free government, since, however great an amount of liberty the citizens might practically enjoy, they could never forget that they held it on sufferance, and by a concession which, under the existing constitution of the state, might at any moment be resumed; that they were legally slaves, though of a prudent or indulgent master.

It is not much to be wondered at if impatient or disappointed reformers, groaning under the impediments opposed to the most salutary public improvements by the ignorance, the indifference, the untractableness, the perverse obstinacy of a people, and the corrupt combinations of selfish private interests, armed with the powerful weapons afforded by free institutions, should at times sigh for a strong hand to bear down all these obstacles, and compel a recalcitrant people to be better governed. But (setting aside the fact that for one despot who now and then reforms an abuse, there are ninety-nine who do nothing but create them) those who look in any such direction for the realization of their hopes leave out of the idea of good government its principal element, the improvement of the people themselves. One of the benefits of freedom is that under it the ruler can not pass by the people's minds, and amend their affairs for them without amending *them*. If it were possible for a people to be well governed in spite of themselves, their good government would last no longer than the freedom of a people usually lasts who have been liberated by foreign arms without their own co-operation. It is true, a despot may educate the people, and to do so really would be the best apology for his despotism. But any education which aims at making human beings other than machines, in the long run makes them claim to have the control of their own actions. The leaders of French philosophy in the eighteenth century had been educated by the Jesuits. Even Jesuit education, it seems, was sufficiently real to call forth the appetite for freedom. Whatever invigorates the faculties, in however small a measure, creates an increased desire for their more unimpeded exercise; and a popular education is a failure if it educates the people for any state but that which it will certainly induce them to desire, and most probably to demand.

I am far from condemning, in cases of extreme exigency, the assumption of absolute power in the form of temporary dictatorship. Free nations have, in times of old, conferred such power by their own choice, as a necessary medicine for diseases of the body politic which could not be got rid of by less violent means. But its acceptance, even for a time strictly limited, can only be excused, if, like Solon or Pittacus, the dictator employs the whole power he assumes in removing the obstacles which debar the nation from the enjoyment of freedom. A good despotism is an altogether false ideal, which practically (except as a means to some temporary purpose) becomes the most senseless and dangerous of chimeras. Evil for evil, a good despotism, in a country at all advanced in civilization, is more noxious than a bad one, for it is far more relaxing and enervating to the thoughts, feelings, and energies of the people. The despotism of Augustus prepared the Romans for Tiberius. If the whole tone of their character had not first been prostrated by nearly two generations of that mild slavery, they would probably have had spirit enough left to rebel against the more odious one.

There is no difficulty in showing that the ideally best form of government is that in which the sovereignty, or supreme controlling power in the last resort, is vested in the entire aggregate of the community, every citizen not only having a voice in the exercise of that ultimate sovereignty, but being, at least occasionally, called on to take an actual part in the government by the personal discharge of some public function, local or general.

To test this proposition, it has to be examined in reference to the two branches into which, as pointed out in the last chapter, the inquiry into the goodness of a government conveniently divides itself, namely, how far it promotes the good management of the affairs of society by means of the existing faculties, moral, intellectual, and active, of its various members, and what is its effect in improving or deteriorating those faculties.

The ideally best form of government, it is scarcely necessary to say, does not mean one which is practicable or eligible in all states of civilization, but the one which, in the circumstances in which it is practicable and eligible, is attended with the greatest amount of beneficial consequences, immediate and prospective. A completely popular government is the only polity which can make out any claim to this character. It is pre-eminent in both the departments between which the excellence of a political Constitution is divided. It is both more favorable to present good government, and promotes a better and higher form of national character than any other polity whatsoever.

Its superiority in reference to present well-being rests upon two principles, of as universal truth and applicability as any general propositions which can be laid down respecting human affairs. The first is, that the rights and interests of every or any person are only secure from being disregarded when the person interested is himself able, and habitually disposed to stand up for them. The second is, that the general prosperity attains a greater height, and is more widely diffused, in proportion to the amount and variety of the personal energies enlisted in promoting it.

Putting these two propositions into a shape more special to their present application—human beings are only secure from evil at the hands of others in proportion as they have the power of being, and are self-*protecting;* and they only achieve a high degree of success in their struggle with Nature in proportion as they are self-*dependent,* relying on what they themselves can do, either separately or in concert, rather than on what others can do for them.

The former proposition—that each is the only safe guardian of his own rights and interests—is one of those elementary maxims of prudence which every person capable of conducting his own affairs implicitly acts upon wherever he himself is interested. Many, indeed, have a great dislike to it as a political doctrine, and are fond of holding it up to obloquy as a doctrine of universal selfishness. To which we may answer, that whenever it ceases to be true that mankind, as a rule, prefer themselves to others, and those nearest to them to those more remote, from that moment Communism is not only practicable, but the only defensible form of society, and will, when that time arrives, be assuredly carried into effect. For my own part, not believing in universal selfishness, I have no difficulty in admitting that Communism would even now be practicable among the *élite* of mankind, and may become so among the rest. But as this opinion is any thing but popular with those defenders of existing institutions who find fault with the doctrine of the general predominance of self-interest, I am inclined to think they do in reality believe that most men consider themselves before other people. It is not, however, necessary to affirm even thus much in order to support the claim of all to participate in the sovereign power. We need not suppose that when power resides in an exclusive class, that class will knowingly and deliberately sacrifice the other classes to themselves: it suffices that, in the absence of its natural defenders, the interest of the excluded is always in danger of being overlooked; and, when looked at, is seen with very different eyes from those of the persons whom it directly concerns. In this country, for example, what are called the working-classes may be considered as excluded from all direct participation in the government. I do not believe that the classes who do participate in it have in general any intention of sacrificing the working classes to themselves. They once had that intention; witness the persevering attempts so long made to keep down wages by law. But in the present day, their ordinary disposition is the very opposite: they willingly make considerable sacrifices, especially of their pecuniary interest, for the benefit of the working classes, and err rather by too lavish and indiscriminating beneficence; nor do I believe that any rulers in history have been actuated by a more sincere desire to do their duty toward the poorer portion of their countrymen. Yet does Parliament, or almost any of the members composing it, ever for an instant look at any question with the eyes of a working man? When a subject arises in which the laborers as such have an interest, is it regarded from any point of view but that of the employers of labor? I do not say that the working men's view of these questions is in general nearer to truth than the other, but it is sometimes quite as near; and in any case it ought to be respectfully listened to, instead of being, as it is, not merely turned away from, but ignored. On the question of strikes, for instance, it is doubtful if there is so much as one among the leading members of either House who is not firmly convinced that the reason of the matter is unqualifiedly on the side of the masters, and that the men's view of it is simply absurd. Those who have studied the question know well how far this is from being the case, and in how different, and how infinitely less superficial a manner the point would have to be argued if the classes who strike were able to make themselves heard in Parliament.

It is an inherent condition of human affairs that no intention, however sincere, of protecting the interests of others can make it safe or salutary to tie up their own hands. Still more obviously true is it that by their own hands only can any positive and durable improvement of their circumstances in life be worked out. Through the joint influence of these two principles, all free communities have both been more exempt from social injustice and crime, and have attained more brilliant prosperity than any others, or than they themselves after they lost their freedom. Contrast the free states of the world, while their freedom lasted, with the contemporary subjects of monarchical or oligarchical despotism: the Greek cities with the Persian satrapies; the Italian republics, and the free towns of Flanders and Germany, with the feudal monarchies of Europe; Switzerland, Holland, and England with Austria or ante-revolutionary France. Their superior prosperity was too obvious ever to have been gainsaid; while their superiority in good government and social relations is proved by the prosperity, and is manifest besides in every page of history. If we compare, not one age with another, but the different governments which coexisted in the same age, no amount of disorder which exaggeration itself can pretend to have existed amid the publicity of the free states can be compared for a moment with the contemptuous trampling upon the mass of the people which pervaded the whole life of the monarchical countries, or the disgusting individual tyranny which was of more than daily occurrence under the systems of plunder which they called fiscal arrangements, and in the secrecy of their frightful courts of justice.

It must be acknowledged that the benefits of freedom, so far as they have hitherto been enjoyed, were obtained by the extension of its privileges to a part only of the community, and that a government in which they are extended impartially to all is a desideratum still unrealized. But, though every approach to this has an independent value, and in many cases more than an approach could not, in the existing state of general improvement, be made, the participation of all in these benefits is the ideally perfect conception of free government. In proportion as any, no matter who, are excluded from it, the interests of the excluded are left without the guaranty accorded to the rest, and they themselves have less scope and encouragement than they might otherwise have to that exertion of their energies for the good of themselves and of the community to which the general prosperity is always proportioned.

Thus stands the case as regards present well-being—the good management of the affairs of the existing generation. If we now pass to the influence of the form of government upon character, we shall find the superiority of popular government over every other to be, if possible, still more decided and indisputable.

This question really depends upon a still more fundamental one, viz., which of two common types of character, for the general good of humanity, it is most desirable should predominate—the active or the passive type; that which struggles against evils, or that which endures them, that which bends to circumstances, or that which endeavors to bend circumstances to itself.

The commonplaces of moralists and the general sympathies of mankind are in favor of the passive type. Energetic characters may be admired, but the acquiescent and submissive are those which most men personally prefer. The passiveness of our neighbors increases our own sense of security, and plays into the hands of our willfulness. Passive characters, if we do not happen to need their activity, seem an obstruction the less in our own path. A contented character is not a dangerous rival. Yet nothing is more certain than that improvement in human affairs is wholly the work of the uncontented characters; and, moreover, that it is much easier for an active mind to acquire the virtues of patience, than for a passive one to assume those of energy.

Of the three varieties of mental excellence, intellectual, practical, and moral, there never could be any doubt, in regard to the first two, which side had the advantage. All intellectual superiority is the fruit of active effort. Enterprise, the desire to keep moving, to be trying and accomplishing new things for our own benefit or that of others, is the parent even of speculative, and much more of practical talent. The intellectual culture compatible with the other type is of that feeble and vague description which belongs to a mind that stops at amusement or at simple contemplation. The test of real and vigorous thinking, the thinking which ascertains truths instead of dreaming dreams, is successful application to practice. Where that purpose does not exist, to give definiteness, precision, and an intelligible meaning to thought, it generates nothing better than the mystical metaphysics of the Pythagoreans or the Veds. With respect to practical improvement, the case is still more evident. The character which improves human life is that which struggles with natural powers and tendencies, not that which gives way to them. The self-benefiting qualities are all on the side of the active and energetic character, and the habits and conduct which promote the advantage of each individual member of the community must be at least a part of those which conduce most in the end to the advancement of the community as a whole.

But, on the point of moral preferability, there seems at first sight to be room for doubt. I am not referring to the religious feeling which has so generally existed in favor of the inactive character, as being more in harmony with the submission due to the divine will. Christianity, as well as other religions, has fostered this sentiment; but it is the prerogative of Christianity, as regards this and many other perversions, that it is able to throw them off. Abstractedly from religious considerations, a passive character, which yields to obstacles instead of striving to overcome them, may not indeed be very useful to others, no more than to itself, but it might be expected to be at least inoffensive. Contentment is always counted among the moral virtues. But it is a complete error to suppose that contentment is necessarily or naturally attendant on passivity of character; and unless it is, the moral consequences are mischievous. Where there exists a desire for advantages not possessed, the mind which does not potentially possess them by means of its own energies is apt to look with hatred and malice on those who do. The person bestirring himself with hopeful prospects to improve his circumstances is the one who feels good-will toward others engaged in, or who have succeeded in the same pursuit. And where the majority are so engaged, those who do not attain the object have had the tone given to their feelings by the general habit of the country, and ascribe their failure to want of effort or opportunity, or to their personal ill luck. But those who, while desiring what others possess, put no energy into striving for it, are either incessantly grumbling that fortune does not do for them what they do not attempt to do for themselves, or overflowing with envy and ill-will toward those who possess what they would like to have.

In proportion as success in life is seen or believed to be the fruit of fatality or accident and not of exertion, in that same ratio does envy develop itself as a point of national character. The most envious of all mankind are the Orientals. In Oriental moralists, in Oriental tales, the envious man is markedly prominent. In real life, he is the terror of all who possess any thing desirable, be it a palace, a handsome child, or even good health and spirits: the supposed effect of his mere look constitutes the all-pervading superstition of the evil eye. Next to Orientals in envy, as in inactivity, are some of the Southern Europeans. The Spaniards pursued all their great men with it, embittered their lives, and generally succeeded in putting an early stop to their successes.* With the

* I limit the expression to past time, because I would say nothing derogatory of a great, and now at last a free people, who are entering

French, who are essentially a Southern people, the double education of despotism and Catholicism has, in spite of their impulsive temperament, made submission and endurance the common character of the people, and their most received notion of wisdom and excellence; and if envy of one another, and of all superiority, is not more rife among them than it is, the circumstance must be ascribed to the many valuable counteracting elements in the French character, and most of all to the great individual energy which, though less persistent and more intermittent than in the self-helping and struggling Anglo-Saxons, has nevertheless manifested itself among the French in nearly every direction in which the operation of their institutions has been favorable to it.

There are, no doubt, in all countries, really contented characters, who not merely do not seek, but do not desire what they do not already possess, and these naturally bear no ill-will toward such as have apparently a more favored lot. But the great mass of seeming contentment is real discontent, combined with indolence or self-indulgence, which, taking no legitimate means of raising itself, delights in bringing others down to its own level. And if we look narrowly even at the cases of innocent contentment, we perceive that they only win our admiration when the indifference is solely to improvement in outward circumstances, and there is a striving for perpetual advancement in spiritual worth, or at least a disinterested zeal to benefit others. The contented man, or the contented family, who have no ambition to make any one else happier, to promote the good of their country or their neighborhood, or to improve themselves in moral excellence, excite in us neither admiration nor approval. We rightly ascribe this sort of contentment to mere unmanliness

---

into the general movement of European progress with a vigor which bids fair to make up rapidly the ground they have lost. No one can doubt what Spanish intellect and energy are capable of; and their faults as a people are chiefly those for which freedom and industrial ardor are a real specific.

and want of spirit. The content which we approve is an ability to do cheerfully without what can not be had, a just appreciation of the comparative value of different objects of desire, and a willing renunciation of the less when incompatible with the greater. These, however, are excellences more natural to the character, in proportion as it is actively engaged in the attempt to improve its own or some other lot. He who is continually measuring his energy against difficulties, learns what are the difficulties insuperable to him, and what are those which, though he might overcome, the success is not worth the cost. He whose thoughts and activities are all needed for, and habitually employed in, practicable and useful enterprises, is the person of all others least likely to let his mind dwell with brooding discontent upon things either not worth attaining, or which are not so to him. Thus the active, self-helping character is not only intrinsically the best, but is the likeliest to acquire all that is really excellent or desirable in the opposite type.

The striving, go-ahead character of England and the United States is only a fit subject of disapproving criticism on account of the very secondary objects on which it commonly expends its strength. In itself it is the foundation of the best hopes for the general improvement of mankind. It has been acutely remarked, that whenever any thing goes amiss, the habitual impulse of French people is to say, "Il faut de la patience;" and of English people, "What a shame!" The people who think it a shame when any thing goes wrong—who rush to the conclusion that the evil could and ought to have been prevented, are those who, in the long run, do most to make the world better. If the desires are low placed, if they extend to little beyond physical comfort and the show of riches, the immediate results of the energy will not be much more than the continual extension of man's power over material objects; but even this makes room, and prepares the mechanical appliances for the greatest intellectual and social achievements; and while the energy is there, some persons will apply it, and it will be applied more and more, to the perfecting, not of outward circumstances alone, but of man's inward nature. Inactivity, unaspiringness, absence of desire, is a more fatal hinderance to improvement than any misdirection of energy, and is that through which alone, when existing in the mass, any very formidable misdirection by an energetic few becomes possible. It is this, mainly, which retains in a savage or semi-savage state the great majority of the human race.

Now there can be no kind of doubt that the passive type of character is favored by the government of one or a few, and the active self-helping type by that of the many. Irresponsible rulers need the quiescence of the ruled more than they need any activity but that which they can compel. Submissiveness to the prescriptions of men as necessities of nature is the lesson inculcated by all governments upon those who are wholly without participation in them. The will of superiors, and the law as the will of superiors, must be passively yielded to. But no men are mere instruments or materials in the hands of their rulers who have will, or spirit, or a spring of internal activity in the rest of their proceedings, and any manifestation of these qualities, instead of receiving encouragement from despots, has to get itself forgiven by them. Even when irresponsible rulers are not sufficiently conscious of danger from the mental activity of their subjects to be desirous of repressing it, the position itself is a repression. Endeavor is even more effectually restrained by the certainty of its impotence than by any positive discouragement. Between subjection to the will of others and the virtues of self-help and self-government there is a natural incompatibility. This is more or less complete according as the bondage is strained or relaxed. Rulers differ very much in the length to which they carry the control of the free agency of their subjects, or the suppression of it by managing their business for them. But the difference is in degree, not in principle; and the best despots often go the greatest lengths in chaining up the free agency of their subjects. A bad despot, when his own personal indulgences have been provided for, may sometimes be willing to let the people alone; but a good despot insists on doing them good by making them do their own business in a better way than they themselves know of. The regulations which restricted to fixed processes all the leading branches of French manufactures were the work of the great Colbert.

Very different is the state of the human faculties where a human being feels himself under no other external restraint than the necessities of nature, or mandates of society which he has his share in imposing, and which it is open to him, if he thinks them wrong, publicly to dissent from, and exert himself actively to get altered. No doubt, under a government partially popular, this freedom may be exercised even by those who are not partakers in the full privileges of citizenship; but it is a great additional stimulus to any one's self-help and self-reliance when he starts from an even ground, and has not to feel that his success depends on the impression he can make upon the sentiments and dispositions of a body of whom he is not one. It is a great discouragement to an individual, and a still greater one to a class, to be left out of the constitution; to be reduced to plead from outside the door to the arbiters of their destiny, not taken into the consultation within. The maximum of the invigorating effect of freedom upon the character is only obtained when the person acted on either is, or is looking forward to become, a citizen as fully privileged as any other. What is still more important than even this matter of feeling is the practical discipline which the character obtains from the occasional demand made upon the citizens to exercise, for a time and in their turn, some social function. It is not sufficiently considered how little there is in most men's ordinary life to give any largeness either to their conceptions or to their sentiments. Their work is a routine; not a labor of love, but of self-interest in the most elementary form, the satisfaction of daily wants; neither the thing done, nor the process of doing it, introduces the mind to thoughts or feelings extending beyond individuals; if instructive books are within their reach, there is no stimulus to read them; and, in most cases, the individual has no access to any person of cultivation much superior to his own. Giving him something to do for the public supplies, in a measure, all these deficiencies. If circumstances allow the amount of public duty assigned him to be considerable, it makes him an educated man. Notwithstanding the defects of the social system and moral ideas of antiquity, the practice of the dicastery and the ecclesia raised the intellectual standard of an average Athenian citizen far beyond any thing of which there is yet an example in any other mass of men, ancient or modern. The proofs of this are apparent in every page of our great historian of Greece; but we need scarcely look farther than to the high quality of the addresses which their great orators deemed best calculated to act with effect on their understanding and will. A benefit of the same kind, though far less in degree, is produced on Englishmen of the lower middle class by their liability to be placed on juries and to serve parish offices, which, though it does not occur to so many, nor is so continuous, nor introduces them to so great a variety of elevated considerations as to admit of comparison with the public education which every citizen of Athens obtained from her democratic institutions, makes them nevertheless very different beings, in range of ideas and development of faculties, from those who have done nothing in their lives but drive a quill, or sell goods over a counter. Still more salutary is the moral part of the instruction afforded by the participation of the private citizen, if even rarely, in public functions. He is called upon, while so engaged, to weigh interests not his own; to be guided, in case of conflicting claims, by another rule than his private partialities; to apply, at every turn, principles and maxims which have for their reason of existence the general good; and he usually finds associated with him in the same work minds more familiarized than his own with these ideas and operations, whose study it will be to supply reasons to his understanding, and stimulation to his feeling for the general good. He is made to feel himself one of the public, and whatever is their interest to be his interest. Where this school of public spirit does not exist, scarcely any sense is entertained that private persons, in no eminent social situation, owe any duties to society except to obey the laws and submit to the government. There is no unselfish sentiment of identification with the public. Every thought and feeling, either of interest or of duty, is absorbed in the individual and in the family. The man never thinks of any collective interest, of any objects to be pursued jointly with others, but only in competition with them, and in some measure at their expense. A neighbor, not being an ally or an associate, since he is never engaged in any common undertaking for the joint benefit, is therefore only a rival. Thus even private morality suffers, while public is actually extinct. Were this the universal and only possible state of things, the utmost aspirations of the lawgiver or the moralist could only stretch to making the bulk of the community a flock of sheep innocently nibbling the grass side by side.

From these accumulated considerations, it is evident that the only government which can fully satisfy all the exigencies of the social state is one in which the whole people participate; that any participation, even in the smallest public function, is useful; that the participation should every where be as great as the general degree of improvement of the community will allow; and that nothing less can be ultimately desirable than the admission of all to a share in the sovereign power of the state. But since all can not, in a community exceeding a single small town, participate personally in any but some very minor portions of the public business, it follows that the ideal type of a perfect government must be representative.

from An Examination
of Sir William Hamilton's
Philosophy, Volume I

CHAPTER 7   *The Philosophy of the Conditioned, As Applied by Mr. Mansel to the Limits of Religious Thought*

Mr. Mansel may be affirmed, by a fair application of the term, to be, in metaphysics, a pupil of Sir W. Hamilton. I do not mean that he agrees with him in all his opinions; for he avowedly dissents from the peculiar Hamiltonian theory of Cause; still less that he has learned nothing from any other teacher, or from his own independent speculations. On the contrary, he has shown considerable power of original thought, both of a good and of what seems to me a bad quality. But he is the admiring editor of Sir W. Hamilton's Lectures; he invariably speaks of him with a deference which he pays to no other philosopher; he expressly accepts, in language identical with Sir W. Hamilton's own, the doctrines regarded as specially characteristic of the Hamiltonian philosophy, and may with reason be considered as a representative of the same general mode of thought. Mr. Mansel has bestowed especial cultivation upon a province but slightly touched by his master—the application of the Philosophy of the Conditioned to the theological department of thought;

the deduction of such of its corollaries and consequences as directly concern religion.

The premises from which Mr. Mansel reasons are those of Sir W. Hamilton. He maintains the necessary relativity of all our knowledge. He holds that the Absolute and the Infinite, or, to use a more significant expression, an Absolute and an Infinite being, are inconceivable by us; and that when we strive to conceive what is thus inaccessible to our faculties, we fall into self-contradiction. That we are, nevertheless, warranted in believing, and bound to believe, the real existence of an absolute and infinite being, and that this being is God. God, therefore, is inconceivable and unknowable by us, and cannot even be thought of without self-contradiction; that is (for Mr. Mansel is careful thus to qualify the assertion), thought of *as* Absolute, and *as* Infinite. Through this inherent impossibility of our conceiving or knowing God's essential attributes, we are disqualified from judging what is or is not consistent with them. If, then, a religion is presented to us containing any particular doctrine respecting the Deity, our belief or rejection of the doctrine ought to depend exclusively upon the evidences which can be produced for the divine origin of the religion: and no argument grounded on the incredibility of the doctrine, as involving an intellectual absurdity, or on its moral badness as unworthy of a good or wise being, ought to have any weight, since of these things we are incompetent to judge. This, at least, is the drift of Mr. Mansel's argument: but I am bound to admit that he affirms the conclusion with a certain limitation; for he acknowledges, that the moral character of the doctrines of a religion ought to count for something among the reasons for accepting or rejecting, as of divine origin, the religion as a whole. That it ought also to count for something in the interpretation of the religion when accepted, he neglects to say; but we must in fairness suppose that he would admit it. These concessions, however, to the moral feelings of mankind, are made at the expense of Mr. Mansel's logic. If his theory is correct, he has no right to make either of them.

There is nothing new in this line of argument as applied to theology. That we cannot understand God; that his ways are not our ways; that we cannot scrutinize or judge his counsels —propositions which, in a reasonable sense of the terms, could not be denied by any Theist—have often before been tendered as reasons why we may assert any absurdities and any moral monstrosities concerning God, and miscall them Goodness and Wisdom. The novelty is in presenting this conclusion as a corollary from the most advanced doctrines of modern philosophy—from the true theory of the powers and limitations of the human mind, on religious and on all other subjects.

My opinion of this doctrine, in whatever way presented, is, that it is simply the most morally pernicious doctrine now current; and that the question it involves is, beyond all others which now engage speculative minds, the decisive one between moral good and evil for the Christian world. It is a momentous matter, therefore, to consider whether we are obliged to adopt it. Without holding Mr. Mansel accountable for the moral consequences of the doctrine, further than he himself accepts them, I think it supremely important to examine whether the doctrine itself is really the verdict of a sound metaphysic; and essential to a true estimation of Sir W. Hamilton's philosophy to inquire, whether the conclusion thus drawn from his principal doctrine, is justly affiliated on it. I think it will appear that the conclusion not only does not follow from a true theory of the human faculties, but is not even correctly drawn from the premises from which Mr. Mansel infers it.

We must have the premises distinctly before us as conceived by Mr. Mansel, since we have hitherto seen them only as taught by Sir W. Hamilton. Clearness and explicitness of statement being in the number of Mr. Mansel's merits, it is easier to perceive the flaws in his arguments than in those of his master, because he often leaves us less in doubt what he means by his words.

To have "such a knowledge of the Divine Nature" as would enable human reason to judge of theology, would be, according to Mr. Mansel,* "to conceive the Deity as he is." This would be to "conceive him as First Cause, as Absolute, and as Infinite." The First Cause Mr. Mansel defines in the usual manner. About the meaning of Infinite there is no difficulty. But when we come to the Absolute we are on more slippery ground. Mr. Mansel, however, tells us his meaning plainly. By the Absolute, he does not mean what Sir W. Hamilton means in the greater part of his argument against Cousin, that which is completed or finished. He means what Sir W. Hamilton means only once (as we have already seen) the opposite of Relative. "By the Absolute is meant that which exists in and by itself, having no necessary relation to any other Being."

This explanation, by Mr. Mansel, of Absolute in the sense in which it is opposed to Relative, is more definite in its terms that that which Sir W. Hamilton gives when attempting the same thing. For Sir W. Hamilton recognizes (as already remarked) this second meaning of Absolute, and this is the account he gives of it: †—"*Absolutum* means what is freed or loosed; in which sense the Absolute will be what is aloof from relation, comparison, limitation, condition, dependence, &c., and thus is tantamount to τὸ ἀπόλυῖον of the lower Greeks." May it not be surmised that the vagueness in which the master here leaves the conception, was for the purpose of avoiding difficulties upon which the pupil, in his desire of greater precision, has unwarily run? Mr. Mansel certainly gains nothing by the more definite character of his language. The first words of his definition, "that which exists in and by itself," would serve for the description of a Nou-

* Limits of Religious Thought, 4th edition, pp. 29, 30.
† Discussions, p. 14, note.

menon; but Mr. Mansel's Absolute is only meant to denote one being, identified with God, and God is not the only Noumenon. This, however, I will not dwell upon. But the remaining words, "having no necessary relation to any other Being," bring him into a much greater difficulty. For they admit of two constructions. The words, in their natural sense, only mean, *capable of existing out of relation to anything else.* The argument requires that they should mean, *incapable of existing in relation with anything else.* Mr. Mansel cannot intend the latter. He cannot mean that the Absolute is incapable of entering into relation with any other being; for he would not affirm this of God; on the contrary, he is continually speaking of God's relations to the world and to us. Moreover, he accepts, from Mr. Calderwood, an interpretation inconsistent with this.* This, however, is the meaning necessary to support his case. For what is his first argument? That God cannot be known by us as Cause, as Absolute, and as Infinite, because these attributes are, to our conception, incompatible with one another. And why incompatible? Because† "a Cause cannot, as such, be absolute; the Absolute cannot, as such, be a cause. The cause, as such, exists only in relation to its effect: the cause is a cause of the effect; the effect is an effect of the cause. On the other hand, the conception of the Absolute involves a possible existence out of all relation." But in what manner is a possible existence out of all relation, incompatible with the notion of a cause? Have not causes a possible existence apart from their effects? Would the sun (for example) not exist if there were no earth or planets for it to illuminate? Mr. Mansel seems to think that what is capable of existing out of relation, cannot possibly be conceived or known in relation. But this is not so. Anything which is capable of existing in relation, is capable of being conceived or known in relation. If

* Limits of Religious Thought, *p.* 200.
† Ibid., p. 31.

the Absolute Being cannot be conceived as Cause, it must be that he cannot exist as Cause; he must be incapable of causing. If he can be in any relation whatever to any finite thing, he is conceivable and knowable in that relation, if no otherwise. Freed from this confusion of ideas, Mr. Mansel's argument resolves itself into this—The same Being cannot be thought by us both as Cause and as Absolute, because a Cause *as such* is not Absolute, and Absolute, as such, is not a Cause; which is exactly as if he had said that Newton cannot be thought by us both as an Englishman and as a mathematician, because an Englishman, as such, is not a mathematician, nor a mathematician, as such, an Englishman.

Again, Mr. Mansel argues,* that "supposing the Absolute to become a cause," since *ex vi termini* it is not necessitated to do so, it must be a voluntary agent, and therefore conscious; for "volition is only possible in a conscious being." But consciousness, again, is only conceivable as a relation; and any relation conflicts with the notion of the Absolute, since relatives are mutually dependent on one another. Here it comes out distinctly as a premise in the reasoning, that to be in a relation at all, even if only a relation to itself, the relation of being "conscious of itself," is inconsistent with being the Absolute.

Mr. Mansel, therefore, must alter his definition of the Absolute if he would maintain his argument. He must either fall back on the happy ambiguity of Sir W. Hamilton's definition, "what is aloof from relation," which does not decide whether the meaning is merely that it can exist out of relation, or that it is incapable of existing in it; or he must take courage, and affirm that an Absolute Being is incapable of all relation. But as he will certainly refuse to predicate this of God, the consequence follows, that God is not an Absolute Being.

The whole of Mr. Mansel's argument for the inconceivabil-

---

* Limits of Religious Thought, p. 32.

ity of the Infinite and of the Absolute is one long *ignoratio elenchi.* It has been pointed out in a former chapter that the words Absolute and Infinite have no real meaning, unless we understand by them that which is absolute or infinite in some given attribute; as space is called infinite, meaning that it is infinite in extension; and as God is termed infinite in the sense of possessing infinite power, and absolute in the sense of absolute goodness, or knowledge. It has also been shown that Sir W. Hamilton's arguments for the unknowableness of the Unconditioned, do not prove that we cannot know an object which is absolute or infinite in some specific attribute, but only that we cannot know an abstraction called "The Absolute" or "The Infinite," which is supposed to have all attributes at once. The same remark is applicable to Mr. Mansel, with only this difference, that he, with the laudable ambition I have already noticed of stating every thing explicitly, draws this important distinction himself, and says, of his own motion, that the Absolute he means is the abstraction. He says,* that the Absolute can be "nothing less than the sum of all reality," the complex of all positive predicates, even those which are exclusive of one another; and expressly identifies it with Hegel's Absolute Being, which contains in itself "all that is actual, even evil included." "That which is conceived as absolute and infinite," says Mr. Mansel,† "must be conceived as containing within itself the sum not only of all actual, but of all possible modes of being." One may well agree with Mr. Mansel that this farrago of contradictory attributes cannot be conceived; but what shall we say of his equally positive averment that it must be believed? If this be what the Absolute is, what does he mean by saying that we must believe God to be the Absolute?

The remainder of Mr. Mansel's argumentation is suitable to this commencement. The Absolute, as conceived, that is,

---

* Limits of Religious Thought, p. 30.
† Ibid. p. 31.

as he defines it, cannot be "a whole* composed of parts," or "a substance consisting of attributes," or "a conscious subject in antithesis to an object. For if there is in the absolute any principle of unity distinct from the mere accumulation of parts or attributes, this principle alone is the true absolute. If, on the other hand, there is no such principle, then there is no absolute at all, but only a plurality of relatives. The almost unanimous voice of philosophy, in pronouncing that the absolute is both one and simple, must be accepted as the voice of reason also, so far as reason has any voice in the matter. But this absolute unity, as indifferent and containing no attributes, can neither be distinguished from the multiplicity of finite beings by any characteristic feature, nor be identified with them in their multiplicity." It will be noticed that the Absolute, which was just before defined as having all attributes, is here declared to have none: but this, Mr. Mansel would say, is merely one of the contradictions inherent in the attempt to conceive what is inconceivable. "Thus we are landed in an inextricable dilemma. The Absolute cannot be conceived as conscious, neither can it be conceived as unconscious: it cannot be conceived as complex, neither can it be conceived as simple: it cannot be conceived by difference, neither can it be conceived by the absence of difference: it cannot be identified with the universe, neither can it be distinguished from it." Is this chimerical abstraction the Absolute Being whom anybody need to be concerned about, either as knowable or an unknowable? Is the inconceivableness of this impossible fiction any argument against the possibility of conceiving God, who is neither supposed to have no attributes nor to have all attributes, but to have good attributes? Is it any hinderance to our being able to conceive a Being absolutely just, for example, or absolutely wise? Yet it is of this that Mr. Mansel undertook to prove the impossibility.

* Limits of Religious Thought, p. 33.

Again, of the Infinite: according to Mr. Mansel,* being "that than which a greater is inconceivable," it "consequently can receive no additional attribute or mode of existence which it had not from all eternity." It must therefore be the same complex of all possible predicates which the Absolute is, and all of them infinite in degree. It "cannot be regarded as consisting of a limited number of attributes, each unlimited in its kind. It cannot be conceived, for example, after the analogy of a line, infinite in length, but not in breadth; or of a surface, infinite in two dimensions of space, but bounded in the third; or of an intelligent being, possessing some one or more modes of consciousness in an infinite degree, but devoid of others." This Infinite which is infinite in all attributes, and not solely in those which it would be thought decent to predicate of God, cannot, as Mr. Mansel very truly says, be conceived. For † "the Infinite, if it is to be conceived at all, must be conceived as potentially everything and actually nothing; for if there is anything general which it cannot become, it is thereby limited; and if there is anything in particular which it actually is, it is thereby excluded from being any other thing. But again, it must also be conceived as actually everything and potentially nothing; for an unrealized potentiality is likewise a limitation. If the infinite can be that which it is not, it is by that very possibility marked out as incomplete, and capable of a higher perfection. If it is actually everything, it possesses no characteristic feature by which it can be distinguished from anything else, and discerned as an object of consciousness." Here certainly is an Infinite whose infinity does not seem to be of much use to it. But can a writer be serious who bids us conjur up a conception of something which possesses infinitely all conflicting attributes, and because we cannot do this without contradiction, would have us believe that there is a contradiction in the idea of infinite goodness, or infinite wisdom? Instead of "the Infinite," sub-

* Limits of Religious Thought, p. 30.
† Ibid. p. 48.

stitute "an infinitely good Being," and Mr. Mansel's argument reads thus: If there is anything which an infinitely good Being cannot become—if he cannot become bad—that is a limitation, and the goodness cannot be infinite. If there is anything which an infinitely good Being actually is (namely good), he is excluded from being any other thing, as from being wise or powerful. I hardly think that Sir W. Hamilton would patronize this logic, learned though it be in his school.

It cannot be necessary to follow up Mr. Mansel's metaphysical dissertation any farther. It is all, as I have said, the same *ignoratio elenchi*. I have been able to find only one short passage in which he attempts to show that we are unable to represent in thought a particular attribute carried to the infinite. For the sake of fairness, I cite it in a note.* All the argument that I can discover in it, I conceive that I have already answered, as stated much better by Sir W. Hamilton.

Mr. Mansel thinks it necessary to declare† that the contradictions are not in "the nature of the Absolute" or Infinite "in itself, but only" in "our own conception of that nature." He did not mean to say that the Divine Nature is itself contradictory. But he says,‡ "We are compelled, by the constitu-

---

* "A thing—an object—an attribute—a person—or any other term signifying one out of many possible objects of consciousness, is by that very relation necessarily declared to be finite. An infinite thing, or object, or attribute, or person, is therefore in the same moment declared to be both finite and infinite. . . . And on the other hand, if all human attributes are conceived under the conditions of difference, and relation, and time, and personality, we cannot represent in thought any such attribute magnified to infinity; for this again is to conceive it as finite and infinite at the same time. We can conceive such attributes, at the utmost, only *indefinitely;* that is to say, we may withdraw our thoughts, for the moment, from the fact of their being limited; but we cannot conceive them as *infinite;* that is to say, we cannot positively think of the absence of the limit; for, the instant we attempt to do so, the antagonist elements of the conception exclude one another, and annihilate the whole."—Limits of Religious Thought, p. 60.

† Ibid. p. 39.

‡ Ibid. p. 45.

tion of our minds, to believe in the existence of an Absolute and Infinite Being." Such being the case, I ask, is the Being, whom we must believe to be infinite and absolute, infinite and absolute in the meaning which those terms bear in Mr. Mansel's definitions of them? If not, he is bound to tell us in what other meaning. Believing God to be infinite and absolute must be believing something, and it must be possible to say what. If Mr. Mansel means that we must believe the reality of an Infinite and Absolute Being in some other sense than that in which he has proved such a Being to be inconceivable, his point is not made out, since he undertook to prove the inconceivability of the very Being in whose reality we are required to believe. But the truth is, that the Infinite and Absolute which he says we must believe in, are the very Infinite and Absolute of his definitions. The Infinite is that which is opposed to the Finite; the Absolute, that which is opposed to the Relative. He has therefore either proved nothing, or vastly more than he intended. For the contradictions which he asserts to be involved in the notions, do not follow from an imperfect mode of apprehending the Infinite and Absolute, but lie in the definitions of them; in the meaning of the words themselves. The contradictions are in the very object which we are called upon to believe. If, therefore, Mr. Mansel would escape from the conclusion that an Infinite and Absolute Being is intrinsically impossible, it must be by affirming, with Hegel, that the Law of Contradiction does not apply to the Absolute; that, respecting the Absolute, contradictory propositions may both be true.

Let us now pass from Mr. Mansel's metaphysical argumentation on an irrelevant issue, to the much more important subject of his practical conclusion, namely, that we cannot know the divine attributes in such a manner, as can entitle us to reject any statement respecting the Deity on the ground of its being inconsistent with his character. Let us examine whether this assertion is a legitimate corollary from the relativity of human knowledge, either as it really is, or as it is understood to be by Sir W. Hamilton and by Mr. Mansel.

The fundamental property of our knowledge of God, Mr. Mansel says, is, that we do not and cannot know him as he is in himself: certain persons, therefore, whom he calls Rationalists, he condemns as unphilosophical, when they reject any statement as inconsistent with the character of God. This is a valid answer, as far as words go, to some of the later Transcendentalists—to those who think that we have an intuition of the Divine Nature; though even as to them it would not be difficult to show that the answer is but skin-deep. But those "Rationalists" who hold, with Mr. Mansel himself, the relativity of human knowledge, are not touched by his reasoning. We cannot know God as he is in himself (they reply); granted: and what then? Can we know man as he is in himself, or matter as it is in itself? We do not claim any other knowledge of God than such as we have of man or of matter. Because I do not know my fellow-men, nor any of the powers of nature, as they are in themselves, am I therefore not at liberty to disbelieve anything I hear respecting them as being inconsistent with their character? I know something of Man and Nature, not as they are in themselves, but as they are relatively to us; and it is as relative to us, and not as he is in himself, that I suppose myself to know anything of God. The attributes which I ascribe to him, as goodness, knowledge, power, are all relative. They are attributes (says the rationalist) which my experience enables me to conceive, and which I consider as proved, not absolutely, by an intuition of God, but phænomenally, by his action on the creation, as known through my senses and my rational faculty. These relative attributes, each of them in an infinite degree, are all I pretend to predicate of God. When I reject a doctrine as inconsistent with God's nature, it is not as being inconsistent with what God is in himself, but with what he is as manifested to us. If my knowledge of him is only phænomenal, the assertions which I reject are phænomenal too. If those assertions are inconsistent with my relative knowledge of him, it is no answer to say that all my knowledge of him is relative. That is no more a reason against disbelieving an alleged fact as unworthy of God, than against disbelieving another alleged fact as unworthy of Turgot, or of Washington, whom also I do not know as Noumena, but only as Phænomena.

There is but one way for Mr. Mansel out of this difficulty, and he adopts it. He must maintain, not merely that an Absolute Being is unknowable in himself, but that the Relative attributes of an Absolute Being are unknowable likewise. He must say that we do not know what Wisdom, Justice, Benevolence, Mercy, are, as they exist in God. Accordingly he does say so. The following are his direct utterances on the subject: as an implied doctrine, it pervades his whole argument.

"It is a fact * which experience forces upon us, and which it is useless, were it possible, to disguise, that the representation of God after the model of the highest human morality which we are capable of conceiving, is not sufficient to account for all the phænomena exhibited by the course of his natural Providence. The infliction of physical suffering, the permission of moral evil, the adversity of the good, the prosperity of the wicked, the crimes of the guilty involving the misery of the innocent, the tardy appearance and partial distribution of moral and religious knowledge in the world—these are facts which no doubt are reconcilable, we know not how, with the Infinite Goodness of God, but which certainly are not to be explained on the supposition that its sole and sufficient type is to be found in the finite goodness of man." In other words, it is necessary to suppose that the infinite goodness ascribed to God is not the goodness which we know and love in our fellow-creatures, distinguished only as infinite in degree, but is different in kind, and another quality altogether. When we call the one finite goodness and the other infinite goodness, we do not mean what the words assert, but

* Limits of Religious Thought, Preface to the fourth edition, p. 13.

something else: we intentionally apply the same name to things which we regard as different.

Accordingly Mr. Mansel combats, as a heresy of his opponents, the opinion that infinite goodness differs only in degree from finite goodness. The notion* "that the attributes of God differ from those of man in degree only, not in kind, and hence that certain mental and moral qualities of which we are immediately conscious in ourselves, furnish at the same time a true and adequate image of the infinite perfections of God" (the word *adequate* must have slipped in by inadvertence, since otherwise it would be an inexcusable misrepresentation), he identifies with "the vulgar Rationalism which regards the reason of man, in its ordinary and normal operation, as the supreme criterion of religious truth." And in characterizing the mode of arguing of this vulgar Rationalism, he declares its principles to be, that † "all the excellences of which we are conscious in the creature must necessarily exist in the same manner, though in a higher degree, in the Creator. God is indeed more wise, more just, more merciful, than man; but for that very reason, his wisdom, and justice, and mercy must contain nothing that is incompatible with the corresponding attributes in their human character." It is against this doctrine that Mr. Mansel feels called on to make an emphatic protest.

Here, then, I take my stand on the acknowledged principle of logic and of morality, that when we mean different things we have no right to call them by the same name, and to apply to them the same predicates, moral and intellectual. Language has no meaning for the words Just, Merciful, Benevolent, save that in which we predicate them of our fellow-creatures; and unless that is what we intend to express by them, we have no business to employ the words. If in affirming them of God we do not mean to affirm these very qualities, differing only as greater in degree, we are neither philosophi-

* Limits of Religious Thought, p. 26.
† Ibid. p. 28.

cally nor morally entitled to affirm them at all. If it be said that the qualities are the same, but that we cannot conceive them as they are when raised to the infinite, I grant that we cannot adequately conceive them in one of their elements, their infinity. But we can conceive them in their other elements, which are the very same in the infinite as in the finite development. Anything carried to the infinite must have all the properties of the same thing as finite, except those which depend upon the finiteness. Among the many who have said that we cannot conceive infinite space, did any one ever suppose that it is *not* space? that it does not possess all the properties by which space is characterized? Infinite Space cannot be cubical or spherical, because these are modes of being bounded: but does any one imagine that in ranging through it we might arrive at some region which was not extended; of which one part was not outside another; where, though no Body intervened, motion was impossible; or where the sum of two sides of a triangle was less than the third side? The parallel assertion may be made respecting infinite goodness. What belongs to it as Infinite (or more properly as Absolute) I do not pretend to know; but I know that infinite goodness must be goodness, and that what is not consistent with goodness, is not consistent with infinite goodness. If in ascribing goodness to God I do not mean what I mean by goodness; if I do not mean the goodness of which I have some knowledge, but an incomprehensible attribute of an incomprehensible substance, which for aught I know may be a totally different quality from that which I love and venerate—and even must, if Mr. Mansel is to be believed, be in some important particulars opposed to this—what do I mean by calling it goodness? and what reason have I for venerating it? If I know nothing about what the attribute is, I cannot tell that it is a proper object of veneration. To say that God's goodness may be different in kind from man's goodness, what is it but saying, with a slight change of phraseology, that God may possibly not be good? To assert in words what we do not think in meaning, is as suitable a definition as can be given of a moral falsehood. Besides, suppose that certain unknown attributes are ascribed to the Deity in a religion the external evidences of which are so conclusive to my mind, as effectually to convince me that it comes from God. Unless I believe God to possess the same moral attributes which I find, in however inferior a degree, in a good man, what ground of assurance have I of God's veracity? All trust in a Revelation presupposes a conviction that God's attributes are the same, in all but degree, with the best human attributes.

If, instead of the "glad tidings" that there exists a Being in whom all the excellences which the highest human mind can conceive, exist in a degree inconceivable to us, I am informed that the world is ruled by a being whose attributes are infinite, but what they are we cannot learn, nor what are the principles of his government, except that "the highest human morality which we are capable of conceiving" does not sanction them; convince me of it, and I will bear my fate as I may. But when I am told that I must believe this, and at the same time call this being by the names which express and affirm the highest human morality, I say in plain terms that I will not. Whatever power such a being may have over me, there is one thing which he shall not do: he shall not compel me to worship him. I will call no being good, who is not what I mean when I apply that epithet to my fellow-creatures; and if such a being can sentence me to hell for not so calling him, to hell I will go.

Neither is this to set up my own limited intellect as a criterion of divine or of any other wisdom. If a person is wiser and better than myself, not in some unknown and unknowable meaning of the terms, but in their known human acceptation, I am ready to believe that what this person thinks may be true, and that what he does may be right, when, but for the opinion I have of him, I should think otherwise. But this is because I believe that he and I have at bottom the same standard of truth and rule of right, and that he probably understands better than I the facts of the particular case. If I thought it not improbable that his notion of right might be my notion of wrong, I should not defer to his judgment. In like manner, one who sincerely believes in an absolutely good ruler of the world, is not warranted in disbelieving any act ascribed to him, merely because the very small part of its circumstances which we can possibly know does not sufficiently justify it. But if what I am told respecting him is of a kind which no facts that can be supposed added to my knowledge could make me perceive to be right; if his alleged ways of dealing with the world are such as no imaginable hypothesis respecting things known to him and unknown to me, could make consistent with the goodness and wisdom which I mean when I use the terms, but are in direct contradiction to their signification; then, if the law of contradiction is a law of human thought, I cannot both believe these things, and believe that God is a good and wise being. If I call any being wise or good, not meaning the only qualities which the words import, I am speaking insincerely; I am flattering him by epithets which I fancy that he likes to hear, in the hope of winning him over to my own objects. For it is worthy of remark that the doubt whether words applied to God have their human signification, is only felt when the words relate to his moral attributes; it is never heard of in regard to his power. We are never told that God's omnipotence must not be supposed to mean an infinite degree of the power we know in man and nature, and that perhaps it does not mean that he is able to kill us, or consign us to eternal flames. The Divine Power is always interpreted in a completely human signification, but the Divine Goodness and Justice must be understood to be such only in an unintelligible sense. Is it unfair to surmise that this is because those who speak in the name of God have need of the human conception of his power, since an idea which can overawe and enforce obedience, must address itself to real feelings; but are content that his goodness should be conceived only as something inconceivable, because they are so often required to teach doctrines respecting him which conflict irreconcilably with all goodness that we can conceive?

I am anxious to say once more, that Mr. Mansel's conclusions do not go the whole length of his arguments, and that he disavows the doctrine that God's justice and goodness are *wholly* different from what human beings understand by the terms. He would, and does, admit that the qualities as conceived by us bear *some likeness* to the justice and goodness which belong to God, since man was made in God's image. But such a semi-concession, which no Christian could avoid making, since without it the whole Christian scheme would be subverted, cannot save him; he is not relieved by it from any difficulties, while it destroys the whole fabric of his argument. The Divine goodness, which is said to be a different thing from human goodness, but of which the human conception of goodness is some imperfect reflection or resemblance, does it agree with what men call goodness in the *essence* of the quality—in what *constitutes* it goodness? If it does, the "Rationalists" are right; it is not illicit to reason from the one to the other. If not, the divine attribute, whatever else it may be, is not goodness, and ought not to be called by the name. Unless there be some human conception which agrees with it, no human name can properly be applied to it; it is simply the unknown attribute of thing unknown; it has no existence in relation to us, we can affirm nothing of it, and owe it no worship. Such is the inevitable alternative.

To conclude: Mr. Mansel has not made out any connection between his philosophical premises and his theological conclusion. The relativity of human knowledge, the uncognoscibility of the Absolute, and the contradictions which follow the attempt to conceive a Being with all or without any attributes, are no obstacles to our having the same kind of knowledge of God which we have of other things, namely, not as they exist absolutely, but relatively. The proposition, that we cannot conceive the moral attributes of God in such a manner as to be able to affirm of any doctrine or assertion that it is inconsistent with them, has no foundation in the laws of the human mind: while if admitted, it would not prove that we should ascribe to God attributes bearing the same name as human qualities, but not to be understood in the same sense: it would prove that we ought not to ascribe any moral attributes to God at all, inasmuch as no moral attributes known or conceivable by us are true of him, and we are condemned to absolute ignorance of him as a moral being.

from Three Essays
on Religion

Nature

Nature, natural, and the group of words derived from them, or allied to them in etymology, have at all times filled a great place in the thoughts and taken a strong hold on the feelings of mankind. That they should have done so is not surprising, when we consider what the words, in their primitive and most obvious signification, represent; but it is unfortunate that a set of terms which play so great a part in moral and metaphysical speculation, should have acquired many meanings different from the primary one, yet sufficiently allied to it to admit of confusion. The words have thus become entangled in so many foreign associations, mostly of a very powerful and tenacious character, that they have come to excite, and to be the symbols of, feelings which their original meaning will by no means justify; and which have made them one of the most copious sources of false taste, false philosophy, false morality, and even bad law.

The most important application of the Socratic Elenchus, as exhibited and improved by Plato, consists in dissecting large abstractions of this description; fixing down to a precise definition the meaning which as popularly used they merely shadow forth, and questioning and testing the common maxims and opinions in which they bear a part. It is to be regretted that among the instructive specimens of this kind of investigation which Plato has left, and to which subsequent times have been so much indebted for whatever intellectual clearness they have attained, he has not enriched posterity with a dialogue περὶ φύσεως. If the idea denoted by the word had been subjected to his searching analysis, and the popular commonplaces in which it figures had been submitted to the ordeal of his powerful dialectics, his successors probably would not have rushed, as they speedily did, into modes of thinking and reasoning of which the fallacious use of that word formed the corner stone; a kind of fallacy from which he was himself singularly free.

According to the Platonic method which is still the best type of such investigations, the first thing to be done with so vague a term is to ascertain precisely what it means. It is also a rule of the same method, that the meaning of an abstraction is best sought for in the concrete—of an universal in the particular. Adopting this course with the word Nature, the first question must be, what is meant by the "nature" of a particular object? as of fire, of water, or of some individual plant or animal? Evidently the *ensemble* or aggregate of its powers or properties: the modes in which it acts on other things (counting among those things the senses of the observer) and the modes in which other things act upon it; to which, in the case of a sentient being, must be added, its own capacities of feeling, or being conscious. The Nature of the thing means all this; means its entire capacity of exhibiting phenomena. And since the phenomena which a thing exhibits, however much they vary in different circumstances, are always the same in the same circumstances, they admit of being described in general forms of words, which are called the *laws* of the thing's nature. Thus it is a law of the nature of water that under the mean pressure of the atmosphere at the level of the sea, it boils at 212° Fahrenheit.

As the nature of any given thing is the aggregate of its powers and properties, so Nature in the abstract is the aggregate of the powers and properties of all things. Nature means the sum of all phenomena, together with the causes which produce them; including not only all that happens, but all that is capable of happening; the unused capabilities of causes being as much a part of the idea of Nature, as those which take effect. Since all phenomena which have been sufficiently examined are found to take place with regularity, each having certain fixed conditions, positive and negative, on the occurrence of which it invariably happens; mankind have been able to ascertain, either by direct observation or by reasoning processes grounded on it, the conditions of the occurrence of many phenomena; and the progress of science mainly consists in ascertaining those conditions. When discovered they can be expressed in general propositions, which are called laws of the particular phenomenon, and also, more generally, Laws of Nature. Thus, the truth that all material objects tend towards one another with a force directly as their masses and inversely as the square of their distance, is a law of Nature. The proposition that air and food are necessary to animal life, if it be as we have good reason to believe, true without exception, is also a law of nature, though the phenomenon of which it is the law is special, and not, like gravitation, universal.

Nature, then, in this its simplest acceptation, is a collective name for all facts, actual and possible: or (to speak more accurately) a name for the mode, partly known to us and partly unknown, in which all things take place. For the word suggests, not so much the multitudinous detail of the phenomena, as the conception which might be formed of their manner of existence as a mental whole, by a mind possessing a complete knowledge of them: to which conception it is the aim of science to raise itself, by successive steps of generalization from experience.

Such, then, is a correct definition of the word Nature. But this definition corresponds only to one of the senses of that ambiguous term. It is evidently inapplicable to some of the modes in which the word is familiarly employed. For example, it entirely conflicts with the common form of speech by which Nature is opposed to Art, and natural to artificial. For in the sense of the word Nature which has just been defined, and which is the true scientific sense, Art is as much Nature as anything else; and everything which is artificial is natural—Art has no independent powers of its own: Art is but the employment of the powers of Nature for an end. Phenomena produced by human agency, no less than those which as far as we are concerned are spontaneous, depend on the properties of the elementary forces, or of the elementary substances and their compounds. The united powers of the whole human race could not create a new property of matter in general, or of any one of its species. We can only take advantage for our purposes of the properties which we find. A ship floats by the same laws of specific gravity and equilibrium, as a tree uprooted by the wind and blown into the water. The corn which men raise for food, grows and produces its grain by the same laws of vegetation by which the wild rose and the mountain strawberry bring forth their flowers and fruit. A house stands and holds together by the natural properties, the weight and cohesion of the materials which compose it: a steam engine works by the natural expansive force of steam, exerting a pressure upon one part of a system of arrangements, which pressure, by the mechanical properties of the lever, is transferred from that to another part where it raises the weight or removes the obstacle brought into connexion with it. In these and all other artificial operations the office of man is, as has often been remarked, a very limited one; it consists in moving things into certain places. We move objects, and by doing this, bring some things into contact which were separate, or separate others which were in contact: and by this simple change of place, natural forces previously dormant are called into action, and produce the desired effect. Even the volition which designs, the intelligence which contrives, and the muscular force which executes these movements, are themselves powers of Nature.

It thus appears that we must recognize at least two principal meanings in the word Nature. In one sense, it means all the powers existing in either the outer or the inner world and everything which takes place by means of those powers. In another sense, it means, not everything which happens, but only what takes place without the agency, or without the voluntary and intentional agency, of man. This distinction is far from exhausting the ambiguities of the word; but it is the key to most of those on which important consequences depend.

Such, then, being the two principal senses of the word Nature; in which of these is it taken, or is it taken in either, when the word and its derivatives are used to convey ideas of commendation, approval, and even moral obligation?

It has conveyed such ideas in all ages. *Naturam sequi* was the fundamental principle of morals in many of the most admired schools of philosophy. Among the ancients, especially in the declining period of ancient intellect and thought, it was the test to which all ethical doctrines were brought. The Stoics and the Epicureans, however irreconcilable in the rest of their systems, agreed in holding themselves bound to prove that their respective maxims of conduct were the dictates of nature. Under their influence the Roman jurists, when attempting to systematize jurisprudence, placed in the front of their exposition a certain *Jus Naturale,* "quod natura", as Justinian declares in the Institutes, "omnia animalia docuit": and as the modern systematic writers not only on law but on moral philosophy, have generally taken the Roman jurists for their models, treatises on the so-called Law of Nature have abounded; and references to this Law as a supreme rule and ultimate standard have pervaded literature. The writers on International Law have done more than any others to give currency to this style of ethical speculation; inasmuch as having no positive law to write about, and yet being anxious to invest the most approved opinions respecting international morality with as much as they could of the authority of law, they endeavoured to find such an authority in Nature's imaginary code. The Christian theology during the period of its greatest ascendancy, opposed some, though not a complete, hindrance to the modes of thought which erected Nature into the criterion of morals, inasmuch as, according to the creed of most denominations of Christians (though assuredly not of Christ) man is by nature wicked. But this very doctrine, by the reaction which it provoked, has made the deistical moralists almost unanimous in proclaiming the divinity of Nature, and setting up its fancied dictates as an authoritative rule of action. A reference to that supposed standard is the predominant ingredient in the vein of thought and feeling which was opened by Rousseau, and which has infiltrated itself most widely into the modern mind, not excepting that portion of it which calls itself Christian. The doctrines of Christianity have in every age been largely accommodated to the philosophy which happened to be prevalent, and the Christianity of our day has borrowed a considerable part of its colour and flavour from sentimental deism. At the present time it cannot be said that Nature, or any other standard, is applied as it was wont to be, to deduce rules of action with juridical precision, and with an attempt to make its application co-extensive with all human agency. The people of this generation do not commonly apply principles with any such studious exactness, nor own such binding allegiance to any standard, but live in a kind of confusion of many standards; a condition not propitious to the formation of steady moral convictions, but convenient enough to those whose moral opinions sit lightly on them, since it gives them a much wider range of arguments for defending the doctrine of the moment. But though perhaps no one could now be found who like the institutional writers of former times, adopts the so-called Law of Nature as the foundation of ethics, and endeavours consistently to reason from it, the word and its cognates must still be counted among those which carry great weight in moral argumentation. That any mode of thinking, feeling, or acting, is "according to nature" is usually accepted as a strong argument for its goodness. If it can be said with any plausibility that "nature enjoins" anything, the propriety of obeying the injunction is by most people considered to be made out: and conversely, the imputation of being contrary to nature, is thought to bar the door against any pretension on the part of the thing so designated, to be tolerated or excused; and the word unnatural has not ceased to be one of the most vituperative epithets in the language. Those who deal in these expressions, may avoid making themselves responsible for any fundamental theorem respecting the standard of moral obligation, but they do not the less imply such a theorem, and one which must be the same in substance with that on which the more logical thinkers of a more laborious age grounded their systematic treatises on Natural Law.

Is it necessary to recognize in these forms of speech, another distinct meaning of the word Nature? Or can they be connected, by any rational bond of union, with either of the two meanings already treated of? At first it may seem that we have no option but to admit another ambiguity in the term. All inquiries are either into what is, or into what ought to be: science and history belonging to the first division, art, morals and politics to the second. But the two senses of the word Nature first pointed out, agree in referring only to what is. In the first meaning, Nature is a collective name for everything which is. In the second, it is a name for everything which is of itself, without voluntary human intervention. But the employment of the word Nature as a term of ethics seems to disclose a third meaning, in which Nature does not stand for what is, but for what ought to be; or for the rule or standard of what ought to be. A little consideration, however, will show that this is not a case of ambiguity; there is not here a third sense of the word. Those who set up Nature as a standard of action do not intend a merely verbal proposition; they do not mean that the standard, whatever it be, should be *called* Nature; they think they are giving some information as to what the standard of action really is. Those who say that we ought to act according to Nature do not mean the mere identical proposition that we ought to do what we ought to do. They think that the word Nature affords some external criterion of what we should do; and if they lay down as a rule for what ought to be, a word which in its proper signification denotes what is, they do so because they have a notion, either clearly or confusedly, that what is, constitutes the rule and standard of what ought to be.

The examination of this notion, is the object of the present Essay. It is proposed to inquire into the truth of the doctrines which make Nature a test of right and wrong, good and evil, or which in any mode or degree attach merit or approval to following, imitating, or obeying Nature. To this inquiry the foregoing discussion respecting the meaning of terms, was an indispensable introduction. Language is as it were the atmosphere of philosophical investigation, which must be made transparent before anything can be seen through it in the true figure and position. In the present case it is necessary to guard against a further ambiguity, which though abundantly obvious, has sometimes misled even sagacious minds, and of which it is well to take distinct note before proceeding further. No word is more commonly associated with the word Nature, than Law; and this last word has distinctly two meanings, in one of which it denotes some definite portion of what is, in the other, of what ought to be. We speak of the law of gravitation, the three laws of motion, the law of definite proportions in chemical combination, the vital laws of organized beings. All these are portions of what is. We also speak of the criminal law, the civil law, the law of honour, the law of veracity, the law of justice; all of which are portions of what ought to be, or of somebody's suppositions, feelings, or commands respecting what ought to be. The first kind of laws, such as the laws of motion, and of gravitation, are neither more nor less than the observed uniformities in the occurrence of phenomena: partly uniformities of antecedence and sequence, partly of concomitance. These are what, in science, and even in ordinary parlance, are meant by laws of nature. Laws in the other sense are the laws of the land, the law of nations, or moral laws; among which, as already noticed, is dragged in, by jurists and publicists, something which they think proper to call the Law of Nature. Of the liability of these two meanings of the word to be confounded there can be no better example than the first chapter of Montesquieu; where he remarks, that the material world has its laws, the inferior animals have their laws, and man has his laws; and calls attention to the much greater strictness with which the first two sets of laws are observed, than the last; as if it were an inconsistency, and a paradox, that things always are what they are, but men not always what they ought to be. A similar confusion of ideas pervades the writings of Mr. George Combe, from whence it has overflowed into a large region of popular literature, and we are now continually reading injunctions to obey the physical laws of the universe, as being obligatory in the same sense and manner as the moral. The conception which the ethical use of the word Nature implies, of a close relation if not absolute identity between what is and what ought to be, certainly derives part of its hold on the mind from the custom of designating what is, by the expression "laws of nature," while the same word Law is also used, and even more familiarly and emphatically, to express what ought to be.

When it is asserted, or implied, that Nature, or the laws of

Nature, should be conformed to, is the Nature which is meant, Nature in the first sense of the term, meaning all which is— the powers and properties of all things? But in this signification, there is no need of a recommendation to act accordin to nature, since it is what nobody can possibly help doing, and equally whether he acts well or ill. There is no mode of acting which is not conformable to Nature in this sense of the term, and all modes of acting are so in exactly the same degree. Every action is the exertion of some natural power, and its effects of all sorts are so many phenomena of nature, produced by the powers and properties of some of the objects of nature, in exact obedience to some law or laws of nature. When I voluntarily use my organs to take in food, the act, and its consequences, take place according to laws of nature: if instead of food I swallow poison, the case is exactly the same. To bid people conform to the laws of nature when they have no power but what the laws of nature give them—when it is a physical impossibility for them to do the smallest thing otherwise than through some law of nature, is an absurdity. The thing they need to be told is, what particular law of nature they should make use of in a particular case. When, for example, a person is crossing a river by a narrow bridge to which there is no parapet, he will do well to regulate his proceedings by the laws of equilibrium in moving bodies, instead of conforming only to the law of gravitation, and falling into the river.

Yet, idle as it is to exhort people to do what they cannot avoid doing, and absurd as it is to prescribe as a rule of right conduct what agrees exactly as well with wrong; nevertheless a rational rule of conduct *may* be constructed out of the relation which it ought to bear to the laws of nature in this widest acceptation of the term. Man necessarily obeys the laws of nature, or in other words the properties of things, but he does not necessarily *guide* himself by them. Though all conduct is in conformity to laws of nature, all conduct is not grounded on knowledge of them, and intelligently directed to the attainment of purposes by means of them. Though we cannot emancipate ourselves from the laws of nature as a whole, we can escape from any particular law of nature, if we are able to withdraw ourselves from the circumstances in which it acts. Though we can do nothing except through laws of nature, we can use one law to counteract another. According to Bacon's maxim, we can obey nature in such a manner as to command it. Every alteration of circumstances alters more or less the laws of nature under which we act; and by every choice which we make either of ends or of means, we place ourselves to a greater or less extent under one set of laws of nature instead of another. If, therefore, the useless precept to follow nature were changed into a precept to study nature; to know and take heed of the properties of the things we have to deal with, so far as these properties are capable of forwarding or obstructing any given purpose; we should have arrived at the first principle of all intelligent action, or rather at the definition of intelligent action itself. And a confused notion of this true principle, is, I doubt not, in the minds of many of those who set up the unmeaning doctrine which superficially resembles it. They perceive that the essential difference between wise and foolish conduct consists in attending, or not attending, to the particular laws of nature on which some important result depends. And they think, that a person who attends to a law of nature in order to shape his conduct by it, may be said to obey it, while a person who practically disregards it, and acts as if no such law existed, may be said to disobey it: the circumstance being overlooked, that what is thus called disobedience to a law of nature is obedience to some other or perhaps to the very law itself. For example, a person who goes into a powder magazine either not knowing, or carelessly omitting to think of, the explosive force of gunpowder, is likely to do some act which will cause him to be blown to atoms in obedience to the very law which he has disregarded.

But however much of its authority the "Naturam sequi"

doctrine may owe to its being confounded with the rational precept "Naturam observare," its favourers and promoters unquestionably intend much more by it than that precept. To acquire knowledge of the properties of things, and make use of the knowledge for guidance, is a rule of prudence, for the adaptation of means to ends; for giving effect to our wishes and intentions whatever they may be. But the maxim of obedience to Nature, or conformity to Nature, is held up not as a simply prudential but as an ethical maxim; and by those who talk of *jus naturæ,* even as a law, fit to be administered by tribunals and enforced by sanctions. Right action, must mean something more and other than merely intelligent action: yet no precept beyond this last, can be connected with the word Nature in the wider and more philosophical of its acceptations. We must try it therefore in the other sense, that in which Nature stands distinguished from Art, and denotes, not the whole course of the phenomena which come under our observation, but only their spontaneous course.

Let us then consider whether we can attach any meaning to the supposed practical maxim of following Nature, in this second sense of the word, in which Nature stands for that which takes place without human intervention. In Nature as thus understood, is the spontaneous course of things when left to themselves, the rule to be followed in endeavouring to adapt things to our use? But it is evident at once that the maxim, taken in this sense, is not merely, as it is in the other sense, superfluous and unmeaning, but palpably absurd and self-contradictory. For while human action cannot help conforming to Nature in the one meaning of the term, the very aim and object of action is to alter and improve Nature in the other meaning. If the natural course of things were perfectly right and satisfactory, to act at all would be a gratuitous meddling, which as it could not make things better, must make them worse. Or if action at all could be justified, it would only be when in direct obedience to instincts, since these might perhaps be accounted part of the spontaneous order of Nature; but to do anything with forethought and purpose, would be a violation of that perfect order. If the artificial is not better than the natural, to what end are all the arts of life? To dig, to plough, to build, to wear clothes, are direct infringements of the injunction to follow nature.

Accordingly it would be said by every one, even of those most under the influence of the feelings which prompt the injunction, that to apply it to such cases as those just spoken of, would be to push it too far. Everybody professes to approve and admire many great triumphs of Art over Nature: the junction by bridges of shores which Nature had made separate, the draining of Nature's marshes, the excavation of her wells, the dragging to light of what she has buried at immense depths in the earth; the turning away of her thunderbolts by lightning rods, of her inundations by embankments, of her ocean by breakwaters. But to commend these and similar feats, is to acknowledge that the ways of Nature are to be conquered, not obeyed: that her powers are often towards man in the position of enemies, from whom he must wrest, by force and ingenuity, what little he can for his own use, and deserves to be applauded when that little is rather more than might be expected from his physical weakness in comparison to those gigantic powers. All praise of Civilization, or Art, or Contrivance, is so much dispraise of Nature; an admission of imperfection, which it is man's business and merit to be always endeavouring to correct or mitigate.

The consciousness that whatever man does to improve his condition is in so much a censure and a thwarting of the spontaneous order of Nature has in all ages caused new and unprecedented attempts at improvement to be generally at first under a shade of religious suspicion; as being in any case uncomplimentary, and very probably offensive to the powerful beings (or, when polytheism gave place to monotheism, to the all-powerful Being) supposed to govern the various phenomena of the universe, and of whose will the course of nature was conceived to be the expression. Any attempt to

mould natural phenomena to the convenience of mankind
might easily appear an interference with the government of
those superior beings: and though life could not have been
maintained, much less made pleasant, without perpetual interferences of the kind, each new one was doubtless made
with fear and trembling, until experience had shown that it
could be ventured on without drawing down the vengeance
of the Gods. The sagacity of priests showed them a way to
reconcile the impunity of particular infringements with the
maintenance of the general dread of encroaching on the divine administration. This was effected by representing each
of the principal human inventions as the gift and favour of
some God. The old religions also afforded many resources
for consulting the Gods, and obtaining their express permission for what would otherwise have appeared a breach of
their prerogative. When oracles had ceased, any religion
which recognized a revelation afforded expedients for the
same purpose. The Catholic religion had the resource of an
infallible Church, authorized to declare what exertions of human spontaneity were permitted or forbidden; and in default
of this, the case was always open to argument from the Bible
whether any particular practice had expressly or by implication been sanctioned. The notion remained that this liberty
to control Nature was conceded to man only by special indulgence, and as far as required by his necessities; and there
was always a tendency, though a diminishing one, to regard
any attempt to exercise power over nature, beyond a certain
degree, and a certain admitted range, as an impious effort to
usurp divine power, and dare more than was permitted to
man. The lines of Horace in which the familiar arts of ship-
building and navigation are reprobated as *vetitum nefas,* indicate even in that sceptical age a still unexhausted vein of
the old sentiment. The intensity of the corresponding feeling in the middle ages is not a precise parallel, on account of
the superstition about dealing with evil spirits with which it
was complicated: but the imputation of prying into the se-

crets of the Almighty long remained a powerful weapon of attack against unpopular inquirers into nature; and the charge of presumptuously attempting to defeat the designs of Providence, still retains enough of its original force to be thrown in as a make-weight along with other objections when there is a desire to find fault with any new exertion of human forethought and contrivance. No one, indeed, asserts it to be the intention of the Creator that the spontaneous order of the creation should not be altered, or even that it should not be altered in any new way. But there still exists a vague notion that though it is very proper to control this or the other natural phenomenon, the general scheme of nature is a model for us to imitate: that with more or less liberty in details, we should on the whole be guided by the spirit and general conception of nature's own ways: that they are God's work, and as such perfect; that man cannot rival their unapproachable excellence, and can best show his skill and piety by attempting, in however imperfect a way, to reproduce their likeness; and that if not the whole, yet some particular parts of the spontaneous order of nature, selected according to the speaker's predilections, are in a peculiar sense, manifestations of the Creator's will: a sort of finger posts pointing out the direction which things in general, and therefore our voluntary actions, are intended to take. Feelings of this sort, though repressed on ordinary occasions by the contrary current of life, are ready to break out whenever custom is silent, and the native promptings of the mind have nothing opposed to them but reason: and appeals are continually made to them by rhetoricians, with the effect, if not of convincing opponents, at least of making those who already hold the opinion which the rhetorician desires to recommend, better satisfied with it. For in the present day it probably seldom happens that any one is persuaded to approve any course of action because it appears to him to bear an analogy to the divine government of the world, though the argument tells on him with great force, and is felt by him to be a great support, in behalf of anything which he is already inclined to approve.

If this notion of imitating the ways of Providence as manifested in Nature, is seldom expressed plainly and downrightly as a maxim of general application, it also is seldom directly contradicted. Those who find it on their path, prefer to turn the obstacle rather than to attack it, being often themselves not free from the feeling, and in any case afraid of incurring the charge of impiety by saying anything which might be held to disparage the works of the Creator's power. They therefore, for the most part, rather endeavour to show, that they have as much right to the religious argument as their opponents, and that if the course they recommend seems to conflict with some part of the ways of Providence, there is some other part with which it agrees better than what is contended for on the other side. In this mode of dealing with the great *à priori* fallacies, the progress of improvement clears away particular errors while the causes of errors are still left standing, and very little weakened by each conflict: yet by a long series of such partial victories precedents are accumulated, to which an appeal may be made against these powerful prepossessions, and which afford a growing hope that the misplaced feeling, after having so often learnt to recede, may some day be compelled to an unconditional surrender. For however offensive the proposition may appear to many religious persons, they should be willing to look in the face the undeniable fact, that the order of nature, in so far as unmodified by man, is such as no being, whose attributes are justice and benevolence, would have made, with the intention that his rational creatures should follow it as an example. If made wholly by such a Being, and not partly by beings of very different qualities, it could only be as a designedly imperfect work, which man, in his limited sphere, is to exercise justice and benevolence in amending. The best persons have always held it to be the essence of religion, that the paramount duty of man upon earth is to amend himself: but all except monkish quietists have annexed to this in their inmost minds (though seldom willing to enunciate the obligation with the same clearness) the additional religious duty of amending the world, and not solely the human part of it but the material; the order of physical nature.

In considering this subject it is necessary to divest ourselves of certain preconceptions which may justly be called natural prejudices, being grounded on feelings which, in themselves natural and inevitable, intrude into matters with which they ought to have no concern. One of these feelings is the astonishment, rising into awe, which is inspired (even independently of all religious sentiment) by any of the greater natural phenomena. A hurricane; a mountain precipice; the desert; the ocean, either agitated or at rest; the solar system, and the great cosmic forces which hold it together; the boundless firmament, and to an educated mind any single star; excite feelings which make all human enterprises and powers appear so insignificant, that to a mind thus occupied it seems insufferable presumption in so puny a creature as man to look critically on things so far above him, or dare to measure himself against the grandeur of the universe. But a little interrogation of our own consciousness will suffice to convince us, that what makes these phenomena so impressive is simply their vastness. The enormous extension in space and time, or the enormous power they exemplify, constitutes their sublimity; a feeling in all cases, more allied to terror than to any moral emotion. And though the vast scale of these phenomena may well excite wonder, and sets at defiance all idea of rivalry, the feeling it inspires is of a totally different character from admiration of excellence. Those in whom awe produces admiration may be æsthetically developed, but they are morally uncultivated. It is one of the endowments of the imaginative part of our mental nature that conceptions of greatness and power, vividly realized, produce a feeling which though in its higher degrees closely bordering on pain, we prefer to most of what are accounted pleasures. But we are quite equally capable of experiencing this feeling towards maleficent power; and we never experience it so strongly towards most of the powers of the universe, as when we have most present to our consciousness a vivid sense of their capacity of inflicting evil. Because these natural powers have what we cannot imitate, enormous might, and overawe us by that one attribute, it would be a great error to infer that their other attributes are such as we ought to emulate, or that we should be justified in using our small powers after the example which Nature sets us with her vast forces.

For, how stands the fact? That next to the greatness of these cosmic forces, the quality which most forcibly strikes every one who does not avert his eyes from it, is their perfect and absolute recklessness. They go straight to their end, without regarding what or whom they crush on the road. Optimists, in their attempts to prove that "whatever is, is right," are obliged to maintain, not that Nature ever turns one step from her path to avoid trampling us into destruction, but that it would be very unreasonable in us to expect that she should. Pope's "Shall gravitation cease when you go by?" may be a just rebuke to any one who should be so silly as to expect common human morality from nature. But if the question were between two men, instead of between a man and a natural phenomenon, that triumphant apostrophe would be thought a rare piece of impudence. A man who should persist in hurling stones or firing cannon when another man "goes by," and having killed him should urge a similar plea in exculpation, would very deservedly be found guilty of murder.

In sober truth, nearly all the things which men are hanged or imprisoned for doing to one another, are nature's every day performances. Killing, the most criminal act recognized by human laws, Nature does once to every being that lives; and in a large proportion of cases, after protracted tortures such as only the greatest monsters whom we read of ever purposely inflicted on their living fellow-creatures. If, by an arbitrary reservation, we refuse to account anything murder but what abridges a certain term supposed to be allotted to human life, nature also does this to all but a small percentage of lives, and does it in all the modes, violent or insidious, in which the worst human beings take the lives of one another. Nature impales men, breaks them as if on the wheel, casts them to be devoured by wild beasts, burns them to death, crushes them with stones like the first christian martyr, starves them with hunger, freezes them with cold, poisons them by the quick or slow venom of her exhalations, and has hundreds of other hideous deaths in reserve, such as the ingenious cruelty of a Nabis or a Domitian never surpassed. All this, Nature does with the most supercilious disregard both of mercy and of justice, emptying her shafts upon the best and noblest indifferently with the meanest and worst; upon those who are engaged in the highest and worthiest enterprises, and often as the direct consequence of the noblest acts; and it might almost be imagined as a punishment for them. She mows down those on whose existence hangs the well-being of a whole people, perhaps the prospects of the human race for generations to come, with as little compunction as those whose death is a relief to themselves, or a blessing to those under their noxious influence. Such are Nature's dealings with life. Even when she does not intend to kill, she inflicts the same tortures in apparent wantonness. In the clumsy provision which she has made for that perpetual renewal of animal life, rendered necessary by the prompt termination she puts to it in every individual instance, no human being ever comes into the world but another human being is literally stretched on the rack for hours or days, not unfrequently issuing in death. Next to taking life (equal to it according to a high authority) is taking the means by which we live; and Nature does this too on the largest scale and with the most callous indifference. A single hurricane destroys the hopes of a season; a flight of locusts, or an inundation, desolates a district; a trifling chemical change in an edible root, starves a million of people. The waves of the sea, like banditti seize and appropriate the wealth of the rich and the little all of the poor with the same accompaniments of stripping, wounding, and killing as their human antitypes. Everything in short, which the worst men commit either against life or property is perpetrated on a larger scale by natural agents. Nature has Noyades more fatal than those of Carrier; her explosions of fire damp are as destructive as human artillery; her plague and cholera far surpass the poison cups of the Borgias. Even the love of "order" which is thought to be a following of the ways of Nature, is in fact a contradiction of them. All which people are accustomed to deprecate as "disorder" and its consequences, is precisely a counterpart of Nature's ways. Anarchy and the Reign of Terror are overmatched in injustice, ruin, and death, by a hurricane and a pestilence.

But, it is said, all these things are for wise and good ends. On this I must first remark that whether they are so or not, is altogether beside the point. Supposing it true that contrary to appearances these horrors when perpetrated by Nature, promote good ends, still as no one believes that good ends would be promoted by our following the example, the course of Nature cannot be a proper model for us to imitate. Either it is right that we should kill because nature kills; torture because nature tortures; ruin and devastate because nature does the like; or we ought not to consider at all what nature does, but what it is good to do. If there is such a thing as *reductio ad absurdum,* this surely amounts to one. If it is a sufficient reason for doing one thing, that nature does it, why not another thing? If not all things, why anything? The physical government of the world being full of the things which when done by men are deemed the greatest enormities, it cannot be religious or moral in us to guide our actions by the analogy of the course of nature. This proposition remains true, whatever occult quality of producing good may reside in those facts of nature which to our perceptions are most noxious, and which no one considers it other than a crime to produce artificially.

But, in reality, no one consistently believes in any such occult quality. The phrases which ascribe perfection to the course of nature can only be considered as the exaggerations of poetic or devotional feeling, not intended to stand the test of a sober examination. No one, either religious or irreligious, believes that the hurtful agencies of nature, considered as a whole, promote good purposes, in any other way than by inciting human rational creatures to rise up and struggle against them. If we believed that those agencies were appointed by a benevolent Providence as the means of accomplishing wise purposes which could not be compassed if they did not exist, then everything done by mankind which tends to chain up these natural agencies or to restrict their mischievous operation, from draining a pestilential marsh down to curing the toothache, or putting up an umbrella, ought to be accounted impious; which assuredly nobody does account them, notwithstanding an undercurrent of sentiment setting in that direction which is occasionally perceptible. On the contrary, the improvements on which the civilized part of mankind, most pride themselves, consist in more successfully warding off those natural calamities which if we really believed what most people profess to believe, we should cherish as medicines provided for our earthly state by infinite wisdom. Inasmuch too as each generation greatly surpasses its predecessors in the amount of natural evil which it succeeds in averting, our condition, if the theory were true, ought by this time to have become a terrible manifestation of some tremendous calamity, against which the physical evils we have learnt to overmaster, had previously operated as a preservative. Any one, however, who acted as if he supposed this to be the case, would be more likely, I think, to be confined as a lunatic, then reverenced as a saint.

It is undoubtedly a very common fact that good comes out of evil, and when it does occur, it is far too agreeable not to find people eager to dilate on it. But in the first place, it is quite as often true of human crimes, as of natural calamities. The fire of London, which is believed to have had so salutary an effect on the healthiness of the city, would have produced that effect just as much if it had been really the work of the "furor papisticus" so long commemorated on the Monument. The deaths of those whom tyrants or persecutors have made martyrs in any noble cause, have done a service to mankind which would not have been obtained if they had died by accident or disease. Yet whatever incidental and unexpected benefits may result from crimes, they are crimes nevertheless. In the second place, if good frequently comes out of evil, the converse fact, evil coming out of good, is equally common. Every event public or private, which, regretted on its occurrence, was declared providential at a later period on account of some unforeseen good consequence, might be matched by some other event, deemed fortunate at the time, but which proved calamitous or fatal to those whom it appeared to benefit. Such conflicts between the beginning and the end, or between the event and the expectation, are not only as frequent, but as often held up to notice, in the painful cases as in the agreeable; but there is not the same inclination to generalize on them; or at all events they are not regarded by the moderns (though they were by the ancients) as similarly an indication of the divine purposes: men satisfy themselves with moralizing on the imperfect nature of our foresight, the uncertainty of events, and the vanity of human expectations. The simple fact is, human interests are so complicated, and the effects of any incident whatever so multitudinous, that if it touches mankind at all, its influence on them is, in the great majority of cases, both good and bad. If the greater number of personal misfortunes have their good side, hardly any good fortune ever befel any one which did not give either to the same or to some other person, something to regret: and unhappily there are many misfortunes so overwhelming that their favourable side, if it exist, is entirely overshadowed and made insignificant; while the corresponding statement can seldom be made concerning blessings. The effects too of every cause depend so much on the circumstances which accidentally accompany it, that many cases are sure to occur in which even the total result is markedly opposed to the predominant tendency: and thus not only evil has its good and good its evil side, but good often produces an overbalance of evil and evil an overbalance of good. This, however, is by no means the general tendency of either phenomenon. On the contrary, both good and evil naturally tend to fructify, each in its own kind, good producing good, and evil, evil. It is one of Nature's general rules, and part of her habitual injustice, that "to him that hath shall be given, but from him that hath not, shall be taken even that which he hath." The ordinary and predominant tendency of good is towards more good. Health, strength, wealth, knowledge, virtue, are not only good in themselves but facilitate and promote the acquisition of good, both of the same and of other kinds. The person who can learn easily, is he who already knows much: it is the strong and not the sickly person who can do everything which most conduces to health; those who find it easy to gain money are not the poor but the rich; while health, strength, knowledge, talents, are all means of acquiring riches, and riches are often an indispensable means of acquiring these. Again, *e converso,* whatever may be said of evil turning into good, the general tendency of evil is towards further evil. Bodily illness renders the body more susceptible of disease; it produces incapacity of exertion, sometimes debility of mind, and often the loss of means of subsistence. All severe pain, either bodily or mental, tends to increase the susceptibilities of pain for ever after. Poverty is the parent of a thousand mental and moral evils. What is still worse, to be injured or oppressed, when habitual, lowers the whole tone of the character. One bad action leads to others, both in the agent himself, in the bystanders, and in the sufferers. All bad qualities are strengthened by habit, and all vices and follies tend to spread. Intellectual defects generate moral, and moral, intellectual; and every intellectual or moral defect generates others, and so on without end.

That much applauded class of authors, the writers on natural theology, have, I venture to think, entirely lost their way, and missed the sole line of argument which could have made their speculations acceptable to any one who can perceive when two propositions contradict one another. They have exhausted the resources of sophistry to make it appear that all the suffering in the world exists to prevent greater—that misery exists, for fear lest there should be misery: a thesis which if ever so well maintained, could only avail to explain and justify the works of limited beings, compelled to labour under conditions independent of their own will; but can have no application to a Creator assumed to be omnipotent, who, if he bends to a supposed necessity, himself makes the necessity which he bends to. If the maker of the world *can* all that he will, he wills misery, and there is no escape from the conclusion. The more consistent of those who have deemed themselves qualified to "vindicate the ways of God to man" have endeavoured to avoid the alternative by hardening their hearts, and denying that misery is an evil. The goodness of God, they say, does not consist in willing the happiness of his creatures, but their virtue; and the universe, if not a happy, is a just, universe. But waving the objections to this scheme of ethics, it does not at all get rid of the difficulty. If the Creator of mankind willed that they should all be virtuous, his designs are as completely baffled as if he had willed that they should all be happy: and the order of nature is constructed with even less regard to the requirements of justice than to those of benevolence. If the law of all creation were justice and the Creator omnipotent, then in whatever amount suffering and happiness might be dispensed to the world, each person's share of them would be exactly proportioned to that person's good or evil deeds; no human being would have a worse lot than another, without worse deserts;

accident or favouritism would have no part in such a world, but every human life would be the playing out of a drama constructed like a perfect moral tale. No one is able to blind himself to the fact that the world we live in is totally different from this; insomuch that the necessity of redressing the balance has been deemed one of the strongest arguments for another life after death, which amounts to an admission that the order of things in this life is often an example of injustice, not justice. If it be said that God does not take sufficient account of pleasure and pain to make them the reward or punishment of the good or the wicked, but that virtue is itself the greatest good and vice the greatest evil, then these at least ought to be dispensed to all according to what they have done to deserve them; instead of which, every kind of moral depravity is entailed upon multitudes by the fatality of their birth; through the fault of their parents, of society, or of uncontrollable circumstances, certainly through no fault of their own. Not even on the most distorted and contracted theory of good which ever was framed by religious or philosophical fanaticism, can the government of Nature be made to resemble the work of a being at once good and omnipotent.

The only admissible moral theory of Creation is that the Principle of Good *cannot* at once and altogether subdue the powers of evil, either physical or moral; could not place mankind in a world free from the necessity of an incessant struggle with the maleficent powers, or make them always victorious in that struggle, but could and did make them capable of carrying on the fight with vigour and with progressively increasing success. Of all the religious explanations of the order of nature, this alone is neither contradictory to itself, nor to the facts for which it attempts to account. According to it, man's duty would consist, not in simply taking care of his own interests by obeying irresistible power, but in standing forward a not ineffectual auxiliary to a Being of perfect beneficence; a faith which seems much better adapted for nerving him to exertion than a vague and inconsistent reliance on an Author of Good who is supposed to be also the author of evil. And I venture to assert that such has really been, though often unconsciously, the faith of all who have drawn strength and support of any worthy kind from trust in a superintending Providence. There is no subject on which men's practical belief is more incorrectly indicated by the words they use to express it, than religion. Many have derived a base confidence from imagining themselves to be favourites of an omnipotent but capricious and despotic Deity. But those who have been strengthened in goodness by relying on the sympathizing support of a powerful and good Governor of the world, have, I am satisfied, never really believed that Governor to be, in the strict sense of the term, omnipotent. They have always saved his goodness at the expense of his power. They have believed, perhaps, that he could, if he willed, remove all the thorns from their individual path, but not without causing greater harm to some one else, or frustrating some purpose of greater importance to the general well-being. They have believed that he could do any one thing, but not any combination of things: that his government, like human government, was a system of adjustments and compromises; that the world is inevitably imperfect, contrary to his intention.* And since the exertion of all his power to make it as little imperfect as possible, leaves

* This irresistible conviction comes out in the writings of religious philosophers, in exact proportion to the general clearness of their understanding. It nowhere shines forth so distinctly as in Leibnitz's famous Théodicée, so strangely mistaken for a system of optimism, and, as such, satirized by Voltaire on grounds which do not even touch the author's argument. Leibnitz does not maintain that this world is the best of all imaginable, but only of all possible worlds; which, he argues, it cannot but be, inasmuch as God, who is absolute goodness, has chosen it and not another. In every page of the work he tacitly assumes an abstract possibility and impossibility, independent of the divine power: and though his pious feelings make him continue to designate that power by the word Omnipotence, he so explains that term as to make it mean, power extending to all that is within the limits of that abstract possibility.

it no better than it is, they cannot but regard that power, though vastly beyond human estimate, yet as in itself not merely finite, but extremely limited. They are bound, for example, to suppose that the best he could do for his human creatures was to make an immense majority of all who have yet existed, be born (without any fault of their own) Patagonians, or Esquimaux, or something nearly as brutal and degraded, but to give them capacities which by being cultivated for very many centuries in toil and suffering, and after many of the best specimens of the race have sacrificed their lives for the purpose, have at last enabled some chosen portions of the species to grow into something better, capable of being improved in centuries more into something really good, or which hitherto there are only to be found individual instances. It may be possible to believe with Plato that perfect goodness, limited and thwarted in every direction by the intractableness of the material, has done this because it could do no better. But that the same perfectly wise and good Being had absolute power over the material, and made it, by voluntary choice, what it is; to admit this might have been supposed impossible to any one who has the simplest notions of moral good and evil. Nor can any such person, whatever kind of religious phrases he may use, fail to believe, that if Nature and Man are both the works of a Being of perfect goodness, that Being intended Nature as a scheme to be amended, not imitated, by Man.

But even though unable to believe that Nature, as a whole, is a realization of the designs of perfect wisdom and benevolence, men do not willingly renounce the idea that some part of Nature, at least, must be intended as an exemplar, or type; that on some portion or other of the Creator's works, the image of the moral qualities which they are accustomed to ascribe to him, must be impressed; that if not all which is, yet something which is, must not only be a faultless model of what ought to be, but must be intended to be our guide and standard in rectifying the rest. It does not suffice them to believe, that what tends to good is to be imitated and perfected, and what tends to evil is to be corrected: they are anxious for some more definite indication of the Creator's designs; and being persuaded that this must somewhere be met with in his works, undertake the dangerous responsibility of picking and choosing among them in quest of it. A choice which except so far as directed by the general maxim that he intends all the good and none of the evil, must of necessity be perfectly arbitrary; and if it leads to any conclusions other than such as can be deduced from that maxim, must be, exactly in that proportion, pernicious.

It has never been settled by any accredited doctrine, what particular departments of the order of nature shall be reputed to be designed for our moral instruction and guidance; and accordingly each person's individual predilections, or momentary convenience, have decided to what parts of the divine government the practical conclusions that he was desirous of establishing, should be recommended to approval as being analogous. One such recommendation must be as fallacious as another, for it is impossible to decide that certain of the Creator's works are more truly expressions of his character than the rest; and the only selection which does not lead to immoral results, is the selection of those which most conduce to the general good, in other words, of those which point to an end which if the entire scheme is the expression of a single omnipotent and consistent will, is evidently not the end intended by it.

There is however one particular element in the construction of the world, which to minds on the look-out for special indication of the Creator's will, has appeared, not without plausibility, peculiarly fitted to afford them; viz. the active impulses of human and other animated beings. One can imagine such persons arguing that when the Author of Nature only made circumstances, he may not have meant to indicate the manner in which his rational creatures were to adjust themselves to those circumstances; but that when he implanted positive stimuli in the creatures themselves, stirring them up to a particular kind of action, it is impossible to doubt that he intended that sort of action to be practised by them. This reasoning, followed out consistently, would lead to the conclusion that the Deity intended, and approves, whatever human beings do; since all that they do being the consequence of some of the impulses with which their Creator must have endowed them, all must equally be considered as done in obedience to his will. As this practical conclusion was shrunk from, it was necessary to draw a distinction, and to pronounce that not the whole, but only parts of the active nature of mankind point to a special intention of the Creator in respect to their conduct. These parts it seemed natural to suppose, must be those in which the Creator's hand is manifested rather than the man's own: and hence the frequent antithesis between man as God made him, and man as he has made himself. Since what is done with deliberation seems more the man's own act, and he is held more completely responsible for it than for what he does from sudden impulse, the considerate part of human conduct is apt to be set down as man's share in the business, and the inconsiderate as God's. The result is the vein of sentiment so common in the modern world (though unknown to the philosophic ancients) which exalts instinct at the expense of reason; an aberration rendered still more mischievous by the opinion commonly held in conjunction with it, that every, or almost every, feeling or impulse which acts promptly without waiting to ask questions, is an instinct. Thus almost every variety of unreflecting and uncalculating impulse receives a kind of consecration, except those which, though unreflecting at the moment, owe their origin to previous habits of reflection: these, being evidently not instinctive, do not meet with the favour accorded to the rest; so that all unreflecting impulses are invested with authority over reason, except the only ones which are most probably right. I do not mean, of course, that this mode of judgment is even pretended to be consistently carried out: life could not go on if it were not admitted that impulses must be controlled, and that reason ought to govern our actions. The pretension is not to drive Reason from the helm but rather to bind her by articles to steer only in a particular way. Instinct is not to govern, but reason is to practise some vague and unassignable amount of deference to Instinct. Though the impression in favour of instinct as being a peculiar manifestation of the divine purposes, has not been cast into the form of a consistent general theory, it remains a standing prejudice, capable of being stirred up into hostility to reason in any case in which the dictate of the rational faculty has not acquired the authority of prescription.

I shall not here enter into the difficult psychological question, what are, or are not instincts: the subject would require a volume to itself. Without touching upon any disputed theoretical points, it is possible to judge how little worthy is the instinctive part of human nature to be held up as its chief excellence—as the part in which the hand of infinite goodness and wisdom is peculiarly visible. Allowing everything to be an instinct which anybody has ever asserted to be one, it remains true that nearly every respectable attribute of humanity is the result not of instinct, but of a victory over instinct; and that there is hardly anything valuable in the natural man except capacities—a whole world of possibilities, all of them dependent upon eminently artificial discipline for being realized.

It is only in a highly artificialized condition of human nature that the notion grew up, or, I believe, ever could have grown up, that goodness was natural: because only after a long course of artificial education did good sentiments become so habitual, and so predominant over bad, as to arise unprompted when occasion called for them. In the times when mankind were nearer to their natural state, cultivated observers regarded the natural man as a sort of wild animal, distinguished chiefly by being craftier than the other beasts of the field; and all worth of character was deemed the result of a sort of taming; a phrase often applied by the ancient philosophers to the appropriate discipline of human beings. The truth is that there is hardly a single point of excellence belonging to human character, which is not decidedly repugnant to the untutored feelings of human nature.

If there be a virtue which more than any other we expect to find, and really do find, in an uncivilized state, it is the virtue of courage. Yet this is from first to last a victory achieved over one of the most powerful emotions of human nature. If there is any one feeling or attribute more natural than all others to human beings, it is fear; and no greater proof can be given of the power of artificial discipline than the conquest which it has at all times and places shown itself capable of achieving over so mighty and so universal a sentiment. The widest difference no doubt exists between one human being and another in the facility or difficulty with which they acquire this virtue. There is hardly any department of human excellence in which difference of original temperament goes so far. But it may fairly be questioned if any human being is naturally courageous. Many are naturally pugnacious, or irascible, or enthusiastic, and these passions when strongly excited may render them insensible to fear. But take away the conflicting emotion, and fear reasserts its dominion: consistent courage is always the effect of cultivation. The courage which is occasionally though by no means generally found among tribes of savages, is as much the result of education as that of the Spartans or Romans. In all such tribes there is a most emphatic direction of the public sentiment into every channel of expression through which honour can be paid to courage and cowardice held up to contempt and derision. It will perhaps be said, that as the expression of a sentiment implies the sentiment itself, the training of the young to courage presupposes an originally courageous people. It presupposes only what all good customs presuppose—that there must have been individuals better than the rest, who set the customs going. Some individuals, who like other people had fears to conquer, must have had strength of mind and will to conquer them for themselves. These would obtain the influence belonging to heroes, for that which is at once astonishing and obviously useful never fails to be admired: and partly through this admiration, partly through the fear they themselves excite, they would obtain the power of legislators, and could establish whatever customs they pleased.

Let us next consider a quality which forms the most visible, and one of the most radical of the moral distinctions between human beings and most of the lower animals; that of which the absence, more than of anything else, renders men bestial; the quality of cleanliness. Can anything be more entirely artificial? Children, and the lower classes of most countries, seem to be actually fond of dirt: the vast majority of the human race are indifferent to it: whole nations of otherwise civilized and cultivated human beings tolerate it in some of its worst forms, and only a very small minority are consistently offended by it. Indeed the universal law of the subject appears to be, that uncleanliness offends only those to whom it is unfamiliar, so that those who have lived in so artificial a state as to be unused to it in any form, are the sole persons whom it disgusts in all forms. Of all virtues this is the most evidently not instinctive, but a triumph over instinct. Assuredly neither cleanliness nor the love of cleanliness is natural to man, but only the capacity of acquiring a love of cleanliness.

Our examples have thus far been taken from the personal, or as they are called by Bentham, the self regarding virtues, because these, if any, might be supposed to be congenial even to the uncultivated mind. Of the social virtues it is almost superfluous to speak; so completely is it the verdict of all experience that selfishness is natural. By this I do not in any wise mean to deny that sympathy is natural also; I believe on the contrary that on that important fact rests the possibility of any cultivation of goodness and nobleness, and the hope of their ultimate entire ascendancy. But sympathetic characters, left uncultivated, and given up to their sympathetic instincts, are as selfish as others. The difference is in the *kind* of selfishness: theirs is not solitary but sympathetic selfishness; *l'egoïsme à deux, à trois, or à quatre;* and they may be very amiable and delightful to those with whom they sympathize, and grossly unjust and unfeeling to the rest of the world. Indeed the finer nervous organizations which are most capable of and most require sympathy, have, from their fineness, so much stronger impulses of all sorts, that they often furnish the most striking examples of selfishness, though of a less repulsive kind than that of colder natures. Whether there ever was a person in whom, apart from all teaching of instructors, friends or books, and from all intentional self-modelling according to an ideal, natural benevolence was a more powerful attribute than selfishness in any of its forms, may remain undecided. That such cases are extremely rare, every one must admit, and this is enough for the argument.

But (to speak no further of self-control for the benefit of others) the commonest self-control for one's own benefit—that power of sacrificing a present desire to a distant object or a general purpose which is indispensable for making the actions of the individual accord with his own notions of his individual good; even this is most unnatural to the undisciplined human being: as may be seen by the long apprenticeship which children serve to it; the very imperfect manner in which it is acquired by persons born to power, whose will is seldom resisted, and by all who have been early and much indulged; and the marked absence of the quality in savages, in soldiers and sailors, and in a somewhat less degree in nearly the whole of the poorer classes in this and many other countries. The principal difference, on the point under consideration, between this virtue and others, is that although, like them, it requires a course of teaching, it is more susceptible than most of them of being self-taught. The axiom is trite that self-control is only learnt by experience: and this endowment is only thus much nearer to being natural than the others we have spoken of, inasmuch as personal experience, without external inculcation, has a certain tendency to engender it. Nature does not of herself bestow this, any more than other virtues; but nature often administers the rewards and punishments which cultivate it, and which in other cases have to be created artificially for the express purpose.

Veracity might seem, of all virtues, to have the most plausible claim to being natural, since in the absence of motives to the contrary, speech usually conforms to, or at least does not intentionally deviate from, fact. Accordingly this is the virtue with which writers like Rousseau delight in decorating savage life, and setting it in advantageous contrast with the treachery and trickery of civilization. Unfortunately this is a mere fancy picture, contradicted by all the realities of savage life. Savages are always liars. They have not the faintest notion of truth as a virtue. They have a notion of not betraying to their hurt, as of not hurting in any other way, persons to whom they are bound by some special tie of obligation; their chief, their guest, perhaps, or their friend: these feelings of obligation being the taught morality of the savage state, growing out of its characteristic circumstances. But of any point of honour respecting truth for truth's sake, they have not the remotest idea; no more than the whole East, and the greater part of Europe: and in the few countries which are sufficiently improved to have such a point of honour, it is confined to a small minority, who alone, under any circumstances of real temptation practise it.

From the general use of the expression "natural justice," it must be presumed that justice is a virtue generally thought to be directly implanted by nature. I believe, however, that the sentiment of justice is entirely of artificial origin; the idea of natural justice not preceding but following that of conventional justice. The farther we look back into the early modes of thinking of the human race, whether we consider ancient times (including those of the Old Testament) or the portions of mankind who are still in no more advanced a condition than that of ancient times, the more completely do we find men's notions of justice defined and bounded by the express appointment of law. A man's just rights, meant the rights which the law gave him: a just man, was he who never infringed, nor sought to infringe, the legal property or other legal rights of others. The notion of a higher justice, to which laws themselves are amenable, and by which the conscience is bound without a positive prescription of law, is a later extension of the idea, suggested by, and following the analogy of, legal justice, to which it maintains a parallel direction through all the shades and varieties of the sentiment, and from which it borrows nearly the whole of its phraseology. The very words *justus* and *justitia* are derived from *jus,* law. Courts of justice, administration of justice, always mean the tribunals.

If it be said, that there must be the germs of all these virtues in human nature, otherwise mankind would be incapable of acquiring them, I am ready, with a certain amount of explanation, to admit the fact. But the weeds that dispute the ground with these beneficent germs, are themselves not germs but rankly luxuriant growths, and would, in all but some one case in a thousand, entirely stifle and destroy the former, were it not so strongly the interest of mankind to cherish the good germs in one another, that they always do so, in as far as their degree of intelligence (in this as in other respects still very imperfect) allows. It is through such fostering, commenced early, and not counteracted by unfavourable influences, that, in some happily circumstanced specimens of the human race, the most elevated sentiments of which humanity is capable become a second nature, stronger than the first, and not so much subduing the original nature as merging it into itself. Even those gifted organizations which have attained the like excellence by self-culture, owe it essentially to the same cause; for what self-culture would be possible without aid from the general sentiment of mankind delivered through books, and from the contemplation of exalted characters real or ideal? This artificially created or at least artificially perfected nature of the best and noblest human beings, is the only nature which it is ever commendable to follow. It is almost superfluous to say that even this cannot be erected into a standard of conduct, since it is itself the fruit of a training and culture the choice of which, if rational and not accidental, must have been determined by a standard already chosen.

This brief survey is amply sufficient to prove that the duty of man is the same in respect to his own nature as in respect to the nature of all other things, namely not to follow but to amend it. Some people however who do not attempt to deny that instinct ought to be subordinate to reason, pay deference to nature so far as to maintain that every natural inclination must have some sphere of action granted to it, some opening left for its gratification. All natural wishes, they say, must have been implanted for a purpose: and this argument is carried so far, that we often hear it maintained that every wish, which it is supposed to be natural to entertain, must have a corresponding provision in the order of the universe for its gratification: insomuch (for instance) that the desire of an indefinite prolongation of existence, is believed by many to be in itself a sufficient proof of the reality of a future life.

I conceive that there is a radical absurdity in all these attempts to discover, in detail, what are the designs of Providence, in order when they are discovered to help Providence in bringing them about. Those who argue, from particular indications, that Providence intends this or that, either believe that the Creator can do all that he will or that he cannot. If the first supposition is adopted—if Providence is omnipotent, Providence intends whatever happens, and the fact of its happening proves that Providence intended it. If so, everything which a human being can do, is predestined by Providence and is a fulfilment of its designs. But if as is the more religious theory, Providence intends not all which happens, but only what is good, then indeed man has it in his power, by his voluntary actions, to aid the intentions of Providence; but he can only learn those intentions by considering what tends to promote the general good, and not what man has a natural inclination to; for, limited as, on this showing, the divine power must be, by inscrutable but insurmountable obstacles, who knows that man *could* have been created without desires which never are to be, and even which never ought to be, fulfilled? The inclinations with which man has been endowed, as well as any of the other contrivances which we observe in Nature, may be the expression not of the divine will, but of the fetters which impede its free action; and to take hints from these for the guidance of our own conduct may be falling into a trap laid by the enemy. The assumption that everything which infinite goodness can desire, actually comes to pass in this universe, or at least that we must never say or suppose that it does not, is worthy only of those whose slavish fears make them offer the homage of lies to a Being who, they profess to think, is incapable of being deceived and holds all falsehood in abomination.

With regard to this particular hypothesis, that all natural impulses, all propensities sufficiently universal and sufficiently spontaneous to be capable of passing for instincts, must exist for good ends, and ought to be only regulated, not repressed; this is of course true of the majority of them, for the species could not have continued to exist unless most of its inclinations had been directed to things needful or useful for its preservation. But unless the instincts can be reduced to a very small number indeed, it must be allowed that we have also bad instincts which it should be the aim of education not simply to regulate but to extirpate, or rather (what can be done even to an instinct) to starve them by disuse. Those who are inclined to multiply the number of instincts, usually include among them one which they call destructiveness: an instinct to destroy for destruction's sake. I can conceive no good reason for preserving this, no more than another propensity which if not an instinct is very like one, what has been called the instinct of domination; a delight in exercising despotism, in holding other beings in subjection to our will. The man who takes pleasure in the mere exertion of authority, apart from the purpose for which it is to be employed, is the last person in whose hands one would willingly entrust it. Again, there are persons who are cruel by character, or, as the phrase is, naturally cruel; who have a real pleasure in inflicting, or seeing the infliction of, pain. This kind of cruelty is not mere hardheartedness, absence of pity or remorse; it is a positive thing; a particular kind of voluptuous excitement. The East, and Southern Europe, have afforded, and probably still afford, abundant examples of this hateful propensity. I suppose it will be granted that this is not one of the natural inclinations which it would be wrong to suppress. The only question would be whether it is not a duty to suppress the man himself along with it.

But even if it were true that every one of the elementary impulses of human nature has its good side, and may by a sufficient amount of artificial training be made more useful than hurtful; how little would this amount to, when it must in any case be admitted that without such training all of them, even those which are necessary to our preservation, would fill the world with misery, making human life an exaggerated likeness of the odious scene of violence and tyranny which is exhibited by the rest of the animal kingdom, except in so far as tamed and disciplined by man. There, indeed, those who flatter themselves with the notion of reading the purposes of the Creator in his works, ought in consistency to have seen grounds for inferences from which they have shrunk. If there are any marks at all of special design in creation, one of the things most evidently designed is that a large proportion of all animals should pass their existence in tormenting and devouring other animals. They have been lavishly fitted out with the instruments necessary for that purpose; their strongest instincts impel them to it, and many of them seem to have been constructed incapable of supporting themselves by any other food. If a tenth part of the pains which have been expended in finding benevolent adaptations in all nature, had been employed in collecting evidence to blacken the character of the Creator, what scope for comment would not have been found in the entire existence of the lower animals, divided, with scarcely an exception, into devourers and devoured, and a prey to a thousand ills from which they are denied the faculties necessary for protecting themselves! If we are not obliged to believe the animal creation to be the work of a demon, it is because we need not suppose it to have been made by a Being of infinite power. But if imitation of the Creator's will as revealed in nature, were applied as a rule of action in this case, the most atrocious enormities of the worst men would be more than justified by the apparent intention of Providence that throughout all animated nature the strong should prey upon the weak.

The preceding observations are far from having exhausted the almost infinite variety of modes and occasions in which the idea of conformity to nature is introduced as an element into the ethical appreciation of actions and dispositions. The same favourable prejudgment follows the word nature through the numerous acceptations, in which it is employed as a distinctive term for certain parts of the constitution of humanity as contrasted with other parts. We have hitherto confined ourselves to one of these acceptations, in which it stands as a general designation for those parts of our mental and moral constitution which are supposed to be innate, in contradistinction to those which are acquired; as when nature is contrasted with education; or when a savage state, without laws, arts, or knowledge, is called a state of nature; or when the question is asked whether benevolence, or the moral sentiment, is natural or acquired; or whether some persons are poets or orators by nature and others not. But in another and a more lax sense, any manifestations by human beings are often termed natural, when it is merely intended to say that they are not studied or designedly assumed in the particular case; as when a person is said to move or speak with natural grace; or when it is said that a person's natural manner or character is so and so; meaning that it is so when he does not attempt to control or disguise it. In a still looser acceptation, a person is said to be naturally, that which he was until some special cause had acted upon him, or which it is supposed he would be if some such cause were withdrawn. Thus a person is said to be naturally dull, but to have made himself intelligent by study and perseverance; to be naturally cheerful, but soured by misfortune; naturally ambitious, but kept down by want of opportunity. Finally, the word natural, applied to feelings or conduct, often seems to mean no more than that they are such as are ordinarily found in human beings; as when it is said that a person acted, on some particular occasion, as it was natural to do; or that to be affected in a particular way by some sight, or sound, or thought, or incident in life, is perfectly natural.

In all these senses of the term, the quality called natural is very often confessedly a worse quality than the one contrasted with it; but whenever its being so is not too obvious to be questioned the idea seems to be entertained that by describing it as natural, something has been said amounting to a considerable presumption in its favour. For my part I can perceive only one sense in which nature, or naturalness, in a human being, are really terms of praise; and then the praise is only negative: namely when used to denote the absence of affectation. Affectation may be defined, the effort to appear what one is not, when the motive or the occasion is not such as either to excuse the attempt, or to stamp it with the odious name of hypocrisy. It must be added that the deception is often attempted to be practised on the deceiver himself as well as on others; he imitates the external signs of qualities which he would like to have, in hopes to persuade himself that he has them. Whether in the form of deception or of self-deception, or of something hovering between the two, affectation is very rightly accounted a reproach, and naturalness, understood as the reverse of affectation, a merit. But a more proper term by which to express this estimable quality would be sincerity; a term which has fallen from its original elevated meaning, and popularly denotes only a subordinate branch of the cardinal virtue it once designated as a whole.

Sometimes also, in cases where the term affectation would be inappropriate, since the conduct or demeanour spoken of is really praiseworthy, people say in disparagement of the person concerned, that such conduct or demeanour is not natural to him; and make uncomplimentary comparisons between him and some other person, to whom it is natural: meaning that what in the one seemed excellent was the effect of temporary excitement, or of a great victory over himself, while in the other it is the result to be expected from the habitual character. This mode of speech is not open to censure, since nature is here simply a term for the person's ordinary disposition, and if he is praised it is not for being natural, but for being naturally good.

Conformity to nature, has no connection whatever with right and wrong. The idea can never be fitly introduced into ethical discussions at all, except, occasionally and partially, into the question of degrees of culpability. To illustrate this point, let us consider the phrase by which the greatest intensity of condemnatory feeling is conveyed in connection with the idea of nature—the word unnatural. That a thing is unnatural, in any precise meaning which can be attached to the word, is no argument for its being blamable; since the

most criminal actions are to a being like man, not more unnatural than most of the virtues. The acquisition of virtue has
in all ages been accounted a work of labour and difficulty,
while the *descensus Averni* on the contrary is of proverbial
facility: and it assuredly requires in most persons a greater
conquest over a greater number of natural inclinations to become eminently virtuous than transcendently vicious. But if
an action, or an inclination, has been decided on other
grounds to be blamable, it may be a circumstance in aggravation that it is unnatural, that is, repugnant to some
strong feeling usually found in human beings; since the bad
propensity, whatever it be, has afforded evidence of being
both strong and deeply rooted, by having overcome that
repugnance. This presumption of course fails if the individual
never had the repugnance: and the argument, therefore, is
not fit to be urged unless the feeling which is violated by the
act, is not only justifiable and reasonable, but is one which
it is blamable to be without.

The corresponding plea in extenuation of a culpable act
because it was natural, or because it was prompted by a
natural feeling, never, I think, ought to be admitted. There
is hardly a bad action ever perpetrated which is not perfectly
natural, and the motives to which are not perfectly natural
feelings. In the eye of reason, therefore, this is no excuse, but
it is quite "natural" that it should be so in the eyes of the
multitude; because the meaning of the expression is, that
they have a fellow feeling with the offender. When they say
that something which they cannot help admitting to be blamable, is nevertheless natural, they mean that they can imagine the possibility of their being themselves tempted to
commit it. Most people have a considerable amount of indulgence towards all acts of which they feel a possible source
within themselves, reserving their rigour for those which,
though perhaps really less bad, they cannot in any way understand how it is possible to commit. If an action convinces
them (which it oftens does on very inadequate grounds)

that the person who does it must be a being totally unlike themselves, they are seldom particular in examining the precise degree of blame due to it, or even if blame is properly due to it at all. They measure the degree of guilt by the strength of their antipathy; and hence differences of opinion, and even differences of taste, have been objects of as intense moral abhorrence as the most atrocious crimes.

It will be useful to sum up in a few words the leading conclusions of this Essay.

The word Nature has two principal meanings: it either denotes the entire system of things, with the aggregate of all their properties, or it denotes things as they would be, apart from human intervention.

In the first of these senses, the doctrine that man ought to follow nature is unmeaning; since man has no power to do anything else than follow nature; all his actions are done through, and in obedience to, some one or many of nature's physical or mental laws.

In the other sense of the term, the doctrine that man ought to follow nature, or in other words, ought to make the spontaneous course of things the model of his voluntary actions, is equally irrational and immoral.

Irrational, because all human action whatever, consists in altering, and all useful action in improving, the spontaneous course of nature:

Immoral, because the course of natural phenomena being replete with everything which when committed by human beings is most worthy of abhorrence, any one who endeavoured in his actions to imitate the natural course of things would be universally seen and acknowledged to be the wickedest of men.

The scheme of Nature regarded in its whole extent, cannot have had, for its sole or even principal object, the good of human or other sentient beings. What good it brings to them, is mostly the result of their own exertions. Whatsoever, in nature, gives indication of beneficent design, proves this beneficence to be armed only with limited power; and the duty of man is to co-operate with the beneficent powers, not by imitating but by perpetually striving to amend the course of nature—and bringing that part of it over which we can exercise control, more nearly into conformity with a high standard of justice and goodness.

Utility of Religion

It has sometimes been remarked how much has been written, both by friends and enemies, concerning the truth of religion, and how little, at least in the way of discussion or controversy, concerning its usefulness. This, however, might have been expected; for the truth, in matters which so deeply affect us, is our first concernment. If religion, or any particular form of it, is true, its usefulness follows without other proof. If to know authentically in what order of things, under what government of the universe it is our destiny to live, were not useful, it is difficult to imagine what could be considered so. Whether a person is in a pleasant or in an unpleasant place, a palace or a prison, it cannot be otherwise than useful to him to know where he is. So long, therefore, as men accepted the teachings of their religion as positive facts, no more a matter of doubt than their own existence or the existence of the objects around them, to ask the use of believing it could not possibly occur to them. The utility of religion did not need to be asserted until the arguments for its truth had in a great measure ceased to convince. People must either have ceased to believe, or have ceased to rely on the belief of others, before they could take that inferior ground of defence without a consciousness of lowering what they were endeavouring to raise. An argument for the utility of religion is an appeal to unbelievers, to induce them to practise a well meant hypocrisy, or to semi-believers to make them avert their eyes from what might possibly shake their unstable belief, or finally to persons in general to abstain from expressing any doubts they may feel, since a fabric of immense importance to mankind is so insecure at its foundations, that men must hold their breath in its neighbourhood for fear of blowing it down.

In the present period of history, however, we seem to have arrived at a time when, among the arguments for and against religion, those which relate to its usefulness assume an important place. We are in an age of weak beliefs, and in which such belief as men have is much more determined by their wish to believe than by any mental appreciation of evidence. The wish to believe does not arise only from selfish but often from the most disinterested feelings; and though it cannot produce the unwavering and perfect reliance which once existed, it fences round all that remains of the impressions of early education; it often causes direct misgivings to fade away by disuse; and above all, it induces people to continue laying out their lives according to doctrines which have lost part of their hold on the mind, and to maintain towards the world the same, or a rather more demonstrative attitude of belief, than they thought it necessary to exhibit when their personal conviction was more complete.

If religious belief be indeed so necessary to mankind, as we are continually assured that it is, there is great reason to lament, that the intellectual grounds of it should require to be backed by moral bribery or subornation of the understanding. Such a state of things is most uncomfortable even for those who may, without actual insincerity, describe themselves as believers; and still worse as regards those who, having consciously ceased to find the evidences of religion convincing, are withheld from saying so lest they should aid in doing an irreparable injury to mankind. It is a most painful position to a conscientious and cultivated mind, to be drawn in contrary directions by the two noblest of all objects of pursuit, truth, and the general good. Such a conflict must inevitably produce a growing indifference to one or other of these objects, most probably to both. Many who could render giant's service both to truth and to mankind if they believed that they could serve the one without loss to the other, are either totally paralysed, or led to confine their exertions to matters of minor detail, by the apprehension that any real freedom of speculation, or any considerable strengthening or enlargement of the thinking faculties of mankind at large, might, by making them unbelievers, be the surest way to render them vicious and miserable. Many, again, having observed in others or experienced in themselves elevated feelings which they imagine incapable of emanating from any other source than religion, have an honest aversion to anything tending, as they think, to dry up the fountain of such feelings. They, therefore, either dislike and disparage all philosophy, or addict themselves with intolerant zeal to those forms of it in which intuition usurps the place of evidence, and internal feeling is made the test of objective truth. The whole of the prevalent metaphysics of the present century is one tissue of suborned evidence in favour of religion; often of Deism only, but in any case involving a misapplication of noble impulses and speculative capacities, among the most deplorable of those wretched wastes of human faculties which make us wonder that enough is left to keep mankind progressive, at however slow a pace. It is time to consider, more impartially and therefore more deliberately than is usually done, whether all this straining to prop up beliefs which require so great an expense of intellectual toil and ingenuity to keep them standing, yields any sufficient return in human well-being; and whether that end would not be better served by a frank recognition that certain subjects are inaccessible to our faculties, and by the application of the same mental powers to the strengthening and enlargement of those other sources of virtue and happiness which stand in no need of the support or sanction of supernatural beliefs and inducements.

Neither, on the other hand, can the difficulties of the question be so promptly disposed of, as sceptical philosophers are sometimes inclined to believe. It is not enough to aver, in general terms, that there never can be any conflict between truth and utility; that if religion be false, nothing but good can be the consequence of rejecting it. For, though the knowledge of every positive truth is an useful acquisition, this doctrine cannot without reservation be applied to negative truth. When the only truth ascertainable is that nothing can be known, we do not, by this knowledge, gain any new fact by which to guide ourselves; we are, at best, only disabused of our trust in some former guide-mark, which, though itself fallacious, may have pointed in the same direction with the best indications we have, and if it happens to be more conspicuous and legible, may have kept us right when they might have been overlooked. It is, in short, perfectly conceivable that religion may be morally useful without being intellectually sustainable: and it would be a proof of great prejudice in any unbeliever to deny, that there have been ages, and that there are still both nations and individuals, with regard to whom this is actually the case. Whether it is the case generally, and with reference to the future, it is the object of this paper to examine. We propose to inquire whether the belief in religion, considered as a mere persuasion, apart from the question of its truth, is really indispensable to the temporal welfare of mankind; whether the usefulness of the belief is intrinsic and universal, or local, temporary, and, in some sense, accidental; and whether the benefits which it yields might not be obtained otherwise, without the very large alloy of evil, by which, even in the best form of the belief, those benefits are qualified.

With the arguments on one side of the question we all are familiar: religious writers have not neglected to celebrate to the utmost the advantages both of religion in general and of their own religious faith in particular. But those who have held the contrary opinion have generally contented themselves with insisting on the more obvious and flagrant of the positive evils which have been engendered by past and present forms of religious belief. And, in truth, mankind have been so unremittingly occupied in doing evil to one another in the name of religion, from the sacrifice of Iphigenia to the Dragonnades of Louis XIV. (not to descend lower), that for any immediate purpose there was little need to seek arguments further off. These odious consequences, however, do not belong to religion in itself, but to particular forms of it, and afford no argument against the usefulness of any religions except those by which such enormities are encouraged. Moreover, the worst of these evils are already in a great measure extirpated from the more improved forms of religion; and as mankind advance in ideas and in feelings, this process of extirpation continually goes on: the immoral, or otherwise mischievous consequences which have been drawn from religion, are, one by one, abandoned, and, after having been long fought for as of its very essence, are discovered to be easily separable from it. These mischiefs, indeed, after they are past, though no longer arguments against religion, remain valid as large abatements from its beneficial influence, by showing that some of the greatest improvements ever made in the moral sentiments of mankind have taken place without it and in spite of it, and that what we are taught to regard as the chief of all improving influences, has in practice fallen so far short of such a character, that one of the hardest burdens laid upon the other good influences of human nature has been that of improving religion itself. The improvement, however, has taken place; it is still proceeding, and for the sake of fairness it should be assumed to be complete. We ought to suppose religion to have accepted the best human morality which reason and goodness can work out, from philosophical, christian, or any other elements. When it has thus freed itself from the pernicious consequences which result from its identification with any bad moral doctrine, the ground is clear for considering whether its useful properties are exclusively inherent in it, or their benefits can be obtained without it.

This essential portion of the inquiry into the temporal usefulness of religion, is the subject of the present Essay. It is a part which has been little treated of by sceptical writers. The only direct discussion of it with which I am acquainted, is in a short treatise, understood to have been partly compiled from manuscripts of Mr. Bentham,* and abounding in just and profound views; but which, as it appears to me, presses many parts of the argument too hard. This treatise, and the incidental remarks scattered through the writings of M. Comte, are the only sources known to me from which anything very pertinent to the subject can be made available for the sceptical side of the argument. I shall use both of them freely in the sequel of the present discourse.

The inquiry divides itself into two parts, corresponding to the double aspect of the subject; its social, and its individual aspect. What does religion do for society, and what for the individual? What amount of benefit to social interests, in the ordinary sense of the phrase, arises from religious belief? And what influence has it in improving and ennobling individual human nature?

The first question is interesting to everybody; the latter only to the best; but to them it is, if there be any difference, the more important of the two. We shall begin with the former, as being that which best admits of being easily brought to a precise issue.

To speak first, then, of religious belief as an instrument of social good. We must commence by drawing a distinction

* "Analysis of the Influence of Natural Religion on the Temporal Happiness of Mankind." By Philip Beauchamp.

most commonly overlooked. It is usual to credit religion *as such* with the whole of the power inherent in *any* system of moral duties inculcated by education and enforced by opinion. Undoubtedly mankind would be in a deplorable state if no principles or precepts of justice, veracity, beneficence, were taught publicly or privately, and if these virtues were not encouraged, and the opposite vices repressed, by the praise and blame, the favourable and unfavourable sentiments, of mankind. And since nearly everything of this sort which does take place, takes place in the name of religion; since almost all who are taught any morality whatever, have it taught to them *as* religion, and inculcated on them through life principally in that character; the effect which the teaching produces as teaching, it is supposed to produce as religious teaching, and religion receives the credit of all the influence in human affairs which belongs to any generally accepted system of rules for the guidance and government of human life.

Few persons have sufficiently considered how great an influence this is; what vast efficacy belongs naturally to any doctrine received with tolerable unanimity as true, and impressed on the mind from the earliest childhood as duty. A little reflection will, I think, lead us to the conclusion that it is this which is the great moral power in human affairs, and that religion only seems so powerful because this mighty power has been under its command.

Consider first, the enormous influence of authority on the human mind. I am now speaking of involuntary influence; effect on men's conviction, on their persuasion, on their involuntary sentiments. Authority is the evidence on which the mass of mankind believe everything which they are said to know, except facts of which their own senses have taken cognizance. It is the evidence on which even the wisest receive all those truths of science, or facts in history or in life, of which they have not personally examined the proofs. Over the immense majority of human beings, the general concurrence of mankind, in any matter of opinion, is all powerful. Whatever is thus certified to them, they believe with a fulness of assurance which they do not accord even to the evidence of their senses when the general opinion of mankind stands in opposition to it. When, therefore, any rule of life and duty, whether grounded or not on religion, has conspicuously received the general assent, it obtains a hold on the belief of every individual, stronger than it would have even if he had arrived at it by the inherent force of his own understanding. If Novalis could say, not without a real meaning, "My belief has gained infinitely to me from the moment when one other human being has begun to believe the same," how much more when it is not one other person, but all the human beings whom one knows of. Some may urge it as an objection, that no scheme of morality has this universal assent, and that none, therefore, can be indebted to this source for whatever power it possesses over the mind. So far as relates to the present age, the assertion is true, and strengthens the argument which it might at first seem to controvert; for exactly in proportion as the received systems of belief have been contested, and it has become known that they have many dissentients, their hold on the general belief has been loosened, and their practical influence on conduct has declined: and since this has happened to them notwithstanding the religious sanction which attached to them, there can be no stronger evidence that they were powerful not as religion, but as beliefs generally accepted by mankind. To find people who believe their religion as a person believes that fire will burn his hand when thrust into it, we must seek them in those Oriental countries where Europeans do not yet predominate, or in the European world when it was still universally Catholic. Men often disobeyed their religion in those times, because their human passions and appetites were too strong for it, or because the religion itself afforded means of indulgence to breaches of its obligations; but though they disobeyed, they, for the most part, did not doubt. There was in those days an absolute and unquestioning completeness of belief, never since general in Europe.

Such being the empire exercised over mankind by simple authority, the mere belief and testimony of their fellow creatures; consider next how tremendous is the power of education; how unspeakable is the effect of bringing people up from infancy in a belief, and in habits founded on it. Consider also that in all countries, and from the earliest ages down to the present, not merely those who are called, in a restricted sense of the term, the educated, but all or nearly all who have been brought up by parents, or by any one interested in them, have been taught from their earliest years some kind of religious belief, and some precepts as the commands of the heavenly powers to them and to mankind. And as it cannot be imagined that the commands of God are to young children anything more than the commands of their parents, it is reasonable to think that any system of social duty which mankind might adopt, even though divorced from religion, would have the same advantage of being inculcated from childhood, and would have it hereafter much more perfectly than any doctrine has it at present, society being far more disposed than formerly to take pains for the moral tuition of those numerous classes whose education it has hitherto left very much to chance. Now it is especially characteristic of the impressions of early education, that they possess what it is so much more difficult for later convictions to obtain—command over the feelings. We see daily how powerful a hold these first impressions retain over the feelings even of those, who have given up the opinions which they were early taught. While on the other hand, it is only persons of a much higher degree of natural sensibility and intellect combined than it is at all common to meet with, whose feelings entwine themselves with anything like the same force round opinions which they have adopted from their own investigations later in life; and even when they do, we may say with truth that it is because the strong sense of moral duty, the sincerity, courage and self-devotion which enabled them to do so, were themselves the fruits of early impressions.

The power of education is almost boundless: there is not one natural inclination which it is not strong enough to coerce, and, if needful, to destroy by disuse. In the greatest recorded victory which education has ever achieved over a whole host of natural inclinations in an entire people—the maintenance through centuries of the institutions of Lycurgus—it was very little, if even at all, indebted to religion: for the Gods of the Spartans were the same as those of other Greek states; and though, no doubt, every state of Greece believed that its particular polity had at its first establishment, some sort of divine sanction (mostly that of the Delphian oracle), there was seldom any difficulty in obtaining the same or an equally powerful sanction for a change. It was not religion which formed the strength of the Spartan institutions. the root of the system was devotion to Sparta, to the ideal of the country or State: which transformed into ideal devotion to a greater country, the world, would be equal to that and far nobler achievements. Among the Greeks generally, social morality was extremely independent of religion. The inverse relation was rather that which existed between them; the worship of the Gods was inculated chiefly as a social duty, inasmuch as if they were neglected or insulted, it was believed that their displeasure would fall not more upon the offending individual than upon the state or community which bred and tolerated him. Such moral teaching as existed in Greece had very little to do with religion. The Gods were not supposed to concern themselves much with men's conduct to one another, except when men had contrived to make the Gods themselves an interested party, by placing an assertion or an engagement under the sanction of a solemn appeal to them, by oath or vow. I grant that the sophists and philosophers, and even popular orators, did their best to press religion into the service of their special objects, and to make it be thought that the sentiments of whatever kind, which they were engaged in inculcating, were particularly acceptable to the Gods, but this never seems the primary consideration in any case save those of direct offence to the dignity of the Gods themselves. For the enforcement of human moralities secular inducements were almost exclusively relied on. The case of Greece is, I believe, the only one in which any teaching, other than religious, has had the unspeakable advantage of forming the basis of education: and though much may be said against the quality of some part of the teaching, very little can be said against its effectiveness. The most memorable example of the power of education over conduct, is afforded (as I have just remarked) by this exceptional case; constituting a strong presumption that in other cases, early religious teaching has owed its power over mankind rather to its being early than to its being religious.

We have now considered two powers, that of authority, and that of early education, which operate through men's involuntary beliefs, feelings and desires, and which religion has hitherto held as its almost exclusive appanage. Let us now consider a third power which operates directly on their actions, whether their involuntary sentiments are carried with it or not. This is the power of public opinion; of the praise and blame, the favour and disfavour, of their fellow creatures; and is a source of strength inherent in any system of moral belief which is generally adopted, whether connected with religion or not.

Men are so much accustomed to give to the motives that decide their actions, more flattering names than justly belong to them, that they are generally quite unconscious how much those parts of their conduct which they most pride themselves on (as well as some which they are ashamed of), are determined by the motive of public opinion. Of course public opinion for the most part enjoins the same things which are enjoined by the received social morality; that morality being, in truth, the summary of the conduct which each one of the multitude, whether he himself observes it with any strictness or not, desires that others should observe towards him. People are therefore easily able to flatter themselves that they are acting from the motive of conscience when they are doing in obedience to the inferior motive, things which their conscience approves. We continually see how great is the power of opinion in opposition to conscience; how men "follow a multitude to do evil;" how often opinion induces them to do what their conscience disapproves, and still oftener prevents them from doing what it commands. But when the motive of public opinion acts in the same direction with conscience, which, since it has usually itself made the conscience in the first instance, it for the most part naturally does; it is then, of all motives which operate on the bulk of mankind, the most overpowering.

The names of all the strongest passions (except the merely animal ones) manifested by human nature, are each of them a name for some one part only of the motive derived from what I here call public opinion. The love of glory; the love of praise; the love of admiration; the love of respect and deference; even the love of sympathy, are portions of its attractive power. Vanity is a vituperative name for its attractive influence generally, when considered excessive in degree. The fear of shame, the dread of ill repute or of being disliked or hated, are the direct and simple forms of its deterring power. But the deterring force of the unfavourable sentiments of mankind does not consist solely in the painfulness of knowing oneself to be the object of those sentiments; it includes all the penalties which they can inflict: exclusion from social intercourse and from the innumerable good offices which human beings require from one another; the forfeiture of all that is called success in life; often the great diminution or total loss of means of subsistence; positive ill offices of various kinds, sufficient to render life miserable, and reaching in some states of society as far as actual persecution to death. And again the attractive, or impelling influence of public opinion, includes the whole range of what is commonly meant by ambition: for, except in times of lawless military violence, the objects of social ambition can only be attained by means of the good opinion and favourable disposition of our fellow-creatures; nor, in nine cases out of ten, would those objects be even desired, were it not for the power they confer over the sentiments of mankind. Even the pleasure of self-approbation, in the great majority, is mainly dependent on the opinion of others. Such is the involuntary influence of authority on ordinary minds, that persons must be of a better than ordinary mould to be capable of a full assurance that they are in the right, when the world, that is, when *their* world, thinks them wrong: nor is there, to most men, any proof so demonstrative of their own virtue or talent as that people in general seem to believe in it. Through all departments of human affairs, regard for the sentiments of our fellow-creatures is in one shape or other, in nearly all characters, the pervading motive. And we ought to note that this motive is naturally strongest in the most sensitive natures, which are the most promising material for the formation of great virtues. How far its power reaches is known by too familiar experience to require either proof or illustration here. When once the means of living have been obtained, the far greater part of the remaining labour and effort which takes place on the earth, has for its object to acquire the respect or the favourable regard of mankind; to be looked up to, or at all events, not to be looked down upon by them. The industrial and commercial activity which advance civilization, the frivolity, prodigality, and selfish thirst of aggrandizement which retard it, flow equally from that source. While as an instance of the power exercised by the terrors derived from public opinion, we know how many murders have been committed merely to remove a witness who knew and was likely to disclose some secret that would bring disgrace upon his murderer.

Any one who fairly and impartially considers the subject, will see reason to believe that those great effects on human conduct, which are commonly ascribed to motives derived directly from religion, have mostly for their proximate cause the influence of human opinion. Religion has been powerful not by its intrinsic force, but because it has wielded that additional and more mighty power. The effect of religion has been immense in giving a direction to public opinion: which has, in many most important respects, been wholly determined by it. But without the sanctions superadded by public opinion, its own proper sanctions have never, save in exceptional characters, or in peculiar moods of mind, exercised a very potent influence, after the times had gone by, in which divine agency was supposed habitually to employ temporal rewards and punishments. When a man firmly believed that if he violated the sacredness of a particular sanctuary he would be struck dead on the spot, or smitten suddenly with a mortal disease, he doubtless took care not to incur the penalty; but when any one had had the courage to defy the danger, and escaped with impunity, the spell was broken. If ever any people were taught that they were under a divine government, and that unfaithfulness to their religion and law would be visited from above with temporal chastisements, the Jews were so. Yet their history was a mere succession of lapses into Paganism. Their prophets and historians, who held fast to the ancient beliefs (though they gave them so liberal an interpretation as to think it a sufficient manifestation of God's displeasure towards a king if any evil happened to his great grandson), never ceased to complain that their countrymen turned a deaf ear to their vaticinations; and hence, with the faith they held in a divine government operating by temporal penalites, they could not fail to anticipate (as Mirabeau's father without such prompting, was able to do on the eve of the French Revolution) *la culbute générale;* an expectation which, luckily for the credit of their prophetic powers, was fulfilled; unlike that of the Apostle John, who in the only intelligible prophecy in the Revelations, foretold to the city of the seven hills a fate like that of Nineveh and Babylon; which prediction remains to this hour unaccomplished. Unquestionably the conviction which experience in time forced on all but the very ignorant, that divine punishments were not to be confidently expected in a temporal form, contributed much to the downfall of the old religions, and the general adoption of one which without absolutely excluding providential interferences in this life for the punishment of guilt or the reward of merit, removed the principal scene of divine retribution to a world after death. But rewards and punishments postponed to that distance of time, and never seen by the eye, are not calculated, even when infinite and eternal, to have, on ordinary minds, a very powerful effect in opposition to strong temptation. Their remoteness alone is a prodigious deduction from their efficacy, on such minds as those which most require the restraint of punishment. A still greater abatement is their uncertainty, which belongs to them from the very nature of the case: for rewards and punishments administered after death, must be awarded not definitely to particular actions, but on a general survey of the person's whole life, and he easily persuades himself that whatever may have been his peccadilloes, there will be a balance in his favour at the last. All positive religions aid this self-delusion. Bad religions teach that divine vengeance may be bought off, by offerings, or personal abasement; the better religions, not to drive sinners to despair, dwell so much on the divine mercy, that hardly any one is compelled to think himself irrevocably condemned. The sole quality in these punishments which might seem calculated to make them efficacious, their overpowering magnitude, is itself a reason why nobody (except a hypochondriac here and there) ever really believes that he is in any very serious danger of incurring them. Even the worst malefactor is hardly able to think that any crime he has had it in his power to commit, any evil he can have inflicted in this short space of existence, can have deserved torture extending through an eternity. Accordingly religious writers and preachers are never tired of complaining how little effect religious motives have on men's lives and conduct, notwithstanding the tremendous penalties denounced.

Mr. Bentham, whom I have already mentioned as one of the few authors who have written anything to the purpose on the efficacy of the religious sanction, adduces several cases to prove that religious obligation, when not enforced by public opinion, produces scarcely any effect on conduct. His first example is that of oaths. The oaths taken in courts of justice, and any others which from the manifest importance to society of their being kept, public opinion rigidly enforces, are felt as real and binding obligations. But university oaths and custom-house oaths, though in a religious point of view equally obligatory, are in practice utterly disregarded even by men in other respects honourable. The university oath to obey the statutes has been for centuries, with universal acquiescence, set at nought: and utterly false statements are (or used to be) daily and unblushingly sworn to at the Custom-house, by persons as attentive as other people to all the ordinary obligations of life. The explanation being, that veracity in these cases was not enforced by public opinion. The second case which Bentham cites is duelling; a practice now, in this country, obsolete, but in full vigour in several other christian countries; deemed and admitted to be a sin by almost all who, nevertheless, in obedience to opinion, and to escape from personal humiliation, are guilty of it. The third case is that of illicit sexual intercourse; which in both sexes, stands in the very highest rank of religious sins, yet not being severely censured by opinion in the male sex, they have in general very little scruple in committing it; while in the case of women, though the religious obligation is not stronger, yet being backed in real earnest by public opinion, it is commonly effectual.

Some objection may doubtless be taken to Bentham's instances, considered as crucial experiments on the power of the religious sanction; for (it may be said) people do not really believe that in these cases they shall be punished by

God, any more than by man. And this is certainly true in the case of those university and other oaths, which are habitually taken without any intention of keeping them. The oath, in these cases, is regarded as a mere formality, destitute of any serious meaning in the sight of the Deity; and the most scrupulous person, even if he does reproach himself for having taken an oath which nobody deems fit to be kept, does not in his conscience tax himself with the guilt of perjury, but only with the profanation of a ceremony. This, therefore, is not a good example of the weakness of the religious motive when divorced from that of human opinion. The point which it illustrates is rather the tendency of the one motive to come and go with the other, so that where the penalties of public opinion cease, the religious motive ceases also. The same criticism, however, is not equally applicable to Bentham's other examples, duelling, and sexual irregularities. Those who do these acts, the first by the command of public opinion, the latter with its indulgence, really do, in most cases, believe that they are offending God. Doubtless, they do not think that they are offending him in such a degree as very seriously to endanger their salvation. Their reliance on his mercy prevails over their dread of his resentment; affording an exemplification of the remark already made, that the unavoidable uncertainty of religious penalties makes them feeble as a deterring motive. They are so, even in the case of acts which human opinion condemns: much more, with those to which it is indulgent. What mankind think venial, it is hardly ever supposed that God looks upon in a serious light: at least by those who feel in themselves any inclination to practise it.

I do not for a moment think of denying that there are states of mind in which the idea of religious punishment acts with the most overwhelming force. In hypochondriacal disease, and in those with whom, from great disappointments or other moral causes, the thoughts and imagination have assumed an habitually melancholy complexion, that topic, falling in with the pre-existing tendency of the mind, supplies images well fitted to drive the unfortunate sufferer even to madness. Often, during a temporary state of depression, these ideas take such a hold of the mind as to give a permanent turn to the character; being the most common case of what, in sectarian phraseology, is called conversion. But if the depressed state ceases after the conversion, as it commonly does, and the convert does not relapse, but perseveres in his new course of life, the principal difference between it and the old is usually found to be, that the man now guides his life by the public opinion of his religious associates, as he before guided it by that of the profane world. At all events, there is one clear proof how little the generality of mankind, either religious or worldly, really dread eternal punishments, when we see how, even at the approach of death, when the remoteness which took so much from their effect has been exchanged for the closest proximity, almost all persons who have not been guilty of some enormous crime (and many who have) are quite free from uneasiness as to their prospects in another world, and never for a moment seem to think themselves in any real danger of eternal punishment.

With regard to the cruel deaths and bodily tortures, which confessors and martyrs have so often undergone for the sake of religion, I would not depreciate them by attributing any part of this admirable courage and constancy to the influence of human opinion. Human opinion indeed has shown itself quite equal to the production of similar firmness in persons not otherwise distinguished by moral excellence; such as the North American Indian at the stake. But if it was not the thought of glory in the eyes of their fellow-religionists, which upheld these heroic sufferers in their agony, as little do I believe that it was, generally speaking, that of the pleasures of heaven or the pains of hell. Their impulse was a divine enthusiasm—a self-forgetting devotion to an idea: a state of exalted feeling, by no means peculiar to religion, but which it is the privilege of every great cause to inspire; a phenomenon belonging to the critical moments of existence, not to the ordinary play of human motives, and from which nothing can be inferred as to the efficacy of the ideas which it sprung from, whether religious or any other, in overcoming ordinary temptations, and regulating the course of daily life.

We may now have done with this branch of the subject, which is, after all, the vulgarest part of it. The value of religion as a supplement to human laws, a more cunning sort of police, an auxiliary to the thief-catcher and the hangman, is not that part of its claims which the more highminded of its votaries are fondest of insisting on: and they would probably be as ready as any one to admit, that if the nobler offices of religion in the soul could be dispensed with, a substitute might be found for so coarse and selfish a social instrument as the fear of hell. In their view of the matter, the best of mankind absolutely require religion for the perfection of their own character, even though the coercion of the worst might possibly be accomplished without its aid.

Even in the social point of view, however, under its most elevated aspect, these nobler spirits generally assert the necessity of religion, as a teacher, if not as an enforcer, of social morality. They say, that religion alone can teach us what morality is; that all the high morality ever recognized by mankind, was learnt from religion; that the greatest uninspired philosophers in their sublimest flights, stopt far short of the christian morality, and whatever inferior morality they may have attained to (by the assistance, as many think, of dim traditions derived from the Hebrew books, or from a primæval revelation) they never could induce the common mass of their fellow citizens to accept it from them. That, only when a morality is understood to come from the Gods, do men in general adopt it, rally round it, and lend their human sanctions for its enforcement. That granting the sufficiency of human motives to make the rule obeyed, were it not for the religious idea we should not have had the rule itself.

There is truth in much of this, considered as matter of history. Ancient peoples have generally, if not always, received their morals, their laws, their intellectual beliefs, and even their practical arts of life, all in short which tended either to guide or to discipline them, as revelations from the superior powers, and in any other way could not easily have been induced to accept them. This was partly the effect of their hopes and fears from those powers, which were of much greater and more universal potency in early times, when the agency of the Gods was seen in the daily events of life, experience not having yet disclosed the fixed laws according to which physical phenomena succeed one another. Independently, too, of personal hopes and fears, the involuntary deference felt by these rude minds for power superior to their own, and the tendency to suppose that beings of superhuman power must also be of superhuman knowledge and wisdom, made them disinterestedly desire to conform their conduct to the presumed preferences of these powerful beings, and to adopt no new practice without their authorization either spontaneously given, or solicited and obtained.

But because, when men were still savages, they would not have received either moral or scientific truths unless they had supposed them to be supernaturally imparted, does it follow that they would now give up moral truths any more than scientific, because they believed them to have no higher origin than wise and noble human hearts? Are not moral truths strong enough in their own evidence, at all events to retain the belief of mankind when once they have acquired it? I grant that some of the precepts of Christ as exhibited in the Gospels—rising far above the Paulism which is the foundation of ordinary Christianity—carry some kinds of moral goodness to a greater height than had ever been attained before, though much even of what is supposed to be peculiar to them is equalled in the Meditations of Marcus Antoninus, which we have no ground for believing to have been in any way indebted to Christianity. But this benefit, whatever it amounts to, has been gained. Mankind have entered into the possession of it. It has become the property of humanity, and cannot now be lost by anything short of a return to primæval barbarism. The "new commandment to love one another;"* the recognition that the greatest are those who serve, not who are served by, others; the reverence for the weak and humble, which is the foundation of chivalry, they and not the strong being pointed out as having the first place in God's regard, and the first claim on their fellow men; the lesson of the parable of the Good Samaritan; that of "he that is without sin let him throw the first stone;" the precept of doing as we would be done by; and such other noble moralities as are to be found, mixed with some poetical exaggerations, and some maxims of which it is difficult to ascertain the precise object; in the authentic sayings of Jesus of Nazareth; these are surely in sufficient harmony with the intellect and feelings of every good man or woman, to be in no danger of being let go, after having been once acknowledged as the creed of the best and foremost portion of our species. There will be, as there have been, shortcomings enough for a long time to come in acting on them; but that they should be forgotten, or cease to be operative on the human conscience, while human beings remain cultivated or civilized, may be pronounced, once for all, impossible.

On the other hand, there is a very real evil consequent on ascribing a supernatural origin to the received maxims of morality. That origin consecrates the whole of them, and protects them from being discussed or criticized. So that if among the moral doctrines received as a part of religion, there be any which are imperfect—which were either erroneous from the first, or not properly limited and guarded in the expression, or which, unexceptionable once, are no longer suited to the changes that have taken place in human relations (and it is my firm belief that in so-called christian morality, instances of all these kinds are to be found) these

---

* Not, however, a new commandment. In justice to the great Hebrew lawgiver, it should always be remembered that the precept, to love thy neighbour as thyself, already existed in the Pentateuch; and very surprising it is to find it there.

doctrines are considered equally binding on the conscience with the noblest, most permanent and most universal precepts of Christ. Wherever morality is supposed to be of supernatural origin, morality is stereotyped; as law is, for the same reason, among believers in the Koran.

Belief, then, in the supernatural, great as are the services which it rendered in the early stages of human development, cannot be considered to be any longer required, either for enabling us to know what is right and wrong in social morality or for supplying us with motives to do right and to abstain from wrong. Such belief, therefore, is not necessary for social purposes, at least in the coarse way in which these can be considered apart from the character of the individual human being. That more elevated branch of the subject now remains to be considered. If supernatural beliefs are indeed necessary to the perfection of the individual character, they are necessary also to the highest excellence in social conduct: necessary in a far higher sense than that vulgar one, which constitutes it the great support of morality in common eyes.

Let us then consider, what it is in human nature which causes it to require a religion; what wants of the human mind religion supplies, and what qualities it develops. When we have understood this, we shall be better able to judge, how far these wants can be otherwise supplied and those qualities, or qualities equivalent to them, unfolded and brought to perfection by other means.

The old saying, *Primus in orbe Deos fecit timor,* I hold to be untrue, or to contain, at most, only a small amount of truth. Belief in Gods had, I conceive, even in the rudest minds, a more honourable origin. Its universality has been very rationally explained from the spontaneous tendency of the mind to attribute life and volition, similar to what it feels in itself, to all natural objects and phenomena which appear to be self-moving. This was a plausible fancy, and no better theory could be formed at first. It was naturally persisted in so long as the motions and operations of these objects seemed to be arbitrary, and incapable of being accounted for but by the free choice of the Power itself. At first, no doubt, the objects themselves were supposed to be alive; and this belief still subsists among African fetish-worshippers. But as it must soon have appeared absurd that things which could do so much more than man, could not or would not do what man does, as for example to speak, the transition was made to supposing that the object present to the senses was inanimate, but was the creature and instrument of an invisible being with a form and organs similar to the human.

These beings having first been believed in, fear of them necessarily followed; since they were thought able to inflict at pleasure on human beings great evils, which the sufferers neither knew how to avert nor to foresee, but were left dependent, for their chances of doing either, upon solicitations addressed to the deities themselves. It is true, therefore, that fear had much to do with religion: but belief in the Gods evidently preceded, and did not arise from, fear: though the fear, when established, was a strong support to the belief, nothing being conceived to be so great an offence to the divinities as any doubt of their existence.

It is unnecessary to prosecute further the natural history of religion, as we have not here to account for its origin in rude minds, but for its persistency in the cultivated. A sufficient explanation of this will, I conceive, be found in the small limits of man's certain knowledge, and the boundlessness of his desire to know. Human existence is girt round with mystery: the narrow region of our experience is a small island in the midst of a boundless sea, which at once awes our feelings and stimulates our imagination by its vastness and its obscurity. To add to the mystery, the domain of our earthly existence is not only an island in infinite space, but also in infinite time. The past and the future are alike shrouded from us: we neither know the origin of anything which is, nor its final destination. If we feel deeply interested in knowing that there are myriads of worlds at an immeasurable, and to our faculties inconceivable, distance from us in space; if we are eager to discover what little we can about these worlds, and when we cannot know what they are, can never satiate ourselves with speculating on what they may be; is it not a matter of far deeper interest to us to learn, or even to conjecture, from whence came this nearer world which we inhabit; what cause or agency made it what it is, and on what powers depend its future fate? Who would not desire this more ardently than any other conceivable knowledge, so long as there appeared the slightest hope of attaining it? What would not one give for any credible tidings from that mysterious region, any glimpse into it which might enable us to see the smallest light through its darkness, especially any theory of it which we could believe, and which represented it as tenanted by a benignant and not a hostile influence? But since we are able to penetrate into that region with the imagination only, assisted by specious but inconclusive analogies derived from human agency and design, imagination is free to fill up the vacancy with the imagery most congenial to itself; sublime and elevating if it be a lofty imagination, low and mean if it be a grovelling one.

Religion and poetry address themselves, at least in one of their aspects, to the same part of the human constitution: they both supply the same want, that of ideal conceptions grander and more beautiful than we see realized in the prose of human life. Religion, as distinguished from poetry, is the product of the craving to know whether these imaginative conceptions have realities answering to them in some other world than ours. The mind, in this state, eagerly catches at any rumours respecting other worlds, especially when delivered by persons whom it deems wiser than itself. To the poetry of the supernatural, comes to be thus added a positive belief and expectation, which unpoetical minds can share with the poetical. Belief in a God or Gods, and in a life after death, becomes the canvas which every mind, according to its capacity, covers with such ideal pictures as it can either invent or copy. In that other life each hopes to find the good which he has failed to find on earth, or the better which is suggested to him by the good which on earth he has partially seen and known. More especially, this belief supplies the finer minds with material for conceptions of beings more awful than they *can* have known on earth, and more excellent than they probably *have* known. So long as human life is insufficient to satisfy human aspirations, so long there will be a craving for higher things, which finds its most obvious satisfaction in religion. So long as earthly life is full of sufferings, so long there will be need of consolations, which the hope of heaven affords to the selfish, the love of God to the tender and grateful.

The value, therefore, of religion to the individual, both in the past and present, as a source of personal satisfaction and of elevated feelings, is not to be disputed. But it has still to be considered, whether in order to obtain this good, it is necessary to travel beyond the boundaries of the world which we inhabit; or whether the idealization of our earthly life, the cultivation of a high conception of what *it* may be made, is not capable of supplying a poetry, and, in the best sense of the word, a religion, equally fitted to exalt the feelings, and (with the same aid from education) still better calculated to ennoble the conduct, than any belief respecting the unseen powers.

At the bare suggestion of such a possibility, many will exclaim, that the short duration, the smallness and insignificance of life, if there is no prolongation of it beyond what we see, makes it impossible that great and elevated feelings can connect themselves with anything laid out on so small a scale: that such a conception of life can match with nothing higher than Epicurean feelings, and the Epicurean doctrine "Let us eat and drink, for to-morrow we die."

Unquestionably, within certain limits, the maxim of the Epicureans is sound, and applicable to much higher things than eating and drinking. To make the most of the present for all good purposes, those of enjoyment among the rest; to keep under control those mental dispositions which lead to undue sacrifice of present good for a future which may never arrive; to cultivate the habit of deriving pleasure from things within our reach, rather than from the too eager pursuit of objects at a distance; to think all time wasted which is not spent either in personal pleasure or in doing things useful to oneself or others; these are wise maxims, and the "carpe diem" doctrine, carried thus far, is a rational and legitimate corollary from the shortness of life. But that because life is short we should care for nothing beyond it, is not a legitimate conclusion; and the supposition, that human beings in general are not capable of feeling deep and even the deepest interest in things which they will never live to see, is a view of human nature as false as it is abject. Let it be remembered that if individual life is short, the life of the human species is not short; its indefinite duration is practically equivalent to endlessness; and being combined with indefinite capability of improvement, it offers to the imagination and sympathies a large enough object to satisfy any reasonable demand for grandeur of aspiration. If such an object appears small to a mind accustomed to dream of infinite and eternal beatitudes, it will expand into far other dimensions when those baseless fancies shall have receded into the past.

Nor let it be thought that only the more eminent of our species, in mind and heart, are capable of identifying their feelings with the entire life of the human race. This noble capability implies indeed a certain cultivation, but not superior to that which might be, and certainly will be if human improvement continues, the lot of all. Objects far smaller than this, and equally confined within the limits of the earth (though not within those of a single human life), have been found sufficient to inspire large masses and long successions of mankind with an enthusiasm capable of ruling the conduct, and colouring the whole life. Rome was to the entire Roman people, for many generations as much a religion as Jehovah was to the Jews; nay, much more, for they never fell off from their worship as the Jews did from theirs. And the Romans, otherwise a selfish people, with no very remarkable faculties of any kind except the purely practical, derived nevertheless from this one idea a certain greatness of soul, which manifests itself in all their history where that idea is concerned and nowhere else, and has earned for them the large share of admiration, in other respects not at all deserved, which has been felt for them by most noble-minded persons from that time to this.

When we consider how ardent a sentiment, in favourable circumstances of education, the love of country has become, we cannot judge it impossible that the love of that larger country, the world, may be nursed into similar strength, both as a source of elevated emotion and as a principle of duty. He who needs any other lesson on this subject than the whole course of ancient history affords, let him read Cicero *de Officiis*. It cannot be said that the standard of morals laid down in that celebrated treatise is a high standard. To our notions it is on many points unduly lax, and admits capitulations of conscience. But on the subject of duty to our country there is no compromise. That any man, with the smallest pretensions to virtue, could hesitate to sacrifice life, reputation, family, everything valuable to him, to the love of country is a supposition which this eminent interpreter of Greek and Roman morality cannot entertain for a moment. If, then, persons could be trained, as we see they were, not only to believe in theory that the good of their country was an object to which all others ought to yield, but to feel this practically as the grand duty of life, so also may they be made to feel the same absolute obligation towards the universal good. A morality grounded on large and wise views of the good of the whole, neither sacrificing the individual to the aggregate nor the aggregate to the individual, but giving to duty on the one hand and to freedom and spontaneity on the other their proper province, would derive its power in the superior natures from sympathy and benevolence and the passion for ideal excellence: in the inferior, from the same feelings cultivated up to the measure of their capacity, with the superadded force of shame. This exalted morality would not depend for its ascendancy on any hope of reward; but the reward which might be looked for, and the thought of which would be a consolation in suffering, and a support in moments of weakness, would not be a problematical future existence, but the approbation, in this, of those whom we respect, and ideally of all those, dead or living, whom we admire or venerate. For, the thought that our dead parents or friends would have approved our conduct is a scarcely less powerful motive than the knowledge that our living ones do approve it: and the idea that Socrates, or Howard or Washington, or Antoninus, or Christ, would have sympathized with us, or that we are attempting to do our part in the spirit in which they did theirs, has operated on the very best minds, as a strong incentive to act up to their highest feelings and convictions.

To call these sentiments by the name morality, exclusively of any other title, is claiming too little for them. They are a real religion; of which, as of other religions, outward good works (the utmost meaning usually suggested by the word morality) are only a part, and are indeed rather the fruits of the religion than the religion itself. The essence of religion is the strong and earnest direction of the emotions and desires towards an ideal object, recognized as of the highest excellence, and as rightfully paramount over all selfish objects of desire. This condition is fulfilled by the Religion of Humanity in as eminent a degree, and in as high a sense, as by the supernatural religions even in their best manifestations, and far more so than in any of their others.

Much more might be added on this topic; but enough has been said to convince any one, who can distinguish between the intrinsic capacities of human nature and the forms in which those capacities happen to have been historically developed, that the sense of unity with mankind, and a deep feeling for the general good, may be cultivated into a sentiment and a principle capable of fulfilling every important function of religion and itself justly entitled to the name. I will now further maintain, that it is not only capable of fulfilling these functions, but would fulfil them better than any form whatever of supernaturalism. It is not only entitled to be called a religion: it is a better religion than any of those which are ordinarily called by that title.

For, in the first place, it is distinterested. It carries the thoughts and feelings of self, and fixes them on an unselfish object, loved and pursued as an end for its own sake. The religions which deal in promises and threats regarding a future life, do exactly the contrary: they fasten down the thoughts to the person's own posthumous interests; they tempt him to regard the performance of his duties to others mainly as a means to his own personal salvation; and are one of the most serious obstacles to the great purpose of moral culture, the strengthening of the unselfish and weakening of the selfish element in our nature; since they hold out to the imagination selfish good and evil of such tremendous magnitude, that it is difficult for any one who fully believes in their reality, to have feeling or interest to spare for any other distant and ideal object. It is true, many of the most unselfish of mankind have been believers in supernaturalism, because their minds have not dwelt on the threats and promises of their religion, but chiefly on the idea of a Being to whom they looked up with a confiding love, and in whose hands they willingly left all that related especially to themselves. But in its effect on common minds, what now goes by the name of religion operates mainly through the feelings of self-interest. Even the Christ of the Gospels holds out the direct promise of reward from heaven as a primary inducement to the noble and beautiful beneficence towards our fellow-creatures which he so impressively inculcates. This is a radical inferiority of the best supernatural religions, compared with the Religion of Humanity; since the greatest thing which moral influences can do for the amelioration of human nature, is to cultivate the unselfish feelings in the only mode in which any active principle in human nature can be effectually cultivated, namely by habitual exercise: but the habit of expecting to be rewarded in another life for our conduct in this, makes even virtue itself no longer an exercise of the unselfish feelings.

Secondly, it is an immense abatement from the worth of the old religions as means of elevating and improving human character, that it is nearly, if not quite impossible for them to produce their best moral effects, unless we suppose a certain torpidity, if not positive twist in the intellectual faculties. For it is impossible that any one who habitually thinks, and who is unable to blunt his inquiring intellect by sophistry, should be able without misgiving to go on ascribing absolute perfection to the author and ruler of so clumsily made and capriciously governed a creation as this planet and the life of its inhabitants. The adoration of such a being cannot be with the whole heart, unless the heart is first considerably sophisticated. The worship must either be greatly overclouded by doubt, and occasionally quite darkened by it, or the moral sentiments must sink to the low level of the ordinances of Nature: the worshipper must learn to think blind partiality, atrocious cruelty, and reckless injustice, not blemishes in an object of worship, since all these abound to excess in the commonest phenomena of Nature. It is true, the God who is worshipped is not, generally speaking, the God of Nature only, but also the God of some revelation; and the character of the revelation will greatly modify and, it may be, improve the moral influences of the religion. This is emphatically true of Christianity; since the Author of the Sermon on the Mount is assuredly a far more benignant Being than the Author of Nature. But unfortunately, the believer in the christian revelation is obliged to believe that the same being is the author of both. This, unless he resolutely averts his mind from the subject, or practises the act of quieting his conscience by sophistry, involves him in moral perplexities without end; since the ways of his Deity in Nature are on many occasions totally at variance with the precepts, as he believes, of the same Deity in the Gospel. He who comes out with least moral damage from this embarrassment, is probably the one who never attempts to reconcile the two standards with one another, but confesses to himself that the purposes of Providence are mysterious, that its ways are not our ways, that its justice and goodness are not the justice and goodness which we can conceive and which it befits us to practise. When, however, this is the feeling of the believer, the worship of the Deity ceases to be the adoration of abstract moral perfection. It becomes the bowing down to a gigantic image of something not fit for us to imitate. It is the worship of power only.

I say nothing of the moral difficulties and perversions involved in revelation itself; though even in the Christianity of the Gospels, at least in its ordinary interpretation, there are some of so flagrant a character as almost to outweigh all the beauty and benignity and moral greatness which so eminently distinguish the sayings and character of Christ. The recognition, for example, of the object of highest worship, in a being who could make a Hell; and who could create countless generations of human beings with the certain foreknowledge that he was creating them for this fate. Is there any moral enormity which might not be justified by imitation of such a Deity? And is it possible to adore such a one without a frightful distortion of the standard of right and wrong? Any other of the outrages to the most ordinary justice and humanity involved in the common christian conception of the moral character of God, sinks into insignificance beside this dreadful idealization of wickedness. Most of them too, are happily not so unequivocally deducible from the very words of Christ as to be indisputably a part of christian doctrine. It may be doubted, for instance, whether Christianity is really responsible for atonement and redemption, original sin and vicarious punishment: and the same may be said respecting the doctrine which makes belief in the divine mission of Christ a necessary condition of salvation. It is nowhere represented that Christ himself made this statement, except in the huddled-up account of the Resurrection contained in the concluding verses of St. Mark, which some critics (I believe the best), consider to be an interpolation. Again, the proposition that "the powers that be are ordained of God" and the whole series of corollaries deduced from it in the Epistles, belong to St. Paul, and must stand or fall with Paulism, not with Christianity. But there is one moral contradiction inseparable from every form of Christianity, which no ingenuity can resolve, and no sophistry explain away. It is, that so precious a gift, bestowed on a few, should have been withheld from the many: that countless millions of human beings should have been allowed to live and die, to sin and suffer, without the one thing needful, the divine remedy for sin and suffering, which it would have cost the Divine Giver as little to have vouchsafed to all, as to have bestowed by special grace upon a favoured minority. Add to this, that the divine message, assuming it to be such, has been authenticated by credentials so insufficient, that they fail to convince a large proportion of the strongest and most cultivated minds, and the tendency to disbelieve them appears to grow with the growth of scientific knowledge and critical discrimination. He who can believe these to be the intentional shortcomings of a perfectly good Being, must impose silence on every prompting of the sense of goodness and justice as received among men.

It is, no doubt, possible (and there are many instances of it) to worship with the intensest devotion either Deity, that of Nature or of the Gospel, without any perversion of the moral sentiments: but this must be by fixing the attention exclusively on what is beautiful and beneficent in the precepts and spirit of the Gospel and in the dispensations of Nature, and putting all that is the reverse as entirely aside as if it did not exist. Accordingly, this simple and innocent faith can only, as I have said, co-exist with a torpid and inactive state of the speculative faculties. For a person of exercised intellect, there is no way of attaining anything equivalent to it, save by sophistication and perversion, either of the understanding or of the conscience. It may almost always be said both of sects and of individuals, who derive their morality from religion, that the better logicians they are, the worse moralists.

One only form of belief in the supernatural—one only theory respecting the origin and government of the universe —stands wholly clear both of intellectual contradiction and of moral obliquity. It is that which, resigning irrevocably the idea of an omnipotent creator, regards Nature and Life not as the expression throughout of the moral character and purpose of the Deity, but as the product of a struggle between contriving goodness and an intractable material, as was believed by Plato, or a Principle of Evil, as was the doctrine of the Manicheans. A creed like this, which I have known to be devoutly held by at least one cultivated and conscientious person of our own day, allows it to be believed that all the mass of evil which exists was undesigned by, and exists not by the appointment of, but in spite of the Being whom we are called upon to worship. A virtuous human being assumes in this theory the exalted character of a fellow-labourer with the Highest, a fellow-combatant in the great strife; contributing his little, which by the aggregation of many like himself becomes much, towards that progressive ascendancy, and ultimately complete triumph of good over evil, which history points to, and which this doctrine teaches us to regard as planned by the Being to whom we owe all the benevolent contrivance we behold in Nature. Against the moral tendency of this creed no possible objection can lie: It can produce on whoever can succeed in believing it, no other than an ennobling effect. The evidence for it, indeed, if evidence it can be called, is too shadowy and unsubstantial, and the promises it holds out too distant and uncertain, to admit of its being a permanent substitute for the religion of humanity; but the two may be held in conjunction: and he to whom ideal good, and the progress of the world towards it, are already a religion, even though that other creed may seem to him a belief not grounded on evidence, is at liberty to indulge the pleasing and encouraging thought, that its truth is possible. Apart from all dogmatic belief, there is for those who need it, an ample domain in the region of the imagination which may be planted with possibilities, with hypotheses which cannot be known to be false; and when there is anything in the appearances of nature to favour them, as in this case there is (for whatever force we attach to the analogies of Nature with the effects of human contrivance, there is no disputing the remark of Paley, that what is good in nature exhibits those analogies much oftener than what is evil), the contemplation of these possibilities is a legitimate indulgence, capable of bearing its part, with other influences, in feeding and animating the tendency of the feelings and impulses towards good.

One advantage, such as it is, the supernatural religions must always possess over the Religion of Humanity; the prospect they hold out to the individual of a life after death. For, though the scepticism of the understanding does not necessarily exclude the Theism of the imagination and feelings, and this, again, gives opportunity for a hope that the power which has done so much for us may be able and willing to do this also, such vague possibility must ever stop far short of a conviction. It remains then to estimate the value of this element—the prospect of a world to come—as a constituent of earthly happiness. I cannot but think that as the condition of mankind becomes improved, as they grow happier in their lives, and more capable of deriving happiness from unselfish sources, they will care less and less for this flattering expectation. It is not, naturally or generally, the happy who are the most anxious either for a prolongation of the present life, or for a life hereafter: it is those who never have been happy. They who have had their happiness can bear to part with existence: but it is hard to die without ever having lived. When mankind cease to need a future existence as a consolation for the sufferings of the present, it will have lost its chief value to them, for themselves. I am now speaking of the unselfish. Those who are so wrapped up in self that they are unable to identify their feelings with anything which will survive them, or to feel their life prolonged in their younger cotemporaries and in all who help to carry on the progressive movement of human affairs, require the notion of another selfish life beyond the grave, to enable them to keep up any interest in existence, since the present life, as its termination approaches, dwindles into something too insignificant to be worth caring about. But if the Religion of Humanity were as sedulously cultivated as the supernatural religions are (and there is no difficulty in conceiving that it might be much more so), all who had received the customary amount of moral cultivation would up to the hour of death live ideally in the life of those who are to follow them: and though doubtless they would often willingly survive as individuals for a much longer period than the present duration of life, it appears to me probable that after a length of time different in different persons, they would have had enough of existence, and would gladly lie down and take their eternal rest. Meanwhile and without looking so far forward, we may remark, that those who believe the immorality of the soul, generally quit life with fully as much, if not more, reluctance, as those who have no such expectation. The mere cessation of existence is no evil to any one: the idea is only formidable through the illusion of imagination which makes one conceive oneself as if one were alive and feeling oneself dead. What is odious in death is not death itself, but the act of dying, and its lugubrious accompaniments: all of which must be equally undergone by the believer in immortality. Nor can I perceive that the sceptic loses by his scepticism any real and valuable consolation except one; the hope of reunion with those dear to him who have ended their earthly life before him. That loss, indeed, is neither to be denied nor extenuated. In many cases it is beyond the reach of comparison or estimate; and will always suffice to keep alive, in the more sensitive natures, the imaginative hope of a futurity which, if there is nothing to prove, there is as little in our knowledge and experience to contradict.

History, so far as we know it, bears out the opinion, that mankind can perfectly well do without the belief in a heaven. The Greeks had anything but a tempting idea of a future state. Their Elysian fields held out very little attraction to their feelings and imagination. Achilles in the Odyssey expressed a very natural, and no doubt a very common sentiment, when he said that he would rather be on earth the serf of a needy master, than reign over the whole kingdom of the dead. And the pensive character so striking in the address of the dying emperor Hadrian to his soul, gives evidence that the popular conception had not undergone much variation during that long interval. Yet we neither find that the Greeks enjoyed life less, nor feared death more, than other people. The Buddhist religion counts probably at this day a greater number of votaries than either the Christian or the Mahomedan. The Buddhist creed recognises many modes of punishment in a future life, or rather lives, by the transmigration of the soul into new bodies of men or animals. But the blessing from Heaven which it proposes as a reward, to be earned by perseverance in the highest order of virtuous life, is annihilation; the cessation, at least, of all conscious or separate existence. It is impossible to mistake in this religion, the work of legislators and moralists endeavouring to supply supernatural motives for the conduct which they were anxious to encourage; and they could find nothing more transcendant to hold out as the capital prize to be won by the mightiest efforts of labour and self-denial, than what we are so often told is the terrible idea of annihilation. Surely this is a proof that the idea is not really or naturally terrible; that not philosophers only, but the common order of mankind, can easily reconcile themselves to it, and even consider it as a good; and that it is no unnatural part of the idea of a happy life, that life itself be laid down, after the best that it can give has been fully enjoyed through a long lapse of time; when all its pleasures, even those of benevolence, are familiar, and nothing untasted and unknown is left to stimulate curiosity and keep up the desire of prolonged existence. It seems to me not only possible but probable, that in a higher, and, above all, a happier condition of human life, not annihilation but immortality may be the burdensome idea; and that human nature, though pleased with the present, and by no means impatient to quit it, would find comfort and not sadness in the thought that it is not chained through eternity to a conscious existence which it cannot be assured that it will always wish to preserve.

John Stuart Mill
A Select Bibliography

Bibliography

Courtney, W. L. *Life of John Stuart Mill.* London, 1889.

MacMinn, N., J. R. Hainds, and J. M. McCrimmon. *Bibliography of the Published Writings of John Stuart Mill.* Evanston, 1945.

Packe, M. St. J. *The Life of John Stuart Mill.* New York, 1954.

Works of John Stuart Mill

PUBLISHED IN MILL'S LIFETIME

The Rationale of Judicial Evidence. From the MSS. of Jeremy Bentham. Edited, with a Preface, by J. Stuart Mill. 5 vols. London, 1827.

The Spirit of the Age. Articles from *The Examiner,* Jan.-May 1831. Reprinted as a volume, with an Introduction by F. A. Hayek. Chicago, 1942.

Notes on Some of the more Popular Dialogues of Plato. Articles from *The Monthly Repository,* Feb. 1834-March 1835. Reprinted as a volume, entitled *Four Dialogues of Plato—J. S. Mill,* with an Introduction by R. Borchard. London, 1946.

A System of Logic. 2 vols. London, 1843. The definitive edition is the 8th. London, 1872.

Essays on Some Unsettled Questions of Political Economy. London, 1844.

Principles of Political Economy. 2 vols. London, 1848. The definitive edition is the 7th. London, 1871. The 7th edition, reissued with

Introduction, notes, and comments on the revisions, by W. J. Ashley, is the most usable. London, 1909.

On Liberty. London, 1859.

Thoughts on Parliamentary Reform. London, 1859. Reprinted in *Dissertations and Discussions,* IV.

Dissertations and Discussions. 4 vols. London, 1859-1875.

Considerations on Representative Government. London, 1861.

Utilitarianism. Reprinted from *Fraser's Magazine,* Oct.-Dec. 1861, as a volume. London, 1863. Reprinted in *Dissertations and Discussions,* III.

An Examination of Sir William Hamilton's Philosophy. 2 vols. London, 1865.

Auguste Comte and Positivism. Reprinted from the *Westminster Review,* April and July, 1865. London, 1865.

Inaugural Address Delivered at the University of St. Andrews. London, 1867. Reprinted in *Dissertations and Discussions,* IV.

England and Ireland. London, 1868.

Analysis of the Phenomena of the Human Mind, by James Mill. Edited, with notes by John Stuart Mill. 2 vols. London, 1869.

The Subjection of Women. London, 1869.

PUBLISHED POSTHUMOUSLY

Autobiography. London, 1873. The definitive version is edited by J. J. Coss. New York, 1924.

Three Essays on Religion. London, 1874.

Chapters on Socialism. Reprinted from the *Fortnightly Review,* 1879, under the title *Socialism—John Stuart Mill,* ed. W. D. P. Bliss. Linden, Mass., 1891.

(The essay, *On Social Freedom,* reprinted with an Introduction by D. Fosdick [New York, 1944], and frequently included among Mill's posthumous works, is almost certainly not by Mill. See the discussion in J. C. Rees' *Mill and His Early Critics,* pp. 38-54.)

Collections

Gibbs, J. W. M. (ed). *Early Essays.* London, 1897.

Laski, H. (ed.). *Autobiography, with an appendix of hitherto unpublished speeches.* London, 1924.

Wishy, B. (ed.). *Prefaces to Liberty.* Boston, 1959.

Letters

d'Eichthal, E. (ed.). *John Stuart Mill, Correspondance inédite avec Gustave d'Eichthal.* Paris, 1898.

Elliot, H. S. R. (ed.). *The Letters of John Stuart Mill.* 2 vols. London, 1910.

Hayek, F. A. *John Stuart Mill and Harriet Taylor.* London, 1951.

Lévy-Bruhl, L. (ed.). *Lettres inédites de John Stuart Mill à Auguste Comte.* Paris, 1899.
Mayer, J.-P. (ed.). *Oeuvres complètes d'Alexis de Tocqueville,* Vol. VI. Paris, 1954.

Biography
Bain, A. *John Stuart Mill, a Criticism.* London, 1882.
Borchard, R. *John Stuart Mill, the Man.* London, 1957.
Courtney, W. L. *Life of John Stuart Mill.* London, 1889.
Holyoake, G. J. *John Stuart Mill, as some of the Working Classes knew him.* London, 1873.
Packe, M. St. J. *The Life of John Stuart Mill.* New York, 1954.

Critical and Expository
Anschutz, R. P. *The Philosophy of J. S. Mill.* Oxford, 1953.
Apchié, M. *Les sources françaises de certains aspects de la pensée économique de John Stuart Mill,* Paris, 1931.
Bain, A. *John Stuart Mill, a Criticism.* London, 1882.
Britton, K. *John Stuart Mill.* London, 1953.
Courtney, W. L. *Life of John Stuart Mill.* London, 1889.
Crawford, J. F. *The Relation of Inference to Fact in Mill's Logic.* Chicago, 1916.
Douglas, C. *J. S. Mill, A Study of his Philosophy.* Edinburgh, 1895.
────── *The Ethics of J. S. Mill.* Edinburgh, 1897.
Green, T. H. "Logic of J. S. Mill," *Works of Thomas Hill Green,* ed. R. L. Nettleship. Vol. II. London, 1900.
Hall, E. W. "The 'Proof' of Utility in Bentham and Mill," *Ethics,* LX (Oct. 1949), 1-18.
Jackson, R. *Examination of the Deductive Logic of J. S. Mill.* Oxford, 1941.
Jevons, W. S. "John Stuart Mill's Philosophy Tested," *Pure Logic and Other Minor Works.* London, 1890.
Kubitz, O. A. *The Development of Mill's System of Logic.* Urbana, Ill., 1932.
Leavis, F. R. "Introduction," *Mill on Bentham and Coleridge.* London, 1950.
Lindsay, A. D. "Introduction," *Utilitarianism, Liberty, and Representative Government,* by John Stuart Mill. New York, 1950.
Mansel, H. L. *The Philosophy of the Conditioned; comprising some remarks on Sir William Hamilton's Philosophy, and on Mr. J. S. Mill's Examination of that Philosophy.* London, 1866.
Mayer, J.-P. "Alexis de Tocqueville and John Stuart Mill," *The Listener,* XL (March 16, 1950), 471-2.
McCosh, J. *Examination of Mr. J. S. Mill's Philosophy.* London, 1866.

Morlan, G. *America's Heritage from John Stuart Mill.* New York, 1936.

Morley, J. "John Stuart Mill: An Anniversary," *Critical Miscellanies,* Vol. IV. London, 1908.

———— "Mr. Mill's Autobiography," *Critical Miscellanies,* Vol. III. London, 1886.

Mueller, I. W. *John Stuart Mill and French Thought.* Urbana, Ill., 1956.

Nagel, E. "Introduction," *John Stuart Mill's Philosophy of Scientific Method.* New York, 1950.

Neff, E. *Carlyle and Mill.* New York, 1926.

Pankhurst, R. K. P. *The Saint-Simonians, Mill and Carlyle.* London, 1957.

Rees, J. C. *Mill and his Early Critics.* Leicester, 1956.

———— "A Re-Reading of Mill on Liberty," *Political Studies,* VIII (June 1960), 113-129.

Russell, B. *John Stuart Mill.* London, 1955.

Saenger, S. *John Stuart Mill. Sein Leben und Lebenswerk.* Stuttgart, 1901.

Spencer, H., et. al. *John Stuart Mill: His Life and Works.* Boston, 1873.

Stephen, J. F. *Liberty, Equality, Fraternity.* London, 1873.

Stephen, L. *The English Utilitarians,* Vol. III. London, 1900.

Street, C. L. *Individualism and Individuality in the Philosophy of John Stuart Mill.* Milwaukee, 1926.

Taine, H. *Le positivisme anglais; étude sur Stuart Mill.* Paris, 1864.

Urmson, J. O. "The Interpretation of the Moral Philosophy of John Stuart Mill," *The Philosophical Quarterly,* 3 (Jan. 1953), 33-39.

Vaysset-Boutbien, R. *Stuart Mill et la sociologie française contemporaine.* Paris, 1941.

Viner, J. "Bentham and J. S. Mill: The Utilitarian Background," *The Long View and the Short.* Glencoe, 1958.

Whewell, W. *Of Induction, with especial reference to Mr. J. Stuart Mill's "System of Logic."* London, 1849.

———— "On Mill's Logic," *On the Philosophy of Discovery.* London, 1860.

Whittaker, T. *Comte and Mill.* London, 1908.

Williams, R. "Mill on Bentham and Coleridge," *Culture and Society 1780-1950.* New York, 1958.

General

Adler, M. *The Idea of Freedom.* Garden City, 1958.

Aiken, H. D. "Definitions, Factual Premises, and Ethical Conclusions," *The Philosophical Review,* LXI (July 1952), 331-348.

Albee, E. *A History of English Utilitarianism.* London, 1901.

Anshen, R. N. (ed.). *Freedom: Its Meaning.* New York, 1940.

Aster, E. V. *Geschichte der englischen Philosophie.* Bielefeld and Leipzig, 1927.

Berlin, I. *Two Concepts of Liberty.* Oxford, 1958.

Bradley, F. H. *Ethical Studies.* London, 1876.

——— *The Principles of Logic.* London, 1883.

Brinton, C. *English Political Thought in the Nineteenth Century.* London, 1933.

Cohen, M. "Berlin and the Liberal Tradition," *The Philosophical Quarterly,* 10 (July 1960), 216-227.

Cohen, M. R. and E. Nagel. *An Introduction to Logic and Scientific Method.* New York, 1936.

Davidson, W. L. *Political Thought in England: Utilitarianism from Bentham to J. S. Mill.* London, 1915.

de Ruggiero, G. *The History of European Liberalism,* trans. R. G. Collingwood. Oxford, 1927.

Dicey, A. C. *Law and Public Opinion in England.* London, 1905.

Fosdick, D. *What Is Liberty?* New York, 1939.

Frege, G. *The Foundations of Arithmetic,* trans. J. L. Austin. Oxford, 1953.

Green, T. H. *Prolegomena to Ethics,* ed. A. C. Bradley. Oxford, 1883.

Grote, J. *An Examination of the Utilitarian Philosophy.* Cambridge, Eng., 1870.

Halévy, E. *The Growth of Philosophical Radicalism,* trans. Mary Morris. London, 1928.

Hart, H. L. A. and A. M. Honoré. *Causation in the Law.* Oxford, 1959.

Hearnshaw, F. J. C. (ed.). *The Social and Political Ideas of some Representative Thinkers of the Age of Reaction and Reconstruction.* London, 1932.

——— *The Social and Political Ideas of some Representative Thinkers of the Victorian Age.* London, 1933.

Hobhouse, L. T. *Liberalism.* New York, 1911.

Leroux, E. and A. Leroy. *La philosophie anglaise classique.* Paris, 1951.

Lewis, C. I. "The Pragmatic Conception of the *A Priori,*" *Readings in Philosophical Analysis,* ed. H. Feigl and W. Sellars. New York, 1949.

Lippincott, B. E. *The Victorian Critics of Democracy.* Minneapolis, 1938.

MacCunn, J. *Six Radical Thinkers.* London, 1907.

Moore, G. E. *Principia Ethica.* Cambridge, Eng., 1903.

Plamenatz, J. *The English Utilitarians.* Oxford, 1958.

Popper, K. R. *The Open Society and its Enemies.* London, 1945.
——— *The Poverty of Historicism.* Boston, 1957.
Rawls, J. "Two Concepts of Rules," *The Philosophical Review,* LXIV (Jan. 1955), 3-32.
——— "Justice as Fairness," *ibid.,* LXVII (April 1958), 164-194.
Robbins, L. *The Theory of Eoonomic Policy.* London, 1953.
Ross, W. D. *Foundations of Ethics.* London, 1939.
Ryle, G. "The Theory of Meaning," *British Philosophy in the Mid-Century,* ed. C. A. Mace. London, 1957.
Sabine, G. *A History of Political Theory.* New York, 1955.
Schumpeter, J. A. *History of Economic Analysis.* New York, 1954.

MODERN LIBRARY GIANTS

A series of sturdily bound and handsomely printed, full-sized library editions of books formerly available only in expensive sets. These volumes contain from 600 to 1,400 pages each.

THE MODERN LIBRARY GIANTS REPRESENT A
SELECTION OF THE WORLD'S GREATEST BOOKS